Practical
Neural Network Recipes
in C++

Practical
Neural Network
Recipes
in C++

Timothy Masters

Academic Press, Inc.
Harcourt Brace Jovanovich, Publishers
Boston San Diego New York
London Sydney Tokyo Toronto

ACADEMIC PRESS, INC.
1250 Sixth Avenue, San Diego CA 92101-4311

United Kingdom Edition published by
ACADEMIC PRESS LIMITED
24-28 Oval Road, London NW1 7DX

Library of Congress Cataloging-in-Publication Data

Masters, Timothy.
    Practical neural network recipes in C++ / Timothy Masters.
        p.   cm.
    Includes bibliographical references and index.
    ISBN 0-12-479040-2
    1. Neural networks (computer science) 2. C++ (computer
program
  language) I. Title.
  QA76.87.M37   1993
  006.3--dc20   92-47469
                                                         CIP

Printed in the United States of America
93 94 95 96 97 EB 9 8 7 6 5 4 3 2 1

LIMITED WARRANTY AND DISCLAIMER OF LIABILITY

This book is dedicated to my cherished wife, Johanna. Her grammatical skills and unselfish giving of time for proofreading were obviously invaluable. But it was her constant support and encouragement that made this work possible.

Contents

Preface

The primary purpose of this book is to serve as a cookbook for neural network solutions to practical problems. It should enable people with moderate programming experience to select a neural network model that is appropriate to solving a particular problem and to produce a working program that implements that network. It will also provide guidance along the entire problem-solving path. This includes designing the training set, preprocessing variables, training and validating the network, and evaluating its performance. A detailed discussion of computation of decision confidences is also provided.

One of the thorniest issues in neural network training is local minima in the error function. Two effective means of addressing this problem are provided. Simulated annealing and genetic optimization are presented in a neural network context. Complete algorithms for implementing these popular stochastic optimization methods are given.

Sometimes highly effective neural networks are discounted because their operation is poorly understood. The vitally important subject of feature identification is covered in detail. Several means of discovering what a neural network sees in the data are discussed. The reader is also steered away from dangerous interpretations.

This book includes a lengthy treatment of practical fuzzy logic, along with examples of how hybrid fuzzy/neural models can outperform either alone. Complete code for implementing all major fuzzy operations is shown. This allows the reader to easily construct fuzzy preprocessors and postprocessors for neural networks.

No background in neural networks is assumed for the reader; all models are presented from the ground up. On the other hand, this book is not intended as a general course in neural networks. Its content is strictly limited to models that have been in existence long enough to have been proven worthy of widespread use. As such, it is intentionally incomplete. Models that are of primarily historical or biological interest are ignored. Also, there are some recent models that show promise, but have not yet withstood the test of time. These, too, are omitted.

The operation of all models is set forth with sufficient mathematics to allow the ambitious reader to understand how they operate and to follow any program code provided. However, full mathematical details are relegated to references cited. This avoids bogging down the majority of readers with unnecessary detail.

The program code in this book is in C++, as this language combines high level, object-oriented structure with nearly the speed and compactness of assembler. An attempt has been made to use structures unique to C++ only when vital. Thus, much of the code can be easily adapted to C compilers. Vector and Matrix classes, as well as operator overloading, have been avoided. Such specialized constructs contribute little or nothing to program efficiency and complicate the lives of programmers who wish to use these algorithms in other languages. Strictly C++ techniques have been used only when they significantly improved program readability or efficiency. Because operation of all programs is thoroughly discussed in the accompanying text and comments within the code, translation to other languages should not be difficult.

The principal focus of this book is the three-layer feedforward network, although several other immensely useful models are presented. The reason for this relatively narrow focus is entirely pragmatic. There is an abundance of books that broadly survey network models. The world would not benefit from yet another such work. The three-layer feedforward network has been the workhorse of many professional arsenals for a decade and hence deserves special recognition. Of course, other network models that have performed well are also included.

All of the C++ code in this book (and on the program disk) has been tested for strict ANSI compatibility. No special, proprietary libraries are ever referenced. The author used Zortech C++ version 3.0. The code has also been compiled with Borland Turbo C++. It is anticipated that any ANSI C++ compiler would be able to compile all of the code correctly.

I would especially like to thank Ms. Kathleen Tibbetts of Academic Press for her valuable assistance during all stages of this book's preparation. She had faith in a first-time author. Then, she supplied the support and encouragement that propelled the project through a seemingly overwhelming agenda. Finally, she efficiently guided the final manuscript preparation. May all beginning authors find such an editor.

1

Foundations

A brief history and overview of neural networks serves as a concise introduction for those readers having little or no experience in this area.

Motivation

From the time of the first primitive computing machines, their designers and users have been trying to push computers beyond the role of automatic calculators and into the realm of "thinking" machines. Unfortunately, just what is meant by "thinking machine" is debatable. The variety of definitions for the popular phrase "artificial intelligence" is astounding. Methods for supposedly implementing humanlike thought processes with a deterministic machine are likewise varied. Neural networks represent one of these approaches.

A biological neuron, shown simplified in Figure 1.1, is a single cell capable of a sort of crude computation. It is stimulated by one or more inputs, and it generates an output that is sent to other neurons. The output is dependent on the strength of each of the inputs and on the nature of each input connection (called a *synapse*). Some synapses may be such that an input there will tend to excite the neuron (increase the output). Others may be inhibitory; an input to such synapses will tend to reduce the neuron's output.

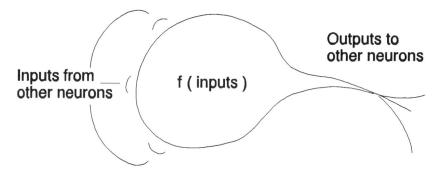

Fig. 1.1: A simplified neuron

The actual relationship between inputs and output can be enormously complex. There can be significant time delays between application of the input stimulus and generation of the output response. Fatigue can set in, so that the neuron does not always respond in the same way to the same inputs. Even random events can influence the operation of a neuron. Luckily, a large body of research indicates that simple models, which account for only the most basic neural processes, can provide excellent solutions to practical problems.

The variety of neural networks being tested today is enormous. Individual neurons can be modeled by a simple weighted sum of inputs, a complex collection of differential equations, or anything in between. Connections between neurons can be organized in layers such that information flows in one direction only, or it can circulate throughout the network in cyclic patterns. All neurons can be updated simultaneously, or time delays can be introduced. All responses can be strictly deterministic, or random behavior can be allowed. The variations are endless.

Many neural network models are of strictly theoretical importance. They may be too slow to be practical, good training algorithms may not exist for them, too much computer memory may be required, or their performance in real life problems may leave much to be desired. On the other hand, some models have been proven to be immensely valuable. Tasks that were formerly performed by statistical techniques like discriminant analysis can now be done faster and more effectively by neural nets.

New Life for Old Techniques

A side effect of the surge in interest in neural networks is that some negelected statistical techniques are being rediscovered. When we say that something is a "neural network", we imply that it has a segmented structure. A neural network is characterized by an architecture in which its operations are distributed among many relatively simple processors. When a complicated procedure can be broken up this way, two benefits are realized:

1)   Simple hardware processors can be constructed. These are typically cheap and fast. This allows economical implementations of what might otherwise be nearly impossible.

2)   The procedure can take advantage of the neural network craze. If an algorithm can be called a neural network, its chances of attracting attention are vastly increased.

The classic example of this is the probabilistic neural network. It is really a decades-old powerful statistical technique. Because its memory and processing requirements are large, it was not accepted when it was first proposed. But when Donald Specht discovered that it could be recast as a neural network, it was propelled to fame. This extremely useful model is discussed in Chapter 12.

Another example is the functional link network. Yoh-Han Pao took ordinary multiple regression, added a nonlinear front-end, applied a nonlinear transformation to the output, and showed how the whole process could be viewed as a neural network. The result is one of the most powerful function-mapping models known. It is discussed in Chapters 13 and 14.

Perceptrons and Linear Separability

The *perceptron* [Rosenblatt, 1958] was the first artificial neural network. It was computationally feasible on the hardware of that time, was based on biological models, and was capable of learning. Unfortunately, it also suffered from a significant weakness: the inability to learn to perform an important family of classification tasks. Since the original perceptron has little practical use today, it will not be presented in detail. However, some discussion of it can contribute to understanding closely related networks that are immensely practical.

Rosenblatt proposed many variations of the perceptron, but the most straightforward consists of three-layers. The first is an input "retina". It is connected to a second layer, composed of what he called "association units", which acts as a feature detector. That layer finally connects to an output response layer. Units (neurons) in his model produce an output that is a thresholded weighted sum of their inputs. This nonlinearity is crucial to most neural networks. It can be shown that if the response function were linear, the middle layer would be superfluous. Some of his models also include inhibitory connections between the response neurons in order to discourage more than one of them being activated at the same time.

Training of the perceptron is accomplished by repeatedly presenting it with a sample input on the "retina", computing the outputs of the middle-layer neurons, using those values to compute the outputs of the response-layer neurons, and then updating the weights through which the middle layer connects to the response layer. The weights connecting the input layer (the retina) to the middle layer are not changed. Thus, although the network has three layers, it actually is more like a two-layer network. The middle layer performs the mundane task of transforming the input to enhance features. In practice, the fixed weights connecting the input to the middle layer may be set to detect known features, or they may be chosen randomly.

In addition to its historical position as the first "practical" artificial neural network, the perceptron has an important claim to fame in the "perceptron convergence theorem." Rosenblatt presented an algorithm by which his perceptron could be trained. He proved that if a set of training patterns is learnable by the perceptron, his algorithm is guaranteed to converge to a set of weights that enable correct response to the training set. As will be seen later, such a powerful training algorithm is rare for artificial neural networks. This theorem, along with some fairly impressive early demonstrations of problem solving, propelled neural network research forward for a short time.

Unfortunately, the perceptron has a serious shortcoming. It is only capable of solving classification problems that are *linearly separable* at the output layer. For each output neuron, the training samples that activate it must be able to be separated from those that do not by means of a hyperplane (whose dimension would, of course, be one less than the number of inputs to that neuron). For example, suppose we have two inputs to a neuron, and the following responses are desired:

in1	in2	out
0	0	1
1	0	0
0	1	1
1	1	1

This training data is shown in the left side of Figure 1.2, along with a line that can separate the set according to whether or not the output is to be activated. This training set can be learned by a perceptron.

Compare this to the XOR (exclusive or) logical function graphed in the right side of that figure. There is no line that can segregate this training set, so it cannot be learned by a perceptron.

in1	in2	out
0	0	0
1	0	1
0	1	1
1	1	0

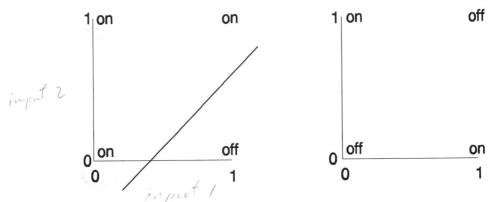

Fig. 1.2: Linearly separable and inseparable sets

Fate then conspired against artificial neural networks. Rosenblatt's former schoolmate, Marvin Minsky, along with Seymour Papert, published the book *Perceptrons* [Minsky and Papert, 1969], which went to great lengths expounding on the weaknesses of the perceptron model. Because of the book's mathematical rigor, and also because the authors were very well known and respected researchers in artificial intelligence, a shadow was cast on neural network research. Soon after, in 1971, Frank Rosenblatt died in a boating accident. Without his support, and in the wake of *Perceptrons*, money for neural network research rapidly dwindled.

During the ensuing years, a few pioneers continued studying neural models, developing much interesting theory but having little practical success. See [Anderson and Rosenfeld, 1988] and [Rumelhart and McClelland, 1986] for an excellent overview of this work. It wasn't until 1986, when David Rumelhart, Geoffrey Hinton, and Ronald Williams published "Learning Internal Representations by Error Propagation" (see [Rumelhart and McClelland, 1986]) that research into artificial neural networks once again began to receive significant recognition and funding. Their development of a multilayer feedforward network that was not restricted to linearly separable training sets, along with a reasonably effective training algorithm for it, demonstrated that artificial neural networks could provide real solutions to practical problems.

Neural Network Capabilities

Imaginative researchers are devising new uses for artificial neural networks daily. Some of the more traditional applications include

Classification - Neural networks can be used to determine crop types from satellite photographs, to distinguish a submarine from a boulder given its sonar return, and to identify diseases of the heart from electrocardiograms. Any task that can be done by traditional discriminant analysis can be done at least as well (and almost always much better) by a neural network.

Noise Reduction - An artificial neural network can be trained to recognize a number of patterns. These patterns may be parts of time-series, images, et cetera. If a version of one of these patterns, corrupted by noise, is presented to a properly trained network, the network can provide the original pattern on which it was trained. This technique has been used with great success in some image restoration problems.

Prediction - A very common problem is that of predicting the value of a variable given historic values of itself (and perhaps other variables). Economic and meteorological models spring to mind. Neural networks have frequently been shown to outperform traditional techniques like ARIMA and frequency domain analysis.

Artificial neural networks are most likely to be superior to other methods under the following conditions:

1) The data on which conclusions are to be based is "fuzzy." If the input data is human opinions, ill-defined categories, or is subject to possibly large error, the robust behavior of neural networks is important.

2) The patterns important to the required decision are subtle or deeply hidden. One of the principal advantages of a neural network is its ability to discover patterns in data which are so obscure as to be imperceptible to human researchers and standard statistical methods. One of the first major commercial uses of neural networks was predicting the credit-worthiness of loan applicants based on their spending and payment history. The correct decision depends on far more than simple factors like salary and debt level. Neural networks were shown to provide decisions superior to those made by trained humans.

3) The data exhibits significant unpredictable nonlinearity. Traditional time-series models for predicting future values, such as ARIMA and Kalman filters, are based on strictly defined models. If the data does not fit the models, results will be useless. Neural networks are marvelously adaptable.

4) The data is chaotic (in the mathematical sense). Chaos can be found in telephone line noise, stock market prices, and a host of other physical processes. Such behavior is devastating to most other techniques, but neural networks are generally robust with inputs of this type.

The excellent performance of artificial neural networks is not surprising when one considers the solid theoretical foundations on which many of them rest. The standard workhorse, the three-layer feedforward network, has powerful function-approximation capabilities. In particular, *any* continuous function defined over a compact subset of $\mathfrak{R}^n$ can be approximated to arbitrary accuracy given sufficient hidden neurons. The importance of this result cannot be overstated. When combined with the robustness of the three-layer feedforward network as regards input errors, it is a powerful tool. Rigorous mathematical discussion of these properties is given in [Hornik, 1991] and [Blum and Li, 1991]. See page 85 of this book for more details.

The probabilistic neural network also has a solid theoretical basis. Under very general conditions, its ability to classify is asymptotically Bayes-optimal. See [Specht, 1990] and page 201 of this book for details.

In summary, many artificial neural networks possess both substantial theoretical foundations and practical utility. Any problem that can be solved with traditional modeling or statistical methods can most likely be solved more effectively with a neural network. It is hoped that the contents of this book will constitute a guide capable of leading the beginning practitioner every step of the way, from initial choice of an appropriate network to efficient implementation of the final program.

Basic Structure of a Neural Network

Several specific neural network models will be presented in later chapters. This section simply seeks to introduce neural networks in a very general way.

Figure 1.3 illustrates the general structure of a neural network. There are one or more (usually many) inputs. These inputs are commonly called input neurons, though in a sense that is a misnomer. They are only hypothetical neurons that produce an output equal to their supposed input. No processing is done by an input neuron. For example, if we show a sample (a vector of numbers) to the network, and this sample's third variable has a value of 0.7, then we act as if input neuron three is producing an output of 0.7. There is no actual input neuron. It is a semantic construct used to represent the input sample.

There are also one or more output neurons, typically very few. These provide the results of the network to the world. Unlike the hypothetical input neurons, the output neurons are very real. Each output neuron accepts inputs (from the outside world and/or from other neurons), processes these inputs, and produces an output.

Figure 1.3 shows the input neurons being connected to the output neurons through a "black box" process. The exact network model determines the nature of this black box. This arrangement is very common, but it is not the only one. Some models omit the intermediary, connecting the inputs directly to the output neurons. In this case, the entire burden of the network's task is taken on by the processing done by the output neurons. Other models allow the output neurons to connect with each other as well as with the previous layer. Still other models do not distinguish so explicitly between input and

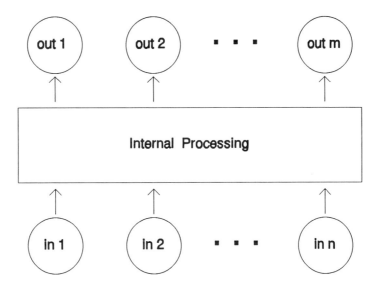

Fig. 1.3: Basic neural network

output neurons. After presentation of a sample to the input layer, the network is allowed to ruminate until it settles down to a conclusion, at which time the former input neurons take on the role of output neurons. However, these other models will not play much of a role in this book. The above figure is representative of the majority of the network models to be discussed.

Training

A neural network is (usually) trained in one of two ways. The most common is *supervised* training. We collect many samples to serve as exemplars. Each sample in this *training set* completely specifies all inputs, as well as the outputs that are desired when those inputs are presented. Then we choose a subset of the training set and present the samples in that subset to the network one at a time. For each sample, we compare the outputs obtained by the network with the outputs we would like it to obtain. After the entire subset of training samples has been processed, we update the weights that connect the neurons in the network. This updating is done in such a way that we (hopefully) reduce a measure of the error in the network's results. One pass through the subset of training samples, along with an updating of the network's weights, is called an *epoch*. The number of samples in the subset is called the *epoch size*. Some researchers use an epoch size of one, meaning that the weights are updated after each training case is presented. The author usually favors using the entire training set for each epoch, as this favors stability in convergence to the optimal weights. Compromises between these extremes are popular. When the epoch size is less than the entire training set, it is important that the subset be selected randomly each time, or ugly oscillations may occur. Epochs of training are repeated until the network's performance is satisfactory, or until patience expires.

The other principal training method is *unsupervised* training. As in supervised training, we have a collection of sample inputs. But we do not provide the network with outputs for those samples. We typically assume that each input arises from one of several classes, and the network's output is an identification of the class to which its input belongs. The process of training the network consists of letting it discover salient features of the training set, and using these features to group the inputs into classes that it (the network) finds distinct. Unsupervised training will be covered lightly in a later chapter, but is generally not as important as supervised training.

There is a third, hybrid training method, which deserves brief mention. *Reinforcement learning* is unsupervised in that the exact outputs desired are not specified. At the same time, it is supervised in that when the network responds to a sample in the training set, it is told whether its response was good or bad. This type of learning will not be discussed in this book.

Validation

It would be foolhardy to train a network then immediately place it into service. Its competence must be evaluated first. This process is called *validation*. The usual procedure is to separate the known cases into two disjoint sets. One is the training set, which is used to train the network. The other is the validation set, which is used to test the trained network. Many specific methods for testing are discussed in Chapter 19, page 343.

Never underestimate the importance of validation. In many respects, proper validation is more important than proper training. It is all too easy to observe wonderfully small error on the training set, and erroneously conclude that all is well with the network. An examination of Figure 1.4 shows why low training-set error can be misleading. If the model has too many free parameters relative to the number of cases in the training set, it can *overfit* the data. Rather than learning the basic structure of the data, enabling it to generalize

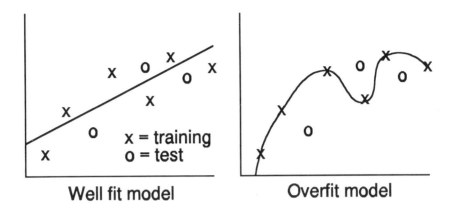

Fig. 1.4: Low training error need not imply good performance

well, it learns irrelevant details of the individual cases. Naturally, we can expect the error on the validation set to exceed slightly that on the training set. But if the difference is large, we must suspect that either the two sets are not representative of the same population, or the model has been overfitted. In either case, disparity in the errors is a warning sign that must not be ignored.

There is a dangerous pitfall into which many practitioners tumble when in the validation phase of a project. It is imperative that the validation set not be used as part of the training procedure in any way whatsoever. Almost nobody "accidentally" lets part or all of the validation set slip into the training set. That is too obvious an error. But a much more subtle error can easily occur if more than one training–testing cycle is done. Suppose that the initially trained network does poorly on the validation set. (We assume that it performs well on the training set, or else we would not consider the network to be trained yet!) The training process may be performed again, this time starting at a different random-weight configuration. It is quite possible that the resulting trained network will have a very different final-weight configuration than did the first trained network. This new network is now tested with the validation set. If it does well, it is accepted. Otherwise, training is done again. This is continued until performance on the validation set is acceptable. *This process has essentially used the validation set as a training set*, rendering it invalid for validation.

Why is the above process illegal? Remember that the purpose of the validation phase is to provide us with an unbiased indication of what can be expected of the network when it is used in the general population. By including it in the training cycle, we have biased it.

We have specifically chosen our final network to be the one which performed best on the validation set. This deprives us of independent confirmation. To accept blindly results obtained in this way is to bury our heads in the sand.

So what do we do if our trained network performs poorly on the validation set? First, we must realize that there is important information to be found in the validation set, information the network has not learned. It may be that a poor random-weight configuration is responsible. But it is much more likely that the training set was incompetently designed. The validation-set information truly belongs in the training set. Therefore, the first step is to combine the training and validation sets into one large training set. The network is then retrained until its performance on this augmented training set is acceptable. Then we bite the bullet and collect a new validation set. This may be expensive, but it probably will not be as expensive as putting an incompetent network into service. Chalk it up as the expense incurred as the result of poor training set collecting, and let the lesson be learned for the next time.

If, by some chance, there is absolutely, positively, no way to collect a new validation set, the best solution to the above problem is to train with the combined set and to trust divine providence. To use any less of the available data for training would be to discard valuable information. In the face of this advice, superficial reasoning would question the utility of initially dividing up the known data into training and validation sets. Why not use it all for training in the first place? The reason is that we only got into this mess by virtue of having an incomplete training set. The initial assumption is that our training and validation sets are good, and *the presence of a validation set tests that assumption as much as it tests the network itself*. If that assumption is false, we punt.

Leave-*k*-out Method

There is a standard method for dealing with small training sets in traditional statistical techniques. It is called the *leave-k-out* method, also called *jackknifing*. This section will explain how it works and why it may not be applicable to neural networks.

Jackknifing is most frequently used in discriminant analysis. The researcher has a collection of samples from several known categories. A model is to be built from which measured variables can be used to predict class membership. Sometimes the actual ability to predict is important. But very often all that is desired is to know the degree to which the measured variables *are capable* of predicting class membership.

Ideally, we have two large sets of known cases. One set is used to train the discriminant analysis. The other set, which is totally independent of the first, is used to test the discriminator. Its performance on that set is taken to be indicative of its performance in the general population. A problem arises when the amount of known data is too small to justify splitting it into two sets. It would obviously be unfair to train and test the discriminator using the same data set. This brings us to the leave-k-out method.

A small fraction of the known cases, often just one case, is held back for testing, and the rest of them are used for training. Then, the cases held back are classified. This is a fair, unbiased test of that particular discriminator's capability. Unfortunately, since just one or at most very few cases are tested, the random error inherent in the sampling procedure guarantees us a high probability of significant error in the performance estimate. So we do it again, this time holding back a different small subset. By repeating this as many times as are needed to test every known case, we have made optimal use of our data, yet we still have a performance estimate that is not biased by ever using the same case for both training and testing — very clever indeed.

The key point to remember here is that each test involves the discriminator whose training was determined by a subset of the known data. At no time do we actually test the discriminator that would be obtained by using the entire data set. This, of course, is of no consequence when our goal is to ascertain the theoretical discrimination ability of the measured variables. On the other hand, this algorithm cannot tell us anything mathematically certain about the ability of a discriminator that was never even constructed!

In practice, for linear discriminant analysis, this is a non-concern. It is well known that except for very unusual cases, adding or deleting one member of a training set has little effect on the discriminator. This is largely due to the fact that the model is deterministically constructed and is based on aggregate information. A fixed set of training cases will always yield exactly the same fixed model, which can be explicitly computed. The effect of changing any measured value in the training set can be rigorously bounded, albeit with considerable difficulty. Thus, we are fairly safe in extrapolating jackknife results to the discriminator that would be obtained from the entire known set.

The above is not true for neural network classifiers. The error of a network, as a function of the weights that define the network, is filled with hills and valleys. A trivial change in the training data can push the weights over the edge into an entirely different region. Even with exactly the same training set, different random starting weights can result in dramatically different final results. Therefore, we do not dare assert that a network trained with all of the known data is essentially identical to networks trained with subsets of the data. It may be that most of the tested networks worked well, but an unlucky quirk in the training of the final network left it lacking. Jackknifing will not inform us of this event.

It is even possible, though uncommon in practice, that the network as designed is capable of learning any subset of the known data, but cannot learn the entire set. We have already discussed linear separability and the infamous XOR (exclusive or) problem. The astute reader will observe that any subset of the four training cases in that problem *is* linearly separable, while the entire set of four is not. Thus, there are simple networks capable of performing perfectly on all four jackknifes obtained by training with three of the four cases, yet incapable of learning all four.

2

Classification

One of the most common uses for neural networks is classification. This includes both simple binary decisions (is a condition present?) and multiple-class identification. This chapter introduces this topic, which will be the main subject of most of the remainder of this book.

Industry, academia, and the military all need classification techniques. A potato chip manufacturer needs to decide if the chips rolling off the line are perfect, overcooked, or undercooked. A tank gunner needs to know if a hot spot detected by an infrared sensor is a friend or foe. Of all the possible uses for neural networks, classification is probably the most common. Many details of classification will be covered throughout this book. This chapter focuses on the general issues common to all network models.

When we refer to a "classification network", we are not necessarily referring to a particular network model that is designed to classify. There are many models, such as the multiple-layer feedforward network, which are adept at a wide variety of tasks other than classification. Rather, we are concerned with the use to which a particular network is put. This chapter will not be directed toward any single model. It is applicable to any model being used for classification.

Binary Decisions

The simplest classification problem is the binary decision. Note that when the choice is between two classes, deciding where a sample belongs is *not* a binary decision if there is the possibility that it belongs to neither class. A true binary decision admits only two possibilities. Such problems are best served by having exactly one output neuron. The network would be trained to produce a high output activation for one decision and a low activation for the other. A common mistake is to use two output neurons, one for each decision, and train so that one is on while the other is off. This gains nothing in performance, costs memory and training time, and adds ambiguity to the decision process. (What if both are on or off?)

It is important that the network be trained to produce realizable activation levels, rather than extreme values that are difficult or impossible to achieve. For example, many network models described later use the logistic activation function:

$$f(x) = \frac{1}{1 + e^{-x}} \qquad\qquad 2\text{-}1$$

In this case, neither the full activation level of 1.0 nor the full off level of 0.0 can ever be attained. If an attempt is made to train the network to achieve these levels, weights will be driven to such large values that numerical instability for borderline cases will result. Also, the derivative of the logistic function approaches zero at extreme activations, so gradient-directed optimization methods slow to a snail's pace.

Finally, mean square error as a measure of performance loses some meaning since it can never reach zero. It is best to train the network to achieve more moderate values. In the case of the logistic activation function, the traditional choices are 0.1 for one decision, and 0.9 for the other decision. Some other activation functions may have different ranges and may require different training levels. For example, the hyperbolic tangent and scaled arctangent functions (page 80) range from -1.0 to 1.0. In this case, training for -0.9 and 0.9 is appropriate.

Making the Decision

When the trained network is put to the test with an unknown sample, we decide between the two possible outcomes based on the activation level achieved by the single output neuron. If the activation is at least as large as a predefined threshold, we choose the decision for which high activation was trained. In many cases, the threshold is set midway between the two trained extremes. This makes intuitive sense and in practice is usually effective in the absence of any additional information. However, we may want to prejudice the decision by setting the threshold closer to one of the extremes. This topic is discussed on page 389.

We must avoid the temptation to introduce a third, "reject" decision into what is *supposed* to be a strictly binary decision by setting two arbitrary thresholds. For example, suppose the network has a logistic activation function, and we have trained for output values of 0.1 and 0.9. We may be tempted to make one decision if the output is at least 0.7, make the other decision if the output is less than 0.3, and consider it undecided if the output lies between 0.3 and 0.7. This policy fails to distinguish between the situation in which the test case clearly belongs to one of the categories but shares many characteristics of the other category, versus the situation in which the test case does not clearly resemble either category. The only reason to use this two threshold policy is in the validation phase, as it indicates inadequate training. When a case is found that activates the output neuron to an intermediate level, that case should be carefully studied. If it is definitely a member of one category, it should be included in the training set for that category, and training repeated. If it is not a member of either category, the choice of a strict binary classification model must be brought into question.

This does not mean that we are forced into a blind decision based on a single threshold. We have recourse. If we are *positive* that there are only two possible categories, we can often use the confidence measures discussed on page 361 to tell us approximately how confident we can be in our decision. This removes the arbitrary nature of a subjective threshold. If, on the other hand, we cannot be positive that it is a strictly binary decision, we must use two output neurons and approach it as a multiple-class problem. This is discussed in the next section. Then, the activations of the two output neurons can help us decide whether a difficult case is a member of one class but is also similar to the other (having both neurons highly activated), or whether it is atypical of both classes (having both neurons nearly off). Unfortunately, we still have the potential problem of both neurons having intermediate activation. In this case, we are back to the situation of inadequate training.

Multiple Classes

A multiple-class model not only allows for several class decisions, but also allows for the possibility of a "reject" decision. Even if only two classes are possible, a multiple-class model must be used if we want to include the possibility of failing to classify into either of the two categories. As was pointed out in the previous section, failing to identify clearly a winner in a single-neuron binary model may be more an indication of inadequate training than it is of failure to fall into either category.

The generally best way to implement a multiple-class model is to use a separate output neuron for each class. Training is done by requiring the neuron corresponding to the class being presented to be highly activated, while all other neurons are required to be nearly off. (See the previous section, Binary Decisions, for a discussion of *highly activated* and *nearly off*.) Thus, for each training example, exactly one output neuron will be trained to be on. The only exception is if we are able also to train for a reject category. Samples from the reject category would require all output neurons to be nearly off.

Reject Category

It can sometimes be helpful to include samples from a reject category in the training collection. Since, as will be seen later, we will reject an unknown sample if all output-neuron activations are below a preordained threshold, we can help the network to reach this rejection decision when appropriate by giving it examples of when to keep all output neurons inactivated. However, we must beware of a hidden danger. The network cannot be expected to reliably reject cases that do not have exemplars in the training collection. It is all too easy to include only a partial representation of what is to be rejected, then become overconfident. When an unknown sample is not clearly rejected, the user may believe that it is significant, when really it is nothing more than a true reject that was not represented in the training collection. Note that this is *not* a theoretical error; it is nearly always better to train with a partial collection of rejects, if such can be had, than with none at all. Rather, it is a human error. We must remember that just because we have trained with *some* rejects, we dare not have excessive confidence in our ability to reject *all* unknown cases that should be rejected.

Making the Decision

When an unknown case is presented to the network, the classification decision is based on the activations of all output neurons. We hope either that exactly one of them is highly activated, and the others are not, or that none of them is highly activated. In the former case, we classify the unknown into the class that corresponds to the highly activated neuron. In the latter case, we reject the unknown from all classes. In particular, the decision rule is

1) If all output neuron activations are less than a specified threshold, reject the unknown sample.

2) Otherwise, classify the unknown into the category whose corresponding output neuron has the highest activation. In the unlikely event of a tie, break it randomly.

Other Encoding Schemes

The traditional encoding scheme in which each class has its own dedicated output neuron has many advantages. Perceived similarity of a sample to each class can be assessed by the degree of activation of that class's neuron. If one or more output neurons are activated nearly as highly as the winner, we know that there is the possibility of confusion. Sometimes we can even estimate confidence in a decision using the techniques described starting on page 361. For these reasons, this encoding is nearly always best. However, there are other possibilities.

If there is a definite order relationship among the classes, we may want to use one neuron encoded so that its activation level corresponds to position in the hierarchy. For example, suppose that the task of a neural network is to grade fruit into one of four categories:

A: Premium quality, destined for select consumers
B: Good quality, for grocery stores
C: Poor quality, for juice
D: Reject

The classes clearly have an order relationship, so using just one output neuron is appropriate. In fact, using four separate output neurons could lead to interpretational difficulties. What if an unknown sample highly activated two neurons? The only advantage would be that in such a case we would justifiably suspect our training procedure and subject the unusual sample to close scrutiny. However, this is a validation issue, not an issue that should have to be dealt with by an end user.

When the categories have an order relationship, we must decide what activation levels to train for. The simplest approach is to space them equally. In the above example of grading fruit, it would be reasonable to train the network so that samples from grade A activate the neuron to 90 percent activation, B to 63 percent, C to 37 percent, and D to 10 percent. In some instances, there may be reasons for unequal spacing and, if so, there is no reason for demanding equal spacing. On the other hand, ad hoc decisions are always dangerous. In the absence of obvious justification, avoid subjective choices of activations.

Another situation in which separate output neurons for each class may not be best is if the classes are defined by two or more binary (or other low radix) variables. One example of this would be blood typing. Three of the medically significant factors that may or may not be present in human blood are the A, B and Rh components. Blood that contains neither the A nor the B components is said to be type O. Otherwise, its type is indicated by the letters A and/or B. If the Rh factor is present, the blood is called positive; otherwise it is negative. Thus, blood that contains all three factors is AB positive, and blood that contains none of them is O negative. There are $2^3 = 8$ possible blood types. Testing is done by mixing antiserums for each of these factors with separate blood samples. If the corresponding factor is present, the blood sample will take on a characteristic clotted appearance. Suppose that our network's input is photographs of all three samples. It would be wasteful to use eight output neurons, one for each type. A much more sensible approach would be to use just three neurons, one for each factor. In fact, it may be faster to train three separate one-output-neuron networks than one three-output-neuron network. But that is an architectural decision, discussed elsewhere. At this point, we are simply dealing with a black box having three photographic inputs and sufficient outputs to determine a blood type. In problems of this type, it is better to use the more compact binary encoding for output classes.

There is no reason to limit compact encoding to binary subclasses, although the situation can rapidly become quite complex. Serious consideration should be given to separate subclasses whenever the classes are separable. For example, consider a network that must listen to a spoken sound and provide some classification information. Its task might be to decide whether the starting articulation was from the lips, tongue, or palate, and whether or not its continuation was nasalized. (This is, of course, a vast simplification of an extremely complex problem.) There are six possible categories. A good design might be to use three output neurons for the articulation, one each for lips, tongue, and palate, and one output neuron for the nasalization, giving a total of four outputs.

Care must be taken that compact encoding not be used in problems that only give the *appearance* of being separable. Perhaps an employee of some government is pulling samples of high altitude photographs of crops from a satellite transmission. These crop photos are fed to a neural network, which must decide the type of crop (corn, wheat, soybeans, et cetera) and whether or not the crop is diseased. It would be tempting to allocate one output neuron for each type of crop and then just one neuron for the health–disease question. But this is not a separable decision. The manifestation of disease could be different for each crop. While such a design *might* be able to be made to work given a sophisticated network, it would be asking a lot. A far better approach would be to have two (or more, if a variety of diseases is possible) output neurons for each crop type. One neuron would be activated for healthy corn, another for diseased corn, and so forth. A large number of neurons would be required, but training time and performance would most likely be better than if one neuron were dedicated to the entire range of crop diseases.

A final possibility is to use *equilateral encoding*. This relatively complex procedure involves projecting the class basis vectors into a lower dimension subspace. It has the advantage that learning is often enhanced when there are many classes. This method of encoding information, which can also be applied to input data, is fully described on page 255.

Supervised versus Unsupervised Training

The preceding discussion has assumed that during the training phase we tell the network the true class membership of each training sample.

Since this is the most common situation, the majority of this book will be devoted to *supervised training* models. The reader should be aware, though, that it is possible to let neural networks discover salient characteristics of training data on their own. Models that are capable of *unsupervised training* can be especially valuable in exploratory work. Sometimes the researcher hypothesizes that distinct classes exist in a collection of samples, but is not sure what those classes are. Another possible situation is that the data falls into defined classes, but it is suspected that some of the classes contain several subclasses. Identification of these subclasses can not only aid in understanding the problem, but can often lead to improved performance by suggesting restructuring of the training set. These and other issues relating to unsupervised training are discussed starting on page 327.

3

Autoassociation

A network can be trained to reproduce its input at its output. This has many applications, such as guided image enhancement and filtering noise from signals.

When a neural network has exactly as many output neurons as input neurons and is trained so that its outputs attempt to match its inputs for every member of a training set, it is said to be an *autoassociative network*. Of what use would such a network be? It seems silly, because if we already know the inputs, why would we want a network to reproduce that input? The answer is that these networks tend not to reproduce just any input pattern applied to them. Rather, they tend to reproduce only those input patterns for which they have been trained. The effect is that if a trained network is presented with an input pattern that resembles a pattern on which it was trained, its output will (hopefully) be close to the training pattern that most closely resembles the trial input. This means that if a trial input is nearly identical to one of the training patterns, except that it has been corrupted by noise or is partly missing, then the network will act as a noise filter or pattern completer.

Autoassociative Filtering

Several of the special applications of autoassociative models described in later sections will require the same algorithm: an autoassociative filter. That algorithm will be described here. Uses for it will follow.

The basic principle involved is that a neural network is trained to reproduce its input for many different offsets of a pattern (or perhaps several patterns). If the data is a time series, these offsets will be time lags (phase angles). If it is an image, the offsets will be in two dimensions. The application will determine how far the offsets must extend and whether or not they extend in more than one direction. That issue will be discussed later as needed. For now we only need to understand that we will require multiple presentations of the pattern(s) to be learned. These presentations will vary in time or space.

After the network is trained using many offsets of a pattern, the test data (signal to be filtered) is applied to the network's inputs in sections using the same offsets as were used in training. For each offset, the computed outputs of the network are then shifted in such a way as to counter the offset at the input. Each point in the filtered result is computed as the mean of all "un-offset" network outputs. *The quality of the filtered result will depend on how many of the trial presentations have a corresponding presentation in the training set.* If every possible version of the pattern that may appear in the trial data appeared in the training data, the filter can perform quite well.

The preceding, confusing description of an autoassociative filter can be clarified with a diagram. Suppose that we wish to teach the network to emphasize a sawtooth wave. We would want to train the network with every possible phase angle, limited only by the discrete sampling. This is because we assume that the trial signal will be relatively long, meaning that the sawtooth pattern will be seen at all phase angles relative to arbitrary starting points. A typical training procedure is shown in Figure 3.1.

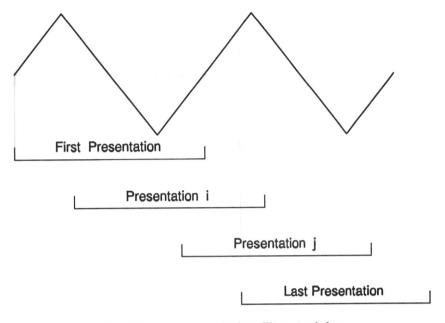

Fig. 3.1: Autoassociative filter training

Each bracketed interval represents one training sample. Every phase angle is in the training set. It is generally best to slide the window one point at a time, so that maximum resolution is obtained. Two arbitrarily chosen sample windows are labeled i and j. These will be referred to when the actual filtering is described later.

Note that the width of the sample window was set equal to the period of the pattern to be learned. This is the minimum necessary to do a reasonable job of filtering. If multiple periods are learned, the quality will improve. However, location of the starting and stopping points of the pattern will become more difficult, as partial patterns are not represented in the training set. The more sample periods contained in the training window, the more this "partial pattern at boundaries" effect will become a problem. This is because more periods in the window mean wider windows, and wider windows mean more opportunities for windows to contain the pattern only partly.

After the network has been trained to reproduce the pattern at all possible offsets, we are ready to filter a signal. The filtering process is diagrammed in Figure 3.2.

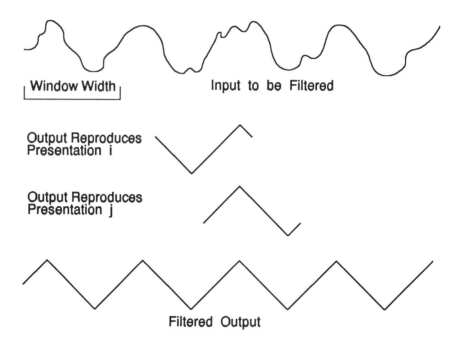

Fig. 3.2: Autoassociative filtering

The top of the figure shows a signal consisting of the sawtooth pattern plus noise. Just under the input, at the left, is the sliding window. This window will be positioned at each discrete sample point. The trial signal subset covered by the window will be presented to the trained network. The outputs produced by the network will be used to compute the filtered output for the exact same window section. Each point in the filtered output signal will be the average of the corresponding network outputs for all window positions that enclose that point. Thus, we see that the first (leftmost) filtered output point will be generated from just one presentation. It will be the leftmost output neuron of the leftmost trial window. The second filtered output point will be the mean of two numbers: the second output neuron of the first trial window, and the first output neuron of the second window. In the interior of the series, each filtered output point will be the average of as many points as there are inputs/outputs in the network (the window width). The components of the average that make up an interior point will extend from the rightmost output neuron of the leftmost trial window enclosing that point, through the leftmost output neuron of the rightmost trial window enclosing that point.

Two of the many window placements in Figure 3.2 are labeled i and j. These correspond to the same training positions in Figure 3.1. When the window is placed on the trial signal at position i, the network will tend to reproduce the training signal closest to the input under that window. That will most likely be the training sample i shown in Figure 3.1. A similar effect will happen for window placement j and all other placements not labeled. Note that the outputs align with each other. That is the key. Although here the reproduction of each window section is shown to be a perfect match to the training sample, in practice it will not be quite so clean. But because the reproductions all line up in the same phase relationship, thanks to including all phases in the training set, errors will tend to cancel each other as the window outputs are averaged, while the trained pattern will be reinforced.

Mathematically, the filtering can be defined as follows: let the window width (number of input/output neurons) be n. Index the window placements from origin zero. In other words, the window covering the first n points (points 0 through n - 1) in the signal is window 0. The window covering points 1 through n is window 1, et cetera. Also number the n output neurons from origin zero. Suppose we present the trial signal to the network using window position i. In other words, the inputs to the network are the trial signal inputs i through $i + n$ - 1. Let us denote as $O_{i,j}$ the achieved activation level of output neuron j for this presentation. Then, as long as we are in the interior of the signal, so that the summation below does not extend past an end, we can compute the value of point k in the filtered output as:

$$\mathrm{FILT}_k = \frac{1}{n} \sum_{i=k-n+1}^{k} O_{i,k-i} \qquad\qquad 3\text{-}1$$

When we compute filtered output points near the ends of the signal, the formula is the same except that the sum obviously does not include points that do not exist, and the divisor of n for finding the mean must be reduced to be equal to the number of terms that actually went into the sum.

Code for Autoassociative Filtering

The following subroutine uses a trained autoassociative network to filter a signal. It calls the external subroutine evaluate to execute the trained network. Only the declaration for evaluate is given here.

```
/*
    This is the declaration for a subroutine which executes a trained auto-
    associative neural network.
*/

void evaluate (                    // Execute trained autoassociative network
   int n ,                         // Number of inputs and outputs
   double *in ,                    // Input to the network
   double *out                     // Outputs returned here
   ) ;


/*
    This is the actual filtering routine
*/

void aut_filt (                    // Autoassociative filter routine
   int n ,                         // N of net ins and outs (window width)
   int m ,                         // Length of the series to be filtered
   double *in ,                    // Input series to be filtered
   double *out ,                   // Output series of filtered input
   double *work                    // Work vector n long
   )

{
   int i, j, n_presentations, lim ;

   for (i=0 ; i<m ; i++)           // Zero output in preparation for
      out[i] = 0. ;                // cumulating window results

   n_presentations = m - n + 1 ;             // This many windows done
   for (i=0 ; i<n_presentations ; i++) {     // Loop does all presentations
      evaluate ( n , in+i , work ) ;         // Run net for this window
      for (j=0 ; j<n ; j++)                  // Cumulate sum of
         out[i+j] += work[j] ;               // all presentations
      }

   if (n_presentations > 1) {                        // Divide to get means
      lim = (n_presentations < n) ? n_presentations : n ; // Max possible
      for (i=0 ; i<m ; i++) {                        // Loop divides each output
         j = m - i ;                                 // If we are at the far end
         if ((i+1) < j)                              // or at the near end we must
            j = i + 1 ;                              // compute the number in sum
         if (j > lim)                                // In the interior the
            j = lim ;                                // max went into the sum
         out[i] /= (double) j ;                      // Divide to get mean
         }
      }
}
```

The above code is straightforward. It starts by zeroing the output array, where the sum of all window presentations will be cumulated to form the filtered output. Then, the presentations are done with a sliding window. The last step is to divide each sum in the filtered output array by the number of presentations that went into that sum, to get a mean. The maximum possible number in each sum is the lesser of the total number of presentations and the width of the window. The first and last filtered points will each have only one presentation. The next points in will each have two components in their sum. The next will have three, et cetera. It will increase until the limit is reached. All interior points will have that limit.

Noise Reduction

One use for autoassociative neural networks is recovery of signals from a noisy environment. Sometimes the expected signals are a member of a fairly small collection of possibilities. Touch-tone telephone codes, for example, are composed of pairs of pure tones. One can easily construct optimal filters for small sets of pure tones by using standard mathematical formulas. But such theoretically derived filters become complex when more than a few tones are involved. And they become nearly impossible to compute when the signals being sought are not pure tones. Wiener filters, for example, are designed based on power spectra and ignore phase information. Suppose that the possible signals are composed of many harmonics arranged in precise phase relationships. Perhaps we are looking for bursts of spikes in particular timings. Theoretical derivation of appropriate filters is difficult at best. On the other hand, a very straightforward approach is to train an autoassociative neural network using samples of the patterns.

Samples for training the network could be artificially produced from known models, or they could be reasonably clean samples of real data. In fact, if enough samples are available, they could even be quite noisy samples of real data (see page 31). Then, when trial samples of a signal are applied to the network's inputs, its outputs will reproduce a trained pattern if that pattern is present in the input, even though it may be corrupted by noise. If none of the trained patterns is present in the input, the output will be relatively low amplitude random noise. This can be dealt with by training the network with several time-shifted versions of each of the example patterns. The trial signal is applied to the trained network several times, with time shifts equal to those used in training the network. If the outputs of these multiple trials are averaged, the reconstructed patterns will be reinforced if present, while the random-noise outputs produced if the pattern is not present will tend to cancel each other out.

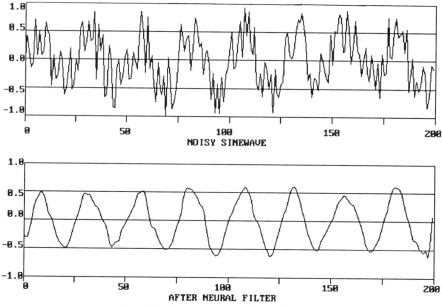

Fig. 3.3: Autoassociative filtering

An example of this type of signal filtering is shown in Figure 3.3. Two hundred points of a sine wave having a period of 25 were generated. Two hundred uniform random numbers on (-1, 1) were also generated. A noisy sine wave was computed as the sum of 40 percent pure sine plus 60 percent random noise. The model chosen was a three-layer feedforward network (described in detail later) having 25 input and output neurons and 10 hidden neurons. The training set consisted of 25 samples of a pure sine wave, with the samples covering 25 equally spaced phase angles. A mean output error of 0.022 percent was obtained after a short training period.

In order to filter the noisy signal, it was presented to the trained network in sets of 25 consecutive points. An output array 200 points long was initialized to 0. For each of the 200 - 25 + 1 = 176 presentations, the network outputs were cumulated in the corresponding position in the output array. So first, points 0 – 24 of the input signal were applied to the network inputs, with the network outputs cumulating into points 0 – 24 of the output array. Then points 1 – 25, then 2 – 26, et cetera, were applied, until finally points 175 – 199 were done. When all presentations were finished, each element in the output array was divided by the number of trials that went into the sum to get a mean. This would be 25 for all interior points, dwindling to just one point at the ends. That filtering procedure has already been described more rigorously starting on page 24. As can be seen in Figure 3.3, results were quite good for this simple filter.

Of course, no competent scientist would use a neural filter for a simple problem like this. Digital filters having all sorts of nice optimality properties exist for this task, and any of them would most likely be superior to an autoassociative neural filter. On the other hand, what if the pattern sought is not a pure wave, but is very complex? And what if there are several possible patterns, which may have very different spectral characteristics? When one considers that all one needs to do is train a network with examples of the patterns in order to get a filter that will emphasize those patterns in the presence of noise, an autoassociative network becomes appealing. An example of this appears in the next section.

Learning a Prototype from Exemplars

In the previous example, the neural network was trained on samples of the exact data it was supposed to reproduce. Sometimes we do not have the luxury of possessing this information. One virtue of autoassociative neural networks is that they are usually capable of learning prototypical patterns from collections of noisy examples of those patterns. As long as all examples of a particular pattern are at least fairly similar to each other and are reasonably different from all examples of any other individual patterns that are to be learned simultaneously, performance should be good.

An important data consideration is that a sufficient number of samples of each pattern should be available so that the network is able to distinguish between the aspects of the samples that are in common (the pattern to be learned), versus the aspects that are not shared (the noise to be rejected). If the same noise pattern happens to appear in a significant fraction of the training samples due to using an excessively small training set, the network certainly cannot be expected to know that it is noise! It will assume that it is part of the pattern to be learned. Such artifacts are called *communal noise*.

To demonstrate the ability of a neural network to learn from noisy samples, four distinctive signal patterns were created. The first two are short bursts of unusual periodic waveforms. The second is the negative of the first. The third pattern is a trivial sine wave. The last is a pair of pulses. They are illustrated in Figures 3.4 through 3.7. In each figure, the top signal is the pure prototype. The bottom signal is a typical example of a training signal, derived from the pure prototype by adding random noise. Each signal contains 100 points.

The network used for this demonstration is a three-layer feedforward network with 10 neurons in the hidden layer. One hundred noisy random samples of each of the 4 prototypes were used to train the network, giving a total of 400 signals in the training set. It is vital to remember that *no pure prototypes were presented to the network*. The network saw only noisy examples, closely resembling the bottom signal in each of Figures 3.4 through 3.7.

After training was complete, the network was presented with noisy samples of each of the four prototypes. The test samples did not duplicate any of the training samples; they were contaminated with new random noise. This input, along with the filtered output, is shown in Figures 3.8 through 3.11.

Exposing Isolated Events

Autoassociative neural networks can be used to make isolated patterns more visible amid a noisy background. This is similar to the general filtering described in a previous section. It is different, however, in that here the focus is on events of short duration, and their position in time (for a signal) or space (for an image) is important. When the filter shown in Figure 3.3 was created, we were able to treat the training signal as a continuous pattern and sample it at a sufficient number of time lags so that every phase angle at which it might appear in the input window was represented in the training set. Each training sample was a complete example of the pattern; only the phase was unique. This yields tremendous reinforcement when the pattern is present for stretches significantly larger than the input window. On the other hand, performance suffers at border areas. When the input window contains part pattern and part nonpattern, due to the pattern just starting or stopping, that presentation will not be represented in the training set. Thus, the output of the network will be unpredictable, and most likely less than excellent. When the event of interest is of short duration, and we need to be able to locate its start and/or stop time, a different training approach is needed.

The problem with treating the input as continuous is that transitions from nonpattern to pattern and back are not in the training set. If these transitions are included, performance at boundaries can be improved. Dilution of the training set with this border information does lessen reinforcement in the interior, though. General performance can be expected to suffer.

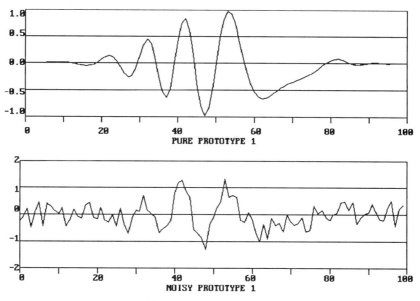

Fig. 3.4: Prototype 1

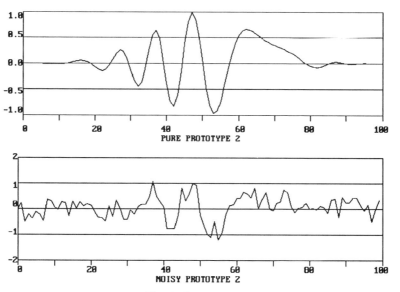

Fig. 3.5: Prototype 2

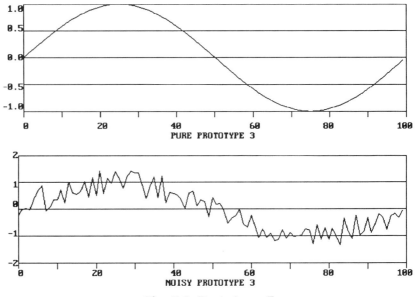

Fig. 3.6: Prototype 3

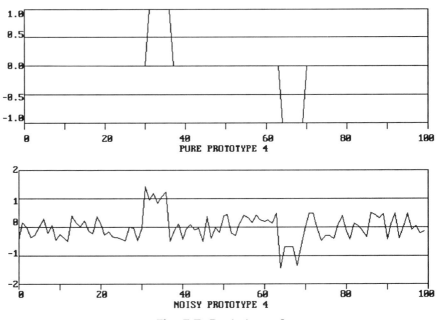

Fig. 3.7: Prototype 4

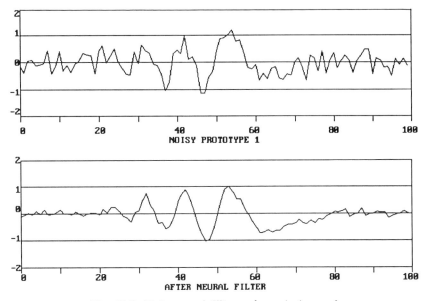

Fig. 3.8: Noisy and filtered prototype 1

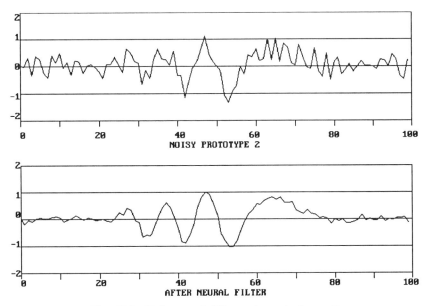

Fig. 3.9: Noisy and filtered prototype 2

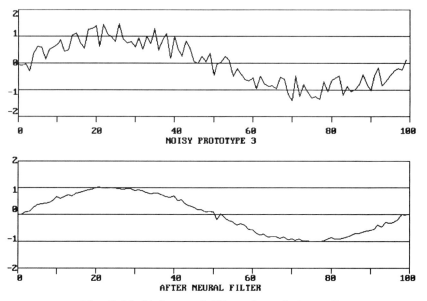

Fig. 3.10: Noisy and filtered prototype 3

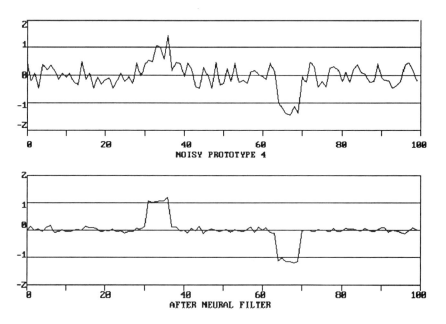

Fig. 3.11: Noisy and filtered prototype 4

Let us take a common case as our example. Suppose that the event is well defined, both in shape and in duration. In order to sample every border condition, as well as the complete event, we must prepend and append nonpattern data of the same length as the event. Then, the length of each training sample would be equal to the length of the event. The first sample is taken from the beginning of the extended series and is entirely nonpattern. The second sample is one to the right and includes the leftmost part of the pattern. This is repeated until the last sample is taken, entirely past the event. For an image, this would be done in two dimensions, entirely around the pattern. Due to the small fraction of the training set occupied by the actual pattern when extended in two dimensions, this rarely works excellently, though it can be good. This extension and sampling method for time series is shown schematically in Figure 3.12.

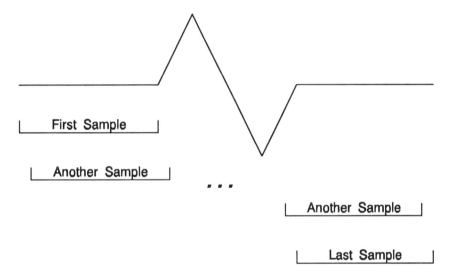

Fig. 3.12: Extending for boundary sampling

In the unusual but possible circumstance that the phase of the signal at the boundary is not fixed, we have a more serious problem. This could happen, for example, if the event is a continuously generated wave that is switched on and off asynchronously. Training simultaneously for every border position and phase is an impracticably large problem. The author is not aware of any practical way of solving this problem. Luckily, in real life, events usually at least start in the same way and often even finish consistently or taper off.

A damped sine wave makes a good example of event filtering. Its transition is sharp on one end and smooth on the other. An instance of such an event is shown in the top half of Figure 3.13.

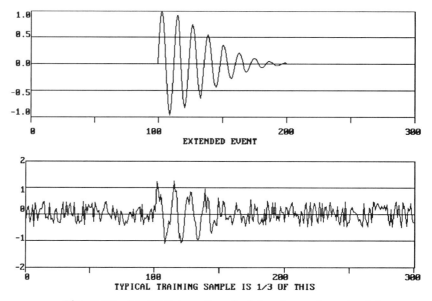

Fig. 3.13: An event, extended for boundary training

To make the problem even more difficult, training is done with noisy exemplars. A typical training sample is shown in the bottom half of that figure. The length of the event is 100 points, so the number of points in the extended pattern is 300 (the event, plus 100 points both before and after). A three-layer feedforward network is used. The hidden layer has 30 neurons. This relatively large number is necessary due to the large number of patterns (border positions) to be learned. In fact, even more would probably be useful. There are 200 possible border positions. (Actually, there could be only 199, as the first and last are pure nonevent.) Ten randomly noisy samples at each position were made. Training is quite slow due to the facts that the input layer is large, that there are many hidden neurons, and that the training set is large. As will be discussed in more detail later, it is the number of hidden neurons, 30, which is the real killer. Unfortunately, many hidden neurons are needed when many complex patterns must be learned.

To test this event filter, the pattern was extended and noise added. Figure 3.14 shows the resultant noisy signal (top half), along with the results of the neural filter. This filtering was done exactly as already described on page 30. Note that the actual filtering process is the same whether we are interested in a continuous signal, as in the earlier example, or in an isolated event, as in this example. The only difference is in how the training set is built.

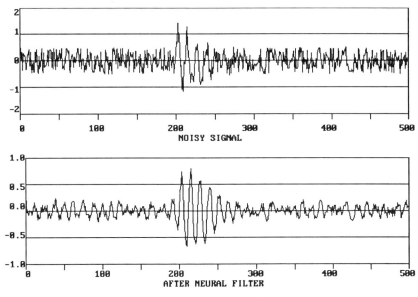

Fig. 3.14: Filtered event

This example illustrates several interesting considerations when doing this sort of filtering. First, observe that the amplitude of the filtered event is less than that of the original event in the input. This is a common effect, largely due to the nonlinearity of the output neuron's activation function. (See page 80 for a discussion of activation functions.) When learning in feedforward networks is described later, it will be seen that the compression at the extremes of the activation function causes learning to be more focused on typical data, rather than on the extremes. While this is responsible for neural networks' tolerance of outliers, it also means that when training is inadequate, performance at the extremes will be sacrificed first. The scaling for the network used in this example ranged from 10-percent to 90-percent activation. Shrinking the active range would alleviate this compression problem, but it would be at the expense of less tolerance to noise. You pay your money and you take your choice. Of course, the real solution would be to use more hidden neurons and train longer. Then performance at the extremes would no longer have to be sacrificed. But that is not always feasible.

A related problem seen here is that the start of the event is not as clearly defined in the filtered output as might be desired. This is mostly due to the fact that the beginning is an extreme value and so is compressed. The same steps taken to cure the compression problem would cure this as well.

The last anomaly is the small but well-defined waveform seen before and after the filtered event. This area contained random noise before filtering, so one would like it still to be random noise. Instead, it bears an uncomfortable resemblance to the event itself. This always happens; however, as seen here, it is usually of such low amplitude that it is not generally serious. It is caused by the fact that even random noise contains components similar to the event. These very low amplitude components are picked up by the filter and purified, while the random components orthogonal to the event are suppressed. The net result is very similar to the well-known Slutzky-Yule effect seen in moving average filters. See [Kendall and Stuart, vol. 3, 1976] for a discussion of this effect.

As a final note, it must be remembered that the purpose of the filter described above is to bring out certain events while reducing random noise. This is not the same thing as *detecting* the event. Detection of an event is a much simpler operation, essentially nothing more than classifying inputs as event versus nonevent. If our goal is simply to locate an event in time (signal processing) or space (image processing), there are much better ways than training an auto-associative network to filter the input. Classification networks are an excellent choice. Even a trivial correlation filter, implemented by convolution of the input series with samples of the event, is superior to using an autoassociative network.

Pattern Completion

Autoassociative neural networks are powerful pattern completers. If a network is trained on examples of complete patterns (or, similar to the previous section, many examples of incomplete patterns), it will tend to reproduce the complete patterns when presented with partial patterns. One recent research focus of this is in facsimile machines. Sometimes line noise or other problems will result in parts of characters being dropped. This can be alleviated by training an autoassociative neural network with a large collection of typical character shapes. Three crude examples are shown in Figure 3.15.

The actual digitization of the characters is in a much finer resolution than shown here, and all possible fonts would need to be represented. It is not a trivial problem. However, the payoff is substantial. If some parts of the character are omitted, a well-trained network will do an excellent job of filling in the missing pieces in order to generate the character the input most resembles.

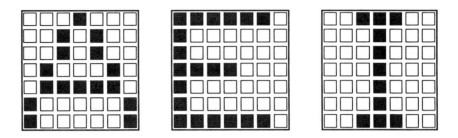

Fig. 3.15: Grid representation of A, E, and I

Error Correction

Autoassociative neural networks are also used for error correction in complex tasks. Since at this time their behavior is not strictly predictable, they are no substitute for rigorous error correction schemes when such schemes are usable. However, there are many problems whose structure does not admit traditional methods. For example, a recent area of research is voice-to-text conversion. Neural networks and other techniques are being used with increasing success to transcribe spoken dialogue into written text. One of the many approaches is to detect phonemes, then translate the phonemes into word parts. Pauses, or other more sophisticated schemes, delineate the actual words. One weakness of this is occasional generation of nonsense words. Straight dictionary lookup can tell if a nonsense word has been produced, but can do little to help otherwise. Many complex procedures have been devised to guess what word is really meant. But these procedures are all rule-based, and their success hinges on the quality of the rules. Sometimes it is better to trust experience rather than subjective rules. Here is where autoassociative networks are appropriate. The network is trained to reproduce all words from the expected vocabulary. Each trial word is presented to the network's input, and the network's output is taken to be the confirmed result. Whenever the input is one of the words on which the network was trained, that exact word will be returned (assuming, of course, that the network was trained well, which can be tested). But when a word outside its vocabulary is presented, the output will usually be one of the trained words that the network feels is closest to the input word.

In all fairness, it should be pointed out that there are several problems with this approach. Unlike a rigorously defined rule base, its actions cannot be easily predicted without actually trying it. This frightens many people.

Another problem is that for many network models, there is no absolute guarantee that the output of the network will be one of the words on which it was trained. In some cases, nonsense words can still be produced. On the other hand, it is interesting that in such cases, they are often "sensible" nonsense words, such as might be written by a young child. For example, suppose the word "karate" is spoken and slightly garbled by the translation algorithm. The nonsense result is input to the autoassociative neural network. The output might be "kroty". In some applications, this output would be superior to something like "crotchety", which might be generated by a rule-based dictionary algorithm.

Encoding Words

The means by which input/output data for an autoassociative neural network is encoded can be critical to operation of the network. Every problem is different, but the subject of word encoding illustrates some of the general areas that should be addressed.

To simplify the problem, assume that we are dealing with only 26 caseless letters of the alphabet. Capitals, numbers, punctuation, and other special characters will be ignored. Some upper limit on the length of a word will need to be established, as that defines, in conjunction with the encoding scheme, the number of input and output neurons. We need a method by which words can be unambiguously translated from a letter representation to a "network-friendly" representation, and back again.

First, we must understand that, despite the fact that we all have memorized our ABCs, the alphabet is truly unordered. B is not greater than (or less than) A. Thus, we should avoid using incremental degrees of activation to represent different letters. It would not do to let 10-percent activation of a neuron represent A, 12-percent be B, et cetera. Binary coding is called for.

The most obvious encoding method is to use one neuron for each letter of the alphabet, for each word position. Thus, if our maximum word length were 4 letters, we would need 4 * 26 = 104 input and output neurons. Exactly one of the first set of 26 neurons would be activated, according to the first letter in the word, while the other 25 would be off. The same would be done for the other letters. If the word were shorter than four letters, the blanks could be represented by all neurons being off. While this is an obviously primitive method, requiring a large number of neurons, this method must not be sniffed at. In many applications, it is the method of choice, for it has a desirable property: if a letter is incorrect, exactly two bits (neurons) will be in error. One bit will be on when it should be off, and another will be off when it should be on. Since most neural network models are directly or indirectly responsive to the number of bits by which a trial pattern differs from an expected pattern, this is significant. As will be seen, other encoding methods may not have this property.

At the opposite extreme from brute force 1-of-26 encoding is optimal binary encoding. The letter A would be represented as 00001, B as 00010, C as 00011, et cetera. We can use just 5 bits (input neurons per letter) to encode all 26 letters, and have $32 - 26 = 6$ characters to spare. This, though, is usually the worst possible choice. Many errors, such as substituting C for B, differ by only one bit. Substituting O for P causes a difference of all 5 bits. This lack of relationship between actual severity of error and perceived severity of error can seriously impact the network's performance.

In many cases, we can circumvent that problem of binary coding by clever choice of the grouping. We may even want to abandon entirely binary division and use some other low-radix classification. In the alphabet example above, we arbitrarily let the highest bit be off if the letter was $A - O$, and on if it was $P - Z$. Suppose we know that the algorithm that gives us our trial word is unlikely to confuse a vowel with a consonant. In other words, if it says a letter is an A, its probable mistakes would be limited to the letter actually being an E, I, O, or U. Now, we could use one bit to signify whether the letter is a vowel or a consonant, then use $26 - 5 = 21$ bits in a 1-of-21 encoding to select the consonant. If the letter is a vowel, we would, of course, need only 5 of those 21 bits. We have reduced the number of bits from 26 to 22 by some binary encoding, but still have correspondence between severity of error and number of erroneous bits. This could be taken further if we subdivided the consonants. Perhaps we know that plosive consonants are unlikely to be confused with gutturals. The 21 bits used for consonants could be subdivided.

There is no vital reason for limiting ourselves to binary divisions. If there is a logical separation into three classes, use a set of three bits and encode the class as 1-of-3. Detail information for each of the three main classes would be encoded in other bits, possibly themselves factored into subclasses. There is no intrinsic limit to our ability to do this, although the larger the radix, the less reduction in bits we get. Nonetheless, it is always in our best interest to attempt to factor the data as much as possible. As long as the encoding classes are defined in such a way that errors across the classes are much less likely than errors within the class, we can maintain a good relationship between the severity of the error and the number of incorrect bits.

Data Compression

Three-layer feedforward networks trained for autoassociative recall are sometimes used for data compression. These networks are discussed in detail starting on page 77, so their inner workings will be glossed over here. All that is important to understand at this point is that this model consists of the usual hypothetical input layer and the actual output layer, with a single layer of neurons hidden between the input and output layers. In general, there are far fewer neurons in the hidden layer than in the input and output layers. A three-layer feedforward network having six input and output neurons and two hidden-layer neurons is shown schematically in Figure 3.16.

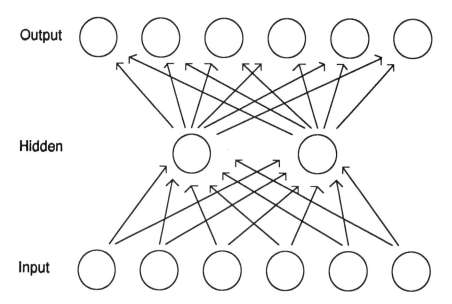

Fig. 3.16: Three-layer network

The principle of compression is as follows. The network is trained in autoassociative mode using blocks of typical samples of the data. If we are compressing signals, we would use short, contiguous sections of many samples of the signal. If we are compressing images, we would use small, rectangular blocks of sample images. (The classic paper describing this technique is [Cottrell, Munro, and Zipser, 1987].) The more our training samples resemble the actual data that will be compressed later, the better the quality of compression will be. After training is complete, we compress data by applying it to the input of the network. For each data sample applied, compute the activations of the hidden neurons. This comprises the compressed data. (Recall that there are fewer hidden neurons than input/output neurons.) To uncompress the data, use the hidden-neuron activations to compute the outputs.

Obviously, there will be a tradeoff between the degree of compression and the quality of reproduction. More hidden neurons will enable more accurate reproduction, but will result in less compression. Also, be aware that the quality of reproduction is directly related to the completeness of the training. As long as all possible data patterns are at least approximately represented and training is sufficiently completed, results will be excellent. On the other hand, if the network is later called upon to compress data that does not resemble anything in its training set, it may not perform well.

The principal problem with this type of compression is that if the blocks are regularly spaced, their seams will be faintly visible on the uncompressed image. Work is being done to alleviate this problem using staggered positions having varying degrees of overlap.

4

Time-Series Prediction

This chapter discusses how neural networks can be used to predict time series. No particular neural model is implied; only the general subject of time-series prediction with neural networks is covered.

Prediction of future values of a time series is an extremely common problem. Economists want to predict economic figures based on current and historical measurements. Meteorologists want to predict the weather based on recent changes in barometric pressure and other data. Communications specialists want to predict future sunspot activity based on recent solar events. And everybody wants to be able to forecast stock market prices. Thus, it should come as no surprise that there is a tremendous body of literature on time-series forecasting. This section will barely scratch the surface of that important field, even when the topic is restricted to use of neural networks for prediction. What will be attempted here is to survey some of the more important aspects of prediction and point the reader in appropriate directions for enrichment.

The first issue to be addressed is the reason for using neural networks at all. There is a fantastic number of prediction algorithms already in existence, most of them having solid theoretical foundations and proof of competence. Neural networks, on the other hand, are poorly understood in many cases. Their correct operation cannot always be rigorously verified. The means by which they do their prediction is often obscure. But once again we come back to the same two primary reasons for choosing a neural network over more traditional techniques:

1)   They are so versatile that they do not require us to choose a model. Rather than having to choose between AR versus MA versus ARIMA versus exponential smoothing versus spectral decomposition versus . . . ad nauseam, we can just throw a mountain of data at the network and let it ruminate. It will choose its own model and generally do a good job of it.

2)   Bizarre noise patterns, including chaotic components having very heavy tails, are tolerated by neural networks far better than they are by most other methods. It is now known that many important time series have significant chaotic components.

The only real danger inherent in many neural network techniques is overfitting. Since most networks contain a large number of free parameters, far more than other traditional models, it is easy to fit the training set accurately while poorly modeling the population. But careful testing, necessary with any technique, can detect this.

The Basic Model

Any neural network that is capable of accepting real-valued vectors as input and producing real-valued outputs may be used for time-series prediction. This chapter will not assume that any particular model is used; treatment of the problem will be applicable to any such network.

For now, we will assume the simplest possible structure. The neural network is a black box having one or more inputs and exactly one output. We are attempting to predict one point ahead in a single time series. Extensions to this simple structure will be discussed later. A typical mapping of a time series to a neural network for prediction is diagrammed in Figure 4.1.

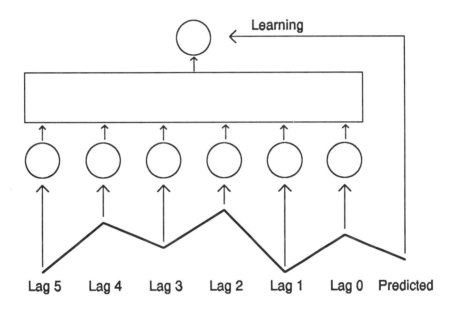

Fig. 4.1: Simple time-series prediction

That figure demonstrates the use of six contiguous points in a time series to predict the next point. A training series is used to generate a large number of individual samples. Each sample for the model shown here would consist of seven points: the current point (lag 0), five historical points (lags 1 through 5), and the following point, which would be used to direct the training of the output neuron. Usually, every set of seven contiguous points available in the training series would be used for training. As can be seen, the training set can become very large. It is also possible to make use of more than one training series to generate the training set.

If use of every contiguous group of points results in what is considered to be an excessive number of training samples, it is reasonable to use a subset. However, extreme care should be taken if a deterministic method is used to choose the subset. Straight decimation (selection of every nth group) can easily cause bias in the training set. It is not uncommon for patterns to vary in cycles. Deterministic sampling can emphasize some patterns, while missing others. A far better approach is to select training samples randomly from the training series.

Figure 4.1 shows the predictors being contiguous points (lags from $0 - 5$). Many practical models will involve some separation. For example, suppose we are doing an economic forecast based on monthly figures. It might be reasonable to use six input neurons: one for each of the last four months (lags $0 - 3$), one for the same month a year ago (lag 12), and one for the same month two years ago (lag 24).

Figure 4.1 also shows the prediction being exactly one point into the future. Many times, we need to predict further out than just one point. That is perfectly reasonable. If we are working with monthly data and want to predict for the same month a year later, use the series point 12 samples ahead rather than 1 sample ahead as the training value. As will be discussed later in this chapter, though, it is usually best to limit a network to having to make only 1 lead prediction, whether that lead is 1 point into the future or 100 points ahead. Although most networks can easily accommodate multiple outputs, it is better not to try to train multiple outputs to learn different lead predictions. Instead, train separate networks for each lead time. In other words, do not design a network with 2 outputs, training 1 of the outputs to predict 1 point ahead, and the other output to predict 12 points ahead. Use 2 networks.

Input Data

On page 253 we will discuss many general details related to proper preparation of neural network input data. This section will deal only with issues specific to time series.

For our purposes, a time series is a sequence of measurements taken at equal intervals. The intervals are usually defined in terms of time, as in the case of audio data sampled 44,000 times per second, or Widget, Inc., sales volume sampled monthly. It need not be time, though. A production facility may measure some property of units coming down the assembly line, looking for deterministic control-process flukes related to the number of units manufactured. A maker of coated paper may measure the thickness of the coating at equi-spaced points along a roll. These are all considered time series, although time may not be directly involved. The only possibly important element is that the measurements must be equally spaced for some techniques to be valid. But even this restriction is not always needed. Sometimes the fact that there is an order relationship inherent in the sampling procedure is all that is required.

In most cases, the variable being measured is a single real number. There is no reason, though, to be limited in this way for neural networks. Vector-valued data can be spread across input neurons as easily as single numbers can be. The input data could conceivably be ordinal or nominal also. If each time-series point can take on one of the three values perfect, cracked, or burned, we could use three input neurons for each sample, turning on exactly one of the three, depending on the series value. If the input's values have an ordinal relationship, such as "pass", "marginal" and "fail", we *may* wish to use just one input neuron for each sample, and encode "pass" as full activation, "marginal" as half activation, and "fail" as no activation. These sorts of choices are discussed more fully starting on page 253, so will not be pursued here.

One vital aspect of time-series processing, especially for neural networks, is that large-scale deterministic components should be eliminated. This includes obvious trends and seasonal variation. The neural network's role should be limited to predicting more subtle effects. Although most neural networks can do an excellent job of modeling trends and seasonal variation, it is counterproductive to ask a network to do many tasks at once. To do so would be rather like teaching a beginning student of a foreign language the fine nuances of composition while simultaneously teaching the first 400 basic vocabulary words. While it can be done, learning is more efficient if the basics are dealt with first, before the advanced material is introduced.

Trend Elimination

Elimination of trend and seasonal variation is a surprisingly complex subject, far too broad to cover well here. A good practical discussion can be found in [Kendall and Stuart, vol. 3, 1976]. It is treated in a highly technical manner in [Brillinger, 1975]. An extremely thorough treatment is done by [Box and Jenkins, 1976]. However, it is so important to good prediction with neural networks that it must be discussed to some degree. There are primarily two reasons for eliminating large-scale trends, and one reason why we *might* want to keep seasonal variation:

- The network will assume that a trend is important information and will attempt to learn to use that information for prediction. That would be fine if it could do so without compromising itself. However, by eliminating trends that are easily predicted and added back in later, we free the network to concentrate on finer details.

- Neural networks are inherently nonlinear. While this is vital to their strength and robust behavior, much of their activity takes place in fairly linear regions of their neurons' activation functions. If large variation is superimposed on more important subtle information, the learning process will tend to scale down overall variation, thus depriving the smaller variation information of the benefits of nonlinearity.

- In some rare cases, the above point can be an argument *for* keeping seasonal variation. A certain local pattern may have one meaning (hence leading to a particular prediction) when the overall series is taking on large values, and another very different meaning (and hence different prediction) when the overall series is taking on small values. A neural network could learn to handle this by setting its bias levels in such a way that one set of neurons is driven to saturation (ignored) for large inputs, while another set is saturated for low inputs. The network would then consist of largely independent groups of neurons, with the group that is active at any time being determined by the overall input level. (Beginners who do not understand the above statement will find it clarified after reading later chapters.)

There are at least two quite different ways of eliminating a linear trend. Higher-order trends will not be considered here; see the previously cited references for that complex topic. These alternative methods often behave very differently, and the choice of which to use should be made carefully. At the minimum, a plot of the series should be examined.

One way to eliminate a linear trend is to do a simple least-squares fit of a line to the series. A variable X is defined to be the ordinal number of a sample point, while Y is the value of the series at a point. If there are n points in the series, the values of X will be 0, 1, ..., n - 1. In other words, $X_i = i$. Each of these X's will have a corresponding Y. We wish to fit a line of the following form:

$$y = mx + b \qquad \text{4-1}$$

We need values for m and b such that we minimize the sum for all X's of the squared differences between the Y predicted by the above equation minus the Y defined by the time series. The method for doing so is well known. First, compute the mean of each variable:

$$\bar{x} = \frac{1}{n} \sum_{i=0}^{n-1} x_i = \frac{n-1}{2}$$

$$\bar{y} = \frac{1}{n} \sum_{i=0}^{n-1} y_i \qquad \text{4-2}$$

Then compute the sum of squares (SS) about the mean, and the cross product:

$$SS_x = \sum_{i=0}^{n-1} (x_i - \bar{x})^2$$

$$SS_{xy} = \sum_{i=0}^{n-1} (x_i - \bar{x})(y_i - \bar{y}) \qquad \text{4-3}$$

The slope, m, and intercept, b, are finally calculated as:

$$m = \frac{SS_{xy}}{SS_x}$$

$$b = \bar{y} - m\bar{x} \qquad \text{4-4}$$

That done, the series is detrended by subtracting this line from each point:

$$\tilde{y}_i = y_i - (mx_i + b) \qquad \text{4-5}$$

The detrended series would be used to train the neural network. The prediction would be done from a similarly detrended series. To convert the network's predicted series into values equivalent to the original data, the predicted series would be retrended by adding the detrend line to each value:

$$y_i = \tilde{y}_i + (mx_i + b) \qquad \text{4-6}$$

The least-squares method just described, though intuitively excellent, has a few annoying shortcomings. It can give incorrect results in some very simple cases. For example, suppose we have a basic sine wave sampled in such a way that an integral number of periods appear. This series obviously has no deterministic trend. But notice that it starts out on a positive cycle and ends on a negative cycle. This will fool a least-squares fit into thinking that it has a downward trend. Using the above equations to detrend five periods of a sine wave will give the results shown in Figure 4.2.

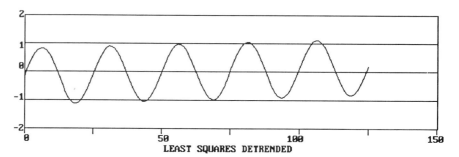

LEAST SQUARES DETRENDED

Fig. 4.2: A "detrended" sine wave

Observe that our "detrended" series now has a small but significant upward trend!

In order to avoid at least partially his and other shortcomings of the least squares method, such as its vulnerability to wild points, a much simpler method is often employed. Rather than basing the fit on the entire series, only the first and last samples are used. The slope and intercept are trivially computed as:

$$m = \frac{y_{n-1} - y_0}{n-1}$$
$$b = y_0$$

4-7

The series is detrended and retrended with the same formulas (Equations 4-5 and 4-6) as used in the least-squares method.

This method has an obviously serious shortcoming also, in that random error at the endpoints will affect results. Examining Figure 4.3, we see that it has a clearly defined upward trend. However, noise has conspired to make the values of the first and last sample points approximately equal. The above formulas will conclude that this series has no trend. Nevertheless, the "endpoints only" method is extremely popular and should be given strong consideration. Keep in mind also that it can be slightly modified to use the average of the first few and last few points. This makes it more immune to noise, yet does not seriously bias it if the series is long.

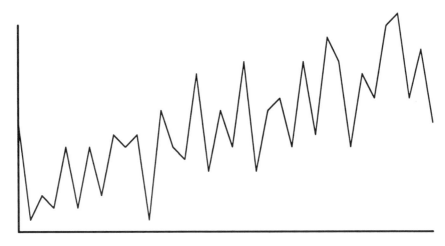

Fig. 4.3: A poor candidate for endpoint detrending

Code for Detrending and Retrending

Several short subroutines are given which use either of the above methods to detrend and retrend a time series. They are presented without explanation, as they are straightforward implementations of the formulas already discussed.

```
/*
   Forward declarations of local routines
*/

void detrend_lsq ( double *source , int n , double *dest ,
                   double *slope , double *intercept ) ;
void detrend_endpt ( double *source , int n , double *dest ,
                   double *slope , double *intercept ) ;

/*
   Main detrending routine
*/

void detrend (
   double *source ,        // Input signal for detrending
   int n ,                 // Its length
   double *dest ,          // Detrended output, may replace input
   int type ,              // 1=lsq, 2=endpt
   double *slope ,         // Output of slope per pt
   double *intercept       // Output of intercept at first point
   )
```

```
{
   if (n < 2) {                 // Degenerate case
      *slope = 0.0 ;
      *intercept = source[0] ;
      return ;
      }

   switch (type) {
      case 1: detrend_lsq ( source , n , dest , slope , intercept ) ; break;
      case 2: detrend_endpt ( source , n , dest , slope , intercept ) ; break;
      }
}

static void detrend_lsq (
   double *source ,
   int n ,
   double *dest ,
   double *slope ,
   double *intercept
   )

{
   int i ;
   double x, y, xmean, ymean, xvar, xy ;

   xmean = (double) (n-1) / 2.0 ;
   xvar = ymean = xy = 0.0 ;

   for (i=0 ; i<n ; i++)
      ymean += source[i] ;
   ymean /= (double) n ;

   for (i=0 ; i<n ; i++) {
      x = (double) i - xmean ;
      y = source[i] - ymean ;
      xvar += x * x ;
      xy += x * y ;
      }

   *slope = xy / xvar ;
   *intercept = ymean - *slope * xmean ;


/*
   Do the detrending here
*/

   for (i=0 ; i<n ; i++) {
      y = *slope * (double) i + *intercept ;
      dest[i] = source[i] - y ;
      }
}
```

```
static void detrend_endpt (
   double *source ,
   int n ,
   double *dest ,
   double *slope ,
   double *intercept
   )

{
   int i ;
   double y ;

   *slope = (source[n-1] - source[0]) / (double) (n-1) ;
   *intercept = source[0] ;

/*
   Do the detrending here
*/

   for (i=0 ; i<n ; i++) {
      y = *slope * (double) i + *intercept ;
      dest[i] = source[i] - y ;
      }
}

/*
   Retrending routine
*/

void retrend (
   double *source ,          // Input signal for retrending
   int n ,                   // Its length
   double *dest ,            // Retrended output, may replace input
   double *slope ,           // Input of slope per pt
   double *intercept         // Input of intercept at first point
   )

{
   int i ;
   double y ;

   for (i=0 ; i<n ; i++) {
      y = *slope * (double) i + *intercept ;
      dest[i] = source[i] + y ;
      }
}
```

The only comment that might be made about the above code is that if peak efficiency is to be traded for clarity of code, it is not strictly necessary to sum the x squares in computing xvar in detrend_lsq. One might use the formula:

$$\sum_{j=1}^{n} j^2 = \frac{n\,(n+1)\,(2\,n+1)}{6} \qquad\qquad 4\text{-}8$$

Seasonal Variation

Removing seasonal variation is even trickier than removing linear trends. Even barely adequate treatment of this subject is far beyond the scope of a book on neural networks. Therefore, the reader is simply reminded that it is usually, but not always, important that seasonal variation be removed, and a few pointers toward the right direction are given.

The single most critical concept in removal of seasonal variation is that *it is inexorably bound up with trend*. Linear (and higher-order, if any) trends MUST be removed either prior to seasonal trend removal or concomitantly with it. The relationship can be seen with a trivial example. Suppose we have monthly sales figures for several years, and they are consistently increasing. This monthly increase is entirely due to the quality of the product and the robustness of the economy; no seasonal trend is involved. A naive approach would be to find the average of all Januaries, the average of all Februaries, et cetera. These 12 figures might be considered the seasonal component. Since all February figures exceed all January figures, and all March figures exceed all February figures, et cetera, what we would have is 12 increasing numbers. This is clearly not a representative seasonal component! If the series were detrended *after* computing a seasonal component this way, then this supposed seasonal component subtracted, the resulting series would be sawtoothed rubbish. In order for the simple method of monthly averages to represent the seasonal component correctly, all deterministic trends must be removed *prior* to computing the averages.

A very common method for computing seasonal variation is to start by applying a low-pass filter to the series. The frequency cutoff of the filter is chosen so that seasonal variation is blocked while lower frequencies are passed. A frequent choice is a moving-average filter. In the fairly unusual case that the number of components m in a complete season cycle is odd, we can filter by summing every contiguous set of m samples and dividing by m to get the mean. In the more usual case of even-length seasons (12 months per year, 4 quarters per year, et cetera), we use a centered filter containing m - 1 weights equal to 2, and an additional weight of 1 at each end. Thus, if our season is 12 months, we would use the 13 weights (1,2,2,...,2,1) applied to every 13 contiguous samples, and divide by 24. After the low-pass filtered series is computed this way, it is subtracted from the original series. This removes all slow trends, leaving only seasonal variation, higher frequency variation to be learned and predicted by the network, and random error.

Once deterministic trends have been removed, as per the above method or some other, we can safely compute monthly averages (or whatever time unit is in use) to estimate the seasonal component. After the average for each month is computed, we center this seasonal component by subtracting its average (the grand mean of all 12 monthly averages) from each of the 12 monthly averages. By insuring that the sum of all 12 seasonal component figures is 0, we avoid confounding a constant offset with a seasonal variation. The centered seasonal component can then be safely removed by subtracting it from the original series. Now we have data that is more ready to be input to a neural network.

The above discussion has assumed that the trend and seasonal components are *additive*. In many practical problems, especially those arising from economic models, they are *multiplicative*. In this case, our best choice is usually to convert it to an additive model by taking logarithms of the series. There are alternative methods. We may determine the trend as before, but instead of subtracting the filtered series from the original series, we divide it into the original series. The monthly component is then computed by averaging and centering as in the additive model. However, this method rapidly becomes very complex. The details concerning this and other methods will not be covered here, as they stray too far from the central topic of neural network time-series prediction.

If the reader is now left with the impression that an important topic has been too lightly glossed over, the author has succeeded in his purpose. A full treatment of trend and seasonality is far beyond the scope of this book. The preceding discussion has been provided mainly to convince the researcher that trend and seasonality are vital considerations when neural networks are used for time-series prediction. The points raised are sufficient to guide the reader in the right initial directions. But it would be foolish to tackle an important problem that contains trend and seasonal components using no more of an arsenal than that dispensed here.

Differencing

One very popular technique for preprocessing time-series data is to compute the difference between successive points. Thus, rather than working with the raw data, we work with its changes. This can have many advantages, but a few dangers lurk about also.

First, note that differencing a time series completely eliminates a constant trend by converting it to a constant offset. Slowly changing trends are usually eliminated enough that they can be ignored. Even seasonal trends, if they have a long enough period, are often eliminated for all practical purposes. All the complexities of the preceding sections on trend can be ignored. This alone is a powerful argument for differencing.

There are many applications in which the notion of working with differences fits naturally into the problem. For example, stock market prediction may sometimes be done best by working with differences, especially if those differences are scaled to be relative to price. A $40 stock may have maximum weekly fluctuations of at most a few dollars for long periods of time. Special scaling would be needed to make these fluctuations in raw price significant enough for a neural network to use them efficiently. On the other hand, using the price *changes* as data would probably be more meaningful. Finally, using the *percent* price change would remove the effect of absolute price, often the best choice of all.

A warning is in order, though. Remember that differencing is a potent high-pass filter. If there is any possibility that low frequency information may be important to the network, we are in trouble. It may be that a particular pattern has one meaning when input values are relatively high, and another meaning when low. Differencing will remove this information. For example, it may be that a sudden price spurt when a stock is already at a relatively high price presages a breakout to new highs, while that same type of price spurt at a low price time means that investors are short covering, and the safety net is about to be taken away. The solution in this case is to use *both* the raw and differenced data as inputs to the network.

Scaling

Some neural networks are limited in the range that their output can attain. For example, the common feedforward network with a logistic activation function is theoretically limited to an output range of 0 to 1. In practice, the range is more like 0.1 to 0.9 at most, with even these values being somewhat difficult to attain. A few networks, such as common versions of the Kohonen model, are limited in the values their inputs can take on. And virtually *all* networks train more efficiently if their inputs and outputs are restricted to a "reasonable" range. This has important implications for time-series prediction.

It is obvious that a network's input/output limitations imply that we must prescale the series to meet these limitations, then comparably unscale the predictions. But there is another not-so-obvious consideration. As will be seen on page 80, many common network models employ sigmoid activation functions. These squasher functions tend to emphasize the importance of intermediate output values, while obscuring fine differences when the outputs are near their extreme high and low values. This means that predictions that approach the limits of the network's output will be less accurate than intermediate predictions. In particular, predicted values near the high end of the range will usually underestimate the best prediction, while those near the low end will overestimate the correct prediction. In other words, the range of predicted values will be compressed relative to what it really should be.

This leads us to assume that we should scale the series to a narrow range near the center of the network's limits, or employ linear output activation functions. But this is often counterproductive. In linearizing the network, we can hamper its ability to recognize patterns. This is not an extremely serious problem, as hidden layers can still operate over their full nonlinear range, which is all that is mathematically required. It is a consideration, though.

Another problem with restricting the range or linearizing the outputs is that immunity to outliers is compromised. The squashing activation functions are largely responsible for neural networks' robust behavior in the presence of unusual noise. Reducing the range of data expands the range that can be covered before squashing takes place. In some cases, excessively wild predictions can result.

The rule of thumb employed by the author is to aim for the series to cover approximately 70 to 90 percent of the theoretical range of the output neuron's activation function range. If predictions are excessively compressed, reduce the range as needed, but only as much as absolutely necessary.

Multiple Prediction

Multiple predictions from one network are possible, but are generally best avoided, especially if the predictions are widely spaced. For example, an electric utility may want to do two sorts of load prediction. One department would like to estimate how much power will be needed next year, based on consumption patterns over the last few decades (and perhaps other data as well). Another group, such as the control room engineers, needs to know how much power will be needed in the next hour. While both predictions could conceivably be made by the same neural network based on the same historical data, there are two reasons for not doing so.

The obvious reason is that the time scaling of the requisite data may be different. The yearly prediction would most likely be based on yearly or monthly data. Any finer resolution would be excess baggage. Also, their history would need to go back many years if large scale patterns were to be detected. In contrast, the hourly prediction would naturally need hourly (or finer) data, and it would at most need to go back several years, perhaps less. Any database used for training a single network to do both predictions would be either so large as to be unwieldy, or too small to do a good job for one of its tasks.

There is another, more subtle problem with multiple prediction. The further out into the future one attempts to predict, the more error is to be expected. Suppose that we want to predict 1 sample ahead and 10 samples ahead. In most cases of practical interest, the average error in the 10-ahead prediction will be significantly greater than that in the 1-ahead prediction. Most training algorithms choose the network's connection weights in such a way that the average error is minimized. Since the 10-ahead error will be the dominant component in the average error, that component will be favored in the training process. Weight changes that could produce a *relatively* large improvement in the 1-ahead error will not be made if they increase the *absolute* error in the 10-ahead prediction by an amount exceeding the absolute improvement in the 1-ahead, even though that may represent a relatively small worsening in the 10-ahead prediction. The net result is that the 1-ahead prediction will almost always be inferior to what it could be if it were done alone.

Multiple Predictors

The most basic time-series predictions are made using lags from a single time series as all predictors. This is easily extended to multiple series if needed. And, of course, there is no reason why the same lags need to be used for all series. An example using a simplistic stock market model is shown in Figure 4.4. That figure shows how several different time series can be combined into a lucrative dream. The series are the closing price of a stock at four different lags, quarterly earnings at two different lags, yearly earnings, and overall market price/earnings ratio. The network would be trained by collecting historical data for the stock and market PE, and using whatever lead time the hopeful millionaire desires as the output training figure.

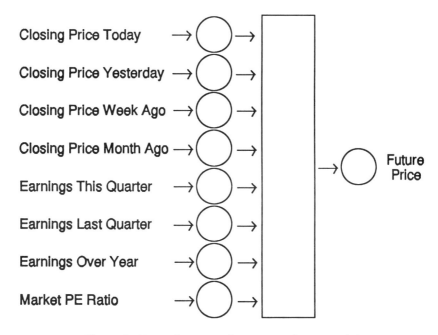

Fig. 4.4: Neural networks can make you rich

The inputs to a time-series prediction model need not be limited to measured values. Identifying information can often be extremely useful. For example, suppose that we are working with an electric utility to predict the next day's need for electricity. We have at our disposal the obvious historical data. We may even have meteorological data, as air conditioners are a major consumer of electric power. But what about holidays, especially those that are not always periodic? The majority of restaurants and households across America have their ovens running full force on Thanksgiving. It might be useful to dedicate a neuron to signifying whether the next day is a historically high consumption day.

Identifying information is not restricted to time domains. Series generated from assembly line measurements may have as input various status flags. Whether or not periodic maintenance was just performed on a critical subsystem could be an important predictor. Always remember that the standard rule of thumb for neural network data is, "If in doubt, throw it in." Let the network decide what is important and what is not. But of course, always save out some training data for verification that the network has learned to generalize, not just learned the training set!

Measuring Prediction Error

Suppose that we have trained a neural network to do time-series prediction. We have a test series with which to evaluate the performance of the trained network. Using groups of known points from the test series, we make predictions. For each prediction, we know the value of the series as predicted by the network, and we know the true value of the series. The problem now is to express the performance of the network in a useful manner.

Most neural network training algorithms work by minimizing the mean square error of the output(s). Naturally, during training this is done in terms of the scaled data that the network actually sees. For our purposes here, we will assume that the network's outputs have been unscaled, so that we are working with the real problem data. The mean square error is computed by finding the difference between the desired target output and the attained output, squaring it, and summing across all trials. The sum is divided by the number of trials to get a mean value. If t_i is the target (true) value of the prediction for trial presentation i, and o_i is the value obtained by the network, the mean square error for n trial presentations is calculated as:

$$\text{MSE} = \frac{1}{n} \sum_{i=0}^{n-1} (t_i - o_i)^2 \qquad\qquad 4\text{-}9$$

For various technical reasons addressed in later chapters, this is usually the easiest error measure to minimize. Therefore, despite the fact that mean square error may not always be the most meaningful figure, it certainly is an important one to understand.

The squaring operation in the above formula, while leading to all sorts of mathematical niceties, makes it difficult for humans to interpret mean square error directly. By taking its square root, we get the "root mean square" (RMS) error. This is an extremely popular error measurement. Electrical and communications engineers are familiar with the utility of expressing signal levels as RMS values. It is nicely interpretable in that it is linear. Doubling all individual errors will double the RMS error. The same doubling operation would quadruple the mean square error, causing difficulty in comparing results.

$$\text{RMS ERR} = \sqrt{\frac{1}{n} \sum_{i=0}^{n-1} (t_i - o_i)^2} \qquad \text{4-10}$$

RMS error is an absolute number in that it is not directly related to the magnitude of the predicted series. An RMS error of 5 is tiny if the series has typical values in the millions, but large if the series hovers around 10. Its scale is tied to the measurement unit of the data. Thus, if one person uses inches as a unit, and another tackles the same problem using millimeters, comparing errors becomes complicated by the fact that we must compensate for the different units. To avoid this, we must somehow divide the error by the predicted series values in order to get a unitless number. There are two common ways of doing this.

One way of expressing the error as a unitless relative quantity is to compute the RMS values of the error term and the series to be predicted, and use their ratio as the error measurement:

$$\text{REL RMS ERR} = \sqrt{\frac{\sum_{i=0}^{n-1} (t_i - o_i)^2}{\sum_{i=0}^{n-1} t_i^2}} \qquad \text{4-11}$$

The above formula is influenced by a constant offset from zero. In other words, adding a constant to the series will reduce the relative error due to an increase in the denominator. Sometimes the constant offset is meaningful, so this is what we want. If not, the mean of the series should be subtracted from each point so that we are working with true variance.

$$\text{REL RMS ERR} = \sqrt{\frac{\sum_{i=0}^{n-1} (t_i - o_i)^2}{\sum_{i=0}^{n-1} (t_i - \bar{t})^2}} \qquad \text{4-12}$$

Which of these formulas to use is problem-dependent. The determining factor is whether or not a constant offset of the series is to be considered meaningful. In most practical problems, it is not, so Equation 4-12 would usually be more appropriate.

Another, less common way of expressing the error as a unitless relative number is by dividing each error value by the target value *before* summing. In this case, the absolute value rather than the square is usually taken. Each term in the sum is the fraction of the true series value represented by the error. The mean of those fractions is usually called the *mean relative error* (MRE).

$$\text{MRE} = \frac{1}{n} \sum_{i=0}^{n-1} \left| \frac{t_i - o_i}{t_i} \right| \qquad\qquad 4\text{-}13$$

Programs for computing the above error must take care to avoid dividing by zero. In nearly all cases in which the above formula would be appropriate, the predicted series will have zero probability of equaling zero. Nonetheless, careful programmers will set a floor below the denominator. A common procedure followed when the denominator is less than a predefined minimum is to set the ratio equal to the numerator, rather than dividing the numerator by the floor value. Which method to use is problem dependent, but both should be considered.

The difference between the relative RMS error (Equation 4-12) and the mean relative error (Equation 4-13) lies principally in the denominator. The decision of which to use depends on the importance of the *variation* of the series versus the *current value* of the series. If we are measuring the position of a particle in a turbulent flow, whether the particle is at one extreme or the other, or near the center of its range, is probably of little interest as regards the error. We would most likely want to compare the degree of error with the overall degree of variation. Therefore, Equation 4-12 would be most appropriate. On the other hand, we may be trying to predict a stock price. In this case, using the total variation in the denominator would not be good. It would be preferable to be able to say that our prediction error is a certain fraction of the actual price. Thus, Equation 4-13 would be more appropriate.

The above error measures are not by any means a complete list of the possibilities. Another is the signal-to-noise ratio, discussed on page 359. The most important consideration is the problem itself. What do we *want* to measure? If it is to be relative to anything, what is it relative to? Does our proposed error measure make sense? Can inexperienced people have at least an intuitive grasp of its meaning? Only by carefully answering these questions can we arrive at the best way of describing the prediction error.

5

Function Approximation

Using neural networks to approximate functions is an extremely broad topic. This chapter will discuss a few diverse examples, but cannot come close to examining all possibilities. The previous major topics, classification, autoassociation and time-series prediction, can all be thought of as specialized forms of function approximation. If we define function approximation in its broadest sense, what we are left with is nearly everything else that a neural network can be used for! The focus here, though, will be on approximating functions that map from the vector-valued real domain to the vector-valued real range.

In one sense, neural networks *are* intrinsically function approximators. They accept one or more inputs and produce one or more outputs. Most networks produce a unique output for a given input, so this qualifies them as functions. Thus, the entire gamut of applications of neural networks falls into the blanket role of function approximation. However, for the purposes of this chapter, we will consider the more specific problem of using neural networks to map real-valued vectors to real-valued vectors. As will be seen, this is still an extremely broad category.

Univariate Function Approximation

Every student of numerical analysis learns how to approximate functions. The basic problem is that we have a function that is difficult to compute. Perhaps the computation is possible, but very slow. Perhaps it can only be measured from a physical process, and the measurements are expensive or haphazard. Perhaps it can be measured, but only approximately due to contamination by random error. What we need is a faster or easier way to compute the function at any point, given its values at some points. Neural networks are often an appropriate solution.

There is at least one class of numerical approximation problems for which there is no reason to try to replace traditional solutions with neural networks. This is simple approximation of transcendental functions. For example, floating-point libraries need to be able to compute trigonometric functions, logarithms, et cetera, rapidly. There is a solid body of numerical methods, including splines, rational approximations, continued fractions, and so forth, which do an excellent job and have their position well secured. Any time that rapid approximators can be explicitly derived, or computation of the underlying function is rapid enough to make standard fitting procedures feasible, those procedures should be used.

The usual difficulty encountered when trying to approximate a function for which only a limited number of collocation points are known is that between these points the approximating function often wiggles excessively. A classic example of a function that exhibits this behavior is the Gaussian function:

$$g(x) = e^{-x^2} \qquad\qquad 5\text{-}1$$

Special fitting methods are required to produce a good approximator for this function. As long as we can acquire as many collocation points as we desire, this is no problem. Custom fitting can be done to any difficult function if our supply of known points is limitless. On the other hand, what if only a few collocation points are all that we have and can get? Then we must use a generic "well-behaved" fitting method and trust that it will do a good job. There are many such methods, such as exponential splines, which have a good reputation. These traditional methods are not to be disparaged. The point being made here is simply that neural networks are generally reliable even in pathological cases and, hence, should be added to our arsenal of robust data-fitters.

The notoriously difficult-to-fit Gaussian function is shown in Figure 5.1.

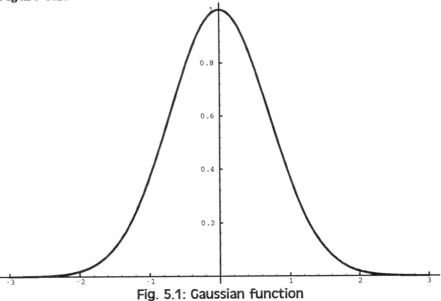

Fig. 5.1: Gaussian function

In order to demonstrate fitting to a limited number of points, 11 equally spaced collocation points were defined: (0, 1), (0.54546, 0.7427), (1.0909, 0.3042), (1.6364, 0.0687), (2.1818, 0.0086), (2.7273, 0.00059) and the five symmetric negative x points. If the primitive method of exactly fitting a tenth-degree polynomial to these 11 points is used, the approximating equation is shown in Figure 5.2.

Observe that the function is unable to remain flat between the outermost collocation points. Such ripples are characteristic of non-custom fits to difficult functions. Even worse, the approximating equation goes wild outside the range of collocation points. The difference between the true function and the approximation is shown in Figure 5.3.

A feedforward network with one hidden layer containing only *two* hidden neurons was trained on these same 11 points. Its approximation and error are shown in Figures 5.4 and 5.5, respectively.

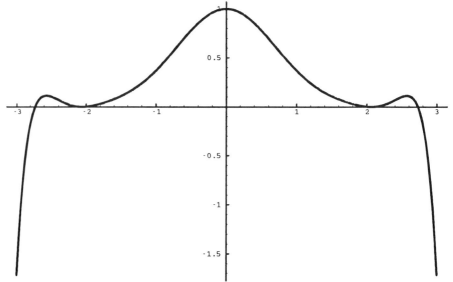

Fig. 5.2: Polynomial approximation to Gaussian function

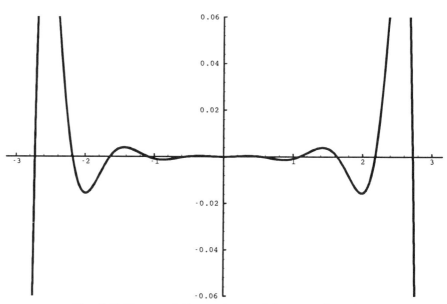

Fig. 5.3: Error of the polynomial approximation

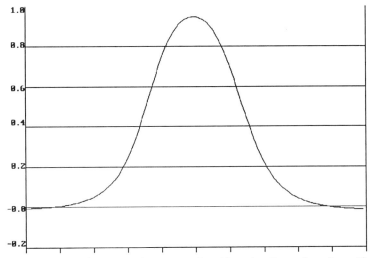

Fig. 5.4: Neural network approximation to Gaussian function

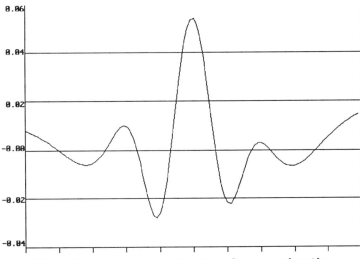

Fig. 5.5: Error of neural network approximation

It is a profound testimony to the approximating power of feedforward networks that such a close and smooth fit is able to be obtained by using only two hidden neurons. The relatively large error that occurs near (0, 1) is partially due to the nonlinearity of the output neuron's activation function. When feedforward networks are used for function approximation where serious noise problems are not expected, the output neurons are usually given linear activation functions. Alternatively, if it is difficult or impossible to change the activation function due to program limitations, the data can be scaled to cover a narrow interval in the center of the activation function's range, where it is nearly linear. Activation functions for feedforward networks are discussed on page 80.

The primary cause of the poor fit near (0, 1), though, is the design of the training set. Six of the 11 training points have Y near 0, while only one training point has Y at 1. Since the mean square error is minimized, there is great favoritism exhibited toward a good fit near Y = 0, at the expense of the fit near Y = 1. Duplicating the (0, 1) point, or including several additional training samples near X = 0, would largely solve this problem.

Inverse Modeling

Sometimes we can accurately model complex physical phenomena. Seismologists can predict the appearance of shock waves for specific types of earthquakes. Molecules have known x-ray diffraction patterns determined by their atomic structure. Radar returns at various polarizations can be predicted if the shape of the reflecting object is known. These pieces of information can be computed because acceptably accurate mathematical models of the underlying process exist. The real problem arises when we want to go in the opposite direction. A seismological pattern is observed. What type of earthquake caused it? A radar return arrives. What is the shape of the object that produced the reflection? Explicit inversion of complex models is frequently impossible.

Neural networks can aid in solving this problem. Suppose that we have a real-valued vector X which describes a condition. X may represent a type of earthquake, or an atomic structure, or a solid shape. Because of this condition X, a result Y is produced. Y may be a shock wave registered on a seismograph, or an x-ray diffraction pattern, or a radar return. Assume that we have a model m by which we can predict Y for any appropriate given X:

$$y = m(x) \qquad \text{5-2}$$

What we do is collect a representative set of X's and apply the model to each. If it is a stochastic model, one whose Y may not be uniquely determined for a given X, we must replicate each X as needed, to generate multiple samples of Y. The issue of what comprises "enough" X's and Y's is, unfortunately, problem-dependent and difficult to answer except by thorough testing of the trained network. The X's and Y's are used as a training set. Each Y is applied to the network's inputs, and the network is trained to produce the corresponding X at its output. This is shown in Figure 5.6.

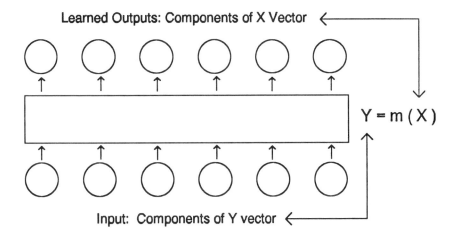

Fig. 5.6: Inverse modeling

After the network has been trained, it must be tested with the same basic procedure. If possible, X's that are different from those used to generate the training set should be chosen. Thorough testing is particularly important if the model is stochastic, as we then must ascertain whether or not the training set adequately sampled the range of random possibilities for Y. It is frequently the case that sampling may be found to be inadequate for only one or a few particular X values. If so, the only option is to generate more Y values for those X's, and retrain.

Multiple Regression

Multiple regression is a standard statistical technique by which one or more *independent* variables are used to predict a single *dependent* variable. For example, we may have n independent variables, X_1, X_2, ..., X_n and a dependent variable Y. Given many $n + 1$ long vectors of observed values for these $n + 1$ variables, the goal of multiple regression is to find values for $n + 1$ coefficients, a_i, $i=0$, ..., n, such that we can predict Y from given X values:

$$\hat{y} = a_0 + \sum_{i=1}^{n} a_i x_i \qquad\qquad \text{5-3}$$

The coefficients are traditionally chosen such that the sum of the squared error for all training samples is minimized. There are several standard techniques for computing these coefficients. They are discussed starting on page 165.

A serious disadvantage of the above technique is that in order for performance to be good, the relationship of the dependent variable to the independent variables must be linear. Any departure from linearity will be reflected in prediction error. If the exact nature of the nonlinearity is known, it can sometimes be compensated for by suitably transforming the independent variables. Unfortunately, we often do not have the luxury of knowing the nature of the nonlinearity. Also, there are many types of nonlinear relationships which cannot be linearized by transformations. In these cases, ordinary multiple regression is worthless.

Many neural network models, especially multiple-layer feedforward networks (page 77), can handle complex nonlinear relationships easily. If any of the nonlinearities is known in advance, a functional link network (page 223) can be used to improve learning. But if the nature of the relationship is totally unknown, it can still be modeled. As an example, consider the following function:

$$f(x,y) = 0.1 + \frac{1.0 + \sin(2x + 3y)}{3.5 + \sin(x - y)} \qquad\qquad \text{5-4}$$

This function is obviously very wiggly. It is graphed over the domain of -2.0 to 2.0 in Figure 5.7.

A training set was constructed from the function by sampling in two dimensions at equally spaced grid points, an interval of 0.2 being used for both X and Y. That spacing corresponds to the tick marks shown in the graph. The NEURAL program listed in the Appendix was used to train several three-layer networks.

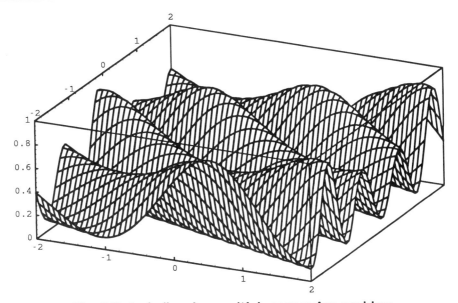

Fig. 5.7: A challenging multiple-regression problem

Hidden Neurons	Training Error	Test Error	RMS Error
1	4.479	4.469	0.2114
2	2.879	2.748	0.1658
3	0.981	0.842	0.0918
4	0.694	0.565	0.0752
5	0.382	0.305	0.0552
10	0.097	0.074	0.0273

The *Training Error* column in the above table shows 100 times the mean square error of the training set. A test set was constructed using grid spacing of 0.05195, a value chosen to avoid replication of training-set points, forcing the network to interpolate. The error for this set is shown in the next column. Note an interesting anomaly. The test-set error is actually less than the training-set error in all cases! In order to understand this highly unusual event, the network's computed outputs must be examined. What happens here is that the predictions are excellent in the interior of the domain, but deteriorate very badly near the borders, especially at the four corners where x and y are near 2.0 or -2.0. Since the test set is much larger than the training set, the mass of good predictions in the interior swamps out the poor predictions at the border to a larger degree in the large test set than in the smaller training set.

The last column in that table is the most important. It is the square root of the test set's mean square error. (Remember that the test error shown in the table is 100 times the actual test error.) As such, it can be considered a sort of average prediction error. Note how few hidden neurons are required to achieve respectable results with this unusually difficult function. This is all the more impressive when one considers that the majority of that error is coming from the extreme areas of the domain.

6

Multilayer Feedforward Networks

This standard workhorse family of networks is described in detail. Efficient algorithms for implementing them are presented. Several training methods are given, and comparisons are made with regard to alternative network architectures within this family.

Basic Architecture

A *multilayer feedforward network* consists of a set of neurons that are logically arranged into two or more layers. There is an input layer and an output layer, each containing at least one neuron. Neurons in the input layer are hypothetical in that they do not themselves have inputs, and they do no processing of any sort. Their activation (output) is defined by the network input. There are usually one or more "hidden" layers sandwiched between the input and output layers. The term "feedforward" means that information flows in one direction only. The inputs to neurons in each layer come exclusively from the outputs of neurons in previous layers, and outputs from these neurons pass exclusively to neurons in following layers.

The output of each neuron in the network is a function of that neuron's inputs. Given an input to such a network, the activations of all output-layer neurons can be computed in one deterministic pass; iteration is not required, and randomness does not play a role.

Some models allow connections to skip layers, in that outputs of neurons in one layer may connect directly to inputs of neurons in layers past the immediately following layer. Such networks will not be discussed in this book.

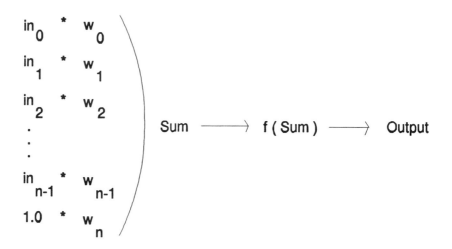

Fig. 6.1: An artificial neuron

A single neuron is shown schematically in Figure 6.1. It has n inputs, labeled from 0 through $n - 1$. It also has one assumed input, called its *bias*, which is always equal to 1.0. The neuron is characterized by $n + 1$ weights which multiply each input, and an *activation function* which is applied to the weighted sum of inputs in order to produce the neuron's output. The weighted sum of inputs, including the bias, is frequently called the *net* input. Thus, if our n inputs are $\{x_i, i = 0, ..., n - 1\}$, the neuron's output is calculated as:

$$out = f(net) = f(\sum_{i=0}^{n-1} x_i w_i + w_n)$$

6-1

The operational characteristics of this neuron are primarily controlled by the weights, w_i. Although the activation function $f(net)$ is also obviously important, it will be seen that in practice the neuron's operation is generally little affected by the exact nature of the activation function as long as some basic requirements are met. Training speed, on the other hand, may be strongly impacted by the activation function. This will be discussed later.

Feedforward networks usually have a single layer of hidden neurons sandwiched between the input and output layers. Such a network is called a three-layer network. Rarely, two hidden layers will be needed. A four-layer network is shown schematically in Figure 6.2.

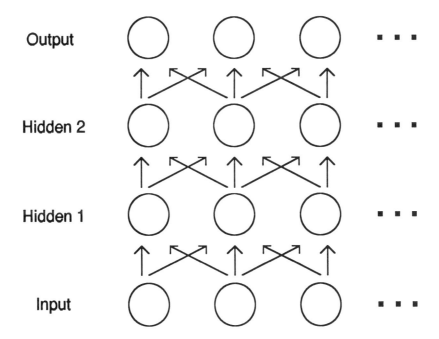

Fig. 6.2: Four-layer feedforward network

Each neuron in a feedforward network, represented by circles in that figure, operates as shown in Equation 6-1. Its inputs come from the previous layer, and its outputs go to the next layer. Nearly always, the same activation function is used for all neurons. It is the weights connecting neurons in one layer to those in the next which primarily determine the behavior of the network.

Recall from the discussion on page 8 that the input neurons are hypothetical constructs. They do not actually do any processing. The inputs to the network are the "outputs" of the theoretical input neurons. Only the hidden (if any) and output neurons operate by combining inputs and generating an output.

Activation Functions

The activation function is a nonlinear function that, when applied to the net input of a neuron, determines the output of that neuron. Its domain must generally be all real numbers, as there is no theoretical limit to what the net input can be. (In practice we can easily limit the net input by limiting the weights, and often do. Nevertheless, activation functions almost always have an unlimited domain.) The range of the activation function (values it can output) is usually limited. The most common limits are $0 - 1$, while some range from $-1 - 1$.

Early neural models, including the original perceptron, used a simple threshold function. If the weighted sum of inputs, the net, is less than the threshold, the neuron's output is 0. Otherwise the output is 1. In some models, such as later versions of the perceptron, the output would be the weighted sum itself if the threshold is exceeded. However, as will be seen shortly, there are great advantages to the function being differentiable, which a threshold certainly is not. Figures 6.3 and 6.4 show a typical threshold activation function and one version of the perceptron activation function, respectively.

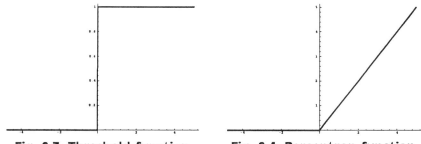

Fig. 6.3: Threshold function   Fig. 6.4: Perceptron function

The majority of current models use a *sigmoid* (S-shaped) activation function. A sigmoid function may be loosely defined as a continuous, real-valued function whose domain is the reals, whose derivative is always positive, and whose range is bounded. The most commonly employed sigmoid function is the *logistic* function.

$$f(x) = \frac{1}{1 + e^{-x}}$$
6-2

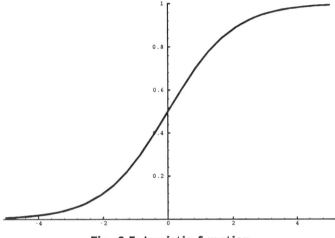

Fig. 6.5: Logistic function

One advantage of this function is that its derivative is easily found:

$$f'(x) = f(x)\ (1 - f(x))$$
6-3

Other sigmoid functions, such as the *hyperbolic tangent* and (scaled) *arctangent*, are sometimes used.

$$\tanh(x) = \frac{e^x - e^{-x}}{e^x + e^{-x}}$$
6-4

In most cases, it has been found that the exact shape of the function has little effect on the ultimate power of the network, though it can have a significant impact on training speed.

[Kenue, 1991] reports that the relatively small derivative of the logistic activation function slows learning in the basic backpropagation algorithm. Two of the alternatives that he proposes, along with their derivatives, are shown in Equations 6-5 and 6-6.

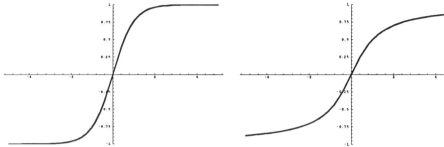

Fig. 6.6: Hyperbolic tangent   **Fig. 6.7: Scaled arctan**

$$f(x) = \frac{2}{\pi} \tan^{-1}(\sinh(x))$$

$$f'(x) = \frac{2}{\pi} \text{sech}(x)$$

6-5

$$f(x) = \frac{2}{\pi} \left(\frac{\tanh(x)}{\cosh(x)} + \tan^{-1}(\sinh(x)) \right)$$

$$f'(x) = \frac{4}{\pi} \text{sech}^3(x)$$

6-6

[Kalman and Kwasny, 1992] make a very eloquent case for choosing the hyperbolic tangent function. They propose and justify four criteria that an ideal activation function should meet, and show that only the tanh function meets all four.

It must be kept in mind that sigmoid functions never reach their theoretical minimum or maximum. For example, neurons that use the logistic function should be considered fully activated at around 0.9, and turned off at about 0.1 or so. It is certainly reasonable to use the extremes of 0.0 and 1.0 as inputs to a network. It is futile, though, to attempt to train a network to achieve extreme values as its output.

Example Network

A three-layer network capable of solving the "exclusive or" problem is shown in Figure 6.8. Recall that this problem, which is not linearly separable, was a major factor in the demise of the perceptron model. As an exercise, let us find the output activation that would result from an input of 0 for the first input neuron, and 1 for the second. We hope

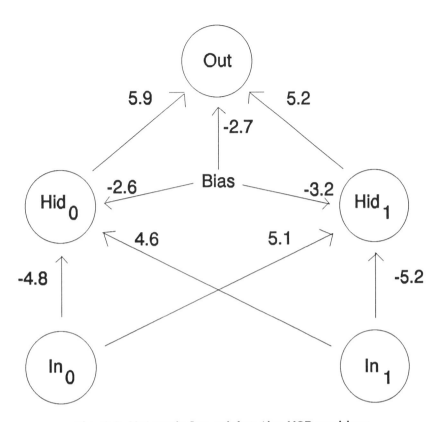

Fig. 6.8: Network for solving the XOR problem

that the output neuron will be fully activated. First, compute the weighted sum going into the first hidden neuron:

$$0.0 * -4.8 + 1.0 * 4.6 - 2.6 = 2.0$$

Applying the logistic function to this gives an activation of 0.88 for the first hidden neuron. Now do the same for the second hidden neuron:

$$0.0 * 5.1 + 1.0 * -5.2 - 3.2 = -8.4$$

The logistic function here drops to nearly 0. Now we compute the weighted sum going into the output neuron:

$$0.88 * 5.9 + 0.0 * 5.2 - 2.7 = 2.5$$

The logistic function of 2.5 is 0.92, so we see that the output neuron may be considered fully activated. It is left to the reader to determine that the output for (1, 0) inputs is 0.86, and the outputs for (0, 0) and (1, 1) are 0.11 and 0.10, respectively (within rounding, of course). The output of this example network is graphed over the entire square input domain in Figure 6.9.

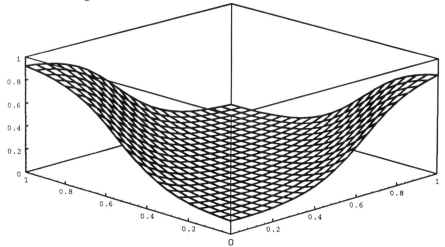

Fig. 6.9: Output of XOR network

Linear Output Neurons

Throughout this book, it is assumed that the output neurons have the same activation function as the hidden neurons, typically the logistic function. This is traditional and is generally recommended. However, it must be emphasized that it is not required. In fact, in some cases, it may be detrimental. Many applications use the identity function, $f(x) = x$, as the activation function of the output-layer neurons. In other words, the output of each of these neurons is equal to its net input. All of the theoretical properties cited in the next section are satisfied by a linear output layer; all that is necessary is that the hidden neurons have a nonlinear activation function. There are several advantages to using linear activation functions in the output layer. When autoassociative filters were discussed on page 24, it was pointed out that the squashing function used in the output layer could cause compression of extreme values. Similar detrimental effects were mentioned with regard to time-series prediction and function approximation. These are all avoided when the identity function, or any linear function, is used.

One of the biggest advantages of a linear output layer is that the regression technique described on page 165 will produce *exactly* optimal output weights. The implication is that nonlinear optimization needs to be done only on hidden-layer weights. For any given set of hidden-layer weights, output-layer weights that deliver the global minimum of the mean square error can be explicitly computed. This is a significant savings, especially if there are many output neurons.

There is one potentially serious drawback to linear activation functions. This concerns noise immunity. Although the squashing functions in the hidden layer provide a fair degree of buffering, the extra amount provided at the output layer can sometimes be valuable. Also, the problems of nonlinear output activation functions cited above are rarely very serious. Intelligent scaling can alleviate undue compression, and regressed output weights for nonlinear neurons are normally quite close to being optimal. The best approach is usually to use squashing functions first, switching to linear functions only if there is a clear reason to do so.

Theoretical Discussion

This section will briefly outline some of the principal theoretical facts currently known about multiple-layer feedforward networks. Details are left for the references cited. The main purpose for including this section is to mollify neural skeptics. Neural networks in general, and multilayer feedforward networks in particular, suffer from some small but annoying shortcomings. It is nearly impossible to specify an effective architecture given the specifications of a problem. That must be done by experimentation. After a network is trained, it may be difficult to understand how it works. Worse yet, the supposition that it will work correctly when presented with any possible test is usually taken on faith. Techniques for strict mathematical verification of a neural network's performance are still in their infancy. Let it be clearly understood that these networks *do* perform well in practice. It is exceedingly rare for a network to be well trained, verified with a reasonable test set, then fail in the line of duty. Performance quality is simply difficult to *prove* at this point in time.

Because of this, it is always heartening when a new, powerful theorem is proved regarding neural networks. Most of the research in this area concerns the capabilities of certain architectures. It is shown that a particular network design is theoretically capable of solving a particular problem. Many of these results are of more theoretical than practical interest. A theorem may show that just one hidden layer is *sufficient* to solve our problem. But it does not inform us whether memory or training requirements for that structure would be impractical, while using two hidden layers would work well. Those sorts of more practical results are rare, but the first hints of them are coming.

We will start by stating in plain English a summary of the principal results currently known about multilayer feedforward networks. These statements are deliberately loose, so that they can be understood by those with little mathematical background. Offended mathematicians should hastily skip ahead.

The results that follow are stated in terms of *what functions a network can learn*. Each problem is posed as a definition of a function that a network is asked to learn. Realize that a multilayer feedforward network implements a function itself. Inputs are applied to it, and deterministic outputs are produced. So we are asking one function, our network, to approximate another function, the problem. The network is said to be able to solve the problem if it is able to learn to approximate the function to arbitrary accuracy.

A function here is taken to be a mapping from the real-valued vector domain $\Re^n$ to the real numbers $\Re$. The more general case of learning a function that maps to vectors is a simple repetition of the results for each component, and so is superfluous.

The meaning of learning to "arbitrary accuracy" can be understood by thinking of a little demon who spouts out more and more unreasonable demands. He says, "Bring the error to within .0001 when measured over the entire domain," and you respond with a network that can bring its output sufficiently close to the correct function values. He in turn responds by asking you to bring it even closer, which you are able to do. We say that the network is able to learn a problem when that demon has a hopeless task. No matter how closely he requires your network to be able to respond with the correct answers, you can show him a network that will do so. Notice that he *cannot* require your network to produce *exactly* the correct solution. That is an unreasonable demand. But he can demand that you come as close to the exact solution as he pleases.

Now that somewhat of a definition of "learning ability" has been set forth, we can proceed by equally rigorously stating the capabilities of multilayer feedforward networks regarding learning a function.

1) If the function consists of a finite collection of points, a three-layer network (one hidden layer) is capable of learning it.

2) If the function is continuous and defined on a compact domain, a three-layer network is capable of learning it. Roughly speaking, "compact domain" means that the inputs have definite bounds, rather than having no limits on what they can be.

3) Many functions that do not meet the above criteria can also be learned by a three-layer network. In particular, discontinuities can be theoretically tolerated under all conditions likely to be met in real life. Also, functions that do not have compact support, such as when the inputs are normally distributed random variables, can be learned by a three-layer network under some conditions.

4) Under very general conditions, all other functions that can be learned by a neural network can be learned by a four-layer (two hidden) network.

Notice that the first two cases above cover the vast majority of practical problems. This means that, theoretically at least, we are always reasonably safe using a single hidden layer. Furthermore, we should never (at least theoretically) need more than two hidden layers. A network having two hidden layers is a universal approximator.

In practice, the need for a second hidden layer comes about in essentially only one way. That is when we need to learn a function that is mostly continuous, but has a few discontinuities. We occasionally are confronted with a function defined on a compact domain that is generally continuous, but has one or more sudden jumps where continuity is lost. These piecewise-continuous functions cannot in general be learned easily by a network having only one hidden layer (though it is theoretically possible). Two hidden layers are usually required.

The most common reason why a function cannot be learned by *any* multilayer feedforward network is when it seriously violates the assumption of a compact domain. We cannot expect a function that keeps on doing things as its inputs wander off toward infinity to be approximated well by ordinary neural networks. Even so, use of trigonometric activation functions can create neural networks that behave like Fourier approximators, thus circumventing even that problem!

The single most important point that the reader should get out of this section is the following:

> *A multilayer feedforward network CAN learn your function. If you have problems, they are NOT due to the model itself. They are due to insufficient training, on insufficient number of hidden neurons, or an attempt to learn a supposed function that is not deterministic.*

The learning and generalization capabilities of multiple-layer feedforward networks are astounding. And it is the experience of the author that surprisingly few hidden neurons are usually required. With proper design of the network and training set, the training time is usually manageable. They are worthy of serious consideration for nearly every neural network task.

Bibliography of Feedforward Network Theory

For those who desire more details than were presented here, the following sources are excerpted from the Bibliography section near the end of this text.

Blum, Edward, and Li, Leong (1991). "Approximation Theory and Feedforward Networks." *Neural Networks* 4:4, 511 – 515.

> *Nice summary of the subject, along with a few new theorems. Demonstration of a piecewise-constant function that cannot be learned by a special class of neural networks.*

Blum, A. L., and Rivest, R. L. (1992). "Training a 3-Node Neural Network Is NP-Complete." *Neural Networks,* **5**:1, 117 – 127.

> *Terrifying demonstration that training even tiny feedforward networks (one hidden layer with two neurons) can be vastly more difficult than we want to believe.*

Cardaliaguet, Pierre and Euvrard, Guillaume (1992). "Approximation of a Function and its Derivative with a Neural Network." *Neural Networks,* **5**:2, 207 – 220.

> *Explicit formulas for weights in a three-layer network mapping $\Re$ to $\Re$, and a four-layer network mapping $\Re^2$ to $\Re$, where both the function and its derivative are approximated. Proves the existence of such networks in higher dimensions, but reverts to back-propagation for weights. Nice example from control theory of why simultaneously approximating derivatives may be important.*

Gallant, Ronald, and White, Halbert (1992). "On Learning the Derivatives of an Unknown Mapping with Multilayer Feedforward Networks." *Neural Networks*, 2:2 129 – 138.

> *Under fairly reasonable asymptotic conditions, ordinary least-squares learning of weights automatically gives a network mapping that also approximates the derivative of the target mapping.*

Hornik, Kurt, Stinchcombe, Maxwell, and White, Halbert (1989). "Multilayer Feedforward Networks are Universal Approximators." *Neural Networks*, 2:5, 359 – 366.

> *Seminal paper that uses the Stone-Weierstrass theorem to prove that three-layer networks (one hidden) having arbitrary squashing activation functions are capable of approximating any Borel measurable function from one finite dimensional space to another to any desired degree of accuracy. Also contains a short but sweet historical bibliography of related material.*

Hornik, Kurt (1991). "Approximation Capabilities of Multilayer Feedforward Networks." *Neural Networks*, 4:2, 251 – 257.

> *Theoretical extension of the results in [Hornik et al; 1989].*

Ito, Y. (1991b). "Approximation of Functions on a Compact Set by Finite Sums of a Sigmoid Function without Scaling." *Neural Networks*, 4:6, 817 – 826.

> *Existential proof based on the Hahn-Banach theorem. Constructive proofs of several corollaries hint at possible algorithms.*

Ito, Y. (1992). "Approximation of Continuous Functions on **R**ⁿ by Linear Combinations of Shifted Rotations of a Sigmoid Function with and without Scaling." *Neural Networks*, **5**:1, 105 – 115.

> *Extension of [Ito, 1991b] to the whole $\Re^n$ space. Especially useful paper in that it contains a highly informative table relating assumptions, methods, and results for various theorems concerning function approximation by three-layer networks.*

Kurkova, Vera (1992). "Kolmogorov's Theorem and Multilayer Neural Networks." *Neural Networks*, **5**:3, 501 – 506.

> *Titillating paper concerning function approximation capabilities of four-layer (two hidden) networks. Constructive proof gives limits (large, but limits nonetheless) on the number of hidden neurons required. Also strong hints of extremely fast learning algorithms. Much promise here.*

Sussmann, Hector J. (1992). "Uniqueness of the Weights for Minimal Feedforward Nets with a Given Input-Output Map." *Neural Networks*, **5**:4, 589 – 593.

> *Mathematical proof that, except for obvious symmetries and degenerate cases, a three-layer feedforward network with tanh activation function is uniquely determined by its mapping.*

Algorithms for Executing the Network

We need to be able to compute the activation of all output neurons in response to an input stimulus presented to the network. This operation, the *raison d'etre* of the network, will also be repeated thousands of times during training. Thus, it behooves us to code it as efficiently as possible.

Execution proceeds by layers. First, we find the activation of each neuron in the layer just after the input layer. These outputs comprise the inputs to the next layer, which is then computed. This continues until the output layer is done.

Activation of a single neuron is computed in two steps. First, the dot product of the inputs (including the bias) with the neuron's weight vector is found. Then, the activation function is applied to this dot product. These operations are summarized in Equation 6-1.

For most practical networks, it is the dot product that requires the most time during both training and recall. Fanatics will certainly code it in assembler. Those who must use a higher-level language should use the loop technique shown in the following code fragment. The naive method simply loops once for each vector element, cumulating the products. This requires numerous decrements of the loop counter, tests for zero, and conditional branches. A better approach is to break the vectors into groups, summing each group during a pass through the loop. For example, suppose the vectors contain 22 elements. We could loop five times, each time summing four products, then finish the last two elements separately. This greatly reduces the number of times a looping decision must be made.

There is another potential advantage of this method compared to the naive approach. Many modern processors, especially RISC, use *pipelining* to speed operations. While one instruction is being executed, the next few are being prepared for execution; operands are fetched, addresses built, et cetera. When a conditional branch is encountered, as would be the case after each pass through the loop, the pipeline is broken. The processor cannot know in advance which direction will be taken. This can profoundly slow such processors. There is much to be gained by minimizing the number of loop passes. The dot product code is as follows:

```
double dotprod (
    int n ,                          // Length of vectors
    double *vec1 ,                   // One of the vectors to be dotted
    double *vec2 )                   // The other vector
{
    int k, m ;
    double sum ;
    sum = 0.0 ;                      // Will cumulate dot product here
    k = n / 4 ;                      // Divide vect into this many gps of 4
    m = n % 4 ;                      // This is remainder of that division

    while (k--) {                    // Do each group of 4
        sum += *vec1 * *vec2 ;
        sum += *(vec1+1) * *(vec2+1) ;
        sum += *(vec1+2) * *(vec2+2) ;
        sum += *(vec1+3) * *(vec2+3) ;
        vec1 += 4 ;
        vec2 += 4 ;
    }
```

```
    while (m--)                    // Do the remainder
      sum += *vec1++ * *vec2++ ;

    return sum ;
  }
```

There are several ways in which this code could be modified. The choice of using blocks of four is fairly arbitrary. Obviously, larger groups will result in slightly more savings. Applications that expect long vectors would certainly benefit from using eight or even more. On the other hand, shorter vectors would lose out, spending much time in the final loop, which cumulates the remainder elements. Also, the point of diminishing returns is reached rapidly. The moral: test several choices with the application, and pick the fastest.

A second area for possible modification is the method by which vector addresses are incremented in the first loop. The code shown here uses constant offsets, *(vec1+1) and so on. The addresses are incremented by four at the end of the loop. This is in deference to many common processors that allow constant offsets in their machine language. Other processors may execute faster by incrementing the addresses as the terms are summed, as is done in the second loop. This is strictly a hardware decision.

Although evaluation of the activation function typically is not as time consuming as the dot product operation, it usually is at least the second most significant. A piecewise linear approximation will in practice work as well as using the exact definition and will be tremendously faster. A second benefit is that this method is easily adapted to virtually any activation function that may be needed. The code shown here will be for the common *logistic* function, but only the initialization code would need to be changed for most other functions. Discontinuous functions, and similar monstrosities, may require special treatment.

The choice of the interpolation table length depends on the amount of memory that may be dedicated to it, and the intended use of the trained network. Obviously, execution time is not affected by the length, since the table is directly addressed, not actually searched. Most modern computers have sufficient memory that the use of 100 entries shown here requires an insignificant fraction of total memory. However, it should be noted that much shorter tables are usually acceptable *if the same table will be used for both training and recall.* It has been observed that in virtually all practical cases, there is nothing special about the exact shape of the activation function as far as final performance is concerned (although training time may be affected). Anything that is even roughly sigmoid can perform as well as any other. Furthermore, small errors in the computed derivative due to approximation errors in the function are swamped out by irregularities in the problem space itself. The only serious problem arises if one table resolution is used for training, and another for recall. Errors in computed activation levels can be detrimental here.

The code for the logistic activation function is as follows:

```
#define F_TABLE_LENGTH 100
#define F_TABLE_MAX 10.0

static double f_factor, f_f[F_TABLE_LENGTH], f_d[F_TABLE_LENGTH] ;

void act_func_init ()
{
  int i ;

  f_factor = (double) (F_TABLE_LENGTH - 1) / (double) F_TABLE_MAX ;
  for (i=0 ; i<F_TABLE_LENGTH ; i++) {
    f_f[i] = 1.0 / (1.0 + exp ( - ((double) i) / f_factor )) ;
    if (i)
      f_d[i-1] = f_f[i] - f_f[i-1] ;
    }
}

double act_func ( double x )
{
  int i ;
  double xd ;

  if (x >= 0.0) {                        // Handle this half of function
    xd = x * f_factor ;                  // Find location in table
    i = (int) xd ;                       // Subscript in table
    if (i >= (F_TABLE_LENGTH - 1))       // If outside table
      return f_f[F_TABLE_LENGTH-1] ;     // hold at highest entry
    return f_f[i] + f_d[i] * (xd - i) ;  // Else interpolate
    }

  else {                       // Handle other symmetric half of function
    xd = -x * f_factor ;
    i = (int) xd ;
    if (i >= (F_TABLE_LENGTH - 1))
      return 1.0 - f_f[F_TABLE_LENGTH-1] ;
    return 1.0 - (f_f[i] + f_d[i] * (xd - i)) ;
    }
}
```

Several aspects of this code should be noted. Most importantly, it does not strictly follow the mathematical definition of the logistic function. Rather than asymptotically approaching the limits of 0 and 1 at extremes, it holds at the outermost table value. Experience indicates that this frequently aids learning. Sometimes during training, one or more weights will become inordinately large in absolute value. If the exact definition were used, this would result in a derivative becoming nearly 0, so that weight would become stuck out in left field. Keeping the function value away from extremes prevents this occurrence. The exact point at which this limit is imposed is not critical; the value of 10 shown here should be generally applicable.

In case there is extremely limited memory available, it is not necessary to precompute f_d, the difference table. This would cut the memory requirement in half. The difference could be computed as f_f[i+1] - f_f[i] when it is needed in the interpolation. Having it available in a table slightly speeds execution, but is certainly not necessary.

One annoyance about the above algorithm is that the programmer must remember to call act_func_init before the act_func routine is called. Otherwise the tables will contain garbage. Even worse, f_factor could contain a negative number, resulting in a serious run-time error when a negative subscript is generated!

When the network is trained, the derivative of the activation function will also be needed. The logistic function has a particularly simple derivative:

$$f'(x) = f(x) \ (1 - f(x)) \qquad\qquad 6\text{-}7$$

It is somewhat unusual in that it is most easily computed from the function value. If the experimenter wishes to try other activation functions for which this is not true, the code for the derivative must be modified appropriately. As will be seen later, only the function value itself is easily available at the time the derivative is needed. Although the net input could be preserved for use in computing derivatives of other activation functions, this is in general a waste of both time and memory.

```
double actderiv (
   double f )                          // f(net), the activation function value
{
   return f * (1.0 - f) ;              // Logistic derivative
}
```

Training the Network

Training a practical network is usually a numerical nightmare. Although many advances have been made since the basic back-propagation with momentum algorithm first described by Rumelhart, Hinton, and Williams [Rumelhart and McClelland, 1986], there is no escaping the underlying problem. We must optimize a very nonlinear system consisting of a large number of highly correlated variables.

False minima abound, and they are usually at the bottom of extremely narrow valleys. Naive algorithms need not apply.

The training process starts by initializing all weights to small non-zero values. Often these are generated randomly. Later it will be shown how *simulated annealing* can be used to select starting values more intelligently. Then, a subset of the collection of training samples is presented to the network, one at a time. A measure of the error incurred by the network is made, and the weights are updated in such a way that the error is reduced. This process is repeated as necessary.

One pass through this [present a subset of the training set ... measure error ... update weights] cycle is called an *epoch*. The size of the subset (number of training samples used per weight update) is called the *epoch size*. Often, the entire training set is used for the epoch. If smaller subsets are used, it is important that they be chosen randomly, or learning may be impaired.

The most common error measure used is the mean square error in output activations. It is easily computed, has proven itself in practice, and perhaps most importantly, its partial derivative with respect to individual weights can be computed explicitly. (Recent experiments indicate that using the log of the mean square error may aid learning.) The mean square error for a single presentation is found by squaring the difference between the attained and target activations for each output neuron, and averaging across them all. The epoch error is computed by averaging the errors of the training presentations within that epoch. In particular, suppose we are processing training pattern p. Let the correct (target) activation of output neuron j be designated as t_{pj}, and the observed activation be o_{pj}. If there are n output neurons, the error for that single presentation is

$$E_p = \frac{1}{n} \sum_{j=0}^{n-1} (t_{pj} - o_{pj})^2 \qquad\qquad 6\text{-}8$$

If there are m presentations in the epoch, the error for that epoch is

$$E = \frac{1}{m} \sum_{p=0}^{m-1} E_p \qquad\qquad 6\text{-}9$$

Derivatives are priceless to the numerical analyst who must optimize a function. If we know the partial derivative of the error with respect to each weight, we know (at least on a local scale) which way the weights must move in order to reduce the error. Mathematical derivation of the derivatives may be found in Chapter 8 of [Rumelhart and McClelland, 1986]. Here we simply state that for a single presentation, the derivative of the output layer weight connecting previous layer neuron i to output neuron j is

$$\frac{\partial E}{\partial w_{ji}} = -o_i \, f'(net_j) \, (t_j - o_j) \qquad\qquad 6\text{-}10$$

where o_i is the output of previous layer neuron i, net_j is the weighted sum coming into output layer neuron j, o_j is that neuron's obtained activation, and t_j is the desired activation for that neuron. Note that we need to know the derivative, f', of the activation function. The above formula is often written in two parts:

$$\delta_j = f'(net_j) \, (t_j - o_j) \qquad\qquad 6\text{-}11$$

$$\frac{\partial E}{\partial w_{ji}} = -o_i \, \delta_j \qquad\qquad 6\text{-}12$$

Partial derivatives with respect to hidden-layer weights may be computed if the δ values for the following layer are known. In the following formula, w_{kj} is the weight connecting neuron j in this hidden layer to neuron k in the next layer. The δ shown with a subscript of k refers to the deltas for the layer following this hidden layer, while the δ having a subscript of j refers to the deltas being computed for this hidden layer. We are computing the partial derivative of the error with respect to w_{ji}, the weight connecting this hidden layer neuron j with previous layer neuron i.

$$\delta_j = f'(net_j) \sum_k (\delta_k \, w_{kj}) \qquad\qquad 6\text{-}13$$

$$\frac{\partial E}{\partial w_{ji}} = -o_i \, \delta_j \qquad\qquad 6\text{-}14$$

It can be seen that evaluation of the derivatives occurs in the opposite order as executing the network. The output layer is done first. Its δ's are then used to compute derivatives for the next layer back, et cetera. It is this *backward propagation* of output errors which inspired the name for a popular training method to be described in a later section. (It unfortunately also inspired a terrible misnomer: since multiple-layer feedforward networks are often trained using these formulas, they have inappropriately come to be called backpropagation networks.)

The above formulas are for a single presentation of an input pattern. To compute the gradient for an entire training epoch, the gradients for each sample are summed. Recall that the derivative of the sum of functions is the sum of their individual derivatives.

The code for executing a network is straightforward. It is best to structure it into two subroutines. One computes the activation of a single layer, given the activations of the previous layer. In C++ this would most likely belong to a general layer network class. The other routine would be for a specific member of this class and would apply the first routine once for each layer. The general activation is computed as follows:

```
void LayerNet::activate_layer (
   int nthis,                    // Number of neurons in this layer
   int nprev,                    // Number of neurons in the previous layer
   double **coefs,               // nthis ptrs to weight vects nprev+1 long
   double *ins,                  // nprev vect of previous layer activations
   double *outs)                 // nthis vector of this layer's activations

{
   int i ;
   double net, *cptr ;

   for (i=0 ; i<nthis ; i++) {   // Do each neuron in layer
      cptr = coefs[i] ;          // Point to its nprev+1 weight vector
      net = dotprod ( nprev , ins , cptr ) + cptr[nprev] ; // include bias
      outs[i] = act_func ( net ) ;
      }
}
```

For each of the nthis neurons in this layer, the dot product of the input vector with the weight vector is computed. The weight vector actually contains nprev+1 elements. The last is the weight for that neuron's bias. The net is then given to the activation function.

The function that executes a particular network given an input presentation is illustrated below for a three-layer network. It simply applies the above routine twice: once to compute the hidden layer given the inputs, then to compute the outputs given the hidden layer. The variables used here are member variables of LayerNet and ThreeLayer classes. To save space and increase clarity, no declarations appear here.

```
void ThreeLayer::present ( double *ins )
{
   activate_layer ( nhid , nin , hidcoefs , ins , hidden ) ;
   activate_layer ( nout , nhid , outcoefs , hidden , outputs ) ;
}
```

Once the network has been executed, we can compute the mean square error of its outputs given a desired target vector. Sample code is shown next.

```
double LayerNet::output_error (
  double *targets )                    // nout vector of target activations

{
  int i ;
  double d, sum ;

  sum = 0.0 ;
  for (i=0 ; i<nout ; i++) {
    d = targets[i] - outputs[i] ;
    sum += d * d ;
    }
  return sum / (double) nout ;
}
```

Note once again that some variables shown in the output error and gradient listings, such as nout and outputs, are member variables of the LayerNet class, and so need not appear in the calling parameter list. Their names should make their function obvious.

Code for computing the gradient exactly follows the equations shown earlier. The grad_output routine would be called first. Then grad_hidden would be called once for each hidden layer, working backwards from the output layer toward the input. This is because computation of the gradient for a hidden layer needs the deltas for the layer that follows it. Both of these routines call the already described routine actderiv, which returns the derivative of the activation function given the value of that function. Note that these gradient routines actually compute the negative gradient. The following routine implements Equation 6-12.

```
void LayerNet::grad_output (
  int nprev,              // Number of neurons in previous layer
  double *prevact,        // nprev vect of previous layer activations
  double *targets,        // nout vector of target activations
  double *deltas,         // nout vector of computed deltas
  double **grad )         // nout vect of ptrs to nprev+1 neg grads

{
  int i, j ;
  double delta, *gradptr ;
```

```
              for (i=0 ; i<nout ; i++) {
                delta = (targets[i] - outputs[i]) * actderiv ( outputs[i] ) ;
                deltas[i] = delta ;
                gradptr = grad[i] ;
                for (j=0 ; j<nprev ; j++)
                  gradptr[j] += delta * prevact[j] ;
                gradptr[nprev] += delta ;   // Bias activation is always 1
                }
            }
```

The delta for each output neuron is computed and saved (as gradient computation for hidden layers will need it). Then the partial derivative for each of the nprev weights connecting the previous layer to this neuron are computed and summed into the epoch total. Finally, the partial derivative for the bias weight is found. Recall that the bias comes from a hypothetical neuron that is always fully activated.

Gradient computation for hidden layers is slightly more complex, as it involves deltas and weights for the layer that follows it, as well as for the layer that precedes it. If savedeltas is nonzero, the deltas are preserved for the hidden layer preceding the one being done. Of course, this is a waste of space (and a tiny amount of time) for the first hidden layer. In this case, savedeltas would be set to zero. The following code implements Equation 6-14.

```
void LayerNet::grad_hidden (
   int nprev,                    // Number of neurons in previous layer
   int nthis,                    // Number of neurons in this layer
   int nnext,                    // Number of neurons in next layer
   int savedeltas,               // Save deltas for doing preceding layer?
   double *prevact,              // nprev vector of prev layer activations
   double *hidact,               // nthis vect of this hidden layer activations
   double *nextdeltas,           // nnext vector of next layer deltas
   double **nextcoefs,           // nnext vect of ptrs to nthis+1 wt vects
   double *deltas,               // nthis vector of computed deltas
   double **grad )               // nthis vect of ptrs to nprev+1 neg grads

{
   int i, j ;
   double sum, delta, *gradptr ;
   for (i=0 ; i<nthis ; i++) {
     sum = 0.0 ;
     for (j=0 ; j<nnext ; j++)
       sum += nextdeltas[j] * (nextcoefs[j])[i] ;
     delta = sum * actderiv ( hidact[i] ) ;
     if (savedeltas)
       deltas[i] = delta ;
     gradptr = grad[i] ;
     for (j=0 ; j<nprev ; j++)
       gradptr[j] += delta * prevact[j] ;
     gradptr[nprev] += delta ;   // Bias activation is always 1
     }
}
```

This section has provided the foundation algorithms for training a multiple-layer feedforward network. The mean square error, given an epoch of input presentations and desired output targets, can be found. The weight gradient vector of this error can also be computed. All that remains is to apply any of several standard numerical techniques to optimize the network. The next sections will focus on the most important such algorithms.

Training by Backpropagation of Errors

Backpropagation was the first practical method for training a multiple-layer feedforward network. Its presentation in [Rumelhart and McClelland, 1986] was almost singlehandedly responsible for the rekindling of serious interest in artificial neural networks. Their original algorithm is still used in many successful programs. For these reasons, it is now described in some detail. However, it must be noted that the conjugate gradient method of the next section is generally faster and more robust. Readers who desire more explicit information on the backpropagation algorithm, such as choice of learning parameters, should consult the previously cited reference.

Motivation for naming this the "backpropagation algorithm" can be seen when we examine the algorithm for computing the gradient, discussed in the previous section. The output-layer errors are successively propagated backwards through the network. In fact, though, it is a poor name in that backpropagation really refers to computation of the gradient, an operation common to many learning algorithms. Unfortunately, history has firmly glued that name to the algorithm now described, so we must honor tradition.

In its most basic form, backpropagation is what numerical analysts call a *gradient descent* algorithm. The gradient of a multivariate function is the direction that is most steeply "uphill". A tiny step in that direction will result in the maximum increase of the function compared to all other possible directions. By the same token, a tiny step in the opposite direction will effect the maximum possible decrease in the function. As discussed in the previous section, our function is the network's error for the training set. Thus, it seems to make sense to compute the gradient of this error function, take a step in the opposite direction (the direction of the negative gradient), and repeat as needed. Since we are always stepping in the optimal direction for reducing the error (at least locally), we would expect to descend to the minimum error location quite quickly. The exact distance to step, often called the *learning rate,* can be critical. If this distance is too small, convergence will be excessively slow. If it is too large, we will jump wildly and never converge.

There are two very serious flaws in the above method. First is the fact that the gradient is an extremely *local* pointer to optimal function change. Even a tiny distance away, the gradient may point in a dramatically different direction. These wild fluctuations can cause the search for the minimum error to meander a distance thousands of times longer (read: slower to compute) than a direct route. The second problem is that it is difficult to know in advance how far to step in the negative gradient direction. If we are conservative and take a tiny step, an inordinate amount of time will be required for all those network evaluations and gradient computations. But if we step too far, we are liable to overshoot and have the error actually increase! As will be seen in the next section, the conjugate gradient algorithm addresses both of these issues. For now, a more heuristic approach is taken.

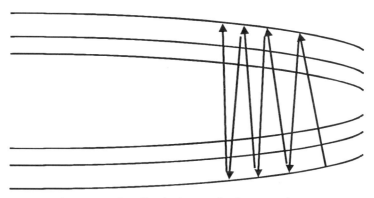

Fig. 6.10: Gradient descent along a chasm

Examine Figure 6.10, which shows typical equal-error contour lines along a chasm in a two-dimensional weight space. The chasm shown in that figure is extremely common in neural networks. Numerical analysts tell us that the gradient is always perpendicular to the equal-error contour lines. Thus, we can easily trace the path taken by a gradient descent algorithm. Such a path will zigzag as shown, bouncing from one wall to the other as it tediously progresses along the canyon toward the distant minimum. This is one of the main reasons that traditional backpropagation learning is so slow.

The most significant modification to the basic method described above is the addition of a *momentum* term. Rather than letting our search direction wildly thrash about as the gradient changes, we impose a momentum on it. Each new search direction is computed as a weighted sum of the current gradient and the previous search direction. This is essentially a low-pass filter applied to the search direction. The idea is that if rapid local fluctuations are filtered out, the remaining trend will be toward a more global minimum. Years of experience indicate that this is an extremely effective technique, often speeding convergence by several orders of magnitude. Yet, it is not a perfect solution. Unless a great deal of momentum is employed, the zigzags shown in the previous figure will still dominate learning. But if too much momentum is used, the algorithm will not be able to follow the twists and turns that are so common in weight space.

Dozens (or is it thousands?) of other modifications to the basic backpropagation algorithm have been proposed. Some of the more popular ones are

1)   Change the learning rate (step size in the negative gradient direction) as learning progresses. Try to keep the steps as large as possible without overshooting.

2)   Modify the formula for the derivative of the activation function so that slightly larger values are obtained. This discourages getting stuck at extreme weight values where derivatives are so tiny that escape is difficult.

3)   Do not update the weights in all layers simultaneously. Update those going into the first (hidden) layer, then recompute the activations for that layer. Use these *new* activations to compute the corrections for the next layer, et cetera. This method, first reported in [Samad, 1988], requires a lot of fancy bookkeeping, but is said to speed convergence greatly.

A common theme in such improvements is that they heap more empirically derived tweaking on top of an already largely empirical algorithm. One is frequently left with a hodgepodge of methods known to "usually work quite well for most problems." A number of parameters must be set by the user, and convergence speed (if not the very *probability* of convergence) is highly dependent on the values chosen. Since the conjugate gradient algorithm has no critical parameters and few noncritical ones, only the basic backpropagation algorithm code, in all its historical glory, is given here.

As in the previous section, just the essential logic of the backpropagation learning code is provided here. *More superfluous aspects, such as allocation of memory for work areas, is omitted for clarity.*

```
double ThreeLayer::backprop (
   int ntrain ,                    // Number of training set presentations
   int maxits ,                    // Maximum iterations allowed
   double rate ,                   // Gradient multiplier
   double mom ,                    // Momentum coefficient
   double errtol ,                 // Quit if error drops this low
   double gradtol )                // Quit if all gradients this small

{
   int i, j, iter, pnum, key ;
   double *outdelta, **outgrad, **hidgrad, **outprev, **hidprev ;
   double corr, error, *ins, *targ, *cptr, *gptr, *pptr, maxgrad ;

/* -----> Allocation of work memory should go here <----- */

/*
   Zero the previous iteration correction.  This vector is used to implement
   momentum.  It has separate parts for the hidden layer (hidprev) and
   output layer (outprev) weights. Its structure is identical to that of the
   weight vectors: each component of the vector corresponds to one neu-
   ron, and is a pointer to a vector whose length is one greater than the
   number of neurons in the previous layer (the extra being for the bias).
*/

   for (i=0 ; i<nout ; i++) {
      gptr = outprev[i] ;
      for (j=0 ; j<=nhid ; j++)
         gptr[j] = 0.0 ;
      }

   for (i=0 ; i<nhid ; i++) {
      gptr = hidprev[i] ;
      for (j=0 ; j<=nin ; j++)
         gptr[j] = 0.0 ;
      }

/*
   Main iteration loop is here.  Normally it will be terminated by either the
   network error falling within 'errtol' or the maximum absolute value of any
   component of the gradient falling within 'gradtol'.  The 'maxits' limit is
   generally used as a safety factor only, and is typically set to a very
   large number.
*/

   for (iter=0 ; iter<maxits ; iter++) { // Each iter is an epoch

      error = find_grad ( ntrain , ins , targ , outdelta , outgrad , hidgrad ) ;

      if (error <= errtol)         // If our error is within user's limit
         break ;                   // then we are done!
```

```
/*
     Correct coefficients and save correction for momentum.  Also check
     grad size.
*/

     maxgrad = 0.0 ;
     for (i=0 ; i<nout ; i++) {         // Do it for output layer weights
       cptr = outcoefs[i] ;
       gptr = outgrad[i] ;
       pptr = outprev[i] ;
       for (j=0 ; j<=nhid ; j++) {
         if (fabs(gptr[j]) > maxgrad)           // Keep track of gradient size
           maxgrad = fabs(gptr[j]) ;            // for convergence test later
         corr = rate * gptr[j] + mom * pptr[j] ; // Compute correction
         cptr[j] += corr ;              // Update weight per correction
         pptr[j] = corr ;              // Save it for momentum on next iteration
         }
       }

     for (i=0 ; i<nhid ; i++) { // Same as above, but for hidden layer
       cptr = hidcoefs[i] ;
       gptr = hidgrad[i] ;
       pptr = hidprev[i] ;
       for (j=0 ; j<=nin ; j++) {
         if (fabs(gptr[j]) > maxgrad)
           maxgrad = fabs(gptr[j]) ;
         corr = rate * gptr[j] + mom * pptr[j] ;
         cptr[j] += corr ;
         pptr[j] = corr ;
         }
       }

/*
   Check biggest gradient against user's limit.  Quit if small enough.
*/

     if (maxgrad <= gradtol)
       break ;

     } // This is the end of the main iteration loop

   return error ;
}
```

The following routine is called by backprop (and perhaps other learning routines) to compute the gradient across an epoch. It simply zeros the gradient, then passes through the training set for a complete epoch. For each of the ntrain members it calls gettrain to return that member's input and output vectors in the supplied work areas ins and targ. The input is presented to the network, and the gradient is cumulated across the epoch.

```
double ThreeLayer::find_grad (
   int ntrain ,
   double *ins ,
   double *targ ,
   double *outdelta ,
   double **outgrad ,
   double **hidgrad
   )

{
   int i, j, pnum ;
   double error, *gptr ;

   for (i=0 ; i<nout ; i++) {        // Zero output gradient in preparation
      gptr = outgrad[i] ;            // for summing across this epoch
      for (j=0 ; j<=nhid ; j++)
         gptr[j] = 0.0 ;
      }

   for (i=0 ; i<nhid ; i++) {        // Similarly zero hidden gradient
      gptr = hidgrad[i] ;
      for (j=0 ; j<=nin ; j++)
         gptr[j] = 0.0 ;
      }

   error = 0.0 ;

   for (pnum=0 ; pnum<ntrain ; pnum++) {   // All presentations in epoch
      gettrain ( pnum , ins , targ ) ;     // Get a training presentation
      present ( ins ) ;                    // Compute all activations
      grad_output ( nhid , hidden , targ , outdelta , outgrad ) ;
      grad_hidden ( nin , nhid , nout , 0 , ins , hidden , outdelta ,
                  outcoefs , (double *) NULL , hidgrad ) ;
      error += output_error ( targ ) ;
      }

   return error / (double) ntrain ;
   }
```

Training by Conjugate Gradients

Imagine that you are standing on the edge of the Grand Canyon. Far below, nearly straight down, is a small river. It flows toward your left, eventually filling a lake 10 miles away. Now suppose that you have to find that lake. It represents the minimum of an error function. Relative to your present location, it is 20 feet ahead and 10 miles to the left. The most direct route would be essentially diagonally down the side of the cliff. The backpropagation algorithm of the previous section would start you off almost straight down. Your first step would perhaps land you three-quarters of the way down the cliff and several inches to your left. The next step might place you halfway up the other side and a few more inches to the left, because a fixed-size step is taken. Your third step would take you halfway back up the starting side and slightly more to the left. Momentum, if used, would damp the side-to-side oscillation to a large degree, but could never entirely eliminate it. The conjugate gradient method, on the other hand, would take you directly to the river at the bottom of the canyon in a few steps of rapidly decreasing size. Once at the bottom, it would send you downriver to the lake in a few more very large steps. Let us now examine this algorithm in some detail.

Minimizing along a Direction

The majority of computation time in this algorithm is spent in one operation: finding the minimum of the error function *when the weight variables are constrained to lie along a line.* In other words, we have a vector containing all of the weights, W_0, and a direction vector, W_d. We now have a problem of minimizing a function $f(W_0 + t\ W_d)$ of one variable, t. Later, it will be shown how the clever choice of the direction W_d is responsible for the rapid convergence of the conjugate gradient algorithm. For now we concentrate on minimizing a function of one variable. This topic is discussed in great detail in [Acton, 1970] and [Press et al., 1988]. The precise algorithm used here draws heavily on [Brent, 1973].

The process of minimizing a univariate function requires two steps. In the first step we bracket the minimum by finding three points such that the middle point is less than (has smaller function value than) its two neighbors. In the second step we refine the interval containing the minimum until satisfied with the accuracy of its location. These two steps are illustrated in Figure 6.11.

Start with point one, then move to point two. The function decreased, so go further, to point three. Again it decreased, so move further still, out to point four. The first of the two steps is now complete, as we know that a minimum exists between points two and four. (The case of more than one local minimum is entirely another issue, which will be addressed in a later section.) The second step commences by using the locations of points two, three, and four to make an intelligent guess as to the exact location of the minimum. This is point five. Since it is less than point four, but still exceeds point three, we can discard point four. The minimum now is known to lie in the smaller interval between points two and five, which includes point three. These three points are again used to "predict" the location of the minimum, resulting in point six. Finally, points three, five, and six are used to find point seven, a satisfactorily close approximation to the true minimum.

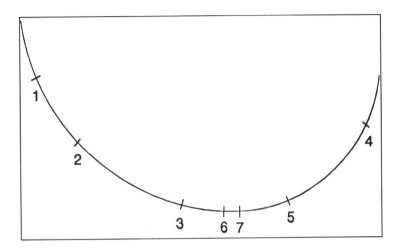

Fig. 6.11: Minimizing along a line

The remainder of this section is an in-depth discussion of what is probably the most popular line-minimization algorithm. It can best be comprehended by following the code listing for direcmin, found on page 437 of the Appendix. Readers not interested in these fine details may skip the rest of this section.

The code for direcmin calls several very short utility subroutines that appear elsewhere in the program listing. Routine preserve saves the weights as they were input to direcmin, so that they can serve as a base X_0 for excursion along the line. Routine step_out is given the parameter t along with the direction X_d and base X_0. It computes the new weights appropriately. Routine trial_error passes through the training set, cumulating the epoch error (the value of the function we are minimizing). Routine negate_dir reverses the search direction. Finally, update_dir multiplies the search direction vector by the specified value of the parameter t, so that it reflects the actual vector difference between the point corresponding to t and the base point X_0.

The first thing done by direcmin is to call preserve, which copies the weights to work area base. The weights are private members of the LayerNet class, so are not explicitly referenced. The base point, X_0, serves as a standard point of departure for the line minimization. The network error (function value) at this point was provided as start_err. A step in the direction direc is now taken to provide a second point. The length of this step is equal to first_step, initialized here to 2.5. The actual value of first_step is not critical to convergence, but can slightly speed the operation if it is optimized for a particular problem. Normally, the error will decrease at this second point, since the search direction has presumably been set to the negative gradient. On the other hand, a robust algorithm is obligated to verify this. We may be very near the minimum and may have stepped too far. In case the function increased, we simply reverse the roles of the two points.

Now that two points are available, with the function at the second less than or equal to the first, a third point beyond the second is found. There is no special rule that *must* be followed regarding placement of this point. [Press et al., 1988] make a good case for using golden ratio spacing, so that method is followed here. In problems in which it is likely that the minimum may be much further out than first_step, a larger jump may be appropriate.

We now have three points, x1, x2, and x3, along with their function values previous_err, current_err, and err. The immediate goal is to bracket a minimum by finding three points such that the function value at the middle is less than those of its neighbors. The while (err < current_err) loop undertakes such a search.

Given three points, it is possible to fit a parabola to those points and explicitly locate the minimum (or maximum!) of that parabola. The variable step is computed to do just that. Of course, if the points are collinear (or nearly so), the estimate will be wild, so precautions are taken. There are four possible locations for this presumed minimum:

1)   It is between x2 and x3. This usually happens near the end of the search. In this case the function is evaluated here and compared to err, the value at x3. Ideally it will be less than err, so we are done. The lower bound x1 and middle point x2 are updated, along with their function values. On the other hand, it may happen that the function value actually exceeds that at x2, current_err. This is no disaster, as we have still bounded the minimum. Simply replace x3 and its function value with the new point. The only real tragedy is if neither of the above happened; the function is somewhere between that of x2 and x3. The function evaluation was a total waste of time. All we can do is step out beyond x3, again using the rather arbitrary golden ratio.

2)   The parabolic estimate is beyond x3, but within the arbitrary large limit. This usually happens a few times early on as we march down the hill. Evaluate the function here. At this point, since we may be rather far from x1 and x2, numerical stability in the parabolic estimate of the next iteration may suffer. Therefore, we take the opportunity to slip in one more point in a golden-ratio extension. Of course this is done only

if the function value decreased. If it did not, there will be no next iteration!

3)   The parabolic estimate is beyond the reasonable limit. Set the step equal to that limit, then proceed as in the step above. Astute programmers will notice that this duplication of code could be avoided by combining cases 2 and 3, including a simple limitation on the size of the step. The code duplication shown here is to facilitate experimentation. It may be desired to skip the golden-ratio jump in case 2. It may work better in some cases to use strictly a golden ratio in case 3, as is done in case 4. This structure simplifies such experimenting. It must be noted, though, that the method is extremely robust regardless.

4)   If the parabolic estimate was anywhere else (namely to the left of x2), then it is obviously wrong. It may actually be a maximum. Use the golden ratio to step out to the new point.

If we didn't bound the minimum via case 1 above, end-of-loop housekeeping shifts the points down one, and the loop starts again. It continues until the minimum (presumably near x2) is bounded between x1 and x3. Finally, if the original direction was reversed at the start, the points are reversed in order to insure that x1 <= x2 <= x3.

The second of the two steps for directional minimization now begins. The size of the interval from x1 to x3 must be reduced until it is acceptably small. For clarity, these variables are renamed xlow and xhigh. The locations of the three best (lowest error) points are kept as xbest, xsecbest and xthirdbest, with their associated function values using "f" rather than "x" in the names. The general procedure is to use these three points iteratively to predict parabolically the location of the minimum. If that predicted point is "reasonable", evaluate the function there. Otherwise split the larger of the two intervals (xlow , xbest) or (xbest , xhigh) with the golden ratio. Evaluate the function at the new point, and update the three best points and (xlow , xhigh) bounds appropriately.

Comments in the code should clarify details glossed over in the above discussion. Further clarification can be obtained from [Press et al., 1988] and [Brent, 1973]. Two points deserve special emphasis, though. First, note that the test for convergence subtly tests both the length of the bounding interval and the proximity of the best estimate to the center of that interval. Do not tamper with that test carelessly, or excessive iteration can result. Second, note that the parabolic fit is used only if on the previous iteration we moved significantly (fabs(prevdist) > tol1) and the size of our steps is shrinking (fabs(step) < fabs(0.5 * testdist)). Otherwise, the golden section is used. These tests prevent slowly creeping toward the minimum, or cycling back and forth on opposite sides of it. Tamper with these tests at your own risk.

Choosing the Direction for Minimization

The best directional minimization scheme in the world (hopefully the one just described!) does no good whatsoever if told to search along inappropriate directions. There is a family of methods, called *conjugate gradient* algorithms, which intelligently choose the search directions. One of the best is the *Polak–Ribiere* algorithm. Its mathematical justifications are too complex to present here. They can be found in [Polak, 1971]. Roughly, it generates a sequence of work vectors "g" and search directions "h" such that the h's are mutually conjugate. It can be proven that if our n-dimensional function to minimize can be expressed as a quadratic form, then minimizing along the first n h's will lead to the exact minimum. Since neural network error functions as described in previous sections are approximately quadratic near local minima, this method can be expected to converge quickly once it is near the minimum.

The remainder of this section is an in-depth discussion of the Polak–Ribiere algorithm. It can best be understood by following the code listing for conjgrad, found on page 433 of the Appendix. Readers not interested in these fine details may skip the rest of this section.

The parameter list contains three means for escape from this subroutine. Maxits sets a limit on the number of iterations allowed. Normally this would be set to a very large number and is for safety only. The usual convergence indicator is reltol. It would be set to a small fraction, such as 0.0001 or so. Iteration terminates when a line minimization fails to reduce the error by approximately this fraction of the actual error. This test is supplemented by a randomization scheme to eject the search from saddle points. Finally, errtol is used to signal convergence if the actual error drops this low. This would normally be set to 0 and reltol used. However, in some cases, errtol may be more appropriate.

The control routine conjgrad is straightforward. The gradient is computed and used to initialize the g and h vectors. Each iteration first checks the absolute error for convergence, then minimizes along the h direction (in grad at that time) and checks the relative error for convergence. The gradient is recomputed at that minimized point. Finally, the constant gamma is calculated and used along with g and the old h to find the search direction for the next iteration. This direction is placed in both h and grad. Note that restricting gamma to the range 0–1 almost always speeds convergence for neural network learning.

Within that loop, we include an insurance policy against getting stuck at a saddle point. If the directional minimization is not effective, first try minimizing directly in the gradient direction. If that fails, try some random directions. Only give up if all fail.

Subroutine find_grad uses the backpropagation Equations 6-12 and 6-14 to compute the gradient. Subroutine gamma computes that constant via the formula

$$\gamma = \frac{(c-g) \cdot c}{g \cdot g} \qquad\qquad 6\text{-}15$$

where c is the negative gradient (which will be g on the next iteration), and g is the current value of the g vector. Finally, subroutine find_new_dir computes the new search direction by adding gamma times the old search direction to the current negative gradient.

The astute observer will notice that the conjugate gradient method just described is strikingly similar to backpropagation with momentum. It differs in two ways. First, the step size is not fixed. Steps are repeated with varying distances until a line minimum is found. Second, the momentum term is called gamma here and varies in a mathematically optimal way rather than being fixed.

Eluding Local Minima in Learning

Every person charged with minimizing a function hopes that it resembles a trampoline with a cannon ball resting in its center. Unfortunately, real-life problems often have cross sections that look more like Figure 6.12. Obviously, any algorithm that relentlessly crawls downward must have a very lucky starting position if it is to settle into the lowest local minimum.

Avoiding false minima requires two separate procedures. First, we must avoid starting in their vicinity. Referring to the figure above, it behooves us to start somewhere in the left half. If we settle into the broad minimum in the right half, it will be very difficult to escape later. Second, we require a procedure for determining whether or not we are in a local minimum, and escaping if we are. This procedure will be constructive in that we simply attempt to escape. If we succeed, we conclude that we were in a local minimum. Otherwise, we assume that we have found the global minimum.

Two very different techniques will be presented in following chapters. The first, *simulated annealing*, is easy to understand and implement and has low memory requirements. It may be used for both initially avoiding and later escaping local minima. The second, a *genetic* algorithm, is more complex and has quite large memory needs,

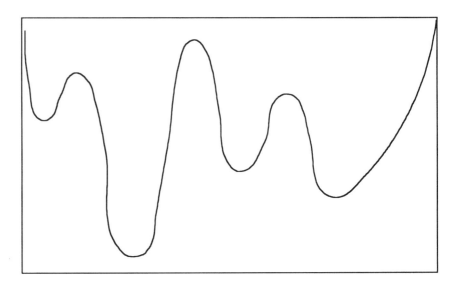

Fig. 6.12: A candidate for simulated annealing

but is generally superior. It is most suitable for finding starting weights.

Local Minima Happen Easily

It is surprisingly easy for gradient algorithms to get stuck in local minima when learning feedforward network weights. Their error surfaces lend a whole new meaning to the term ill-conditioned. Even tiny problems can sport local minima far inferior to global minima, and these minima can be very broad, attracting us in from distant locations. This means that we should *always* repeat the learning process from several different starting positions. It is criminally reckless to use just one starting-weight configuration, assuming that the minimum to which it leads is the best that we can do.

This is a good time to remind the reader that, unlike many other problems, these neural networks always have many equally good global minima. This is because of the numerous symmetries inherent in the architecture. Swapping weight vectors among hidden neurons obviously yields identical networks in terms of input/output mapping. Other symmetries are possible. These multiple global minima are no problem and must not be confused with the serious problem of inferior local minima.

[Gori and Tesi, 1990] give a fascinating demonstration of just how easily local minima can arise. The details in their proof are tedious and so will not be reproduced here. But one of their main results is definitely worth presenting.

Consider the good old XOR (exclusive or) problem. We have two inputs and one output. The training set consists of four cases, being each of the four possible combinations of 1 and 0 which the two inputs can take on. The output is on if and only if exactly one of the two inputs is 1. This is shown graphically in Figure 6.13.

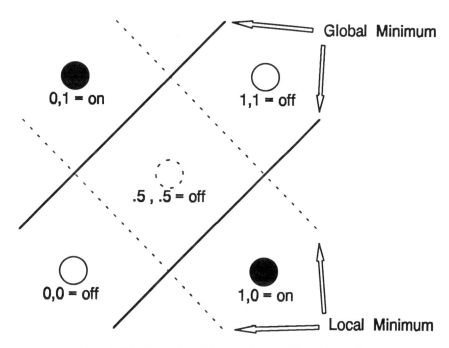

Fig. 6.13: A local minimum in gradient learning

The four corner circles in that figure represent the classical XOR problem. For now, ignore the fifth circle in the center.

The minimal feedforward network capable of solving this problem has two hidden neurons. Such a network operates by partitioning its bivariate input domain into three regions. The two outer regions correspond to one output state, while the inner region is the other output state. Two such partitionings are shown in that figure, one with dark lines, and the other with light lines. Observe that either will solve the XOR problem, so they both correspond to global minimum-weight configurations. Look back at Figure 6.9 for an example of the output function's appearance over the entire square input domain.

Now add a fifth training case. We ask that the output be off when each input is half-activated. This case is the circle in the center of Figure 6.13. The weights corresponding to the dark-line partitioning still solve this augmented problem and thus comprise a global minimum. However, the weights for the light line do not solve it. The key point is that Gori and Tesi show that those latter weights are a local minimum for the new problem and have a significant domain of attraction. They then go on to show even smaller problems, one with only three training cases, which exhibit the same phenomenon — scary.

Mistaken Minima

A minimization difficulty closely related to local minima is that of mistaken minima. We are tempted to decide that we are at a minimum (be it local or global) when the gradient is essentially zero. But just how close to zero do we need to be? That is a particularly important question for neural network learning. Network error functions have broad expanses of plains that are nearly flat, but do definitely slope downward toward a distant minimum. When a gradient descent algorithm finds itself in such an area, it has double trouble. First, since the gradient is so small, the algorithm may wrongly assume that it is at a minimum. This tells us that *we must never accept convergence based on a tiny gradient*. Rather, we should vigorously pursue the (negative) gradient direction, however small it may be, until it turns uphill. We might just drop off a cliff a little further along.

A more serious problem is that when the function is nearly flat in several dimensions, the gradient is poorly defined from a numerical point of view. Roundoff errors can easily conspire to twist the gradient shamefully away from its true direction. The result is that marching in the supposedly correct direction will take us slightly uphill immediately, and our presence at a minimum will be erroneously confirmed. A crude but often effective solution to the problem of a tiny (negative) gradient leading uphill is to choose a handful of alternative directions randomly. Conclude that we are at a minimum only if advancing in each of these directions is unproductive. This method is a waste of time for many numerical problems, but is surprisingly worthwhile for neural network learning.

There is much circumstantial evidence that local minima have gotten a bum rap in neural network learning. In practice, it seems that optimization algorithms are far more likely to become trapped in nearly flat areas, perhaps at the bottom of a deep and narrow channel in some dimensions, but in the midst of a great plain in other dimensions. Figure 6.14 is a cross section of the error surface of an actual neural network.

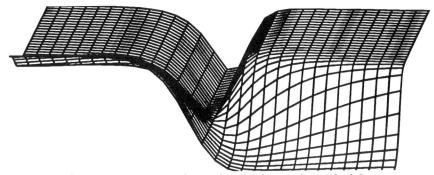

Fig. 6.14: Error surfaces have channels and plains

Because the gradient is tiny in many regions, and because numerical instability may cause it to point uphill, the algorithm may falsely conclude that it is trapped in a local minimum. At present, there is only one known solution: use as much numerical precision as possible. Certainly, eight bytes should be considered an absolute minimum. On hardware that supports it, higher precision is definitely worthwhile. This increased precision causes the gradient to be computed more accurately, allowing us to slowly but surely march out of the flatland so that we can resume our journey downward.

Other Means of Escape

This book focuses on a specialized version of simulated annealing for escape from areas that cause problems for direct optimization algorithms. The author has enjoyed much success with this method. However, there are other possibilities. The Alopex algorithm is a standard stochastic optimization method for large combinatorial problems. [Unnikrishnan and Venugopal, 1992] show how this algorithm can be applied to multiple-layer feedforward network learning. Their method avoids problems with local minima by its stochastic nature. Furthermore, it is not limited to optimizing mean square output error. It can be easily applied to any error criterion. They provide some examples showing how alternative error functions may have intrinsically fewer local minima, a significant improvement in itself.

One of the most exciting developments that this author has seen in learning is the method of [Baba and Kozaki, 1992]. They present a hybrid algorithm. It combines the local power of the conjugate gradient algorithm with the global power of a stochastic method having probability one of finding a global minimum among local minima. There is potential here.

When to Use a Multiple-Layer Feedforward Network

This model has a well-deserved reputation for being *the* neural network. It is a universal function approximator. We can, theoretically at least, teach anything learnable to this network. Thus, it is reasonable to consider this network for any problem.

Another advantage of the multiple-layer feedforward network is that its execution speed is among the fastest of all models currently in use. Many models, none of which is presented in this book, use iteration to converge to a decision, making them abominably slow. If real-time processing is needed, this network may be the only practical choice.

The principal disadvantage of this model is that at the time of this writing there does not exist a fast and reliable training algorithm. The conjugate gradient algorithm shown here usually converges to the nearest minimum significantly faster than traditional gradient descent, but still can be frustratingly slow. And there is no guarantee that the achieved minimum is global. Finding a global minimum is unfortunately a hit-or-miss operation.

There is the compensation that both training and executing a multiple-layer feedforward network is inherently parallel. This is true at two levels. At very small granularity, we have the property that most time is expended in computing dot products, something for which special processors are widely available. At larger granularity, the entire minimization can be distributed across processors, each using a different random starting point. As parallel processors become more common, even on desktop machines, training time will become less of an issue.

In summary, this network should be chosen when rapid execution is needed, slow training will not be a problem, and no special conditions dictate use of an alternative.

7

Eluding Local Minima I: Simulated Annealing

This chapter will discuss a simple yet effective method for avoiding local minima, as well as escaping from them if necessary. The algorithm discussed is a variation of traditional simulated annealing, optimized for the error surfaces encountered in neural network learning. The code given here will be an implementation of that algorithm written for general function minimization, and is primarily for education. The specific code for learning in multiple-layer networks can be found in the Appendix on page 429.

Overview

Annealing is a term from metallurgy. When the atoms in a piece of metal are aligned randomly, the metal is brittle and fractures easily. In the process of annealing, the metal is heated to a high temperature, causing the atoms to shake violently. If it were cooled suddenly, the microstructure would be locked into a random unstable state. Instead, it is cooled very slowly. As the temperature drops, the atoms tend to fall into patterns that are relatively stable for that temperature. Providing that the temperature drop is slow enough, the metal will eventually stabilize into an orderly structure.

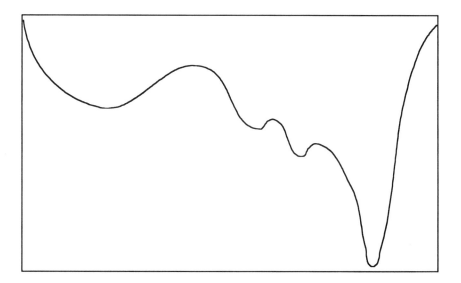

Fig. 7.1: Typical cross section of network error function

The analogue of this process in optimization may be seen by examining Figure 7.1. Suppose one were to toss a ball onto that function and shake it strongly. After each shake, the ball might land anywhere. If the strength of the shaking is reduced, eventually the ball will land somewhere in the right half, and henceforth be unable to jump high enough to move to the left half. If it lands in one of the small pockets in the right side, relatively little shaking will be needed to toss it over the edge into a deeper pocket. Once down low, the relatively weak shaking will be unable to toss it into a higher pocket. This process continues until it eventually settles into the lowest pocket.

Simulated annealing can be performed in optimization by randomly perturbing the independent variables (weights in the case of a neural network) and keeping track of the best (lowest error) function value for each randomized set of variables. A relatively high standard deviation for the random number generator is used at first. After many tries, the set that produced the best function value is designated to be the center about which perturbation will take place for the next temperature. The temperature (standard deviation of the random number generator) is then reduced, and new tries done. (Note that this is slightly different from some traditional methods, which may employ stochastic acceptance of improvement and/or may allow occasional wandering away from improved points. See the final section of this chapter for a discussion.)

There are some optimization problems for which simulated annealing (or other random number techniques) is the only available solution method. However, when more direct methods are available, it is best to employ them as much as possible for the sake of speed. This is the case for learning feedforward network weights, as the conjugate gradient algorithm is very effective at finding a local minimum. Therefore, it is best to interleave the two algorithms. We start by using simulated annealing (or the genetic technique discussed later) to find good starting weights. Conjugate gradient learning then rapidly propels us to the nearest local minimum. Once there, simulated annealing casts about, trying to escape to a lower point. This alternation is continued until we are unable to escape from a local minimum. We then conclude that the local minimum is indeed the global minimum. This algorithm is shown as a flowchart in Figure 22.1 on page 409.

Choosing the Annealing Parameters

Each trial of a random weight set can be very time consuming. Thus, we wish to use as few trials as possible. The total number of trials in our method is equal to the product of the number of temperatures times the number of iterations at each temperature. The obvious question is how we choose each of these quantities. Recall that after iterations at a particular temperature are complete, the best weights at that temperature become the center of iteration for the next temperature. So we must consider how quickly we want to become locked into an area. We also need to choose a starting and ending temperature.

The proper choice of these quantities depends on our purpose. If we are initially selecting weights for a starting point, we want to search a broad area. Also, we are not interested in optimizing by slowly dropping the temperature. That task is best left to the conjugate gradient algorithm. Thus, we would choose very few temperatures. Two, or at most three, are best. Also, a high starting and stopping temperature would be most appropriate. On the other hand, if we have already progressed to a local minimum and are trying to escape, it is better to use a few more temperatures, perhaps four or so. This is more because of the variety needed, rather than because we want to avail ourselves of the optimization gained by many temperatures. We simply do not know how far we must jump in order to escape the local minimum. It may be very broad, requiring a high temperature. Or it may be a small pocket in a narrow channel. In this case, a high temperature would nearly always toss us too far afield. By using a moderately high starting temperature and a low stopping temperature, we are more likely to hit the lucky spot.

If the optimization problem does not have a good direct solution, making simulated annealing our *only* choice, then we must use many temperatures, and cover a wide range. The tradeoff now becomes one of "How sure do we want to be that we have *the* global minimum?" versus "How accurately do we need to estimate the minimum?" If we prefer a rough approximation in exchange for high probability of having the global minimum, then 5 to 10 temperatures, with a fairly high stopping temperature, may be best. On the other hand, if we need high accuracy, we are forced to use many temperatures and drop low. The price we pay is fewer iterations at each temperature, making it more likely that we will become trapped in a local minimum.

The final issue considered here is that of reducing the temperature. How do we progress from the starting temperature to the stopping temperature? One method is by multiplying by a constant factor each time. This factor is computed as:

$$c = e^{\frac{\ln(stop/start)}{n-1}} \qquad\qquad 7\text{-}1$$

where *start* and *stop* are the starting and stopping temperatures, and *n* is the number of temperatures. Note that this temperature-reduction method is chosen for the particular task of neural network learning and is quite different from that employed in many traditional versions of simulated annealing.

Implementation in Feedforward Network Learning

The actual implementation of simulated annealing in network learning is straightforward. No useful purpose would be served by listing sample code here. The interested reader can find it on page 429 of the Appendix. Several special points will be made, though.

There is rarely any need for extremely large weights. In fact, large weights can lead to extreme activation levels (near the theoretical limits of the activation function). This in turn gives rise to very small derivatives of the activation function, which in turn tends to paralyze that weight. For this reason, it is good to impose a limit on the magnitude of all weights, especially in the initialization phase. The temperature (starting standard deviation of the random perturbation) should not exceed approximately three. Each time a new random weight is generated by adding a random number to its current value, the new value should be tested against an absolute upper limit of approximately five. The absolute value of the new weight should not be allowed to exceed this limit. A limit of five is sufficiently large to permit wide variation, yet small enough to let gradient techniques pull it in later if necessary.

The other point to consider in any optimization problem is which parameters need to be randomly perturbed and which can be explicitly computed (or at least estimated). In many problems they must all be subjected to randomization. In the case of feedforward network learning, though, this is not the case. Only weights leading into the hidden layer(s) need to be randomly set. Given those weights, nearly optimal output-layer weights can be explicitly computed. The network error as a function of the output-layer weights, for fixed hidden-layer weights, is a very well-behaved function. Although the nonlinearity of the output neuron's activation functions prevents us from directly minimizing the actual network error, we can use traditional regression to minimize the error in the domain of the activation function. To do this, after randomly setting the hidden-layer weights, we compute and save the activation of each hidden neuron for each training sample, then compute the singular-value decomposition of that matrix. We apply the *inverse* activation function to the target activation of each output neuron for each training sample. Multiplication of the computed singular-value decomposition matrix by this vector gives the output weights that minimize the mean square error of the input to the activation function. Though this will not be exactly the same as minimizing the actual output error, it will certainly be far better than anything that could be expected from random choice of output weights! This regression technique is described in detail starting on page 165.

A Sample Program

A general optimization subroutine using simulated annealing is given here. It can easily be modified to minimize any multivariate function. The principle involved is exactly the same as in learning network weights, and the reader's understanding of the algorithm is enhanced by avoiding the overhead of a complete network learning program. Again note that this algorithm departs from traditional techniques in several ways. See the last section of this chapter for a discussion.

```
#define RANDMAX 32767
static void shake ( int nvars, double *center, double *x, double temp ) ;

double anneal (
    double (*func)( int n , double *x ) ,  // Function to be minimized
    int ntemps,                  // Number of temperatures to use
    int niters,                  // Number of iters at each temperature
    int setback,                 // Set back iters this much if improved
    int maxcalls,                // Limit num of func calls (due to setback)
    double fquit,                // Quit if function reduced to this amount
    double starttemp,            // Starting temp (standard deviation)
    double stoptemp,             // Stopping temperature
    int nvars,                   // Number of variables in x
    double *x,                   // Set to start when called; returns best
    double *cent                 // Work vector nvars long
    )
{
    int i, iter, seed, bestseed, improved, itemp ;
    double tempmult, temp, fval, bestfval ;


/*
    For every temperature, the center around which we will perturb is the
    best point so far.  This is kept in 'cent', so initialize cent to the user's
    starting estimate.   Also, initialize 'bestfval', the best function value so
    far, to be the function value at that starting point.
*/

    for (i=0 ; i<nvars ; i++)
        cent[i] = x[i] ;

    bestfval = (*func) ( nvars , x ) ;
```

```
/*
    This is the temperature reduction loop and the iteration within tempera-
    ture loop. We use a slick trick to keep track of the best point at a given
    temperature. We certainly don't want to replace 'cent' every time an
    improvement is had, as then we would be moving our center about,
    compromising the global nature of the algorithm. We could, of course,
    have a second work area in which we save the 'best so far for this
    temperature' point. But if there are a lot of variables, the usual case,
    this wastes memory. What we do is to save the seed of the random
    number generator which created the improvement. Then later, when
    we need to retrieve the best, simply set the random seed and regener-
    ate it. This technique also saves a lot of copying time if many improve-
    ments are made for a single temperature.
*/


temp = starttemp ;
tempmult = exp ( log ( stoptemp / starttemp ) / (ntemps-1) ) ;

for (itemp=0 ; itemp<ntemps ; itemp++) { // Temp reduction loop

    improved = 0 ;                            // Flags if this temp improved

    for (iter=0 ; iter<niters ; iter++) {     // Iters per temp loop

        seed = rand () ;                      // Get a random seed
        srand ( seed ) ;                      // Brute force set it
        shake ( nvars , cent , x , temp ) ;   // Randomly perturb
        fval = (*func) ( nvars , x ) ;        // evaluate function there

        if (fval < bestfval) {                // If this iteration improved
            bestfval = fval ;                 // then update the best so far
            bestseed = seed ;                 // and save seed to recreate it
            improved = 1 ;                    // Flag that we improved
            if (bestfval <= fquit)            // If we reached the user's
                break ;                       // limit, we can quit
            iter -= setback ;                 // It often pays to keep going
            if (iter < 0)                     // at this temperature if we
                iter = 0 ;                    // are still improving
        }

        if (! --maxcalls)                     // This is for safety in case
            break ;                           // setback causes excess loop
    }

    if (improved) {                           // If temp saw improvement
        srand ( bestseed ) ;                  // set seed to what caused it
        shake ( nvars , cent , x , temp ) ;   // and recreate that point
        for (i=0 ; i<nvars ; i++)             // which will become center
            cent[i] = x[i] ;                  // for next temperature iters
        srand ( bestseed / 2 + 999 ) ;        // Jog seed away from best
    }
```

```
        if (bestfval <= fquit)              // If we reached the user's
            break ;                          // limit, we can quit

        if (! maxcalls)                      // This is for safety in case
            break ;                          // setback causes excess loop

        temp *= tempmult ;                   // Reduce temp for next pass
        }                                    // through this temp loop

    for (i=0 ; i<nvars ; i++)                // Return the best point in x
        x[i] = cent[i] ;

    return bestfval ;
}

/*
--------------------------------------------------------------------

    SHAKE - Randomly perturb the point

--------------------------------------------------------------------
*/

static void shake ( int nvars , double *center , double *x , double temp )
{
    double r ;

// Recall that the variance of a uniform deviate on 0-1 is 1/12.
// Adding four such random variables multiplies the variance by 4,
// while dividing by 2 divides the variance by 4.
// Note that SQRT(12)=3.464...

    temp *= 3.464101615 / (2.*(double) RANDMAX) ;

    while (nvars--) {
        r = (double) rand() + (double) rand() -
            (double) rand() - (double) rand() ;
        *x++ = *center++ + temp * r ;
        }
}
```

The parameters passed to the annealing routine are

func - A pointer to the function that will be minimized.

ntemps - The number of temperatures to use. Larger values should be used if there is a great difference in starttemp and stoptemp. Values of 2 to 15 are typical.

niters - The number of iterations at each temperature. If the setback parameter is greater than 0, the actual number of iterations may exceed this quantity. This should be set as large as possible, with the largest values being necessary for problems with extensive false minima.

setback - As long as improvement is being had at a particular temperature, it makes sense to continue at that temperature. We should conclude that we have minimized as much as is reasonably possible there only when many iterations fail to cause improvement. Thus, it behooves us to reward improvement by setting back the iteration counter (but not below 0) each time we improve. A typical value for this parameter is about half of niters.

maxcalls - It is unlikely, but possible, that a series of widely spaced improvements may cause setback to slow operation excessively. This parameter limits the total number of times the objective function is evaluated. Generally this parameter would be set extremely large and used as insurance only.

fquit - It may be that the user is concerned only with minimizing the function to a certain value and does not care about precisely locating the minimum. Operation will cease if the function value drops to this amount. Generally this would be set to an extremely small value and all temperatures processed.

starttemp - This is the standard deviation of the random perturbation used first. It should be set to several times the maximum expected distance between the starting guess and the global minimum point.

stoptemp - This is the final standard deviation. It should be of the order of magnitude of the desired accuracy in the location of the best point.

nvars - The number of independent variables (length of the x vector).

x - A vector of length nvars. An initial guess should be in this vector when anneal is called. The point that minimized the function will be returned here.

cent - A work vector nvars long.

The constant RANDMAX is defined here as 2^{15} - 1. This is the maximum possible value for rand(), the random number generator. Some implementations may use other values, such as 2^{31} - 1.

The first step in the anneal subroutine is to copy the input guess in x to the work vector cent. The objective function is evaluated at this guess, and the function value preserved as the best so far. The temperature (standard deviation of the random perturbation) is initialized to the user's starting temperature, and the reduction factor is computed.

At the start of each pass through the temperature loop, the improved flag is set to zero. When all iterations at that temperature are complete, the perturbation center for the next temperature will be updated only if that flag was set to one due to improvement. Otherwise, the same center will be used again.

Each iteration at a given temperature starts by calling rand() for a random number. We then call srand() to set explicitly the random seed to this value. This step may not be necessary, as most implementations automatically use each generated number as the seed for the next call. However, it is very cheap insurance. Also, since the same call to srand() will be used later to recreate the best point, it is good programming style to make the call now.

The local routine shake is used to perturb around the center point. It sums four uniform deviates to realize a more bell-shaped curve than would be attained with one deviate alone. By adding two and subtracting two, the random variable has mean zero. The variance of a uniform deviate on 0–1 is 1/12. Adding four such random variables multiplies the variance by 4. Thus, we multiply the specified temperature by sqrt(12)/2 in order to produce a random variable whose standard deviation equals the input temperature.

If the new trial point has a superior function value, update the best function value and save the random seed that gave us this point. Set the improved flag to indicate that we had a success at this temperature. If the function has been minimized enough to suit the user, break out of the loop. Finally, set back the iteration counter to give us more tries at this temperature. Regardless of whether or not we improved, verify that we have not called the objective function the limiting number of times.

When all iterations at a temperature are complete, test the improved flag. If we improved, set the random seed to the seed that gave us the best point, and call shake again to recreate that point. Move the center for the next temperature to that new best point. It is also nice to jog the random seed so that we don't exactly reproduce the same sequence of perturbations.

A Sample Function

An interesting test function is shown in Figure 7.2. It is inverted for visual clarity. Minimizing the function whose code is shown below corresponds to maximizing the displayed function. It has a very

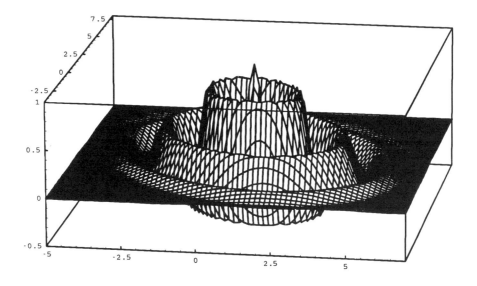

Fig. 7.2: Difficult function to optimize

narrow global extreme, which is surrounded by multiple ridges of false extrema.

```
double func ( int nvars , double vars[] )
{
  double x, y, d, mult, f ;

  x = vars[0] - 1.0 ;
  y = vars[1] - 2.0 ;

  d = x * x  +  y * y  +  0.5 * x * y ;
  mult = exp ( -d / 8. ) ;
  f = cos ( 4. * sqrt(d) ) ;

  return 1. - mult * f ;
}
```

   If the anneal routine is used to minimize a function written by the reader, several points must be kept in mind. First, the same standard deviation random variable is used to perturb each independent variable. Thus, the variables should be scaled in such a way that this is reasonable. If the function is extremely sensitive to small changes in one variable, while large changes are required in another variable in order to effect a significant change in the function value, the algorithm will probably fail. Also, remember to set a starting temperature large enough that the global minimum can be found. As a rule of thumb, the starting temperature should approximately equal twice the maximum anticipated distance between the starting guess and the best point.

Random Number Generation

Random numbers play an important role in neural network learning. In the simplest cases, they are used to initialize weights in preparation for learning. More sophisticated programs use them in simulated annealing and genetic optimization, discussed in the next chapter. Some neural network models even use random numbers as a central ingredient in their operation, rather than only in training. For these reasons, and because simulated annealing is especially dependent on good random numbers, they will be briefly discussed in this section.

No attempt will be made here to define *randomness* thoroughly, nor to present truly excellent random number generators. The definitive source for detailed information on this topic is [Knuth, 1981]. The material in this section is largely based on [Press et al., 1988].

The simulated annealing routine previously shown makes use of the system routine rand() to produce the random numbers it needs. For small problems, this is entirely sufficient. However, large problems that require a large number of truly independent trials will not be adequately served by such a primitive random number generator.

The random-number generator rand() supplied by the vast majority of compiler vendors uses the *linear congruential* algorithm, which operates in the following way. It has three fixed constants: the multiplier a, the increment c, and the modulus m. Given a non-negative integer p_n, which less than m and is taken to be a member of a random sequence, the next integer in the random sequence is computed as

$$p_{n+1} = (a\,p_n + c) \bmod m \qquad\qquad 7\text{-}2$$

where mod m above means the remainder after division by m. This algorithm does a surprisingly good job of generating random numbers, given its simplicity and speed of computation. For many purposes, it is quite sufficient. However, for more exacting tasks, it has several serious drawbacks.

The most serious problem for us is more an implementation problem than an algorithm problem. Obviously, the random numbers generated by this method can never equal or exceed m. ANSI C only requires that m be at least $2^{15} = 32,768$. Nearly every C and C++ compiler that the author has seen uses this minimum value. Compilers using 16-bit integers by default cannot easily use anything larger.

The sad truth is that for many algorithms that rely on a large quantity of random numbers, 32,768 possibilities are not very many.

The above problem is made even worse by the fact that the linear congruential algorithm is periodic. Whenever a particular value appears in the random sequence, the exact same value will always follow it. This means that if m is 32,768, we are not just hampered by having at most that many possible random numbers. We also can have at most that many possible random *sequences*! This means that if we use a deterministic algorithm to produce network weights from a sequence of random integers, we can have at most 32,768 different weight sets. That is really not very many. Consider the following:

1) Unless we explicitly set unique seeds, there is no guarantee that if we generate 32,768 weight sets they will all be different. If the generation process uses exactly 32,768 / 4 = 8,192 random integers to create a weight set, we will get four different weight sets, each repeated 8,192 times! Such duplication occurs suprisingly often, wasting valuable time and space.

2) When a particular random integer occurs at the time that a hidden weight vector is about to be computed, the weights for that vector, and all hidden weight vectors which follow it, are determined. When that same particular integer randomly occurs at the start of another hidden weight vector, the same sequence appears. This means that across trials there will be tremendous duplication of weight vectors. That is hardly random.

Given the above, it can be seen that the run-of-the-mill random number generator like rand() is grossly inadequate for serious simulated annealing.

The linear congruential algorithm has a third problem, which is probably not as serious for our purposes as those just pointed out, but which nonetheless deserves mention. It has *serial correlation*. In other words, close neighbors in the series of random numbers it generates are related to each other in potentially troublesome ways. In particular, suppose that we take successive k-tuples from the series. Each set of k consecutive "random" numbers defines a point in k-space. Our hope is that the space will be filled uniformly. Alas, this does not happen. Rather, the points will lie on k-1–dimensional hyperplanes. There can be at most approximately $m^{1/k}$ such hyperplanes. If the constants a, c, and m are not carefully chosen, there will be far fewer hyperplanes than that.

Serial correlation is especially troublesome in Monte Carlo integration, where it prejudices the search space in ways that absolutely must be accounted for. Although there is no blatantly obvious problem with small-scale serial correlation in random sequences used for neural network weight generation, the possibility cannot be ignored. The random integers used to define the subsets of the weight vector for a single hidden neuron define k-tuples in a very high dimension space, and k'th roots are very small when k is large. Just how serious is it that all subsets of each hidden neuron weight vectors are determined from points that lie on one of very few hyperplanes? That question is sufficiently disquieting that we should consider eliminating serial correlation from our random sequence.

The random number generator shown here addresses all three of the above problems. It increases the number of random integers to 714,025, better than the usual 32,768 by a factor of over 20. Far more importantly, it effectively eliminates periodic repetition. For all practical purposes, this random number generator never repeats itself. This is crucial to achieving variety in network weight vectors. And it practically eliminates serial correlation. The price paid in speed is very little, considering the gain.

This algorithm can be criticized in one tiny way. It uses long integers (32 bits), but does not make use of all possible nonnegative values that 32-bit integers can have. For our purposes, this is irrelevant. Elimination of periodicity is of paramount importance, and that is taken care of. It is nearly impossible for a high-level program to do better than this one does. An assembler program could make use of double-register arithmetic to avoid overflow, a luxury not afforded by C or C++. If the reader is one of the fortunate few whose compiler provides random numbers covering all 2^{31} values, and this asset must be retained, then the program here can be trivially modified by calling the system random routine rather than generating table entries with the local code.

The following program operates by shuffling the random numbers produced by an ordinary linear congruential generator. When pf_rand (for *period free*) is called the first time, or when the seed is explicitly reset by calling pf_srand, a table of random numbers is built. A local seed, reserved exclusively for the local linear congruential generator, is kept. Because pf_rand is not periodic, the table must be rebuilt if the user calls pf_srand to reset the local seed. After the table is built, a local value that is the "previously returned random number" is also initialized with the local generator.

Successive calls to pf_rand use the previously returned random integer to index the table of random numbers. The indexed table entry is returned as the current random number, and that table entry is refilled from the local generator. It is important that the index in the table be found as shown in the program. That method uses the high-order bits of the previous random number. It is tempting to use the mod function to define the index. But that would make use of the low-order bits. It is well known that serial correlation in linear congruential random numbers is more pronounced in the low bits than it is in the high bits. While the shuffling process inherent in the table lookup is largely able to remove this correlation, it is better not to tempt fate.

```
#define IM 714025L            // These constants are from Press et. al.
#define IA 1366L              // "Numerical Recipes in C"
#define IC 150889L            // Do not tamper unless you are an expert
#define TABLE_LENGTH 97       // Length of shuffle table

static long seed = 797 ;          // Keep the current seed here
static long randout ;             // Random output
static long table[TABLE_LENGTH]; // Keep shuffle table here
static int table_initialized = 0 ;   // Has it been initialized?

/*
  Set the random seed
*/

void pf_srand ( long iseed )
{
   seed = iseed ;             // We keep the static seed here
   table_initialized = 0 ;    // Must also rebuild table with it!
}

/*
  Return the maximum random number
*/

long pf_randmax ()
{
   return IM - 1L ;
}

/*
  This is the actual random number generator
*/

long pf_rand ()     // Return the next random number

{
   int i ;

   if (! table_initialized) { // Initialize shuffle table before use
      table_initialized = 1 ; // Flag to avoid more inits
```

```
      for (i=0 ; i<TABLE_LENGTH ; i++) { // Fill entire table
        seed = (IA * seed + IC) % IM ;  // Make a random number
        table[i] = seed ;               // Put it in the table
        }

      seed = (IA * seed + IC) % IM ;    // One more random number
      randout = seed ;                  // for upcoming first use
      }

   i = (int) ((double) TABLE_LENGTH * (double) randout / (double) IM) ;
   randout = table[i] ;            // This output comes from table
   seed = (IA * seed + IC) % IM ;  // Make new random number
   table[i] = seed ;               // to replace used entry
   return randout ;                // then return old entry
}
```

As was previously pointed out, the local linear congruential random number generator does not need to be used in order for this shuffling routine to remove periodicity and serial correlation. If the user is in possession of a full 32-bit rand(), calls to it can be substituted for the three "seed=" lines that locally generate random numbers. The static variable seed would, of course, no longer be needed, as the rand() local seed would take its place. But don't forget to modify the line in pf_rand() which computes the table index. Now you must divide by 2^{31} rather than by IM. And certainly don't just call your srand(seed) to reset the pf_rand() seed. You must also reinitialize the table!

Going on from Here

Of necessity, this chapter's treatment of simulated annealing has been very superficial. Those who crave more sophistication should see the classic text [Aarts and van Laarhoven, 1987]. A very advanced work, for the mathematically inclined only, is [Azencott, ed., 1992]. A superb discussion of techniques specific to function minimization can be found in [Styblinski and Tang, 1990]. That reference also contains a nice bibliography in which some of the pioneering work by H. Szu is cited. This section will entice the reader with a few hints of advanced techniques.

First, it must be clearly stated that the algorithm presented in this chapter contains several significant perversions of fundamental simulated annealing algorithms. In a few traditional versions, improvements are accepted stochastically, rather than deterministically. The temperature controls not only the random variation, but also the probability of accepting an improved point. In many other versions, we always accept improvements, but we can wander away from improved points with probabilities determined by the temperature. These techniques discourage hill climbing, which can cause convergence to a local minimum. The author chooses a deterministic route because, for neural network applications, it apparently gives superior results. In fact, many specific details of the algorithm, for better or for worse, are the result of neural network experimentation by the author and may reflect the spirit, but not the particulars, of traditional annealing. Readers who intend to use the program provided here for more general purposes may want to consult the above references for guidance in slightly modifying the code.

An important comment involves stopping the algorithm, both within temperature loops and across temperatures. The program given here uses a preordained number of temperatures and iterations within each temperature. Setting back the iteration counter after success adds a little more sophistication to the procedure, but we can do even better. The best algorithms will gather information on the energy surface (roughly speaking, the function being minimized) during annealing and determine when to advance to a new temperature or stop the annealing entirely, based on that information.

Another subject often debated is the temperature reduction schedule. Many current implementations use the exponential reduction used here. It has proven itself effective in practice. However, it does have some annoying theoretical shortcomings. Theory would seem to dictate a much slower logarithmic temperature reduction. Alas, experience disagrees with that theory. Compromise schedules, incorporating sublayers of logarithmic schedules, are being investigated. All that is known for sure at this point is that there is no such thing as a universally optimal schedule. The optimum is extremely problem dependent. Interested graduate students should note that adaptive strategies are a promising area for investigation.

The exact nature of the random perturbations can affect speed of convergence. Here we use sums of uniform random deviates, providing a very roughly normal distribution. [Styblinski and Tang, 1990] claim that using a Cauchy distribution gives superior results. This distribution is also said to allow a faster reduction of temperature.

Finally, one of the most fascinating aspects of simulated annealing concerns partitioning it into separate processes. Suppose that we have a fixed amount of computational resources. We do not have the luxury of indefinite computation time, waiting for some stopping criterion to be attained. Intuition leads us to believe that the best use of these resources is to devote them all to a single shot at annealing. If we plan on using n temperatures, devote $1/n$ of the total time to each temperature or perhaps use some other biased allocation. That may *not* be the best approach. We are often better off splitting the computational resources into several parts and performing totally independent annealings, start to finish, within each part. Our final result is chosen to be the best among the different attempts.

The above result has especially important implications for parallel processing. The naive programmer would use a single annealing, distributing the work for each temperature among the processors. After all processors have completed their work for a temperature, they would communicate their results to a central controller, which would then distribute updated work to all processors for the next temperature. But in most cases, especially if communication is expensive, we would be far better off letting each processor complete its own totally autonomous annealing. The only communication would be at the end, when the central controller would choose the best result from among the processors.

8

Eluding Local Minima II: Genetic Optimization

This chapter will discuss a relatively complex method for avoiding local minima. The code here will be for general function minimization and is primarily for education. The specific code for learning in multiple-layer feedforward networks can be found on page 443 in the Appendix.

Overview

Ever since it was discovered that ill-behaved functions could be optimized with methods analogous to those that drive evolution to produce superior individuals, research into such methods has flourished. One chapter of a book cannot begin to do justice to what promises to be a fertile new field. The interested reader is directed to [Davis, 1991] for a very readable and broad introduction to genetic algorithms. More mathematical rigor and explicit programs can be found in [Goldberg, 1989].

The program presented in this section is designed to minimize an arbitrary function. This allows the reader to use it for a variety of problems and also simplifies understanding of its operation. A specific application of genetic optimization for neural network learning is included in the program listing on page 443 of the Appendix.

In nature, evolution is driven by survival of the fittest. Weak individuals tend to die before reproducing, while the stronger ones live longer and bear many offspring, who often inherit the qualities that enabled their parents to survive. Artificial genetic optimization operates in a similar manner. The parameters of the function to be optimized are encoded as *genes* in a *chromosome*. A random population pool of individuals (chromosomes here) is created. Then, pairs of individuals are selected from this pool based on their performance in optimizing the function. The selected pairs reproduce, creating children whose genetic structure shares characteristics of both parents. Perhaps some *mutation* (unexpected random change) takes place in the creation of a child. The children replace their parents. As this proceeds, inferior traits in the pool die out due to lack of reproduction. At the same time, strong traits tend to combine with other strong traits to produce children who perform well.

Terminology becomes confusing at times, since there is not a perfect correspondence between natural and artificial genetic processes. Also, not all authors agree completely in their use of terms. The following generally accepted meanings will be used in this book:

Chromosome - This is the complete genetic description of an individual. It is a collection of primitive features called genes. During reproduction, the chromosome that defines an individual will be split in half, donating half of this individual's genes to each of two children.

Gene - This is a single feature within a chromosome. It may take on any of several values called *alleles*.

Allele - This is a particular value that may be taken on by a gene. Different genes will in general have different alleles. For example, the gene that determines hair color may have alleles of red, blond, brown, et cetera, while the gene that determines eye color may have alleles of blue, brown, and so forth.

Genotype - This is the explicit genetic structure of a chromosome.

Phenotype - This is the physical expression of the genotype. A person has a specific genetic structure that perhaps someday can be mapped in a graphic display. That apparent structure is the person's *genotype*. The actual person (tall, red hair, etc.) is the *phenotype*. For an example closer to the task at hand, a chromosome may have the genotype "00001001" which decodes to a parameter value (phenotype) of 9.

Objective function - This is the function we wish to minimize. In neural networks, it would typically be the mean square error of the network as a function of its connection weights.

Fitness - This is a measure of how well a parameter set (such as a particular set of weights in a neural network) performs. The fitness is generally an inverse function of the value of the objective function; small values of the objective function imply greater fitness, since our goal is minimization.

Schema (plural schemata) - Loosely speaking, this is a collection of genes in a chromosome having certain specified values. For a detailed discussion, see [Goldberg, 1989]. For our purposes, a schema is a small subset of the genes in a chromosome which, when they take on specified values, act as a unit to produce an effect.

Like some of its terminology, the exact nature of genetic optimization is still open to debate. Some practitioners demand strict binary representation within chromosomes. The mathematics of such representation is more tractable and has some nice optimality properties. Other practitioners prefer less constraint. There are numerous algorithms for evaluating the objective function to measure an individual's fitness. Countless methods of reproduction and mutation exist. Even the basic processes of birth and death can vary. However, genetic optimization can generally be characterized by the following steps:

Initialization - Randomly generate a population.

Evaluation - Test each individual, using the objective function. Compute a *fitness* value, which is a measure of how well the individual optimizes the function.

Parent selection - Choose pairs of individuals from the population in such a way that those with higher fitness will be chosen more often.

Reproduction - Generate (usually two) children from each pair of parents. Each parent contributes half of its genetic makeup to each child.

Mutation - Randomly change a tiny amount of the genetic information in each child.

A complete pass through the above steps is a *generation*. After each generation is complete, a new one starts with the *evaluation* of each of the children. Each of the above steps will be described in more detail. But first, we must prepare a solid foundation by careful design of our parameter representation.

Designing the Genetic Structure

Probably the most important consideration in designing a genetic optimization procedure is deciding how the parameters will be encoded in the chromosome. This can make the difference between an algorithm that performs well versus one that is nearly worthless.

The first decision to be made is how to trade off number of genes versus number of alleles for each gene. Many practitioners favor a strictly binary approach. Each gene can have one of two alleles: 0 or 1. Each parameter is encoded as a binary number, and all parameters are strung together as one long string. Theorems concerning properties of various genetic algorithms can usually be proven more easily when this structure is employed. It can be shown that under some conditions this is the optimal structure in that using fewer genes with more allele values to represent the same information will result in inferior expected performance. Finally, it has been the author's experience with practical problems that using more genes with fewer alleles tends to produce slightly more effective algorithms in most cases.

There is much to be said, though, for coarser encoding. The opposite extreme from binary coding is direct parameter storage.

There is one gene for each parameter, and the allele values for that gene are the possible values of that parameter. Conversion between the genotype (internal representation of a chromosome) and the phenotype (parameter values represented by the chromosome) is trivial, since they are one and the same. The operations of crossover and mutation, discussed later, are simplified. In many cases, especially if the population size is large, performance does not significantly suffer as compared to finer encodings. The demonstration program shown later in this section implements this encoding for simplicity. The more sophisticated neural network algorithm listed in the Appendix uses the more effective binary encoding.

A useful compromise is to encode floating-point parameter values as decimal digits. Each gene will represent one significant digit of one parameter. The allele values for that gene will be the decimal digits 0 through 9 (plus a sign for the most significant digit). The demonstration program presented later in this section optionally uses this technique in a very primitive way.

The second consideration in designing the chromosome structure is assignment of genes to positions in the chromosome. Traditional methodology treats the chromosome as a linear structure. Reproduction chops the string at a single point, and every gene on one side of this crossover point goes to one child, while the genes on the other side go to the other child. (More complex operators, such as *inversion*, will not be discussed here.) The implication is that genes physically near each other tend to remain together in children, while those more distant are often assigned to different children. Thus, if we have prior knowledge that some parameters interact with others, we should attempt to assign their genes to close locations on the string. Parameters that are more independent would be placed further apart. Naturally, in many cases, we do not know in advance which parameters will interact. If we do, though, it is important to position them in tight groups according to their expected interactions. In genetic parlance, we want important schemata to be as compact as possible, so that reproduction does not disrupt them. One version of the program shown later in this section demonstrates the effect of failure to assign positions in the chromosome intelligently.

Evaluation

The process of evaluating the fitness of an individual consists of the following five steps:

1) Convert the chromosome's genotype to its phenotype.
2) Evaluate the objective function.
3) Convert the objective function's value to a raw fitness.
4) Convert the raw fitness to a scaled fitness.
5) Convert the scaled fitness to an expected frequency of selection as a parent.

Each of these operations will now be discussed.

Converting a chromosome's genotype to its phenotype is trivial if the simple coding scheme of "one gene equals one parameter" is used. The sample optimization program presented later in this section uses this scheme. It also demonstrates one poor but educational method for handling decimal digit coding. Full binary coding is used in the neural program in the Appendix.

The second evaluation step is to evaluate the objective function at the parameter point. The function should be defined in such a way that all parameter values have roughly the same effect on the function value. If the function is extremely sensitive to one parameter, while very large changes are needed in another parameter to effect significant changes in the function, the genetic algorithm will suffer. Of course, perfect scaling is never possible, but obvious inequities should be dealt with by prescaling in the objective function.

The third evaluation step is to convert the objective function's value to a raw fitness. Recall that we are attempting to minimize the objective function, so we want smaller function values to produce larger fitness values. Also, later calculations will be simplified if the fitness is never negative. The best conversion function can be somewhat problem-dependent. However, one function that has been found to be generally useful is the exponential:

$$f(v) = e^{Kv} \qquad\qquad 8\text{-}1$$

where K is a negative number. In neural network problems where the network error v ranges from 0–1, using -20 for K is effective. This would map an error of .001 to a raw fitness of .98, .01 to .82, and .1 to .14. Problems in which very small values of v could not be expected might benefit from K closer to zero.

The fourth evaluation step is converting the raw fitness to a scaled fitness. If the raw fitnesses were used to determine parent-selection probabilities, two problems could arise. One is that in the first few generations, one or a very few extremely superior individuals usually appear. Their fitness values are so high that they would be selected as parents too many times. Their genetic material would quickly dominate the gene pool. Population diversity, which is crucial to genetic optimization, would be lost early on. The second problem is just the opposite. After many generations, clearly inferior individuals will have been weeded out. The population will consist of individuals who have relatively high raw fitness. The maximum fitness will usually be only slightly greater than the average. As a result, the most fit individuals will not be selected as parents in the high proportions necessary for continued rapid improvement. Scaling solves both of these problems.

The basic scaling principle used here involves applying a linear transform to the raw fitnesses such that the average fitness remains unchanged, but the maximum scaled fitness becomes a fixed multiple of the average. A multiple of two is widely used, while the author prefers three. The only potential problem with this method is that occasionally a very small raw fitness may be mapped to a negative scaled value. One solution is to truncate at zero; if a scaled fitness is negative, set it equal to zero. The approach used here if this happens is to compute an alternative scaling function which again maps the average fitness to itself, but maps the minimum fitness to zero. The scaling formula is

$$f(x) \ = \ slope * x + const \qquad\qquad 8\text{-}2$$

$$slope \ = \ \frac{(mult - 1) * avg}{(max - avg)} \qquad\qquad 8\text{-}3$$

$$const \ = \ \frac{avg * (max - mult * avg)}{max - avg} \qquad\qquad 8\text{-}4$$

where $f(x)$ is the function that converts raw fitness to scaled fitness, *mult* is the factor by which the maximum fitness is favored over the average, *avg* is the average raw fitness, and *max* is the maximum raw fitness. If this formula results in negative scaled fitnesses, an alternative formula is used that maps the minimum raw fitness to zero while leaving the average fitness unchanged.

$$slope = \frac{avg}{avg - min} \qquad\qquad 8\text{-}5$$

$$const = \frac{-min * avg}{avg - min} \qquad\qquad 8\text{-}6$$

The final evaluation step is to convert the scaled fitnesses to expected frequency of selection as parents. This is simple. Just divide each scaled fitness by the average scaled fitness. It is trivial to show that the sum of these final fitness values is equal to the number of individuals in the population pool, and the relative values of the expected selection frequencies are proportional to the scaled fitnesses.

A complete subroutine that converts the objective function values to raw fitnesses, then to scaled fitnesses, and finally to expected selection rates, is shown below.

```
void fval_to_fitness (
    int popsize ,                  // Length of fvals, fitness vectors
    double favor_best ,            // Fact for favoring best over avg (2-3)
    double fitfac ,                // Factor converts fval to raw fitness (-20)
    double *fvals ,                // Input popsize vect of vals of obj func
    double *fitness                // Output popsize vect of fitnesses (rates)
    )

{
    int individual ;
    double fit, avgfitness, minfitness, maxfitness, ftemp, tmult, tconst ;

/*
    The first step is to convert the objective function value (which is to be
    minimized) into a raw (unscaled) fitness value.  The best method can
    be problem dependent.  Certainly, the mapping function must be de-
    creasing, as we want smaller values of the objective function to map to
    larger values of fitness.  Also, later calculations are simplified if the
    fitness is always positive.

    The conversion function used here is f(v) = exp ( k * v ) where k is a
    negative number.  For objective functions which range from zero to one,
    as would be the case of a relative error function, a constant of about
    -20 is appropriate.  This would map .001 to .98, .01 to .82 and .1 to .14.
*/

    avgfitness = 0.0 ;
    maxfitness = -1.e30 ;
    minfitness = 1.e30 ;
```

```
            for (individual=0 ; individual<popsize ; individual++) {
              fitness[individual] = fit = exp ( fitfac * fvals[individual] ) ;
              avgfitness += fit ;
              if (fit > maxfitness)
                maxfitness = fit ;
              if (fit < minfitness)
                minfitness = fit ;
              }

            avgfitness /= (double) popsize ;

  /*

            The second step is to apply a linear transform to these fitnesses to
            prevent extraordinarily fit individuals from dominating early on, and at
            the same time still favor the most fit later in the run when a large
            number of individuals are very fit.

            This transform is:  f' = tmult * f + tconst.

            The coefficients are chosen so that the transformed maximum fitness is
            favor_best times the transformed average, while the average after
            transform is equal to that before.  A typical value for favor_best is 2-3.

            One problem is that late in the run, when the average is close to the
            max, very small fitnesses may map negative.  In this case, map the
            smallest to zero and do the best we can for the max.

            Note that a common alternative is to use the mapping just described,
            and truncate transformed fitnesses at zero.  However, the method
            shown here is usually superior, as it preserves genetic diversity.
  */

            ftemp = maxfitness - avgfitness ;

            if (ftemp > 1.e-20) {  // Insurance: average may equal max!
              tmult = (favor_best - 1.0) * avgfitness / ftemp ;
              tconst = avgfitness * (maxfitness - favor_best * avgfitness) / ftemp ;
              }

            else {
              tmult = 1.0 ;
              tconst = 0.0 ;
              }

  /*
            The 'ideal' scaling factor was just computed.  Use it to map the mini-
            mum fitness.  If it comes out negative, compute an alternative scaling
            factor which will map the minimum to zero and keep the average un-
            changed.
  */

            if (tmult * minfitness + tconst < 0.0) {  // Do not allow negative fitness
              ftemp = avgfitness - minfitness ;
```

```
            if (ftemp > 1.e-20) {
               tmult = avgfitness / ftemp ;
               tconst = -minfitness * avgfitness / ftemp ;
               }
            else {
               tmult = 1.0 ;
               tconst = 0.0 ;
               }
            }

/*
      The scaling factors have been computed.  Do the scaling now.  The
      truncation at zero is theoretically unnecessary, as we avoided negatives
      when we computed the scaling factor above.  However, floating point
      problems can sometimes still produce a 'negative zero'.  In deference to
      possible user modifications which DEMAND nonnegative fitnesses, it is
      good programming practice to enforce this.
*/

         avgfitness = 0.0 ;

         for (individual=0 ; individual<popsize ; individual++) {
            fit = tmult * fitness[individual] + tconst ;
            if (fit < 0.0)
               fit = 0.0 ;
            fitness[individual] = fit ;
            avgfitness += fit ;
            }

         avgfitness /= (double) popsize ;

/*
      The final step is to normalize the fitnesses by dividing each by the
      average fitness.  The effect is that then each fitness can be interpreted
      as the expected number of times it would be chosen from the popula-
      tion pool if its probability of selection were proportional to its fitness.
*/

         for (individual=0 ; individual<popsize ; individual++)
            fitness[individual] /= avgfitness ;
      }
```

Parent Selection

We have evaluated the fitness of each individual, expressing that
fitness as an expected number of times it will be selected as a parent.
Now we must actually choose the parents. One simple method is the
roulette wheel approach. Assign each individual a slot whose
probability is proportional to the fitness of that individual, and spin
the wheel each time a parent is needed. This method was used in
many of the first genetic algorithms. It rapidly became apparent that
chance played too much of a role in this method. One unlucky genera-

tion, in which an important, highly fit individual failed to be selected, could wipe out generations of progress.

The method used here is more reliable in that it guarantees that the most fit individuals will be selected, and that the actual number of times each is selected will be within one of its expected frequency. It uses a work array whose length is equal to the population size and which contains the selected parents. This array is generated by first filling it with the parents that *must* be there due to having an expected frequency of at least one. Those whose expected frequency is two-point-something will appear twice in this array, et cetera. When only individuals with fractional expectations remain, the rest of the array will be filled by randomly selecting parents with probability equal to their expectation. Note that the order in which parents appear in this array is not random, and that this is *not* roulette wheel selection. The unconventional algorithm for handling fractional expectation is based on [Goldberg, 1989]. Code for computing the array of parent choices, given their expected frequencies, is shown below.

```
void fitness_to_choices (
   int popsize ,                 // Length of fitness, choices vectors
   double *fitness ,             // Input array of expected select freqs
   int *choices                  // Output array of parents
   )

{
   int individual, expected, k ;
   double rn ;


/*
   We build the choices array in two steps.  This, the first step, assigns
   parents according to the integer part of their expected frequencies.
*/

   k = 0 ;                       // Will index choices array

   for (individual=0 ; individual<popsize ; individual++) {
      expected = (int) fitness[individual] ;   // Assign this many now
      fitness[individual] -= expected ;        // Save fractional remainder
      while (expected--)                       // Forcibly use int expected
         choices[k++] = individual ;           // quantity of this individual
      }
```

```
/*
    The second step is to take care of the remaining fractional expected
    frequencies.  Pass through the population, randomly selecting members
    with probability equal to their remaining fractional expectation. It is
    tempting to think that the algorithm below could loop excessively due to
    a very small fitness.  But recall that the sum of the fitnesses will be AT
    LEAST as large as the number remaining to be selected, and generally
    much more.  Thus, the ones with very small fitness (likely to cause
    trouble) will never become the only remaining possibilities.
*/

    while (k < popsize) {                          // Select until choices is full
        rn = (double) rand () / ((double) RANDMAX + 1.0) ; // 0-1 random
        individual = rn * popsize ;                // Randomly select individual

        if (fitness[individual] > 0.0) {           // Try members having expect
            rn = (double) rand () / ((double) RANDMAX + 1.0) ; // 0-1 random
            if (fitness[individual] >= rn) {       // Selects with this probability
                choices[k++] = individual ;        // Bingo!  Select individual
                fitness[individual] -= 1.0 ;       // and make inelig in future
                }
            }
        }
    }
```

After the array of parent choices has been built, we need to
select parents randomly from it. We cannot simply fetch them in
order, as the highest fitness members of the array were placed in it in
order. Only the fractional expectation members are random. Also, we
need to select parents *without replacement* if we are to maintain the
desirable property of actual frequencies being close to expected
frequencies. Code for implementing this is shown below.

```
void pick_parents (
    int *nchoices ,             // Number of choices returned dec'd by 2
    int *choices ,              // Nchoices array of parent candidates
    int *parent1 ,              // One parent returned here
    int *parent2                // and the other here
    )

{
    int k ;
    double rn ;

    rn = (double) rand () / ((double) RANDMAX + 1.0) ; // Random 0-1
    k = rn * *nchoices ;                    // Select pos in choices array
    *parent1 = choices[k] ;                 // Then return that parent
    choices[k] = choices[--*nchoices] ;     // without replacement
```

```
rn = (double) rand () / ((double) RANDMAX + 1.0) ; // Ditto parent 2
k = rn * *nchoices ;
*parent2 = choices[k] ;
choices[k] = choices[--*nchoices] ;
}
```

Reproduction

The program presented here uses the trivial genetic coding in which each parameter is represented by exactly one gene. This makes the reproduction operation very easy. Full binary reproduction is covered in the *Advanced Topics* section of this chapter. The principle here is exactly the same as in binary encoding, but we avoid the complexities of breaking a parameter in the midst of its binary code. The algorithm shown here has the educational advantage of simple clarity and should usually perform nearly as well as binary coding if large populations are used.

Recall that two parents will be called upon to generate two children. When the first child is needed, a crossover point along the chromosome is randomly selected. Both parents will be split at this point. Half of the genes on one side of this point in one parent will be given to the child. The other half of the child's genes will come from the other side of the crossover point in the other parent. Note that if we reach the end of the chromosome, we loop around to the beginning. When the second child is generated, the same process is used except that the crossover point is not random; the same point that was used for the first child is chosen. Also, the half of each parent which was not used for the first child is the half that is used for the second child. This method guarantees that there is no loss of genetic material. Randomly selecting a new crossover point for each child could result in valuable genes in a parent being lost forever. Code for reproduction is shown below:

```
void reproduce (
    double *p1 ,              // Pointer to one parent
    double *p2 ,              // and the other
    int first_child ,        // Is this the first of their 2 children?
    int nvars ,              // Number of vars in objective function
    double *child ,          // Output of a child
    int *crosspt             // If first_child, output xover pt, else input
    )

{
    int i, n1, n2 ;
    double rn, *pa, *pb ;
```

```
if (first_child) {
    rn = (double) rand () / ((double) RANDMAX + 1.0) ; // Random 0-1
    *crosspt = rn * nvars ;  // Randomly select crossover point
    pa = p1 ;
    pb = p2 ;
    }

else {                              // Second child, so reverse role of parents
    pa = p2 ;
    pb = p1 ;
    }

n1 = nvars / 2 ;                    // This many genes in first half of child
n2 = nvars - n1 ;                   // and this many in second half
i = *crosspt ;

while (n1--) {
    i = (i+1) % nvars ;
    child[i] = pa[i] ;
    }

while (n2--) {
    i = (i+1) % nvars ;
    child[i] = pb[i] ;
    }
}
```

Mutation

The first thing that must be said here is that *mutation is dangerous*. This cannot be overemphasized. In life, mutation causes birth defects and cancer. In functional optimization, correctly implemented mutation almost always takes a perfectly good chromosome and ravages it so much that it dies in the next generation. Yet mutation plays a vital role in genetic optimization. It introduces new genetic material into a heterogeneous population. In life, the same process that often creates fatally flawed organisms can also occasionally produce an organism that is uniquely suited to its environment and that goes on to procreate a whole new line of superior organisms.

Mutation should always be used in extreme moderation. At the same time, it should be profound in its effect when it happens. There is a common misconception about the role of mutation in genetic optimization. Some practitioners use small mutations with relatively high probability, believing its purpose to be to "touch up" parameter values. This is closer to simulated annealing and rarely has any place in true genetic optimization. The real purpose of mutation is the introduction of new genetic material, or the recreation of good genes that were lost by chance through poor selection of mates. In order to do this effectively, the effect of a mutation must be profound. At the same time, the valuable gene pool must be protected from wanton destruction. Thus, the probability of mutation should be tiny. A subroutine for mutation is shown below:

```
void mutate (
    double *child ,              // Input/Output of the child
    int nvars ,                  // Number of vars in objective function
    double stddev ,              // Standard deviation of mutation
    double pmutate               // Probability of mutation
    )

{
    double rn ;

    while (nvars--) {
        rn = (double) rand () / ((double) RANDMAX + 1.0) ;// Random 0-1
        if (rn < pmutate) {            // Mutate this gene?
            rn = (double) rand() + (double) rand() -
                (double) rand() - (double) rand() ;
            child[nvars] +=
                rn * stddev * 3.464101615 / (2. * (double) RANDMAX ) ;
        }
    }
}
```

A Genetic Minimization Subroutine

The various subroutines for implementing the major components of genetic optimization have been presented. Now it is time to use them to produce a subroutine capable of minimizing an arbitrary function. This routine uses the coarsest possible genetic coding; each parameter is represented by one gene. Relatively few changes would be needed to implement finer coding. In fact, one of the demonstration functions shown later does this in a crude way. The interested reader could be guided by the genetic weight initialization code in the neural network program in the Appendix. However, this coarse coding method should perform nearly as well for most functions, especially if large populations are used. The subroutine is as follows:

```
double genetic (
    double (*func)( int n , double *x ) , // Function to be minimized
    int ngens ,                  // Number of complete generations
    int popsize ,                // Number of individuals in population
    int climb ,                  // Do we hill climb via elitism?
    double stddev ,              // Standard deviation for initial population
    double pcross ,              // Probability of crossover (.6-.9 typical)
    double pmutate ,             // Probability of mutation (.0001 to .001)
    double favor_best ,          // Factor for favoring best over avg (2-3)
    double fitfac ,              // Factor for fval to raw fitness (-20)
    double fquit ,               // Quit if function reduced to this amount
```

```
        int nvars ,                    // Number of variables in x
        double *x ,                    // Set to start when called; returns best
        double *best,                  // Work vector nvars long
        int *choices ,                 // Work vector popsize long
        double *fvals ,                // Work vector popsize long
        double *fitness ,              // Work vector popsize long
        double *pool1,                 // Work vector nvars * popsize long
        double *pool2 )                // Work vector nvars * popsize long

{
    int i, istart, individual, best_individual, generation, n_cross ;
    int first_child, parent1, parent2, improved, crosspt, nchoices ;
    double fval, bestfval, *oldpop, *newpop, *popptr, *temppop ;
    double avg ;

/*
    Generate initial population pool.

    We preserve the best point across all generations, as this is what we
    will ultimately return to the user.  Its objective function value is bestfval.
*/

    bestfval = 1.e30 ;             // For saving best (across all individuals)
    best_individual = 0 ;          // Safety only

    for (individual=0 ; individual<popsize ; individual++) {

        popptr = pool1 + individual * nvars ;   // Build population in pool1
        shake( nvars, x, popptr, stddev) ;      // Random perturb about init x
        fval = (*func) ( nvars , popptr ) ;     // Evaluate function there
        fvals[individual] = fval ;              // Keep function value of each

        if (fval < bestfval) {                  // Keep track of best
            bestfval = fval ;                   // as it will be returned to user
            best_individual = individual ;      // This is its index in pool1
            }

        if (fval <= fquit)
            break ;
        }

/*
    The initial population has been built in pool1.
    Copy its best member to 'best' in case it never gets beat (unlikely
    but possible!)
*/

    popptr = pool1 + best_individual * nvars ;      // Point to best
    memcpy ( best , popptr , nvars * sizeof(double) ) ; // and save it
```

```
/*
    This is the main generation loop.  There are two areas for population
    pool storage: pool1 and pool2.  At any given time, oldpop will be set to
    one of them, and newpop to the other.  This avoids a lot of copying.
*/

    oldpop = pool1 ;              // This is the initial population
    newpop = pool2 ;              // The next generation is created here

    for (generation=0 ; generation<ngens ; generation++) {

        if (fval <= fquit)        // We may have satisfied this in initial pop
            break ;               // So we test at start of generation loop

        fval_to_fitness ( popsize , favor_best , fitfac , fvals , fitness ) ;
        fitness_to_choices ( popsize , fitness , choices ) ;

        nchoices = popsize ;      // Will count down as choices emptied
        n_cross = pcross * popsize ;// Number crossing over
        first_child = 1 ;         // Generating first of parent's 2 children?
        improved = 0 ;            // Flags if we beat best

        if (climb) {              // If we are to hill climb
            memcpy( newpop, best, nvars * sizeof(double)) ; // start with best
            fvals[0] = bestfval ;  // Record its error
            istart = 1 ;          // and start children past it
            }
        else
            istart = 0 ;

/*
   Generate the children
*/

        for (individual=istart ; individual<popsize ; individual++) {

            popptr = newpop + individual * nvars ; // Will put this child here

            if (first_child)  // If this is the first of 2 children, pick parents
                pick_parents ( &nchoices , choices , &parent1 , &parent2 ) ;

            if (n_cross-- > 0)    // Do crossovers first
                reproduce( oldpop+parent1*nvars , oldpop+parent2*nvars ,
                        first_child , nvars , popptr , &crosspt ) ;

            else if (first_child) // No more crossovers, so just copy parent
                memcpy( popptr , oldpop + parent1 * nvars ,
                    nvars * sizeof(double));

            else
                memcpy( popptr , oldpop + parent2 * nvars ,
                    nvars * sizeof(double));
```

```
         if (pmutate > 0.0)
            mutate ( popptr , nvars , stddev , pmutate ) ;

         fval = (*func) ( nvars , popptr ) ;        // Evaluate func for this child
         fvals[individual] = fval ;                 // and keep value of each

         if (fval < bestfval) {                     // Keep track of best
            bestfval = fval ;                       // It will be returned to user
            best_individual = individual ;          // This is its index in newpop
            improved = 1 ;                          // Flag so we copy it later
            }

         if (fval <= fquit)
            break ;

         first_child = ! first_child ;
         } // For all individuals in population
/*
      We finished generating all children.  If we improved (one of these
      children beat the best so far) then copy that child to the best. Swap
      oldpop and newpop for the next generation.
*/

      if (improved) {
         popptr = newpop + best_individual * nvars ;      // Point to best
         memcpy ( best , popptr , nvars * sizeof(double) ) ; // and save it
         }

      temppop = oldpop ;   // Switch old and new pops for next gen
      oldpop = newpop ;
      newpop = temppop ;
      }
/*
   We are all done.  Copy the best to x, as that is how we return it.
*/

   memcpy ( x , best , nvars * sizeof(double) ) ;  // Return best
   return bestfval ;
}

/*
--------------------------------------------------------------------

   SHAKE - Randomly perturb the point

--------------------------------------------------------------------
*/

static void shake ( int nvars , double *center , double *x , double temp )
{
   double r ;
```

```
// Recall that the variance of a uniform deviate on 0-1 is 1/12.
// Adding four such random variables multiplies the variance by 4,
// while dividing by 2 divides the variance by 4.

// SQRT(12)=3.464...
  temp *= 3.464101615 / (2.*(double)RANDMAX) ;

  while (nvars--) {
    r = (double) rand() + (double) rand() -
       (double) rand() - (double) rand() ;
    *x++ = *center++ + temp * r ;
    }
}
```

Most of the variables in the subroutine's parameter list are self-explanatory. The few that merit special discussion are examined here.

The **climb** parameter would almost always be set to zero, which facilitates a wide search for the global minimum. It would be set to a nonzero value if the user believes that the global minimum is quite well defined, and wishes to speed its location at the price of a less thorough search. The name "climb" comes from the fact that we never regress. After each generation, we preserve the best individual, an elitist strategy, starting the next generation with that individual. Therefore, we are guaranteed a source of good genetic material for each generation. On the surface this seems like a good idea. Without this elitism, we can lose very fit individuals due to poor mate selection, and performance can actually decrease from one generation to the next. However, this elitism effects a strong pull toward that individual. That single individual produces an abundance of progeny, to the exclusion of potentially superior genetic building blocks that have simply not yet found the right partners. In the presence of multiple false minima, the effects can be devastating. Use this option with great care.

As in simulated annealing, the **stddev** parameter should be set as small as possible, yet large enough that the initial population can easily contain individuals whose parameter values are near the global minimum. Something on the order of twice the maximum expected distance between the starting estimate and the global minimum is reasonable.

The **pcross** parameter is the probability of crossover (reproduction by splitting parents and recombining as already discussed). The trivial reproduction method of simply copying the parents is also sometimes effective in small doses. This leaves open the possibility that highly fit individuals can be preserved unchanged, without the danger of mating with an inappropriate mate, while still avoiding the hazards of elitism. Experience indicates that a crossover probability around 0.8 or so is generally good.

The first step in the genetic subroutine is to build the initial population. We keep track of the best individual at all times, both now and later. We may need this individual if the climb parameter is non-zero. More importantly, it is this individual, not necessarily the best in the current generation, which will be returned to the user when operation is complete. While the initial population is being built, we only need to note the index of the best, rather than its actual parameter values. After the population is complete, the best member (pointed to by this index) will be preserved in the best work area.

Two population work areas are maintained. At any given time, one will hold the old, parent generation, while the new children will be placed in the other. The pointers oldpop and newpop will initially be set to pool1 and pool2, then swapped after each generation.

For each generation, the first operation is to convert the objective function values, computed while oldpop was being created, into fitnesses. The array of function values fvals is then no longer needed and can be used to store the function values for the new generation as it is produced. Once the fitnesses are computed, the array of parent choices can be found. We then initialize the number of remaining parent choices to the population size, compute the number of children that will be generated by crossover reproduction, and set a flag to indicate that we are about to produce the first of two children and a flag saying that we have not yet seen any improvement in this generation. Now we are ready to make children.

If the user wishes to hill-climb, the first child in the new generation is simply the best from the old generation. We copy it into the new population, copy its objective function value also, and set istart so that children are placed starting at the next position in the new population.

As we generate children, we check to see if this is the first of two. If so, pick its parents. The second child will use the same parents as the first. Then we reproduce using those two parents. Take care of crossover reproduction first. This nonrandomness is fine, since the parents were selected randomly. After the required number of children have been generated via crossover reproduction, we simply copy the parents to complete the generation.

After a child has been created, we apply the mutation operator, then evaluate the objective function for that child. If it beats the best so far, update the best and set the improved flag so that it will be copied later. Finally, after generating each child, we flip the first_child flag so that we alternate between first and second children.

After all children in this new generation have been created, we check the improved flag. If set, we copy the new best individual. Last of all, we swap newpop and oldpop in preparation for the next generation.

Some Functions for Genetic Optimization

This section will present three similar functions for the genetic optimization routine to minimize. Although they differ in only small ways, their behavior under genetic optimization is significantly different. These differences are especially great if the crossover probability is high and the population size is moderate (500–1000). It behooves the interested reader to study these functions carefully and understand what is responsible for their varying behavior.

In the section on designing the chromosome's structure, it was pointed out that genes which interact should be placed physically close to each other. The following function does this.

```
double func ( int nvars , double vars[] )
{
    double a, b, c, d, dist, mult, f ;

    a = vars[0] - 1.0 ;
    b = vars[1] - 2.0 ;
    c = vars[2] - 2.0 ;
    d = vars[3] - 1.0 ;

    dist = (a-b) * (a-b)  +  (c-d) * (c-d) ;

    mult = exp ( -dist / 8. ) ;
    f = cos ( 4. * sqrt(dist) ) ;

    return 1. - mult * f ;
}
```

The function above is quite similar to the one used to demonstrate simulated annealing. In the two-dimensional subspace of (a - b) and (c - d) it has a single small global minimum which is totally surrounded by multiple local minima. This obviously makes it very difficult to minimize. Here, we throw in the complication that there is no unique global minimum. The function depends only on *differences* in its parameters. Any parameters such that vars[1] - vars[0] = 1 and vars[2] - vars[3] = 1 will produce a global minimum of zero. Thus we see that rather than needing particular parameter values, what we need is *cooperation* between parameters. The first two need to be related, as do the second two. This function can be minimized quite well by the algorithm just given.

Now make a seemingly trivial change in the objective function. Replace the first four lines of code with the following:

```
    a = vars[0] - 1.0 ;
    b = vars[2] - 2.0 ;
    c = vars[1] - 2.0 ;
    d = vars[3] - 1.0 ;
```

The only difference is that we inverted the order of the second and third genes. Such a change would make no difference in simulated annealing or in virtually any other minimization algorithm. Yet genetic minimization applied to this function performs noticeably worse than on the first function. Why? Consider the operation of crossover reproduction on a very fit parent. A fit parent will have either a good first pair of genes or a good second pair of genes, or both. In the first function shown, crossover would have only a 50-50 chance of breaking up this good pair. Half of the time this superior genetic material (a pair of genes whose allele values differ by one) would be passed on to a child. But in the second function, crossover will *always* destroy good genetic material. Our beautiful genetic algorithm will be reduced to little more than a random walk in search of a chance good individual.

This may seem like an extreme example, and certainly it was contrived to illustrate this point. Nevertheless, it is an important point. If the user has any prior knowledge about interactions among genes, it is important that these interacting genes be placed near each other in the chromosome.

The last function shown here is deceptive in that it is a crude improvisation constructed to demonstrate finer genetic coding without actually altering the genetic minimization subroutine already presented. It triples the number of parameters, using three "sub-parameters" to represent three significant digits of each actual parameter. Of course, any serious user would revise the genetic minimization routine to use integer or even character variables to hold these digits, rather than wasting time and space using a double variable to hold one digit. Otherwise, the program would be identical. The function is modified by replacing the same four lines by the code shown below:

```
a1 = (int) vars[0] ;
a2 = 0.1  * (((int) (100. * fabs(vars[1]))) % 10) ;
a3 = 0.01 * (((int) (100. * fabs(vars[2])) % 10)) ;
a = a1 + a2 + a3 - 1.0 ;

b1 = (int) vars[3] ;
b2 = 0.1  * (((int) (100. * fabs(vars[4])) % 10)) ;
b3 = 0.01 * (((int) (100. * fabs(vars[5])) % 10)) ;
b = b1 + b2 + b3 - 2.0 ;

c1 = (int) vars[6] ;
c2 = 0.1  * (((int) (100. * fabs(vars[7])) % 10)) ;
c3 = 0.01 * (((int) (100. * fabs(vars[8])) % 10)) ;
c = c1 + c2 + c3 - 2.0 ;
```

```
d1 = (int) vars[9] ;
d2 = 0.1  * (((int) (100. * fabs(vars[10])) % 10)) ;
d3 = 0.01 * (((int) (100. * fabs(vars[11])) % 10)) ;
d = d1 + d2 + d3 - 1.0 ;
```

This function uses the first variable for the one's digit and sign of the first parameter. The second variable is the tenth's digit, and the third is the hundredth's. The next three variables determine the second parameter, et cetera. Especially for small-to-moderate populations, it will be seen that this function is minimized more easily than the first function.

In case the reader uses this crude technique to minimize another function, note that the factor of 100 was chosen to bring out a lower, more random digit in the floating point representation. This factor may need to be changed if the scaling of the variables is significantly different.

Advanced Topics in Genetic Optimization

This section discusses several topics that are too advanced to be comfortably presented in the preceding tutorial program, but are nonetheless important. These techniques are all used in the neural program listed in the Appendix. The code shown in this section is excerpted from that program.

Gray Codes

In the dawn of automatic computation, data input was largely mechanical. Switches opened and closed, transmitting streams of numbers. The traditional binary representation of numbers sometimes caused problems when small changes in numerical values required large changes in switch status. For example, the number 127 in 8 bit binary is 01111111, while 128 is 10000000. A unit change in the number required all eight bits to change. To alleviate this problem, a new coding system, called *Gray code* after its inventor, was devised. In this system, a unit change in the number causes exactly one bit to change. A short table of Gray codes is as follows:

Decimal	Binary	Gray
0	0000	0000
1	0001	0001
2	0010	0011
3	0011	0010
4	0100	0110
5	0101	0111
6	0110	0101
7	0111	0100
8	1000	1100

Many years later, Gray coding has been found useful in genetic representation of numerical parameters. See [Caruana and Schaffer, 1988] for empirical studies. One group of researchers (Lucasius et al. in [Davis, 1991]) even claims that Gray coding of certain numerical parameters is "indispensable" in some cases. For this reason, eight-bit Gray codes are used to represent weights in the genetic initialization phase of the neural network program. The conversion from genotype (eight-bit Gray code) to phenotype (double precision floating point number) is accomplished by looking up the gray code in a translation table to find its binary equivalent, then scaling the binary number (subtract 127.5 and multiply by 0.0392). Code for building a conversion table is shown next:

```
for (n=0 ; n<256 ; n++) {    // N is a one byte Gray code here
   gray = (unsigned char) n ; // though this algorithm is valid
   sum =  0 ;                 // for any number of bits
   bit = 128 ;                // Value of highest bit
   parity = 0 ;               // Even or odd number of 1's from left
   while (bit) {              // Work our way left to right
      if (bit & gray)         // Keep track of even/odd count of 1's
         parity = ! parity ;  // True means odd number
      if (parity)             // As long as odd number of 1's
         sum |= bit ;         // add in this bit value
      bit = bit >> 1 ;        // We do bits left to right
   }                          // End of conversion loop
   gray_code_table[n] = sum ; // Sum is binary equiv of Gray code n
}
```

For the relatively crude operation of weight initialization, one-byte representation is certainly sufficient. Other problems may require several bytes. The above algorithm is correct for any number of bits.

Overinitialization

If the initial population is randomly generated, as is usually the case, it will almost certainly contain many individuals who are dismal failures. The genetic material of individuals whose fitness is extremely low is almost guaranteed to be worthless to future generations. The fitness-driven parent-selection procedure makes it less likely that these individuals will be mated. However, it can still happen by random chance. Furthermore, eliminating many low fitness individuals from the first generation has the undesirable effect of limiting the gene pool from which all future generations will be built. These problems can be alleviated by randomly generating more than the required population size, then discarding the worst. For example, suppose that our population size is to be 100. We could generate 150 individuals, and keep the best 100. In this way we would start with a higher quality gene pool, but still have the diversity that is so crucial to genetic methods. The extra computation time required is a fraction of the total time after several generations, while the gain in both quality and diversity is significant.

This technique should not abused, though. It is usually a waste of computer time to generate an immoderate number of extra individuals. Fifty to 100 percent more is generally optimal. The time required to exceed this would be better spent on another generation or larger population size.

Two-Point Crossover

The tutorial program presented earlier in this chapter uses the traditional reproduction method of *one-point crossover*. A single point is randomly selected in the chromosome, and the genes on one side of it are donated to one child, while the half on the other side goes to the other child. This method has the important property that genes that are close to each other on the chromosome are likely to be passed together to children. In genetic parlance, important *schemata* are likely to be preserved. One of the demonstration functions shown in a previous section showed how important this can be. A crucial question arises, though. What if a schema important to successful optimization consists of several sets of genes that are widely separated? Of course, if a schema is haphazardly scattered across the chromosome, its preservation is difficult to impossible. But more orderly separation is common in neural networks and many other practical optimization problems. For example, suppose we have a network whose single hidden layer has four neurons. If we take the conventional approach of concatenating the weight vectors into a chromosome, then the weights that connect each of the four hidden neurons to the first input neuron will be at the beginnings of the first, second, third, and fourth quarters of the chromosome, respectively. Traditional one-point crossover will result in the weights for the first and third hidden neurons *always* splitting up into different children. (To see this, draw a picture of the chromosome). The same holds true for the second and fourth. Yet it is quite likely that there could be important interaction between these weights.

To remedy this situation, let us consider another type of crossover reproduction. Two-point crossover splits the chromosome into four quarters. The first and third quarters go to one child, while the second and fourth go to the other child. Pictorially, this happens as shown below:

PARENT A: A_1 A_2 A_3 A_4 A_5 A_6 A_7 A_8 A_9 A_{10} A_{11} A_{12} A_{13} A_{14} A_{15} A_{16}

PARENT B: B_1 B_2 B_3 B_4 B_5 B_6 B_7 B_8 B_9 B_{10} B_{11} B_{12} B_{13} B_{14} B_{15} B_{16}

CHILD 1: A_1 A_2 A_3 A_4 B_5 B_6 B_7 B_8 A_9 A_{10} A_{11} A_{12} B_{13} B_{14} B_{15} B_{16}

CHILD 2: B_1 B_2 B_3 B_4 A_5 A_6 A_7 A_8 B_9 B_{10} B_{11} B_{12} A_{13} A_{14} A_{15} A_{16}

Of course, two-point crossover alone is not the solution. Careful examination of the above mating chart will show that genes that are exactly four apart will always be separated into different children. One problem was solved and another created! The solution is obtained when we allow *either* of the two methods to be used, with the choice being randomly made. If single-point crossover is used two-thirds of the time, and two-point used one-third of the time, we can limit the worst case probability of splitting a schema to two-thirds. Of course, this is not great, but it is better than having some potentially vital schemata invariably excluded from reproduction.

Note that we are concerned here with groups of separated genes remaining together. This is somewhat different from the traditional view of schemata, in which *all* genes in a contiguous string are included in the schema. Especially for neural networks, ours is a more realistic view. Just because a gene at the beginning of the chromosome interacts with one in the middle does not mean that all intervening genes are also involved.

The graph in Figure 8.1 shows the probability that a pair of genes will remain together, as a function of their relative distance along the chromosome. The traditional one-point crossover is the best at preserving close genes, but fails miserably for distant genes. Two-point crossover has an interesting V shape, doing poorly for moderately separated pairs. Combining them produces a reproduction method that does a very respectable job at preserving close pairs, yet still allows a reasonable probability that *any* pair of genes, regardless of their position, can be preserved.

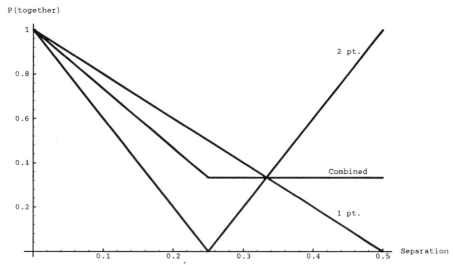

Fig. 8.1: Probability of remaining together vs. separation

A subroutine for performing combined crossover on binary chromosomes is shown next. If this is the first child, randomly generate the gene location and the bit within that gene at which crossover will take place. If the chromosome is large enough, randomly choose one- or two-point crossover. Flag two-point crossover by negating the crossover location. (This is why we use origin 1 rather than 0 for the crossover point.)

```
void reproduce (
    char *p1 ,              // Pointer to one parent
    char *p2 ,              // and the other
    int first_child ,       // Is this the first of their 2 children?
    int chromsize ,         // Number of genes in chromosome
    char *child ,           // Output of a child
    int *crosspt ,          // If first_child, output xover pt, else input
    int *split              // In/out of within byte splitting point
    )

{
    int i, n1, n2, n3, n4 ;
    char left, right, *pa, *pb ;
    double rn ;

    if (first_child) {

        *split = rand() % 8 ;                    // Will split border bytes here
```

```
                    rn = (double) rand () / ((double) RANDMAX + 1.0) ; // Random 0-1
                    *crosspt = 1 + rn * chromsize ;          // Random select crossover pt

                    if ((chromsize >= 16)  &&  (rand() < (RANDMAX/3))) // Two point?
                       *crosspt = -*crosspt ;                 // flag this for second child

                    pa = p1 ;
                    pb = p2 ;
                    } // If first child

                  else {                                      // Second child
                    pa = p2 ;                                 // so parents reverse roles
                    pb = p1 ;
                    }

          /*
             Prepare for reproduction
          */

                  if (*split) {                    // Create left, right splitting masks
                    right = 1 ;
                    i = *split ;
                    while (--i)
                       right = (right << 1) | 1 ;
                    left = 255 ^ right ;
                    }

                  if (*crosspt > 0) {              // Use one point crossover
                    n1 = chromsize / 2 ;           // This many genes in first half of child
                    n2 = chromsize - n1 ;          // and this many in second half
                    n3 = n4 = 0 ;                  // We are using one point crossover
                    i = *crosspt - 1 ;             // We will start building child here
                    }

                  else {                           // Use two point crossover
                    n1 = n2 = n3 = chromsize / 4 ; // This many in first three quarters
                    n4 = chromsize - n1 - n2 - n3 ; // And the last quarter gets the rest
                    i = -*crosspt - 1 ;            // 2 point method was flagged by neg
                    }


          /*
             Do reproduction here
          */
```

```
        if (*split) {
          i = (i+1) % chromsize ;
          child[i] = (left & pa[i]) | (right & pb[i]) ;
          --n1 ;
          }

      while (n1--) {
        i = (i+1) % chromsize ;
        child[i] = pb[i] ;
        }

      if (*split) {
        i = (i+1) % chromsize ;
        child[i] = (left & pb[i]) | (right & pa[i]) ;
        --n2 ;
        }

      while (n2--) {
        i = (i+1) % chromsize ;
        child[i] = pa[i] ;
        }

      if (n4) {                    // Two point crossover?

        if (*split) {
          i = (i+1) % chromsize ;
          child[i] = (left & pa[i]) | (right & pb[i]) ;
          --n3 ;
          }

        while (n3--) {
          i = (i+1) % chromsize ;
          child[i] = pb[i] ;
          }

        if (*split) {
          i = (i+1) % chromsize ;
          child[i] = (left & pb[i]) | (right & pa[i]) ;
          --n4 ;
          }

        while (n4--) {
          i = (i+1) % chromsize ;
          child[i] = pa[i] ;
          }

        } // If two point crossover
  }
```

The reproduction part of the above code is four repetitions of the same pair of operations. First we combine the two partial bytes of the parents into one child byte. Then we simply copy the remaining bytes for this section of the child. That pair of operations is done twice, which completes reproduction if the one-point method is being used. Two-point crossover requires that we do the other two quarters.

9

Regression and
Neural Networks

This chapter reviews the standard statistical technique of multivariate linear regression. A more robust version of regression, using *singular value decomposition* rather than the traditional LU decomposition, is presented. Application of regression to estimating weights in a multilayer feedforward network is discussed.

Overview

Linear regression is the process by which linear combinations of the values of one or more *independent* variables are used to predict the value of a *dependent* variable. For example, a dietician may want to estimate the calorie requirement of a person given his or her height and weight. A suitable equation may take the form:

$$\text{Calories} = a * \text{Height} + b * \text{Weight} + c$$

The constants a, b, and c may be estimated by measuring the height, weight, and calorie intake of a representative collection of people, then applying certain mathematical operations to this data.

Suppose that we sample n representative cases. The independent variables are usually represented as a matrix A having n rows and as many columns as independent variables, plus one extra column that is entirely set to 1. This number of columns will be called m, so there are $m - 1$ independent variables. The measured dependent variable, Y, is arranged as a column vector (n x 1 matrix), and the coefficients to be estimated, ß, are a column vector (m x 1). The basic regression equation can thus be written:

$$A \; \beta = Y \qquad\qquad\qquad 9\text{-}1$$

Linear algebra tells us that this equation has an exact solution ß (perhaps not unique) if and only if Y lies in the subspace spanned by the columns of A. In the uncommon case that $n = m$ (the number of samples equals the number of parameters to be estimated), we may find that A is nonsingular, in which case ß can be found (terribly inefficiently) by inverting A and multiplying that by Y:

$$\beta = A^{-1} \; Y \qquad\qquad\qquad 9\text{-}2$$

In most practical regression problems, the number of samples, n, greatly exceeds the number of parameters, m. In a world filled with random sampling errors, it is highly unlikely that the dependent variable vector Y will lie fully in the subspace spanned by the columns of A when n exceeds m. Therefore, we must be content to find a solution ß that approximately solves the regression equation. Without derivation, we state here that an excellent choice for ß is

$$\beta = (A'A)^{-1} \; A' \; Y \qquad\qquad\qquad 9\text{-}3$$

Derivation of the above formula can be found in nearly any intermediate level statistics text, which will show that the above choice for ß minimizes the mean square error in the predicted values of Y. In other words, if that ß is applied to each training sample to predict the value of the dependent variable, and an error is computed by subtracting the predicted value from the actual value in the sample, then the sum of squares of those errors will be minimized relative to any other possible ß. Note that this is exactly the same criterion used in gradient learning of neural network weights.

Only the poorest programs would compute ß by inverting $A'A$ in the above formula. That involves far more computation than needed. Good programs will use the more economical method of LU decomposition. Still better programs will use the more robust method of QR decomposition. But the very best programs will use the method described in the next section.

Singular-Value Decomposition

There is a problem lurking in linear regression which is so hideous, so mysterious, and so dangerous, that few speak of it. Very few regression programs, professional in every other way, make true provision for it. It is a perilous topic, for it involves taking actions that run counter to intuition, and it sometimes involves seemingly arbitrary decisions. Yet any responsible user of regression techniques will pay close attention to the problem of *near singularity*.

The previous section hinted at this problem when it was stated that "the regression equation has an exact solution ß (perhaps not unique) if and only if Y lies in the subspace spanned by the columns of A." The key words here are "perhaps not unique." Let us consider a small example. Suppose that we have two independent variables, X_1 and X_2 that are used to predict Y. We have four samples as shown:

X_1	X_2	Y
2	1	3
4	2	6
6	3	9
8	4	12

If our regression equation is $aX_1 + bX_2 + c = Y$, we immediately see that (a = 1; b = 1; c = 0) is a solution. But what about (a = 2; b = -1; c = 0)? That works just as well. For that matter, so does (a = 1,000,000,000; b = -1,999,999,997; c = 0).

The problem just described came about because there is an exact linear relationship between X_1 and X_2. Most regression programs will detect this, warn the user, and gracefully refuse to continue. The *serious* problem occurs when the matrix of independent variables is only marginally singular. This would happen in the above example if the values of X_2, rather than being 2, 4, 6, and 8, were instead 2.00001, 3.99997, 5.99996, and 8.00003, or some such values. In this case, most programs will dutifully attempt to compute ß in such a way that the mean square error is minimized down to the last decimal point. The ß produced this way will probably contain values in the six figure range or more! The fit to the *training sample* data will be excellent, but when this crazy ß is used for other data, the results will most likely be wildly inaccurate. What to do?

The solution starts with finding an orthonormal basis, U, for the subspace spanned by the columns of A. In the process, we also find a vector of m weights, usually written as an m x m diagonal matrix W, which measure the importance of each of the m basis vectors in representing the A matrix. Columns of U which contribute greatly to spanning the subspace defined by the columns of A will have a large corresponding weight in the diagonal of W. If the rank of A is less than m, say p, then m - p weights will be zero. Their corresponding columns in U will span the nullspace of A. Finally, we construct an m x m orthonormal matrix V which allows us to reconstruct the A matrix:

$$A = U\ W\ V^T \qquad\qquad 9\text{-}4$$

Irresponsible, trouble-prone regression algorithms use the A matrix directly to estimate ß. Responsible programs compute the above *singular-value decomposition* of A, then use only the most important (largest weight in W) columns of U to compute ß. In particular, when all weights (diagonals of W) are "reasonably" large, meaning that all columns of U are kept, the equation below provides the same ß as the traditional regression formula.

$$\beta = V\ W^{-1}\ U^T\ Y \qquad\qquad 9\text{-}5$$

There is philosophical distress with the above formula when some of the weights are very small. Columns of U which have small (or zero) weights in W are unimportant to spanning A, and hence should be discarded by setting their corresponding diagonal in W^{-1} to zero. But these are precisely the elements of W^{-1} which would be largest, since the reciprocal of a tiny number is huge! How can we in good conscience replace the largest numbers in this formula with zeros? We must remember that it is these discarded columns that are least important and are most likely nothing more than noise. If they were preserved, the computed ß would be inflated into delicately balanced, gigantic values that squeeze the last bit of fit out of the training set, but are worthless in the general population.

It is unfortunate that determination of a "good" cutoff on the minimum weight allowed is fairly arbitrary and problem dependent. Certainly we are always safe in discarding only zeros, as those contribute nothing. That alone is a major improvement over the traditional regression method, as it sacrifices nothing, but gains the important advantage of eliminating all problems of singular matrices. Another generally agreed-upon principle is that the cutoff must be set relative to the *largest* weight, rather than simply being some arbitrary number. Also, the ratio of the cutoff to the largest weight should be large relative to the machine's floating-point precision. Beyond those guidelines, it becomes a choice of how closely do we fit the training set versus how well do we want it to perform for other samples. The author typically uses a ratio of 1.e-6 or so. Elements of the W matrix which are less than that figure times the largest weight in W are changed to zero in the inverse matrix.

In summary, one vital fact must be kept in mind. *In a well-designed regression experiment, the A matrix will be clearly non-singular, and this whole discussion will be irrelevant!* All of the weights will be comfortably nonzero, so no columns of U will be discarded. The whole purpose of singular-value decomposition, with discards of nearly null basis vectors, is to protect against careless experimental design or random subversion of the training set. However, as will be seen in the next section dedicated to regression in neural networks, the user will have little control over the A matrix, so this technique is important to neural networks.

Derivation of the preceding formulas is well presented in [Press et al., 1988]. The mathematics of singular-value decomposition is exceedingly complex and is only briefly discussed in that reference. Detailed treatment can be found in [Forsythe et al., 1977]. A complete subroutine for performing singular-value decomposition is listed on page 470 in the Appendix.

Regression in Neural Networks

Neural networks are explicitly nonlinear. In fact, feedforward networks with linear transfer functions for all neurons are incapable of learning training sets that are not linearly separable. Even though nonlinearity is not strictly needed for output neurons, considerations of robustness dictate that we usually use nonlinear output activation functions. Thus, we cannot use linear regression to directly find optimal network weights. On the other hand, the operation of passing the output activations of one layer to the input of the next layer *is* linear. In particular, the input applied to an output-layer neuron is a linear combination of the activations of the neurons in the previous layer. If we treat that hidden layer's activations as the independent variables, and have a known desired input to an output neuron as the dependent variable, we have a linear regression problem. The weight vector connecting that output neuron to the previous layer is the ß vector computed by linear regression. This weight vector will be optimal in that it minimizes the mean square error of the *input* to the output neuron. Of course what we really want to minimize is the mean square error at the *output*, so this is no panacea. It can be immensely useful, though. Let us see how.

Simulated annealing and genetic optimization are discussed in other chapters as methods for avoiding local minima in the network error function. Naive practitioners would apply those randomization techniques to *all* weights in the network. That is an extremely inefficient approach, though. The essence of neural networks is that they activate hidden neurons based on patterns in the input data. What we are really interested in is the weights that connect the inputs to the hidden layer (and interconnect hidden layers if more than one is used). Once these weights are determined, computation of the weights that lead to the output layer is almost an afterthought. The error of an output neuron, as a function of the weights connecting it to the previous layer, is in general a well-behaved function having only one local minimum, which, of course, is the global minimum. It would be pointless to choose these weights randomly if optimal values can be computed.

We cannot directly compute optimal output weights because of the nonlinear transfer function of the output neurons. Only relatively slow iterative methods, like the conjugate gradient algorithm, can do this. Doing so is not recommended. The time is better spent with more random trials, followed by iterative techniques on all weights simultaneously. What we can do, though, is to use linear regression to approximate the optimal weights. These weights will be vastly superior to what would be attained by random methods, and they certainly provide an excellent starting point for iterative methods applied to all weights later.

What we need to do is to allocate memory sufficient to hold the activations of each hidden neuron in the layer just prior to the output layer, for every member of the training set. We also need memory to hold desired values for each output neuron's input, for every member of the training set. This should be organized as a separate vector for each output neuron. We then pass through the training set. For each member, compute the activation of each neuron in the last hidden layer, storing that in our *A* matrix. This matrix will have as many rows as there are training samples, and as many columns as there are neurons in the last hidden layer, plus one additional column which is always set to 1. This column corresponds to the bias term in neural network parlance and to the constant term in regression parlance. Also, for each training sample, compute the *inverse* transfer function of its desired output for each output neuron. This is the desired input to the output neuron and will be placed in a separate Y vector for each output neuron. Finally, compute the singular-value decomposition of A, and use the method of the preceding section to compute ß for each Y, which will be the weights for that output neuron. Remember that these weights do not necessarily minimize the mean square error of the *outputs*, which is our ultimate goal. However, they do minimize the error on the *input* side of the output neurons, which is a major accomplishment. Fully commented code for implementing this operation can be found on page 468 of the Appendix.

10

Designing Feedforward Network Architectures

Certain problems are more easily solved by particular network architectures. For multiple-layer feedforward networks, the number of hidden neurons can mean the difference between success and failure. While there are no hard formulas known at this time, this chapter briefly discusses some rules of thumb for choosing an appropriate network model and defining specific characteristics of that model.

This chapter discusses the difficult problem of deciding on the structure and training of a feedforward network. It is assumed that the problem to be solved indicates that a multiple-layer feedforward network is the most appropriate model. Given that assumption, we must design the network. While there are no hard and fast rules for defining network parameters, we can generally be safe if we follow three guidelines:

1)   Use one hidden layer.
2)   Use very few hidden neurons.
3)   Train until you can't stand it any more.

Let us now examine these guidelines more closely.

How Many Hidden Layers?

It has already been seen (page 85) that there is no theoretical reason *ever* to use more than two hidden layers. It has also been seen that for the vast majority of practical problems, there is no reason to use more than one hidden layer. Those problems that require two hidden layers are only rarely encountered in real-life situations. But the question arises as to how the *theoretical* requirement relates to the *practical* requirement. Are there problems for which learning benefits by having more than the minimum theoretically required number of hidden layers?

It has been the author's experience that using more than one hidden layer is almost never beneficial. The problem is that training often slows dramatically when more hidden layers are used. This is due to two effects:

1)   The additional layer through which errors must be back-propagated makes the gradient more unstable. The success of any gradient-directed optimization algorithm is dependent on the degree to which the gradient remains unchanged as the parameters (weights in a neural network) vary.

2)   The number of false minima usually increases dramatically. This means that there is a higher probability that after many time-consuming iterations, we will find ourselves stuck in a local minimum and have to escape or start over.

There is, of course, the possibility that a problem exists somewhere such that a network with many hidden layers of just a few neurons each is excellent, while using any fewer hidden layers requires too many neurons in each layer to be practical. It is just that the author has never knowingly encountered any problem that would benefit from having more than two hidden layers, and precious few that would require even two.

In the theory section, page 85, it was pointed out that the only time two hidden layers may be required in practice is when the network must learn a function having discontinuities. A sawtooth function like the one shown in Figure 10.1 is a good example.

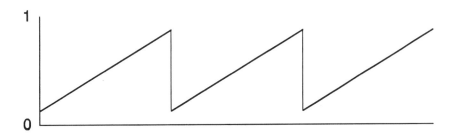

Fig. 10.1: Discontinuities invite two hidden layers

Several different networks were trained using 301 equally spaced points from this function. The results are shown below.

Hidden Neurons	Training Error	Test Error	RMS Error
1	4.313	4.330	0.2081
2	2.714	2.739	0.1655
3	2.136	2.148	0.1465
4	0.471	0.485	0.0697
5	0.328	0.349	0.0590
10	0.319	0.447	0.0668
3,7	0.398	0.414	0.0643
5,5	0.161	0.200	0.0447
7,3	0.113	0.163	0.0403

The first column is the number of hidden neurons, with the quantities in the first and second layers shown for four-layer networks. The *Training Error* column shows 100 times the mean square error of the training set. A test set was constructed using 1,002 points, a value chosen to avoid replication of training-set points, forcing the network to interpolate. The error for this set is shown in the next column. The last column in that table is the square root of the test set's mean square error. As such, it can be considered a sort of average error.

The first thing to notice is that for the three-layer network, there is a magic number of hidden neurons needed. Performance takes a leap when the number of hidden neurons goes from three to four. This is not unusual when dealing with training data having strong features. Smaller networks simply do not have the theoretical capability needed to separate the problem space. More importantly, observe that there appears to be a floor that cannot be breached by adding more neurons. In fact, the test-set error actually starts to increase when a lot of hidden neurons are used.

Using a second hidden layer enables us to break through that floor. It is obvious that the network prefers having the majority of its neurons in the first hidden layer. This is common in four-layer networks.

In summary, it is strongly recommended that one hidden layer be the first choice for any practical feedforward network design. If using a large number of hidden neurons does not satisfactorily solve the problem, then it may be worth trying a second hidden layer and possibly reducing the total number of hidden neurons.

How Many Hidden Neurons?

Choosing an appropriate number of hidden neurons is extremely important. Using too few will starve the network of the resources it needs to solve the problem. Using too many will increase the training time, perhaps so much that it becomes impossible to train it adequately in a reasonable period of time. Also, an excessive number of hidden neurons may cause a problem called *overfitting*. The network will have so much information processing capability that it will learn insignificant aspects of the training set, aspects that are irrelevant to the general population. If the performance of the network is evaluated with the training set, it will be excellent. However, when the network is called upon to work with the general population, it will do poorly. This is because it will consider trivial features unique to training set members, as well as important general features, and become confused. See Figure 1.4 in the first chapter for an example of this. Thus, it is imperative that we use the absolute minimum number of hidden neurons which will perform adequately.

One rough guideline for choosing the number of hidden neurons in many problems is the *geometric pyramid* rule. It states that, for many practical networks, the number of neurons follows a pyramid shape, with the number decreasing from the input toward the output. Of course, this is not true for autoassociative networks, which have the same number of inputs as outputs. But many other networks follow this pattern. This is illustrated in Figure 10.2.

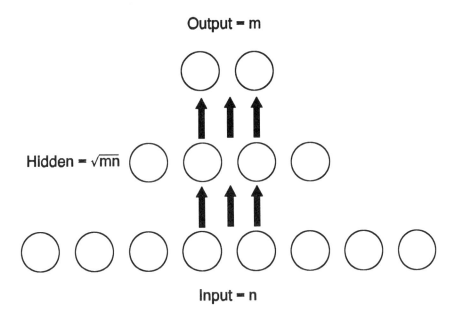

Fig. 10.2: A typical three-layer network

The numbers of neurons in each layer follow a geometric progression. Thus, if we have a three-layer network with n input neurons and m output neurons, the hidden layer would have sqrt(mn) neurons. A similar rule applies to four-layer networks, as seen in Figure 10.3. In this case, computation of the number of hidden-layer neurons is slightly more complex:

$$r = \sqrt[3]{\frac{n}{m}}$$
$$\text{NHID}_1 = m\,r^2$$
$$\text{NHID}_2 = m\,r$$

10-1

The above formulas are only rough approximations to the ideal hidden-layer size. If there are very few inputs and outputs, and the problem is complex, they may underestimate the number required. For example, approximating a complicated function of one variable involves just one input and output neuron, but may require a dozen or more hidden neurons. On the other hand, if it is a simple problem with many inputs and outputs, fewer neurons will often suffice. Do not

Output = m

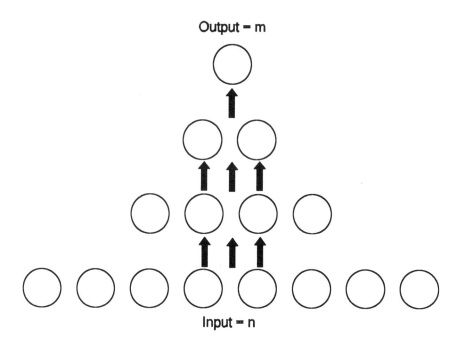

Input = n

Fig. 10.3: A typical four-layer network

treat these formulas as rigorous. It is just that a great number of practical problems solvable with neural networks have many inputs and few outputs. In such cases, the pyramid rules stated above are often applicable.

The best approach to finding the optimal number of hidden neurons is time-consuming, but should always be followed for important tasks. Start with a number of neurons which is definitely too small. If coming up with a good guess for "too small" is impossible, start with two neurons! Choose an appropriate criterion for evaluating the performance of the network. (See page 343 for help in that choice.) Train and test the network, recording its performance. Then slightly increase the number of hidden neurons, and train and test again. Repeat this until the error is acceptably small, or no significant improvement is noted, whichever comes first. It's brute force and it's slow, but it works. If validation sets are easily obtained, we may want to try adding neurons past the point of acceptable results, counting on the validation procedure to warn us of overfitting. Otherwise, we should be content with using the bare minimum number of hidden neurons necessary to achieve acceptable performance. Increasing the number beyond that minimum will often cause deterioration in generalization ability. A more rigorous description of the above procedure is given on page 183. A flowchart is shown in Figure 10.5.

There is a dangerous pitfall to avoid in the above procedure. It is tempting to preserve the learned weights for the next test. In other words, suppose that we have trained a network having five hidden neurons. When we add a sixth, keep the same weights for the first five. Initialize the weights for the new, sixth neuron to small random numbers, and continue training from there. The rationalization is that we already have learned a lot. Don't throw it away. Just use the new neuron to take care of what's not yet learned. *Don't do it* unless you are willing also to try totally random initialization. Although there are some problems for which this will work, there are many situations in which this will rapidly lead to a false minimum. The optimal weights for *n* hidden neurons rarely are even close to being a subset of those for *n* + 1 hidden neurons. If neural networks were linear, this would be an excellent procedure, with each addition taking a bite out of the error subspace left behind by its predecessors. But the profound nonlinearity of these networks prevents this from happening. When a new neuron is added, the upgraded reasoning capability usually means that the network should have an entirely different approach to the solution.

Of course, there is no reason not to at least try keeping the old weights, *as long as in addition to that, other RANDOM starting points are tried.* The problem only arises when the previous weights form the only starting point for additional optimization.

A lot of effort is currently being devoted to the design of *self-pruning* networks. A wide variety of methods has been proposed, but most have in common the simultaneous minimization of output error and minimization of the number of hidden neurons. Many of these methods define an auxiliary criterion based on the number of hidden neurons, or on the size of the weights connecting hidden neurons to other layers, or on hidden-neuron activation distributions. The function that is optimized is a composite of the output error with the hidden-neuron economization criterion. It is the opinion of the author that these methods can be easily abused. They do not directly address the issue of overfitting. Naturally, this issue is indirectly addressed, in that using fewer hidden neurons decreases the likelihood of overfitting. However, that fact may inspire a false sense of security. Also, the choice of how to weigh economy versus training accuracy can be uncomfortably arbitrary. On the other hand, self-pruning algorithms are relatively young. Developments are certainly worth following. In particular, [Fakhr, Kamel, and Elmasry, 1992] propose what seems to be an excellent step in the right direction.

One last point should be made. Most beginners are surprised by their first few problems when they see how few hidden neurons are required. The tendency is invariably to overestimate the requirement. It is not at all unusual to have a problem with hundreds of input neurons and several output neurons which only requires five or so hidden neurons. When in doubt, start low and work up as needed. It is unfortunate that using fewer hidden neurons often increases the likelihood of the learning algorithm becoming trapped in a local minimum. Additional weights can create new channels through which gradient descent is able to pursue a global minimum. In practice, though, the tradeoff is rarely worthwhile. Stick with the minimum number necessary to solve the problem, and emphasize thorough training.

How Long Do I Train This Thing???

There is a dangerous common misconception concerning iterative training. It says that neural networks can be overtrained. It says that there is an optimal amount of training, and that continuing past that point will improve performance on the training set, but degrade performance in the general population. This idea is particularly hazardous because it does have an element of truth in it, for if the network and/or training set has been incorrectly designed, the myth will be reality. Let us briefly examine how the concept of overtraining came into being, why it is usually (if not always) an inappropriate notion, and how we can detect and avoid the common problem which masquerades as overtraining.

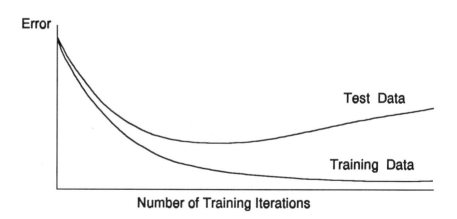

Fig. 10.4: Manifestation of overtraining

Figure 10.4 plots the error of a neural network for two different sets of data as a function of the number of iterations of training done.

One set of data is the training set. As expected, the error for that set monotonically decreases, approaching an asymptote. The other data set, called the validation set, is drawn from the same population as the training set, but is not used for the training. Again, its error decreases at the start of training. But, to our surprise, continuing the training past a certain point causes the validation set's error to *increase*! Since the validation set is presumably representative of the population to which the network will ultimately be applied, this is not good. If we have no alternative, the apparently obvious solution is to stop training when the validation set error bottoms out. However, doing so is often a case of the cure being worse than the disease.

We saw in the previous section that using too many hidden neurons can cause overfitting. Rather than learning only the general patterns needed to produce the correct decision, the network focuses excessively on idiosyncrasies of individual samples. When these prove worthless in its later work, performance suffers. Since it takes considerable time to learn these idiosyncrasies, while the important patterns are more likely to be at least partially learned quickly, the quality of the network often reaches a peak as training progresses, then deteriorates. Thus was born the myth of excessive training. However, there are two reasons why we should never limit training in hopes of finding that elusive peak:

1) It is treating the symptom, not the disease. Reduce the number of hidden neurons to the point that the network does not have the capacity to learn idiosyncrasies, or increase the size and variety of the training set, and the disease is cured.

2) Never forget that we usually start the training with *random* initial weights. When we prematurely stop training, we may have adequately learned what we need to know. Then again, maybe we have not. And we will never know for sure.

The second point deserves deeper examination. When we use a training set to represent an entire population, we are trusting that the trained neural network will be able to interpolate between training samples when it encounters unknown cases that are not identical to training cases. This implies a smooth transition between neighboring training cases. Since we typically start the training process with small random weights, the derivatives of the outputs with respect to the inputs will be small, leading to the desired smoothness. However, just as using higher-degree polynomials in function approximation allows more wiggling due to larger derivatives, using more hidden neurons also allows more wiggling. When all of the hidden layer's resources are not needed just to insure adequate performance, some neurons can learn to specialize. As training continues, their weights can be driven to such extremes that these neurons come into play only for idiosyncratic features of the training set. The derivatives of the outputs with respect to the inputs become large, and smooth interpolation is lost. The philosophy behind halting training early is to prevent weights from taking on extreme values.

Superficially, this seems reasonable. It is an indisputable fact that, in such cases, continuing training *does* degrade performance on the validation set and hence will probably also degrade performance on the entire population. But the flaw in this reasoning stems from the fact that the initial weights were randomly chosen. We do not *know* that we are approaching the optimal weights from a good direction. It may be that we must pass through a region in which the validation set performs poorly, but that it will improve if we continue. And we certainly have no basis for claiming that stopping training when the validation set's error bottoms out leads to any sort of practical optimality. That's cheating! It is in effect using what is supposed to be the final judge of quality as a surrogate training set. We might as well have merged it into the training set. Any degree to which the validation set is not representative of the population will be reflected in our trained network if we base our stopping decision on that set. Our estimated performance will be unduly optimistic.

The worst approach of all is simply stopping training when the training set error begins to flatten out, hoping that all is well in weight space. That act must be reserved for ostriches. *There is no basis for believing that, having started at a random point, stopping before convergence is obtained will leave us near the best point.* And the real tragedy is that we cannot even verify optimal performance. Suppose that we apply the "trained" network to the independent validation set. If the performance is about the same, we *cannot* conclude that training was successful. For all we know, more iterations would have significantly improved performance on both the training and the validation sets. On the other hand, if we then continue training to wait for a bottom in the validation set error, or if we observe inferior performance on the validation set and restart with new random weights, we have committed a grave sin. We have used the validation set to influence training. Now, to be totally honest, we need another independent validation set.

The moral of the story is that we should use as few hidden neurons as possible. Start out with what is known to be too few, then add more as needed to ensure adequate performance on the training set. Never start out with a lot of hidden neurons and then see how many can be taken away while still keeping up the performance.

We must also take great care that the training set adequately represents the population. If it does not, the phenomenon seen in Figure 10.4 will almost always appear, regardless of the number of hidden neurons. Accurately training the network will be a hopeless task.

In summary, correct training is done as follows. For each trial number of hidden neurons, generate random initial weights and train until improvement is negligible. Then generate more random initial weights and train again. And again. And again. When a moderate number of these repetitions in a row fails to improve the performance any more, we can be fairly sure that we have trained the network as best as can be done *for the training set*. Then check it out with an independent validation set. If, after all that training, its performance on the validation set is significantly worse than on the training set, either the training set is defective (too small or not representative of the population), or there are too many hidden neurons. The network was not overtrained.

It must always be remembered that *overfitting is a reflection of the training set not being totally representative of the population*. There cannot be overfitting if the training set consists of the entire population. Naturally, that is a practical impossibility. Nonetheless, thorough training sets make overfitting less problematic.

Also remember that *overfitting results when the training set is small relative to the number of hidden neurons*. We compensate for a paucity of training data by limiting the number of hidden neurons. The training set size and hidden-layer size are inexorably tied together. When they are unbalanced in one direction, the network is unable to learn as well as it should. When unbalanced the other way, the network learns too much and generalizes poorly. There must be a balance. One way of achieving that balance is now discussed.

In the fortuitous event that we can easily collect large quantities of known data, there is an effective training procedure that can be followed. A bonus of this procedure is that we can also use it to select the optimal number of hidden neurons. We still collect an initial training set and an independent validation set that will be used to judge the final network. But we also allow collection of a third type of set, called the *training test set*. This set is used to check the generalization ability of a supposedly trained network. If performance of the network on the training test set is significantly worse than on the training set, we conclude that either overfitting has occurred, or that important information present in the test set was not present in the training set. In either case, the solution is to merge the test set into the training set, and retrain. This is made explicit in the flowchart shown in Figure 10.5.

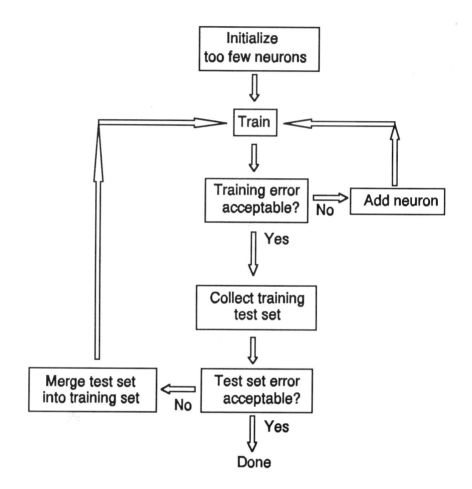

Fig. 10.5: Training when known cases are cheap

Note that the above algorithm depends on the training test set being representative of the population *and* being independent of the training set. If sampling error conspires to provide us with a test set that is extremely similar to the training set, we are in trouble. Therefore, we must take two precautions. First, make sure that the sets are large enough to make such problems unlikely. Second, do not skip final validation. It is tempting to look upon the last training test set as the validation set. While we can often get away with this shortcut, we will sleep better at night if a comprehensive validation is done before delivering the network.

Finally, observe that the above procedure can also be used to help us squeeze as much performance as possible from the network. Suppose that we start out with a fairly good standard of performance, and follow the algorithm until that performance level is obtained. At this time, do not validate the network. Save it and then demand better performance. Obviously, we will immediately add a hidden neuron. A new training test set may then have to be merged into the training set. The algorithm is run until either we get sick of dealing with a huge training set, or our new expectation is met. As long as the fundamental assumption of the quality of the test sets is met, our actions are legal. Our performance goal is limited only by our ability to collect new data and by our computational resources. The number of hidden neurons will increase as needed, and overfitting will be prevented by the test sets.

11

Interpreting Weights:
How Does This Thing Work?

Neural networks are often criticized because their operation is veiled by complexity. This is especially true of multiple-layer feedforward networks. The fact that a particular network *works* may be overshadowed if it is not known *how* it works. This chapter attempts to address some of these issues.

Many researchers mistrust techniques that they do not understand. Often this is senseless, for life is rich in things we do not understand yet blindly accept on faith. However, sometimes understanding is important. If an expert system, neural or otherwise, is guiding a life-support system, we had best understand it at least enough to guarantee its correct operation under all possible conditions.

If classification is being done with ordinary discriminant analysis, we can talk about positions along discriminant axes, and identify those axes. If decisions are made by a rule-based expert system, we can follow the exact line of reasoning which leads from input data to an output conclusion. But if we are using a multiple-layer feedforward network, all we have is a (usually gigantic) collection of weights connecting neurons. The complexity inherent in such a model makes understanding its operation difficult at best. Thus, it should come as no surprise that the contents of this chapter will be as much negative as positive.

When we ask how a feedforward network does its job, we are really asking what it looks at in the data. We assume that some features of the data are irrelevant, while other features are critical to the network's decisions. Thus, the subject of *features* in the data merits more detailed discussion.

First, it must be remembered that the importance of a particular input variable must always be considered in conjunction with other input variables. It is dangerous to assume that each variable stands alone and thus try to come up with individual measures of importance. For example, suppose we train a network to classify people as overweight or normal weight, based on four variables: Height, Hair Color, Eye Color, and Weight. Using some of the techniques described later, we may find that Hair Color and Eye Color are not important to the network's decision. The other two variables need more careful analysis, though. Certainly Height alone tells us nothing about obesity. Even Weight alone tells us little. But taken together, they tell all. So do we call Height an important feature? How do we treat a feature like "Height along with Weight"? This may seem like a trite point, but when our network has dozens of variables, many of which are very esoteric and may exhibit obscure interactions, this becomes a most serious consideration.

The converse of the above point must also be considered. Suppose that in addition to the four variables named, we also measure Arm Length. There is a very high correlation between Arm Length and Height. Now what is our vital feature? Is it "Arm Length along with Weight", or is it "Height along with Weight"? We already saw that Height alone is worthless, but in conjunction with Weight it becomes very important. Does the addition of Arm Length diminish the importance of Height? Once again, with large and complex networks, the possibility (near certainty?) of multiple equivalent features must be considered.

This situation becomes even more complex when we realize that there may be an infinite number of networks that perform practically equivalently, but that look at very different features in the data due to random variations in the initial weight state before training began. Given the above five variables, one training run may produce a network that looks at only Height and Weight. Another training run, with different starting-weight randomization, may produce a network that looks only at Arm Length and Weight. Do we care about this possibility? Are we interested only in the particular network we have in hand, or are we interested in the larger question of what information *might* be used because it is important? These are two totally different questions, and they require different approaches in order to be answered.

A somewhat more practical example may clarify these issues. Suppose that we have a network with 49 inputs arranged as a 7 x 7 grid of pixels. Somebody writes either an X or an O, and this character is projected onto the grid. The task of our neural network is to decide which character has been written. A naive training set might consist of the two examples illustrated in Figure 11.1.

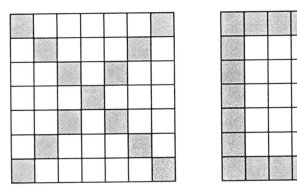

Fig. 11.1: Primitive handwriting recognition

Clearly, the four corner pixels are worthless features for this training sample. The value of any single border pixel or any diagonal pixel (other than the corners) is sufficient to classify the drawing. All other pixels have no contribution to make. A well-designed *statistical* technique would probably look at all of the diagonal and border pixels and base its decision of those values. Unfortunately, it would not be at all unusual for a neural network trained on this data to fixate on one or on a very few important pixels. Whether or not this matters in the design or understanding of the network is a decision that can only be made by the experimenter in the context of the overall problem. It is vital that this be realized, though. Beginning practitioners may be used to traditional statistical techniques, which generally operate in a more sensible and predictable manner.

The root of the O–X feature problem just described is this training set. We need samples of X in which the lines stray from the diagonals. We need O's that are round instead of square. We need some characters with missing parts (pens do skip). A thoroughly diverse training set would improve the robustness of the network by decreasing the chance that it focuses on features that are unique to the training set, improperly ignoring features that may be important in the general population. If effective methods can be employed to determine the features used by a given network, the designer can be more assured of the general applicability of the network.

Features Used by Networks in General

If the question to be answered is the general one of what features are present which *could* be used by a neural network, as opposed to the specific question of what features are being used by a *particular* network, then the only methods known to the author are brute force techniques related to stepwise discriminant analysis. One approach is to try each input alone, retraining the network for each. The single input that performs best alone is kept. This procedure is then repeated by adding a second input, trying each of the remaining possible inputs. Inputs are added until no significant improvement in the trained network is found. This method is obviously computationally intensive. If the network trains slowly, or if there are many inputs, it is impractical. It also shares the disadvantage of stepwise discriminant analysis that some variables may be so worthless alone that they are never chosen; yet if only they could be paired with another, they might be powerful.

If computation time is not a serious limitation, the problem of variables being important only in groups can be addressed by reversing the stepwise procedure. Start with all of the inputs being used. Eliminate one input at a time, retraining the network each time. The input whose elimination causes the least decrease in performance is removed. This procedure is repeated until there is no remaining input whose elimination can be tolerated. This algorithm is even more computationally intensive than the first, since we are starting with all inputs rather than just one. There are few practical problems for which this is a viable solution, although it can be effective when it is used.

The author has had some success with a genetic selection technique. Randomly choose a subset of the inputs, train a network with this subset, and save the results. Repeat this for as many random subsets as time and memory allow. Then use the genetic algorithms previously described (page 135) to select pairs of superior subsets. For each such pair, generate a pair of child subsets by selecting inputs that were present in the parent subsets. As generations pass, useless inputs will tend to be weeded out, while valuable inputs will appear more and more frequently. The behavior of this method, and ways to optimize its performance, are certainly promising areas for research. Graduate students take note.

Features Used by a Particular Network

The question of which features in the training set are used by a particular feedforward network can be excruciatingly difficult to answer. It is easier to discuss tempting methods that *do NOT work* than it is to find methods that do, so that will be done first.

Examination of Weight Vectors

The most obvious candidate is direct examination of the weights connecting the input layer to the hidden layer. One would like to say that inputs having large absolute values are important, while those near zero are not important. Experienced statisticians know that the analogous problem of assessing importance based on regression coefficients is a tricky business at best. And regression is nothing but a neural network with no hidden layer and a linear activation function for the output. When one adds the complication of nonlinearity, plus a hidden layer, statisticians will appreciate the problem. But for nonstatisticians, some discussion is in order.

The presence of a large weight connecting an input to a hidden neuron does not necessarily mean that input is important. Perhaps that hidden neuron has a very low weight connecting it to the output, making its own activation unimportant. Or that input may connect strongly to one or more other hidden neurons, which in turn connect to the output in opposing ways. Different values of that input could then cancel each other by the time the output layer is reached, meaning that the input is for all practical purposes ignored.

Similarly, weights near zero do not necessarily mean that the input is unimportant. Several small weights for that input, each leading to a different hidden neuron, can add up to a significant effect. Also, a small weight may mean that the input affects a hidden neuron only slightly. But that hidden neuron may be connected to an output with a large weight, causing the input to have a significant effect on the output.

Things become even worse if there are highly correlated input variables, a frequent occurrence. Even if neither of a pair of correlated inputs is important to determining the output, they may both have very large weights connecting them to hidden neurons. This is because they are important in a very different sense: they are important in that they must cancel each other out. Perhaps in the learning process, one of the input's weights became trapped with a large absolute value. The other input then is forced to have a large weight so that it can exert a balancing influence.

If this section has led the reader to mistrust weights as a measure of importance, then it has succeeded. Of course, there are cases in which input features clearly map to hidden neurons, and the hidden neurons activate the outputs in meaningful ways. [Eberhart and Dobbins, 1990] present several detailed examples. [Rumelhart and McClelland, 1986] describe numerous carefully contrived experiments to demonstrate meaningful feature mapping. Such cases are the rare exception though, not the rule.

Hinton Diagrams

Now that the reader has been thoroughly warned against scrutinizing weight vectors, we will present a popular method for effectively displaying these vectors, should the need arise. In those rare but delightful cases when an interesting and meaningful mapping is learned, bosses, coworkers, and journal editors will be impressed. This is all the more true if the mapping is novel in that it is not easily noticed by humans. Therefore, it is worthwhile to devise a means of clearly visualizing neuron connection strengths.

Hinton diagrams are named after the neural network pioneer Geoffrey Hinton, who first popularized this method of displaying weights. There are several variations, but they all have in common the attribute that individual squares are used to represent weights. The size of each square is proportional to the strength of the connection weight. Black and white displays typically use filled squares for negative weights, and unfilled squares for positive weights. Color displays may use red and blue, or some other scheme.

The variation in Hinton diagram appearance comes from the placement of the squares. The following two examples are based on the sample XOR network shown in Figure 6.8 on page 83. That network should be examined in conjunction with the next two figures.

The most straightforward format involves displaying the entire network as one group. Sources for connections are placed horizontally along the bottom of the chart. Destinations are arranged vertically, labeled along the left side of the chart. Every connection from a particular source to a particular destination is represented by a square at the intersection of the source column with the destination row. This can be seen in Figure 11.2.

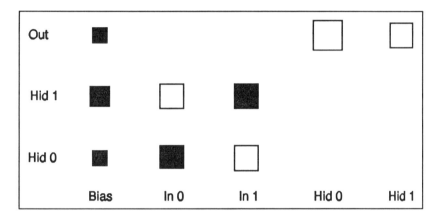

Fig. 11.2: **Full network displayed as a Hinton diagram**

That format can be difficult to interpret, though. It is often more effective to display neurons individually. In this way, an optimal layout of the weights can be arranged, and observers can more easily focus their attention. Conscientious creators of such a display will always include a key along with the display, rather than simply explaining the layout in accompanying text. See Figure 11.3 for an example of single-neuron grouping.

The secret to effective use of a Hinton diagram lies in the arrangement of the squares. If the network's input is an optical grid, it would not do to string out the inputs in a single line. They should be arranged in an identically dimensioned grid so that input patterns are clearly visible. Also, keep in mind that use of squares is traditional, but not mandatory. If the inputs are contiguous points in a time series, it may make sense to represent input weights for a hidden neuron as a time series also! Imagination is clearly called for.

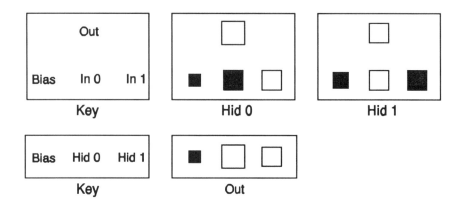

Fig. 11.3: Individual neuron grouping in a Hinton diagram

Clustering

The patterns detected by hidden neurons can sometimes be discovered by clustering the training set based on activation levels of all hidden neurons. Simultaneous use of all hidden-neuron activations is usually preferable to examination of individual neurons, as is done with Hinton diagrams, because it takes into account interactions that cannot be seen on an individual basis.

    The process is as follows. First, present each training input to the network and compute the activation level of each hidden neuron. This gives us a new data set. Each case is a vector having as many components as there are hidden neurons. Now cluster this data set using any of the wide variety of techniques described in standard data analysis texts. Hierarchical clustering is the best if it is compu-tationally feasible. Compute the mean, or some other measure of central location, of the *original* input variables for each cluster (not the hidden-neuron activations on which the clusters are based). Our hope is that these centroids will be meaningful in some sense. If we can pin a name on each cluster by examining the typical values of each of its variables, we have come a long way toward understanding what the network sees.

    If we are willing to narrow our focus down to individual neurons, we can take the above process one step further. Select a hidden neuron for study. Present each of the discovered centroids to that neuron's inputs, and note its achieved activation level. By seeing which input patterns activate it highly, and which do not, we define a feature to which this neuron is sensitive. If we are lucky, the feature may have profound philosophical significance. Note, by the way, that this method of assigning features to hidden neurons is similar but not quite identical to direct examination of its input weight vector. Obviously, its weight vector will define the quintessential input for activating that neuron, at least in terms of vector direction. However, there are two subtle distinctions regarding use of cluster centroids. First, we are limiting ourselves to these training set centroids. It is quite possible that none of these centroids will be exceptionally collinear with the weight vector. This may make it easier to assign a name to the feature. Second, we may have already assigned names to each cluster. In this case, our new naming task can be based solely on existing names if that clarifies things. These two advantages may enable us to give a name to something that does not exist in terms of the exact weights.

Sensitivity Analysis

One simple but relatively effective method for assessing the importance of inputs is sensitivity analysis. The network error for the entire training set is evaluated with one of the inputs clamped to a fixed value for all training samples. The importance of that input can be gauged by the effect on the output error. If the error remains about the same as it was with that input free, we can conclude that the input is not important *as far as THAT particular measure of error is concerned*. Note that an input that has essentially no effect on mean square error (or some other measure) may still have an important effect. If there is more than one output neuron, clamping an input may actually decrease the error for one or more of them enough to nearly offset an increased error in others. Thus, the safest approach to sensitivity analysis is to measure the change in each output neuron for each training sample. The careful experimenter may reap surprisingly rewarding information here.

It may not be easy to decide what value to use for the clamping activation. It is generally best to use a level midway between zero and full activation. The mean value of that input across the training set may also be a good choice. Certainly, extreme values should be avoided, as they can drive hidden neurons into saturation, causing other inputs to be ignored. The unfortunate fact is that all too often the value at which the input is clamped has a significant effect on results. This is even true for inputs that are relatively unimportant, as their activation level can influence the effect of other inputs due to diverse interactions. This is the most serious drawback of this otherwise attractive technique.

One variation of sensitivity analysis attempts to discover which inputs are important to certain classes. Rather than clamping an input to an intermediate level, it is first clamped to one extreme, then the other. If the output neuron corresponding to a certain class tends to become more activated (across the training set) when the input is clamped fully activated, then it appears that activation of that input is a feature important to classification into that class. Due to the unpredictable nature of interactions among inputs, this is a dangerous technique and is easily abused.

Another version of sensitivity analysis presents a case to the network, then observes the effect of varying individual inputs while all others are fixed. Changing some inputs may have little effect on the outputs, while changing others may have a profound effect. Be warned, though, that conclusions reached with this method must be limited to the input patterns in effect when the test was performed. Presenting the network with a different case may dramatically alter the results as various hidden neurons go in and out of saturation. As long as it is realized that observed sensitivities are conditional on the state of other inputs, this is a valid technique. However, in practice, that is often an excessively confining restriction. It is most useful when analyzing borderline cases. Present the network with a case that is just barely correctly (or incorrectly) handled. Now try varying each input. This can provide valuable clues as to what the network is looking for in tipping the scales.

The user must remember that the network's outputs not only are nonlinear functions of the inputs, but they may even be non-monotonic. The following scenario is not at all impossible. Suppose that we have binary inputs. A particular input is fully activated for a given case. We slightly reduce the activation and see an output change significantly. We conclude that the perturbed input is important. But if we drop that input all the way down to the other binary value, we see the affected output go right back to where it was originally! Now, the fatal question: is that input important to that output? Sometimes life can be very difficult.

In practice, it is often easiest to use simple numerical methods if we want to compute the sensitivity of an output to an input. Just slightly vary the input and see what happens to the output! But for those who do not faint at the sight of ghastly equations, [Hashem, 1992] gives explicit formulas for computing partial derivatives of outputs with respect to inputs. This would certainly be the fastest approach computationally.

Finally, the reader must be warned to avoid using sensitivity analysis in conjunction with the stepwise discriminant analysis and genetic methods of the previous section, *Features Used by Networks in General*. In other words, do not clamp groups of inputs, trying to judge the effect of clamping and freeing some neurons while others are clamped. When we are examining a particular network, remember that its training was based on all of the inputs. It is reasonable to remove one, or at most a few inputs, by clamping. However, if more than a few are eliminated, the results will be meaningless. The absence of many inputs can easily drive hidden neurons into nonlinear or totally saturated regions from which they will exhibit fatally distorted responses to the remaining inputs.

Stereotypical Inputs

When we train a multiple-layer feedforward network, our usual goal is to find an optimal set of connection weights. But we can go one step beyond. After the trained weights are found, we can find optimal *input* patterns for producing any desired output pattern. The results of this extension can be very enlightening.

First, it should be emphasized that the function defined by a neural network's input-to-output mapping is generally not invertible. Many different inputs can give exactly the same output. Thus, we cannot ask for the one and only input that will produce a given output. We can, however, ask for that input in the neighborhood of some given input which minimizes the output error with regard to some given output. This is what we will be doing here.

Finding the ideal input pattern to match a specified output is not difficult. Simply imagine that the input neurons are actually a new hidden layer at the front of the network. There is a single input to this layer, having a constant value of 1. Also, the old-input-layer / new-hidden-layer neurons have an activation function which is just the identity function. Then it can be seen that the inputs to the original network are equivalent to the weights connecting this new front layer to the new input neuron having unit activation. Thus, we can apply the exact same algorithm by which we learned the network weights to learn this additional set of weights. Of course, we would hold the original network weights constant throughout the iterative process. We would only update the new layer weights, which are really the inputs. This structure is illustrated in Figure 11.4.

The philosophy behind this approach is a search for stereotypes. We humans unfortunately have over the years developed fixed ideas concerning certain groups. Each of us may have in our mind's eye an image of the archetypical drug pusher, or accountant, or computer jock, or any of a million other such groups. We have been exposed to examples from these classes and have merged the examples into one composite representative. A neural network does much the same thing. We want to get an idea of its composite impressions.

In practice, we do the following. First, train the network. All results that follow will be with respect to *that particular network* and

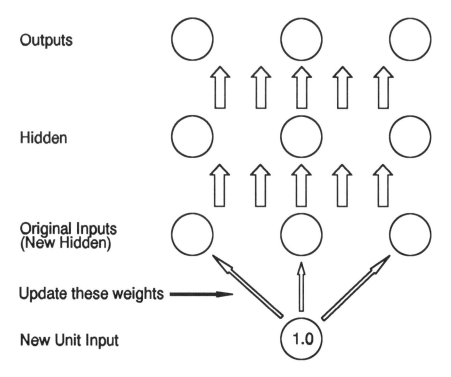

Outputs

Hidden

Original Inputs
(New Hidden)

Update these weights ——————►

New Unit Input

Fig. 11.4: Append a single neuron layer to optimize an input

in general will not be indicative of the behavior of other networks
trained on exactly the same data but starting from a different random-
weight configuration. Then we select a training case in which we are
interested. That training case will determine the initial weight
estimates for the phony front layer, as well as the target outputs for
the network. Now apply exactly the same learning algorithm that was
used to train the network, except for one modification. Do not adjust
the weights that were already learned. Instead, apply the backpropagation algorithm one more time to compute the gradient for the
front layer. Update these weights, which are actually inputs to the
original network. Iterate until convergence to the minimum output
error is obtained. The final weights will be the network's stereotype
inputs for that training case.

　　　The above procedure can be carried one step further when the
inputs are binary (and perhaps even when they are not binary).
Binary inputs are very common, especially for shape and pattern
recognition problems. What we do is compute the ideal input for a
training case, as described above. Then we slightly perturb all
idealized inputs toward their center value. Those that are large are

made a little smaller. Those that are small are made larger. The idea is to wash out the information in the inputs by making them all more mediocre. Then apply the optimization again, starting the search for the best input pattern at this new, less-stimulating pattern. Repeat this sequence of pushing toward mediocrity followed by optimization until no significant change is observed after both phases are performed. What will happen is that those inputs *required* by the network to be high or low in order to achieve the correct response will keep being pulled back away from mediocrity by the optimization. Those the network does not care about will be allowed to slip quietly into obscurity. Most experimenters will be surprised by the tiny amount of input information which the network really uses.

Probabilistic Neural Networks

This chapter presents a decades-old, extremely powerful classification algorithm that can be cast in the form of a neural network. Learning speed for this model is fast to instantaneous. However, classification time may be slow, and memory requirements are large. Performance is generally excellent and is asymptotically Bayes optimal.

Overview

Nearly all standard statistical classification algorithms assume some knowledge of the distribution of the random variables used to classify. In particular, the multivariate normal distribution is frequently assumed and the training set used only to estimate the mean vectors and covariance matrix of the populations. While some deviation from normality is tolerated, large deviations usually cause problems. In particular, multimodal distributions cause even most nonparametric methods to fail. One of the beauties of neural networks is that they can typically handle even the most complex distributions. The three- (and four-) layer feedforward network already described has been shown to be an excellent classifier. However, it has two problems. One is that little is known about how it operates and what behavior is theoretically expected of it. That bothers some researchers, even in the face of its superb performance. A more pragmatic criticism is that its training speed can be seriously slow. This chapter presents an alternative network that has superb mathematical credentials, trains orders-of-magnitude faster, and classifies as well as or better than feedforward networks. Its principal disadvantages are that it is relatively slow to classify and it requires large amounts of memory.

The network described here is actually a statistical algorithm proposed several decades ago. It is described in [Meisel, 1972], although it existed in other related forms even earlier. Although its theoretical and practical power was known at that time, the state of computer technology precluded its widespread use. Even moderate size problems required memory and CPU speed far beyond what was available then. Thus it fell into disregard until Donald Specht revived it in the form of a neural network [Specht, 1990] which he dubbed a "probabilistic neural network" in homage to its roots in probability theory. He showed that by organizing the flow of operations into "layers", and assigning primitive operations to individual "neurons" in each layer, the algorithm can be made to resemble a four-layer feedforward network with exponential activation functions. This chapter will present the method in a form closer to its roots, as this is more straightforward and easier understand.

We start by formally stating the general classification problem. We sample an m-component multivariate random vector $X = [x_1, ..., x_m]$. The K populations from which our samples are drawn will be indexed by k, $k = 1, ..., K$. The prior probability of an unknown sample being drawn from population k is h_k. The cost associated with misclassifying a sample from population k is c_k. Note that in many applications, the prior probabilities, h_k, are treated as being equal, and hence can be ignored. The same is true of the costs, c_k. The training set consists of n_1 samples known to be from population 1, and n_2

samples known to be from population 2, and so forth, through n_K samples from population K. The problem is to devise an algorithm for determining the population from which an unknown sample is taken. If we can devise an algorithm whose expected misclassification cost is less than or equal to that of any other, it is said that our algorithm is *Bayes optimal*.

In the fortuitous event that we know the probability density functions $f_k(X)$ for all populations, the Bayes optimal decision rule is to classify X into population i if

$$h_i \, c_i \, f_i(X) > h_j \, c_j \, f_j(X) \qquad\qquad 12\text{-}1$$

for all populations j not equal to i.

The above decision rule is derived in many intermediate level statistics books and will not be justified here. Also note that the possibility of equality is ignored. In practice, ties are randomly broken.

Unfortunately, we usually do not know the probability density functions $f_k(X)$. Sometimes we are willing to assume that they are members of a particular family of distributions, such as the normal distribution. In this case the training set is used to estimate the parameters of the distribution. But all too often we dare not assume even a rough shape for the distribution. This is especially true if the distribution may be multimodal (have more than one area around which samples are clustered). Our only recourse is to estimate the population density functions with the training samples.

At this point it is instructive to digress for the purpose of laying an intuitive foundation for the classification algorithm soon to be described. Examine the bivariate scatter plot in Figure 12.1. The X's represent training samples from one population, the O's from another. The question mark is an unknown sample to be classified. Observe first that, given this training set, classification in general *should* be fairly easy. With only one real exception, the populations seem to be clustered into isolated groups. However, nearly any conventional classification algorithm would fail miserably with this data set because of the multiple modes (clusters).

Let us now think about how we might classify unknowns, given training data like this. Probably the most straightforward way would be to check the distance (Euclidean or some other measure) separating our unknown from each member of the training set. The unknown would then be classified into the population to which the closest training set member belongs. This *nearest neighbor classifier* is in fact an extremely popular method. It is conceptually simple, easy to program, and in practice it performs reasonably well. On the other hand, it has a weakness. In the above example, the unknown would

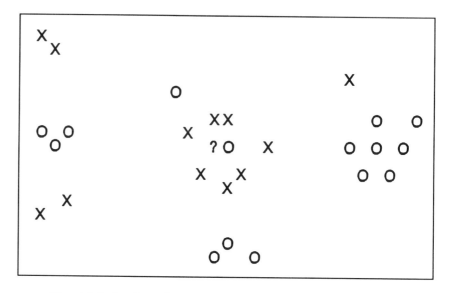

Fig. 12.1: Scatterplot of knowns (X,O) and unknown (?)

be classified into the O population because its nearest neighbor belongs to that class. The fact that the unknown is in the midst of a large cluster of X's is ignored; the single isolated O controlled the classification. A better classifier would consider more than just the unknown's immediate neighborhood. It would take into account more distant neighbors. Of course, the influence of training samples would diminish according to their distance from the unknown. What we need is a "sphere-of-influence" function of the distance separating an unknown point from a training sample point. This function would have a peak at zero distance and diminish to zero as the distance increased. An intuitively good classifier would find the sum of this function for all training set members of each population and classify the unknown into the population that has the largest sum. In the above example, the single member of O near the unknown would make a substantial contribution to the sum for O, but it would be the only contribution. All other members of O would be so far from the unknown that their function values would be essentially zero. On the other hand, the X's surrounding the unknown would each make a smaller contribution, but their quantity would overwhelm the single O, so the unknown would be classified into X. This idea can now be solidified with mathematics.

It was previously stated that if the probability density functions of the populations are known, a Bayes optimal classification scheme can be easily implemented. [Parzen, 1962] showed how to estimate a univariate probability density function from a random sample.

[Cacoullos, 1966] extended Parzen's method to the multivariate case. It is shown that the estimated density converges asymptotically to the true density as the sample size increases. Thus, we have a tool for constructing an asymptotically Bayes optimal classifier even when the parent density functions are unknown. Use Parzen's technique on the training sample to find estimates, $g_k(X)$, of the density function of each population. Then classify an unknown X into population i if

$$h_i \, c_i \, g_i(X) > h_j \, c_j \, g_j(X) \qquad \text{12-2}$$

for all populations j not equal to i. Recall that h_i and c_i are prior probabilities and error costs, as previously defined.

Parzen's PDF estimator is in essence the "sphere-of-influence" weighting function of the intuitive classifier already described. He uses a "weight" function (called a "potential function" in [Meisel, 1972]) that has its largest values for small distances between the unknown and training sample points and decreases rapidly toward zero as the distance increases. His PDF estimator is a scaled average of that function across the training set. In particular, for a single population whose sample size is n, the estimated density function for that population is

$$g(x) = \frac{1}{n\sigma} \sum_{i=0}^{n-1} W\left(\frac{x - x_i}{\sigma}\right) \qquad \text{12-3}$$

The scaling parameter σ (sigma) controls the width of the area of influence and would typically be set to smaller values for larger sample sizes.

A common choice for the weighting function W is the Gaussian function. This choice has nothing to do with assumptions of normal distributions. The Gaussian function is simply a well behaved, easily computed function that satisfies the conditions required by Parzen's method, and it has been shown in practice to perform well. An infinite number of other choices is possible, and some may be superior.

In the multivariate case, the estimator of the probability density function using the Gaussian weighting function is

$$g(x) = \frac{1}{(2\pi)^{p/2} \sigma^p n} \sum_{i=0}^{n-1} e^{-\frac{|x - x_i|^2}{2\sigma^2}} \qquad \text{12-4}$$

It can be seen from the above formula that the population density function estimated from the sample is nothing more than the average of separate multivariate normal distributions, one for each training sample. Of course, the population density would be estimated *separately* for each population. Once again it must be stressed that the choice of a normal distribution (Gaussian weighting function) has no special significance beyond being computationally and mathematically convenient, as well as being proven in practice.

Classification algorithms, like life in general, always have *some* fly in the ointment. For this algorithm, it is σ, the scaling parameter. Its value can be crucial to good performance, yet there is no universal, mathematically rigorous method for choosing the "best" value. Consider a bivariate sample of eight points from a single population. Suppose the population has two distinct modes, and our sample contains four points from each. The density functions estimated with the Gaussian weighting function, for several different values of σ, are shown below.

-3 -2	3 2
-3 -3	3 3
-2 -2	2 2
-2 -3	2 3

Fig. 12.2: Data points

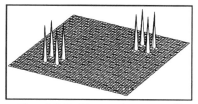

Fig. 12.3: Sigma too small

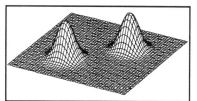

Fig. 12.4: Good sigma

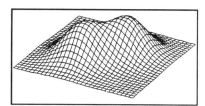

Fig. 12.5: Sigma too large

Figure 12.2 lists eight points in a hypothetical sample. Figure 12.3 shows the effect of the scaling parameter being too small. The effect of neighbors in a cluster is totally eliminated. We are left with essentially a nearest-neighbor classifier. Figure 12.4 shows a good choice for σ. Each of the two population modes is well defined, the samples work together to represent the mode, and the wilderness between the modes (where members of other populations may perhaps lie) remains isolated. Figure 12.5 shows the effect of σ being too large. The population density is blurred so badly that unless the other populations were extremely well separated from this, confusion would surely result.

There are some general guidelines that should be followed if we expect to find values of σ that result in good performance. First, it almost goes without saying that the individual components of a multivariate sample vector should be comparably scaled to some "unit" variation. This equalizes the contributions of each variable. It also eliminates interaction between choice of σ and scaling due to measurement, which has no effect on classification ability, but can help the experimental design by keeping σ in reasonable ranges. For example, if the measured variables are the height and weight of persons, it would be ludicrous to use units of kilograms for weight and millimeters for height. If the distributions are unimodal with no distant outliers, the variables could each be divided by their sample standard deviation so as to produce variables having unit standard deviation. If outliers are present, it may be preferable to divide by their interquartile range. If the distribution is multimodal, some more empirically derived scaling factor may have to be devised. Of course, exact scaling is not crucial. It is only important that the individual variables have similar variation.

It is helpful from an interpretational point of view if the effect of the number of variables on the actual width of the weight function is removed, so that only σ affects it. In other words, suppose we have a bivariate sample, each of whose components has unit variance. We may choose an appropriate value for σ. Suppose now that our sample vectors have 100 components, each with unit variance. The same value for σ in this case would be much too small, as the length of the difference vector X-X_i would usually be much greater than it would be in the bivariate case. We could, of course, remember to use larger values of σ for longer vectors. A better method is to normalize the distance measure by dividing it by the number of variables that went into it before dividing by σ and plugging it into the weight function. This makes the value of σ more uniformly meaningful across problems.

The user must remember that even if all variables are standardized, the optimal value of σ is very problem dependent. In some cases it may be on the order 10; in others it may be .00001 or less! It is vital that some means be devised for estimating a value appropriate to the problem at hand.

[Meisel, 1972] presents a method for choosing σ such that the weighting functions for each sample point overlap to a "moderate" degree. Unfortunately, that method replaces one subjective decision (the value of σ) with another (the degree of overlap). Also, it can be very slow to compute. Finally, it in no way "optimizes" anything. It simply chooses σ so that an arbitrarily selected amount of overlap occurs. Its chief advantage is that if the experimenter is totally unfamiliar with the data, it can usually produce a reasonably effective value of σ.

The author has had very good success with an heuristic technique for optimizing σ. This method, described in a later section, can be slow. However, unlike training other networks, it does not need to be run every time the training set is updated. It is usually sufficient to run it once with a representative training set, so that a value of σ appropriate to the general problem is found. Then, unless there is reason to believe that new training sets from the same populations have radically different distributions, the same σ can continue to be used. At worst, a quick touch-up will be all that is needed. A subroutine that implements this method is presented on page 213.

Computational Aspects

This section discusses several points regarding efficient means for performing classification with the probabilistic neural network. A complete subroutine for classifying is presented later. Here we only focus on a few specific areas. It will be assumed that the usual Gaussian weight function is used. If a problem has few variables and many samples and fast classification is critical, it may be preferable to use another function in order to avoid computing the relatively expensive exponential function. However, most practical problems have so many variables that the time taken to form dot products swamps out the time spent computing the exponential function.

Examine once again the formula given above for estimating the probability density function of a population. The first thing to notice is that the factor involving π will be the same for all populations. Thus, for classification purposes it can be ignored. Also, it is nearly always best to use the same value for σ in all populations. In this case, the factor in front of the sum which involves σ can be ignored. Our classification function (which, strictly speaking, can no longer be called an estimator of a probability density) now reduces to the following general formulation:

$$g(x) = \frac{1}{n} \sum_{i=0}^{n-1} W\left(\frac{d(x,x_i)}{p\sigma}\right) \qquad \text{12-5}$$

In the above equation, W is our familiar weighting function, and $d(x, x_i)$ is a function that measures the distance between the points X and X_i. Most commonly, the distance function is the Euclidean distance between the vectors, and the weighting function is the (unnormalized) Gaussian function:

$$W(z) = e^{-z^2} \qquad \text{12-6}$$

The number of components of the multivariate sample vector is p. This makes σ less dependent on the dimensionality of the sample, as discussed previously.

A special case in which computation can be reduced should be mentioned. First, note that the squared Euclidean distance between two vectors X and Y can be written in vector notation as

$$d^2(X,Y) = (X-Y) \cdot (X-Y) = X \cdot X + Y \cdot Y - 2 X \cdot Y \qquad \text{12-7}$$

In many problems, the sampled vector will always lie on the surface of a sphere of fixed radius. In other words, the length of X and Y will be constant. In this case, the $X \cdot X$ and $Y \cdot Y$ terms in the above expansion will be constant. Only the dot product of the unknown with each training sample needs to be computed. The vector subtraction can be avoided. In particular, this will be the case if all inputs are binary and are coded as -1 and 1. In fact, finding the dot product of two binary vectors involves nothing more than counting the number of variables in the two points which have the same value, thus avoiding even the multiplication!

Optimizing Sigma

A method for finding an optimal value of σ, which avoids subjective choice of parameters, can be based on a standard statistical technique called *jackknifing*. Let us start by discussing the jackknifing method in general.

Users of all classification algorithms share a dilemma. How can its performance be truly tested in an honest, unbiased way? Certainly it would be unfair to judge a classifier based on its performance in classifying its training set. Its performance would probably be better than could be expected in the general population. The most common solution is to save out a sizable fraction of the known cases, training with only part of the known set. The cases saved out are then classified. The classifier's performance on this test set is a much fairer (unbiased) measure of what it can do in the general population. But if the training set is small, as is often the case in real life problems, saving out part of them may be considered wasteful. Random chance may cause an important subset of the population to be excluded from the training. The classifier will then fail to take these cases into account and will misclassify them during the test phases. If the fraction held back for testing is kept small, that problem is less likely to occur, though at the cost of a less reliable measure of performance. Such tradeoffs can lead to painful decisions by the researcher.

There is a better way: jackknifing. If only *one* known sample is held back from the training, there will be minimal impact on quality. This single sample could then be classified to provide an unbiased indicator of the performance of the classifier. Of course, it alone would provide a uselessly small amount of information. Thus, we put it back into the training set and remove a different sample. The classifier is retrained and tested on the new sample. By doing this for every case, we have the economy of being able to use every known sample for both training and testing, yet still have an indicator of performance which, for many classification schemes, is unbiased. Of course, there is a high price in computer time. The process of retraining and classifying for every training sample can sometimes be prohibitive. But it is often a price worth paying.

Jackknifing can be used to test the efficacy of a value of σ in probabilistic neural network classification. Thus, to optimize σ, we simply select many values and choose the one that performs best on the jackknife test. It must be emphasized that *the performance measure found this way is NOT unbiased*, since the jackknife test itself is involved in the choice of σ. However, there is no simple alternative. The test case *must* be excluded from the training set, or else the procedure could degenerate to a nearest-neighbor classifier as the test case gravitated toward itself in the training set. A subroutine for optimizing σ with this technique is presented on page 213.

Related Models

The most straightforward approach to training a probabilistic neural network involves using a single σ (sigma) for all populations, as well as ignoring covariances. It also uses a mixture of distributions centered on each sample point. Some more sophisticated variations are currently being studied. The simplest extension is to use a separate σ for each population. If a large number of samples is available, we can even employ full covariance matrices. Finally, we need not assume a separate distribution centered at every sample. It may be better to impose a limit on the number of distributions and assume a form for them. For example, we may want to treat the population as a mixture of normal distributions, and estimate the parameters of the distributions. These, and other enhancements, are summarized in [Specht, 1992]. Also, [Musavi, Kalantri, and Ahmed, 1992] present an interesting way of estimating covariance matrices.

Finally, it should be pointed out that [Kim and Arozullah, 1992] have proposed a sweeping generalization of the entire probabilistic neural network paradigm. They estimate the underlying probability density functions based on the Gram-Charlier series expansion, with optional use of Parzen windows. Significantly improved performance is claimed.

A Sample Program

This section offers a subroutine for classifying using the probabilistic neural network (Parzen–Bayes classifier). A subroutine for automatically choosing an optimal value for the scaling parameter σ is also given.

```
int pnn (
    int nvars ,              // Number of variables in x
    int npops ,              // Number of populations
    int *ntrain ,            // npops vect of n of samples of each pop
    double **tsets ,         // npops vector of ptrs to training sets
    int model ,              // Distance/Weight model (normally 1)
    double sigma ,           // Scale parameter
    double *unknown ,        // nvars vector to be classified
    double *outputs          // npops vector of classification func vals
    )

{
    int i, n, ipop, icase, ibest ;
    double diff, dist, *tptr, *optr, best ;

    sigma *= (double) nvars ;    // Keep sigma meaningful
    best = -1. ;                 // Keep track of best mean function

    for (ipop=0 ; ipop<npops ; ipop++) { // Evaluate for each population

        n = ntrain[ipop] ;       // Number of samples of this pop
        tptr = tsets[ipop] ;     // Point to them
        optr = outputs+ipop ;    // Cumulate mean weight function here
        *optr = 0.0 ;

        for (icase=0 ; icase<n ; icase++) { // Do all cases in this population

            dist = 0.0 ;             // Will sum distance measure here

            if (model == 2) {        // Use sum of absolute differences
                for (i=0 ; i<nvars ; i++) { // Compute the distance measure
                    diff = unknown[i] - *tptr++ ;
                    dist += fabs ( diff ) ;
                    }
                dist /= sigma ;
                }
```

```
      else {                          // Use squared Euclidean distance
        for (i=0 ; i<nvars ; i++) { // Compute the distance measure
          diff = unknown[i] - *tptr++ ;
          dist += diff * diff ;
          }
        dist /= sigma * sigma ;
        }

      if (model < 3)                  // Use exponential weighting
        *optr += exp ( - dist ) ;
      else                            // Use alternative weight function
        *optr += 1. / (1. + dist ) ;
      }

    *optr /= (double) n ;             // Mean function value for this population

    if (*optr > best) {               // Keep track of best for classification
      best = *optr ;
      ibest = ipop ;
      }
    }

  return ibest ;
}
```

The pnn program listed above starts by multiplying the user's sigma (σ) by the number of variables. This makes the effect of sigma less influenced by the number of variables. The rest of the program just loops across each population, computing the mean weight function for each. The largest is kept in best. The value of each is returned to the user in outputs so that they can be weighted according to prior probabilities or cost functions if full Bayes classification is desired.

For each case, the distance between that case and the unknown is computed. Model 2 uses an absolute-value distance, while models 1 and 3 use the squared Euclidean distance. Then, the weight function is applied to the distance. Models 1 and 2 use the exponential function, while model 3 uses a faster alternative. Thus, model 1 is the usual Gaussian model, while models 2 and 3 are alternatives that are slightly faster to compute. The mean for each population is found, and the identity of the best returned.

The above program makes no provision for prior probabilities or cost functions. When the mean for each population is found by dividing optr by n, equal priors and costs are implied. If we were to use the sum rather than the mean, classification results would be biased to reflect prior probabilities proportional to the training sample size for each population. Alternatively, we could use the mean, but multiply each population mean in optr by the prior probability times the misclassification cost for that population. No other changes would be necessary to implement such biasing.

Optimizing Sigma

A subroutine for choosing an optimal value of σ is now shown. It uses the jackknife method previously described. The parameter list of this routine is almost identical to that of the pnn subroutine. The only additions are related to the optimizing procedure itself.

```
static int evaluate ( int nvars , int npops , int *ntrain , double **tsets ,
                int model , double sigma , double *outputs ) ;

int pnnlearn (
      int nvars ,                   // Number of variables in x
      int npops ,                   // Number of populations
      int *ntrain ,                 // npops vector of n of samples each pop
      double **tsets ,              // npops vector of ptrs to training sets
      int model ,                   // Distance/Weight model (normally 1)
      int nsigs ,                   // Number of sigmas for initial search
      int maxits ,                  // Max number of iterations
      double sigmin ,               // Minimum value to try for sigma
      double sigmax ,               // And max
      double *sigma ,               // Returned best scale parameter
      double *outputs               // Work vector npops long
      )

{
   int i, score, ibest, left_score, mid_score, right_score, prev, iter ;
   int try_score ;
   double sig, sigmult, left, mid, right, try ;


   sigmult = exp ( log ( sigmax / sigmin ) / (nsigs-1) ) ;
   sig = sigmin ;


/*
   Evaluate confusion for nsigs sigmas ranging from sigmin to sigmax,
   with their values spaced by equal ratios (sigmult).  Keep track of the
   best sigma in 'mid' and its subscript so we know if it is the first or last.
   Also keep track of the best score and its neighbors.
*/

   prev = 0 ;                     // Shuts up compilers over use before init
   mid_score = -1 ;               // Keep track of best here

   for (i=0 ; i<nsigs ; i++) {

      score = evaluate ( nvars , npops , ntrain , tsets , model , sig ,
                    outputs ) ;
```

```
        if (score > mid_score) {
           mid = sig ;
           ibest = i ;
           mid_score = score ;
           left_score = prev ;
           }

        else if (i == (ibest+1))
           right_score = score ;
        prev = score ;
        sig *= sigmult ;
        }

   left = mid / sigmult ;
   right = mid * sigmult ;

/*

   At this point we (probably) have three sigmas (left, mid, right) with their
   scores (left_score, mid_score, right_score) such that the mid has the
   highest score.
   There is another possibility.  If ibest=0 it means the best score was had
   at the extreme low end of the user's sigma range, and left_score is
   unknown. Bail out the silly user by shrinking until either we get a three
   point tie (in which case we quit, choosing the center sigma as the best)
   or until our score drops, in which case we just go on to the refinement
   phase.  Also, we have the same possibility at the high end.
*/

   if (! ibest) {   // Best at low end, so keep going down

      for (;;) {

         left_score = evaluate ( nvars , npops , ntrain , tsets , model , left ,
                              outputs ) ;

         if ((left_score == mid_score)  &&  (right_score == mid_score))
            goto DONE ;  // Totally flat, so quit trying

         if (left_score < mid_score) // Trio with mid best, so go refine
            break ;

         right = mid ;                   // Still getting better, so move on down
         right_score = mid_score ;
         mid = left ;
         mid_score = left_score ;
         left = mid / sigmult ;
         }
      }
```

```
       else if (ibest == (nsigs-1)) {     // Best at high end, so keep going up

          for (;;) {

              right_score = evaluate( nvars , npops , ntrain , tsets , model , right,
                                outputs ) ;

              if ((left_score == mid_score)  &&  (right_score == mid_score))
                 goto DONE ;  // Totally flat, so quit trying

              if (right_score < mid_score) // Trio with mid best, so go refine
                 break ;

              left = mid ;                  // Still getting better, so move on up
              left_score = mid_score ;
              mid = right ;
              mid_score = right_score ;
              right = mid * sigmult ;
              }
          }

/*
    At this point we definitely have three sigmas (left, mid, right) with their
    scores (left_score, mid_score, right_score) such that the mid has the
    highest score.  Refine.

*/


       for (iter=0 ; iter<maxits ; iter++) {

          if (mid / left  >  right / mid)  { // Left interval larger, so split it

              try = sqrt ( mid * left ) ;   // Split ratio in half
              try_score = evaluate ( nvars , npops , ntrain , tsets , model , try ,
                                outputs ) ;

              if ((try_score > mid_score)  ||
                 ((try_score == mid_score)  &&  (left_score > right_score))) {
                 right = mid ;
                 right_score = mid_score ;
                 mid = try ;
                 mid_score = try_score ;
                 }

              else {
                 left = try ;
                 left_score = try_score ;
                 }
              }
```

```
      else {                                    // Right interval larger, so split it
        try = sqrt ( mid * right ) ; // Split ratio in half
        try_score = evaluate ( nvars , npops , ntrain , tsets , model , try ,
                      outputs ) ;

        if ((try_score > mid_score) ||
           ((try_score == mid_score)  &&  (left_score < right_score))) {
          left = mid ;
          left_score = mid_score ;
          mid = try ;
          mid_score = try_score ;
          }

        else {
          right = try ;
          right_score = try_score ;
          }
        }

      if ((left_score == mid_score)  &&  (right_score == mid_score))
        break ;  // Totally flat, so quit trying
      }
DONE:
  *sigma = mid ;
  return mid_score ;
}



/*
----------------------------------------------------------------

  evaluate - Local routine to evaluate performance for a given sigma

----------------------------------------------------------------
*/


static int evaluate (
      int nvars ,                    // Number of variables in x
      int npops ,                    // Number of populations
      int *ntrain ,                  // npops vect of n of samples of each pop
      double **tsets ,               // npops vector of ptrs to training sets
      int model ,                    // Distance/Weight model (normally 1)
      double sigma ,                 // Scale parameter
      double *outputs                // Work vector npops long
      )

{
  int i, tclass, ipop, score, popscore, n, exclude ;
  double *tptr, temp, *v1ptr, *v2ptr ;
```

```
              score = 0 ;
              for (ipop=0 ; ipop<npops ; ipop++) { // Evaluate for each population
                 popscore = 0 ;              // Score each pop separately
                 n = ntrain[ipop] ;          // Cases from this population
                 tptr = tsets[ipop] ;        // Point to them
                 --ntrain[ipop] ;            // Temporarily exclude test case

                 exclude = n ;               // Test with this case
                 while (--exclude >= 0) {    // Exclude each case
                    if (exclude < n-1) {     // Do not need to swap last case!
                       v1ptr = tptr + exclude * nvars ;
                       v2ptr = tptr + (n-1) * nvars ;
                       for (i=0 ; i<nvars ; i++) {
                          temp = *v1ptr ;
                          *v1ptr++ = *v2ptr ;
                          *v2ptr++ = temp ;
                          }
                       }

                    tclass = pnn ( nvars , npops , ntrain , tsets , model , sigma ,
                              tptr+(n-1)*nvars , outputs ) ;

                    if (tclass == ipop)
                       ++popscore ;

                    } // For all excludes


                 ++ntrain[ipop] ;            // Restore to correct value
                 score += popscore ;         // Cumulate overall score
                 } // For all pops

           return score ;
           }
```

The pnnlearn routine implements a trivially simple linear optimization algorithm. It starts by evaluating the performance (counting the number of correct classifications) at nsigs values of σ ranging from sigmin to sigmax. These values are spaced geometrically rather than arithmetically. The factor sigmult is the ratio of adjacent values. The best score is kept in mid_score, and its associated σ in mid. The variable prev is used to hold the score for the previous iteration so that we will also know the score of the σ to the left of the best. Also, for the sigma one past the best, we save right_score. Thus, when all nsigs sigmas have been tested, we have a trio of adjacent values such that the center is the best.

Attainment of such a trio will fail if the best happens to be at sigmin or sigmax. If this happens, continue testing sigmas in that direction as long as improvement happens. If three sigmas in a row have equal scores, conclude that the curve is so flat that further testing is a waste, and quit. Otherwise, performance will eventually drop, in which case we have a trio with the best in the center.

Once a trio of sigmas is captured, with the best in the middle, do a few iterations to refine the interval. The primitive method of bisecting the largest of the two intervals is used. After each bisection, a new trio is defined based on the score of the new point. This continues until either all three points have equal scores or maxits bisections have been done.

There are many refinement algorithms far superior to the bisection method used here. Fibonacci splits with quadratic projection, as used in the direcmin routine for conjugate gradient learning, is an obvious candidate. However, such sophistication is definitely not needed and may actually be more expensive than bisection if projection failure causes unnecessary retries. The majority of computation time is spent in the initial search from sigmin to sigmax. Very few iterations of refinement are needed. Typically, nsigs should be *at least* 15 to be sure that the global optimum is located. A value of 5 or so for itmax is nearly always sufficient. In practice, convergence is usually reached within two or three bisections. However, it would not be unreasonable to initially search a range of 0.00001 to 10.0 for sigma.

Other Optimization Criteria

The above program optimized σ based on the primitive criterion of correctness. There are other possibilities, but in general they have so many potential dangers that they should be approached only with great caution. (Students in search of a thesis topic, take note.) The first temptation to be wary of is computing the criterion with misclassification errors weighted by some notion of prior probabilities and/or misclassification costs. A far better approach, if this is needed, is to include these bias terms in the classification decision itself by weighting the mean for each population as already described. Alternatively, use the sum of the window function for each population, rather than the mean. Then use a training set that has each population represented in proportion to its prior probability times its misclassification cost.

Another bit of unstable ground is computing more exotic criteria based on *how much* each winner won by, rather than on a simple count of how many wins were scored. Intuition might whisper to us that it is more useful to know the margin of the win, so that we can choose σ to provide larger margins. But who is to set priorities that would let us weigh large wins for some cases against loss of narrow victories in others? Any such scheme must be very carefully designed.

In summary, it must be emphasized that the author does *not* mean to discourage careful experimentation to determine better optimization criteria. Certainly the simple counting method given here is primitive. All that is intended is a stern warning that coming up with something better will not be a trivial task.

Bayesian Confidence Measures

In most practical classification problems, there is a possibility that unknown samples may not be drawn from any of the trained classes. A submarine sonar classifier may have been trained to identify several types of subs, but no attempt was made to include whales, boulders, et cetera. In this case it is impossible to compute confidence estimates based directly on Parzen density estimates. The techniques discussed starting on page 361 may be applied in some cases, but that is the best that can be done.

Sometimes, though, the classes are mutually exclusive and exhaustive; i.e., they completely cover all possibilities and do not overlap. In this fortuitous but uncommon event, we can apply Bayes' theorem to directly compute posterior probabilities:

$$P[A|X] \; = \; \frac{g_A(X)}{\displaystyle\sum_k g_k(X)} \qquad\qquad 12\text{-}8$$

Each of the density estimates, $g_k(X)$, in the numerator and denominator of the above formula could, of course, be multiplied by prior probabilities and/or cost constants if such biasing is desired. The chapter on computing confidence measures (page 361) discusses the relevant issues, so they will not be repeated here. It should be emphasized, though, that the contents of that chapter are primarily for the case of a simple yes–no decision. If there are multiple, mutually exclusive outcomes for which confidences are needed, by far the best approach is to use a probabilistic neural network and base the confidences on the above formula.

Autoassociative Versions

As should be obvious by now, the probabilistic neural network is fundamentally a classifier. However, there are at least two simple but often effective ways in which it can be used in an autoassociative mode. Which of these methods is chosen depends on the nature of the training data.

Of course, the class assigned to the input is no longer considered the output of the network. Now, the output is a vector of the same length as the input. We compute that output vector after the classification has been done.

If the training samples for each class are noisy versions of a single prototype for that class, it is reasonable to use the mean of all inputs for that class as the output. One case in which this would be appropriate is when we are doing an autoassociative filter (page 24) and learning several prototypes from noisy exemplars (page 31). Each presentation of the sliding window would call upon the probabilistic neural network to decide which prototype class was most likely. After that decision was made, the averaging process within that prototype class would reduce the noise. The author has had varying degrees of success with this method.

Another possible scenario is that the training samples for each class are noise free. Rather, they are slightly different variations on the same theme. For example, an image may contain any of several different types of object. Each type of object may come in a small variety of sizes and shapes. In this case, we would certainly not want to average the input samples within a class to generate the network's output! The average of two legal shapes for a class may be a nonsense shape. Besides, how does one average a shape anyhow? That in itself is a thorny issue. In this situation, we take a slightly different approach. As in the noisy case, we let the probabilistic neural network choose the prototype class. The underlying assumptions are no longer fully valid, since the training set cannot be considered simply noisy versions of a fundamental truth. However, the author has had excellent results despite this. After the classification is done, we make a second pass through the training set. But this time we ignore all members of other classes. We compute the distance metric only for members of the chosen class. Pick the training set member having the minimum distance from the input. This is a nearest neighbor classifier limited to the members of one class. The network's outputs would be set equal to that training set member's inputs. In other words, we return an exact member of the training set, rather than a composite. The probabilistic neural network chose the class, and a nearest neighbor classifier chose the exact member of the class.

When to Use a Probabilistic Neural Network

This model is fairly specialized, not having the wide applicability of the multiple-layer feedforward network. However, in some situations, it is ideal.

First, this model is intrinsically a classifier. Modifications exist that allow it to interpolate between decisions, making it a more universal function approximator, but these tend to be less than elegant. Also, as described above, we can force it into an auto-associative mode. However, this is often inelegant. Thus, in general, we should primarily consider this model for classification problems.

The principal advantage of the probabilistic neural network is that usually little or no training time is required. At worst, sigma optimization may be performed, which can be slow for large training sets. However, training a multiple-layer feedforward network for the same training set would nearly always be many times slower. And a perfect choice of sigma is usually not critical to performance. Experienced users can sometimes guess a good value just by examining histograms. Also, a perfectly acceptable sigma can often be chosen using just a subset of the entire training set.

A second advantage of this network model is that a byproduct of its computations is Bayesian posterior probabilities. If we need confidence estimates for the network's decisions, this model is a strong candidate. While confidences can be squeezed out of many other models, only this model has the solid theoretical foundation to support these estimates.

Another situation in which this network is favored is if the data is likely to contain outliers, points that are very different from the majority. Unless extremely large values of sigma are used, outliers will have no real effect on decisions regarding the more frequent cases, yet will be properly handled if they are valid data.

The probabilistic neural network has three possibly serious drawbacks. First, because of the way it uses potential functions around clusters of training data, its performance depends strongly on having a thoroughly representative training set. Of course, any neural network model benefits from having a comprehensive training set. But this model is far pickier than most. If only a few training samples are available, we can train a multiple-layer feedforward network having very few hidden neurons, and the network will probably do a good job of generalizing far from known points. The same cannot be said of the probabilistic neural network.

The other disadvantages stem from the fact that the entire training set must be stored, as well as processed, each time an unknown case is classified. This means that memory requirements are large, and execution speed is poor. This model is rarely suitable for real-time applications, unless a large array of fast parallel processors is available. Luckily, the algorithm is strongly parallel in that the training cases can be distributed among processors.

In summary, we would want to choose the probabilistic neural network model when the problem is one of classification and the training set is so extensive that training other models would be impracticably slow. We would also strongly favor this model when confidences are needed for classification decisions. Finally, we would reject this model if execution speed is critical or memory is limited.

13

Functional Link Networks

A simple transformation of the input data for a feedforward network often dramatically speeds training. The input layer becomes much larger, sometimes impractically so. However, the number of hidden neurons can usually be greatly decreased, or eliminated entirely.

This chapter is largely based on material contained in [Pao, 1989]. That book is highly recommended not only as a source of additional information about functional link networks, but also because it is an excellent reference on neural networks and classification techniques in general.

The basic strategy of the functional link net is to generate additional, synthetic inputs for a standard feedforward network by applying functions to the original, raw inputs. This is illustrated for a single functional link neuron in Figure 13.1.

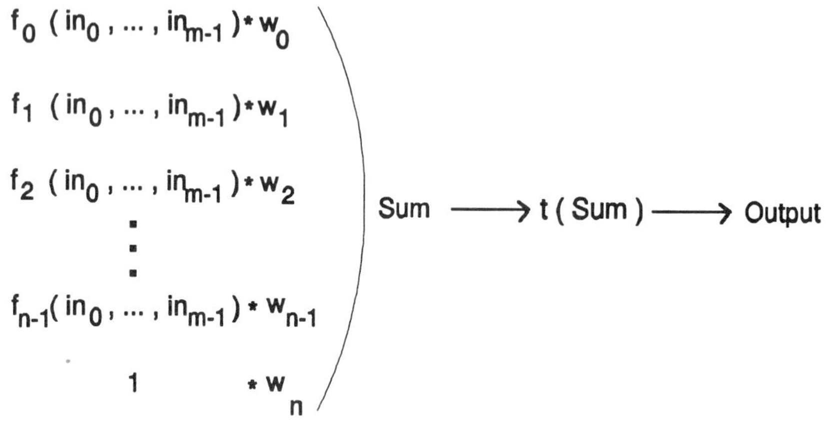

$$f_0\ (in_0,\dots,in_{m-1})*w_0$$

$$f_1\ (in_0,\dots,in_{m-1})*w_1$$

$$f_2\ (in_0,\dots,in_{m-1})*w_2$$

$$\vdots$$

$$f_{n-1}(in_0,\dots,in_{m-1})*w_{n-1}$$

$$1 \qquad *w_n$$

$$\text{Sum} \longrightarrow t\,(\,\text{Sum}\,) \longrightarrow \text{Output}$$

Fig. 13.1: One neuron in a functional link network

These functions may be applied to individual inputs. They may also be functions of more than one input, generating interaction components. The hope is that with the input information presented to the network in such a variety of forms, no hidden layer will be required to decode the complex patterns in the raw data. To train such a network, the regression technique already described can supply excellent initial estimates of the weights connecting the function outputs to the output neurons. The conjugate gradient algorithm then touches up these weights so as to minimize the error of the outputs.

How does one choose the functions that extend the input data? Pao divides the choices into two categories, though he correctly emphasizes that these categories are somewhat artificial and restrictive. The main purpose of this division is to simplify the problem. Models from these categories can be recursively applied to themselves and/or to models from the other category. This allows great generalization.

The first of his two models involves products of the inputs with each other. He calls this the *outerproduct* or *tensor* model. The lowest-order version of this model forms products of all pairs of inputs.

For example, suppose there are three inputs, $\{x_0, x_1, x_2\}$. Then, the feedforward network would be presented with six inputs: $\{x_0, x_1, x_2, x_0x_1, x_0x_2, x_1x_2\}$. Higher-order versions of this model are formed by multiplying in triples or more. However, it is obvious that the number of terms generated this way rapidly increases beyond the limits of practicality. In fact, even the lowest-order model using only pairs becomes unwieldy for any but very small input vectors. If there are n raw inputs, there will be $n + n * (n - 1) / 2$ function values to present to the actual network. It is interesting to note, though, that the infamous XOR problem can be solved without a hidden layer by using $\{x_0, x_1, x_0x_1\}$ as the input to the network.

The second of Pao's categories does not involve any interaction between inputs. It simply applies one or more univariate functions to each input. These functions may or may not be the same for all inputs. He calls this the *functional expansion* model. Users of polynomial regression do this when they take an input variable x and generate additional inputs of x^2, x^3, et cetera. In fact, the only difference between polynomial regression and a functional link net using polynomial functions is that regression treats the weighted sum of polynomial functions as the desired output. The functional link net applies a nonlinear activation function, such as the logistic function already described, to the weighted sum of polynomials to produce the output. This makes the network approach more robust than straight regression in many practical problems involving noisy data, though it does unfortunately mean that iterative techniques like the conjugate gradient algorithm must be used to find the optimum weights.

It must be emphasized that *in practice there is no reason to limit oneself to one of these two models*. Suppose we have three inputs: $\{x_0, x_1, x_2\}$. It would be perfectly legitimate to present the network with a collection of inputs like $\{x_0x_1, \sin(x_1), x_1 \cos(x_0x_2\text{-}x_1), ...\}$. This leads, though, to a serious criticism of the functional link net approach. If there are more than a few raw inputs, nearly always the case in practice, there is often no rigorous method for choosing our functions from the infinite number of possibilities. One of the beauties of networks that send the raw inputs directly to a complex hidden-neuron layer is that the user is relieved of the responsibility of choosing meaningful representations or pattern matchers. The hidden layer does that, and usually does a very good job. The functional link net is, in one sense, a step backwards. The user is in the unenviable position of either carefully choosing functions and hoping that good choices are made, or generating a vast excess and throwing them all at the network. This is particularly dangerous, as overfitting can easily lead to a network that performs well on the training set but fails miserably when applied to the general population.

Application to Nonlinear Approximation

Experimenters are frequently required to approximate an unknown function based on noisy data. For example, it may be known that some observed physical process is governed by a rule $Y = f(X)$, where X is an easily measured independent variable, Y is a dependent variable that can only be measured with difficulty, and $f(X)$ is an unknown function. If it is important to be able easily to estimate Y given X, we may collect a set of (x, y) measurements and use these to formulate a model for estimating Y by measuring X. In practice, the experimentally measured values of Y (and perhaps even X) are contaminated by noise. Since this is such a common problem, it has received extensive study.

The traditional solution to this problem is to compute several functions of the input variable, such as $\ln(x)$, $\sin(x)$, et cetera. Regression is then used to predict Y from these transformed inputs. If the noise contaminating the measurements is approximately normally distributed, this method can do quite well. It is known, though, that ordinary regression fails if the noise is chaotic or has asymmetric or abnormally heavy tails. Many methods for dealing with "outliers" in the data have been proposed. However, they are nearly all rather subjective, and each has its drawbacks. There should be a better way.

Recently, it has been found that feedforward networks with one or two hidden layers can often solve this problem very well, even in the presence of chaotic noise. Another advantage of using such networks is that the experimenter does not need to supply functions. The network would have one input, a dozen or so hidden neurons in a single hidden layer, and one output. The hidden layer will find appropriate functions on its own. This method has two disadvantages, though. One is that training time can be large. Regression can be done in a fraction of a second. Training a network with a dozen hidden neurons, given perhaps hundreds of training samples, can take significant amounts of computer time. The other problem is that it may be difficult to validate the network. We may believe that it will correctly generalize to points that were not in our training sample, but we may not be able to *prove* it. A simple regression equation based on a few well-defined functions can be analyzed. Limits can be placed on its values and derivatives. But the sheer complexity of a practical network with many hidden neurons can make it virtually impossible to say what results it will come up with for unforeseen data points. The overwhelming body of experience in this area indicates that it will nearly always perform excellently. But what if our network is performing a critical task? Sometimes we need more assurance.

The functional link net comes to the rescue here. We are back to the problem of having to supply the functions that transform the raw input data. However, the nonlinear transfer function of the output neuron makes this network much more tolerant of chaotic noise contaminating the measured data, as compared to ordinary regression. Yet we retain the advantage of practicable validation, as a functional link network is nothing but ordinary regression followed by a simple activation function whose behavior is well known.

The entire preceding discussion has been based on the premise that the purpose of the input functions is to *eliminate* the hidden layer. However, it must be pointed out that sometimes it is still beneficial to use a hidden layer. We may simply get away with a much smaller layer by supplying the network with extra functional inputs. The main reason for using a hidden layer in a functional link net is when the user does not feel confident of having just the right functions available. In this case, the powerful pattern detection abilities of a hidden layer can be put to use. This is more fully discussed in the next chapter, *Hybrid Networks*.

Mathematics of the Functional Link Network

Now that the intuitive foundation for functional link networks has been laid, it is time to define formally this network model. It cannot be done in full generality, since nobody has ever done so, and this author will not presume to set forth his own definition. [Pao, 1989] focuses on applying the functions to a feedforward network without a hidden layer, but admits the possibility of other architectures. It is even possible to produce more unusual combinations, such as following a functional link layer with a probabilistic neural network. (This has worked well for the author.) Therefore, our discussion will focus on a single neuron whose output is determined by the functional link network model. Very often the search stops here. There are many successful applications of functional link networks which consist of exactly one neuron. The output of this single neuron determines the decision made by the network. The most common extension of this simple model is to use more than one neuron. This would be done if there are multiple decisions to be made. A less common extension is to use the outputs of the functional link network as inputs to another layer, implementing a hidden layer in a feedforward network. Although this can be enormously useful in some cases, especially when important functions for the links are known a priori, it has the danger of being a "worst of both worlds" approach and should only be used with caution. Functional link nets in which a function layer feeds another layer have the disadvantage of requiring careful function selection, along with the disadvantage of slow training due to the extra layer.

Suppose that we have m raw inputs to our network. We must define n functions $\{f_i(x_0, ..., x_{m-1}), i = 0, ..., n - 1\}$. Usually n will be much greater than m. We also define an activation function for the network. Typically this is the logistic function, although other functions are sometimes used.

$$t(a) = \frac{1}{1 + e^{-a}}$$
                    13-1

Then the activation of our single-neuron functional link network is

$$A(x_0, ..., x_{m-1}) = t\left(\sum_{i=0}^{n-1} w_i f_i(x_0, ..., x_{m-1}) + w_n\right)$$
                    13-2

where $\{w_i, i = 0, ..., n\}$ are $n + 1$ constant weights which determine the response of the network. The network is trained by finding effective values for these weights.

Some special cases of the above model should be noted. First, observe that if the transfer function is the identity, $t(a) = a$, optimal values for the weights can be found by simple regression. Even if the transfer function is nonlinear, regression can be used to provide good approximations to the weights by regressing onto the inverse transfer function values. This is described in the regression chapter, page 165. Then, a nonlinear optimization algorithm, such as the conjugate gradient method, can be used to trim up the weights optimally.

Another special case is Pao's *outerproduct* or *tensor* model [Pao, 1989]. In this case, $n = m + m * (m - 1) / 2$. The first m functions are simple identities:

$$f_i(x_0, ..., x_{m-1}) = x_i, \quad i = 0, ..., m-1$$
                    13-3

The next $m - 1$ functions are the products of x_0 with each of the other x's:

$$f_i(x_0, ..., x_{m-1}) = x_0 x_{i-m+1}, \quad i = m, ..., 2m-2$$
                    13-4

The next $m - 2$ functions are the products of x_1 with x_2 through x_{m-1}, et cetera. This set of functions, trivial though it may seem, can sometimes be extremely powerful.

The remaining important special case is Pao's *functional expansion* model. In this model, one or more univariate functions are defined for each input. None of the functions acts on more than one input.   There is no restriction that the same function or set of functions must be used for each input. Thus, we can have

$$f_i(x_0, ..., x_{m-1}) = g_{0,i}(x_0), \quad i = 0, ..., k-1,$$
$$f_{i+k}(x_0, ..., x_{m-1}) = g_{1,i}(x_1), \quad i = 0, ..., l$$

13-5

and so forth for all desired functions.

There are two commonly used sets of functions for this model. One is the polynomial series:

$$g_{j,k}(x) = x^{k+1}, \quad j = 0, ..., m-1; \quad k = 0, ...$$

13-6

A few words about the polynomial series are in order. If powers higher than three or so are used (not generally recommended), the system of equations starts to become numerically unstable. Rather than using individual polynomial terms, it is better to use *orthogonal polynomials*. Full details are beyond the scope of this text. See any standard regression textbook, such as [Draper and Smith, 1966], for details.

The other common set of functions is the trigonometric series:

$$g_{j,2k}(x) = \sin((k+1)cx), \quad j = 0, ..., m-1; \quad k = 0, ...$$
$$g_{j,2k+1}(x) = \cos((k+1)cx), \quad j = 0, ..., m-1; \quad k = 0, ...$$

13-7

where the constant c is chosen to normalize the input data in a way that is meaningful to the problem.

When to Use a Functional Link Network

Because this model is such a tremendously variable hybrid, it is difficult to specify conditions under which this model is particularly good or bad. Its training speed can be extremely fast if a good choice of functions allows us to avoid a hidden layer, *always our foremost goal*. Or, its training time can be terribly slow if we must blindly use a large number of functions but still feel the need for a hidden layer. Its execution speed can be fast if the functions are fast to compute and use of these functions allows a small following network. Or, it can be slow if the functions are slow to compute.

The hardware on which it runs can also strongly affect its performance relative to its primary competitor, the traditional multiple-layer feedforward network. Machines that have high-speed dot-product accumulators will favor the traditional network. The functional link network typically expends most of its effort computing the functions, with relatively few dot products being involved.

The most compelling reason for choosing this model is if it is known a priori that certain functional transformations of the data will expose its salient features. In this case, by all means apply those functions and attempt to eliminate the hidden layer. On the other hand, if we do not know in advance that particular functions are appropriate, we are rarely better off guessing. Give the raw data to another network model.

14

Hybrid Networks

Sometimes a modest hybrid, a combination of several separate neural networks, can perform better than a single large network.

Some problems are so complex, involving so much data of such diverse variety, and/or in such complex relationships, that a single neural network may not be practical. If we are using a multilayer feed-forward network because of its run-time speed, the training time may be too long. If we are using a probabilistic neural net to avoid long training, or perhaps because we desire Bayesian confidences, run-time speed may be unacceptably slow. It may even be that our problem simply breaks down into several parts in a natural way, and we are interested in exploiting that physical structure. These are the principal reasons for considering hybrid network models.

There is an endless number of ways in which neural networks can be combined with each other and even combined with traditional statistical methods and expert systems. This chapter makes no pretense of completely outlining the possibilities. What is described here are some of the more common hybrids, structures that have been shown to work well in practical problems. If the reader has an idea for a hybrid that is not shown here, do not take that as discouragement. Try it. It will probably work well.

There is one caveat to be mentioned. It is generally not wise to split a model into several separate parts just for the sake of splitting it. If the training time, run-time speed, and other properties of the unified model are acceptable, performance of the unified model will usually be at least slightly superior to that of the hybrid. That statement assumes, of course, that the unified model is given sufficient facilities (hidden neurons) to handle the problem. When we break up a problem, what we are doing in essence is telling the network its job. Remember that a sufficiently large single network is capable of breaking up a problem on its own and, given enough training, can probably do a better job of fragmenting it than you can. The only reason for manually splitting it is if the requisite size of a single network makes it too slow, or if you know that there is hard physical justification for splitting.

Functional Link Net as a Hidden Layer

One of the most useful network pairings is so widely accepted as a network structure that it is almost incorrect to call it a hybrid. Many people would call it a single model. But since it is constructed from two very different types of neurons, each having its own unique operation, it is presented here as a hybrid.

The functional link net is fully described starting on page 223, so it will be only briefly reviewed here. A single neuron in this network has m inputs. We define n transformation functions $\{f_i(x_0, ..., x_{m-1}), i = 0, ..., n-1\}$. Usually n will be much greater than m. We also define an activation function $t(net)$ for the network. Then, the output activation of our single-neuron functional link network is

$$A(x_0, ..., x_{m-1}) = t\left(\sum_{i=0}^{n-1} w_i f_i(x_0, ..., x_{m-1}) + w_n\right) \qquad 14\text{-}1$$

where $\{w_i, i = 0, ..., n\}$ are $n + 1$ constant weights which determine the response of the network. This is illustrated in Figure 13.1.

Many applications are well served by a single functional link neuron. As pointed out in the functional link network chapter, this network can be trained rapidly. The weights can be approximated by regressing the function values onto the target outputs transformed by the inverse activation function. Then they can be fine-tuned by nonlinear optimization. This traditionally difficult operation is usually simple here because the nonlinearity is well behaved, and good starting estimates are already known from the regression.

Unfortunately, sometimes one neuron, powerful as it is, may not be sufficient. We need the additional power of a hidden layer. The usual reason is that we do not possess ideal functions. We often have to guess at what might be effective, and our guess is less than excellent. However, we may have sufficient belief in the utility of our chosen functions that we do not want to revert to a plain old feed-forward network. Thus, we create a hybrid. We use more than one functional link neuron and treat each as if it were a hidden neuron in a feedforward network.

Figure 14.1 illustrates a typical hybrid model. Each functional link output, shown across the top of the box in that illustration, is the output of a single functional link neuron. If we index these neurons with j, their outputs are computed as

$$A_j(x_0, ..., x_{m-1}) = t\left(\sum_{i=0}^{n_j-1} w_{ij} f_{ij}(x_0, ..., x_{m-1}) + w_{n_j j}\right) \qquad 14\text{-}2$$

Observe that the functions, and even n, the number of functions, are indexed by j. In practice, this is not usually done. The same functions are used for all hidden functional link neurons. (Of course, different weights, w_{ij}, are used for each, or the network would be degenerate.) This uniformity is done purely for convenience, though. If the designer believes that there would be some purpose to using several different sets of functions, that is perfectly reasonable.

Each output of the hybrid network is computed by finding the net sum of all k hidden functional link neuron outputs and acting on that sum by an activation function.

Outputs

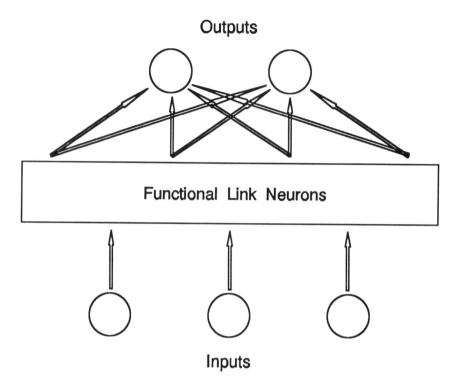

Inputs

Fig. 14.1: Functional link neurons as a hidden layer

$$\text{OUT}_p = t\left(\sum_{j=0}^{k-1} w_{jp} A_j + w_{kp}\right)$$ 14-3

In the above equation, the activation function $t(net)$ is usually the same as that used for the hidden neurons, but need not be.

    If the same functions are used for all hidden functional link neurons, this model is essentially nothing more than an ordinary three-layer network whose inputs are computed by applying a set of functions to the original inputs. Therefore, it is trained in exactly the same way as a three-layer net would be trained. The function outputs are computed for each training sample. Then, the user's choice training algorithm is used to find all of the weights. Since the function values will be needed many times, it is usually best to compute them once in advance, using the stored values during training.

    In the more general case of different functions for different hidden neurons, the training procedure requires only trivial modification. Most canned routines for training feedforward networks assume that the same input values are applied to all hidden neurons. This is no longer the case. But the exact same formulas are still appropriate. The subroutine that computes the correction terms must be modified to use the inputs to each individual hidden neuron when updating the weights for that neuron. Also, if the n's are different, every routine that references the number of inputs must be modified to use the correct n.

Fast Bayesian Confidences

In order to compute Bayesian confidence levels for classification decisions, one must be able to compute estimates of the probability density function. An excellent way to do this is with the Parzen window approximator (page 205) which is the foundation of the probabilistic neural network (page 201). Unfortunately, if there are many input variables and the training set is large, this computation can be slow. Real-time applications often require the speed of a multilayer feedforward network. Enter the hybrid.

Classification time of the probabilistic neural network is proportional to the product of the number of inputs times the number of cases in the training set. Since it is assumed that we are not willing to decimate the training set, the only hope of speeding things up is to reduce the number of its input variables. This can be done by using a multiple-layer feedforward network as a "front end" data-reducer. If the number of output neurons in this network is much fewer than the number of inputs, a highly likely possibility, then we can speed the probabilistic network by using the layer network's outputs as the PNN's inputs. This is illustrated in Figure 14.2.

The next issue to be addressed is the choice of the number of output neurons and the method by which the layer network is trained. A favorite methodology is to start by ignoring the PNN and just designing the layer network as a standard classifier. Use as many output neurons as there are classes, training it so that exactly one output neuron comes on for each case. Design of classification networks is covered in more detail starting on page 15. Considerations concerning completeness are discussed starting on page 376 and should be reviewed carefully.

It is the unproven opinion of the author that the method just described for implementing the feedforward layer network part of the hybrid is generally the best. It has the advantage of elegant simplicity. Also, we may not always need confidences. That method allows us to use the layer network for classification and to take the time to execute the probabilistic net only when called for. Finally, it alerts us

PNN Outputs

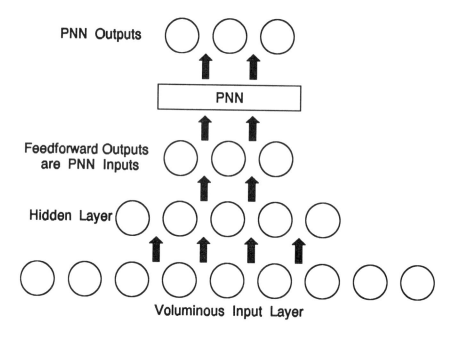

Feedforward Outputs
are PNN Inputs

Hidden Layer

Voluminous Input Layer

Fig. 14.2: Layer network feeding PNN

to trouble if we get the anomalous result of different classifications being done by the two networks! If one output neuron from the layer net is a clear winner, but the highest mean density achieved by the PNN is attained by a neuron corresponding to a different class, we know that the training data bears closer examination.

It may be that there are so many classes that even the data reduction effected by the layer net with the above class coding does not sufficiently speed the probabilistic neural net. In this case, we may wish to explore denser coding timidly. If we limit ourselves to binary output responses, always a good idea, we can encode n classes into $\log_2 n$ neurons by expressing each class ID as a binary number. If we do not limit ourselves in this way, we could even get away with using a single output neuron by encoding each class as an incremental degree of activation! This would not be illegal theoretically, although conversion of a nominal variable to an interval variable sends shudders through the spine. It should be apparent that an infinite variety of encoding schemes, embodying different combinations of the above, is possible. The author has never had to resort to any of them, but he cannot help but feel that they would all be inferior to the one-of-n method first described. Furthermore, they would not have the additional advantages of the one-of-n coding which were previously pointed out.

An astute reader may well ask why this relatively complex data reduction method is necessary. It is time consuming to train a layer network. Why not just use a few linear combinations of the original inputs as PNN inputs? The first few principal components of the training set would spring forth in the mind of a statistician. Perhaps the first few linear discriminant functions would be even more effective inputs to the PNN. The answer to this question lies in the concept of statistical *power*.

A full description of power is far beyond the scope of this book. Here, we must be satisfied with a loose definition. Power is the ability of a test procedure to detect what it is looking for. When a classifier computes the confidences that an unknown observation belongs to each of several classes, we want it to be sure of itself. If there are two classes, we will not be happy if a classifier tells us that an observed case has a 50–50 chance of being from each class. Even a 60–40 split is not very impressive. Something more like a 99-percent confidence is what we want. The ability of the probabilistic neural network to come up with high confidences when warranted depends on the quality of the training data. If all of the classes in the training set look alike as far as the data is concerned, an unknown observation will have approximately the same mean estimated density for all classes. If there are n classes, the computed confidence in each class will be about $1/n$. This classifier has very low power and hence is worthless. On the other hand, suppose that the data samples for each class are well separated by class. Then, an observed case will have a high density estimate for its correct class, and near-zero density for all other classes. This will lead to a high confidence. This classifier has great power.

It is assumed that the impracticably large original data vector contains sufficient information to classify satisfactorily. Otherwise there is no point in pursuing the matter. Presumably, a probabilistic neural network would do an acceptable job if trained on that raw data. The problem is that the sheer size of each observation makes the network too slow. When we reduce the amount of data by shrinking the length of the input vectors, we are implicitly casting most of the information aside. Our hope is that we keep that fraction of the information which is important to correct classification, discarding only superfluous variation. If we fail in this endeavor, the power of the PNN classifier will be compromised.

Now that we understand that the data reduction front-end must preserve the information that is important to classification, providing variables that are *different* for each class but *similar* within a class, we can understand why a neural network trained as a classifier is such a good choice for the data-reducer. The first few principal components certainly explain the majority of the variation in the data, but that implies nothing about classification ability. For all we know, the classification information may reside in the *last* principal component! The choice of linear discriminant functions for data reduction is obviously an improvement over principal components, but still not the solution. Our whole premise is that the data is so complex that linear solutions are unsatisfactory. Thus, there is no point in trusting linear discriminant functions to retain the important information. A trained network, on the other hand, has been optimized to do just that. Its nonlinearity enables it to outperform linear discriminant analysis. And the fact that it was trained in such a way that output activations are strongly affected by class implies that the network's outputs convey good classification information. This means that a probabilistic neural network fed with this information can be very powerful.

Training

Since there are two entirely separate neural networks, two training sessions are involved. First, we must train the feedforward network to activate optimally its output neurons. Then, we must provide the PNN with a training set on which to base its classifications. Ideally, these should be two *independent* sets of data. The reason is that a fundamental assumption of the PNN is that its training set is comprised of fair, randomly obtained samples from the underlying class populations. If the same training set is used for both networks, this assumption will not be met. The act of training the feedforward network will produce output vectors that are certainly not random. They will be prejudiced toward their target values. If those output vectors are used to train the PNN, they will not be representative of the values which would be obtained by presenting independent random samples to the feedforward network and training the PNN with the outputs so produced. Thus, we see that implementing this hybrid network is done as follows:

1) Design a multilayer feedforward network architecture suitable for classification.

2) Collect a set of training data, and train the above network with that set.

3) Collect a new, totally independent set of training data. Apply each sample to the trained feedforward net. Save the outputs of the network for each case.

4) Use the above outputs to train a probabilistic neural network.

5) To classify an unknown, present it to the trained feed-forward network. Then present the outputs of that network to the inputs of the probabilistic neural network. If the decision reached is different from that indicated by the maximally activated output neuron of the feedforward net, suspiciously examine both training sets.

Attention-based Processing

When human beings look at a printed page, they do not spend much time taking in the whole gestalt. Rather, they flit about, focusing on different areas and taking in different levels of detail. When they first glance at the page, they may notice that there is an interesting picture in the upper right corner. Their attention rapidly moves to that picture. After just a moment spent on the complete picture, they move on to a detail within the picture. Close examination of several other details in the picture tells them all they care to know about it for now, so their eyes pass to another moderate size feature on the page. This disjoint attention to multiple levels of detail is highly characteristic of the human visual system.

Artificial neural systems charged with the task of processing large volumes of data can benefit from the same methodology. There are two major advantages to be had.

1) Execution time can be tremendously shortened. High-level processes can quickly screen out vast stretches of unimportant territory. Middle-level processes can remove much of what remains. The typically slow lowest-level processes need not waste their time examining unpromising material.

2) Specialization enables us to develop networks that have a relatively narrow focus. This may mean more networks, but each has less memory use, faster training, faster run-time speed, and superior performance.

Figure 14.3 shows how this procedure might be used to extract the zip code from an address. The silly way to read a zip code would be to train a neural network to read five-digit zip codes in one shot from a rectangular field, and then to scan this rectangle across the entire envelope and wait patiently until it finally hits its target. A better

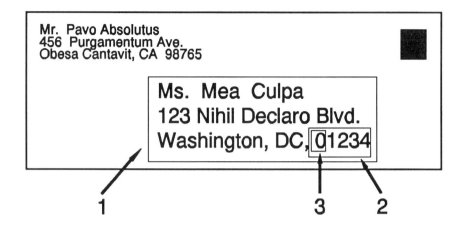

Fig. 14.3: Attention-based address reading

way would be to use three separate algorithms. The first would locate the destination address on the envelope. This might be done with a nonneural algorithm, or we might train a network to locate edges. Other, more sophisticated neural methods are possible, but are beyond the scope of this section. Once the address has been located, a second algorithm would find the zip code at the end of the bottom line. A third algorithm would interpret each individual digit in the code. The specialization of each separate task facilitates not only greater speed, but increased accuracy as well.

One frequent property of attention-based schemes which we should always exploit when possible is that the more global decisions can often be reached based on lower resolution sampling. Full resolution is needed only by the lowest level of processing. Decimating the input data can significantly reduce the workload by itself. If the data is an image, remember that the reductions are squared. Examining every second pixel vertically and horizontally results in only one quarter of the work.

Suppose we have a signal processing problem. Here, we need to detect occasional short pulses. They rise quickly to a peak, then plunge to a negative peak. Their length is so short that high resolution sampling is necessary. But we have some help. We know that these *micro* features are always preceded by a moderate span of slightly higher than normal samples. We will call them *macro* features because they cover a larger area and hence are detectable at lower resolution sampling. Note that the appearance of this macro feature does not necessarily guarantee that the micro feature will appear. It is simply a precondition for appearance of the micro feature. Figure 14.4 illustrates the problem.

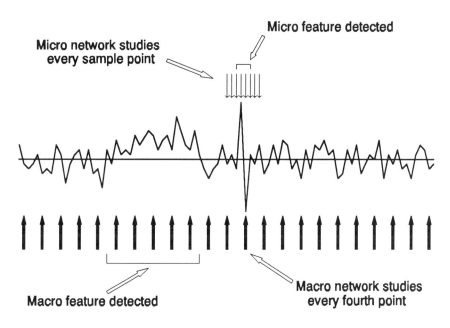

Fig. 14.4: Attention-based signal processing

A good solution would be to use two separate neural networks. One would be trained to detect the macro pattern of successive high samples. It would work with low resolution sampling, such as every fourth point, as shown in that figure. The other network would be trained to detect the micro feature, and it would use full resolution data. This second network would only be called into play when the first network detected the macro feature.

Remember that there are *two* ways that the above scheme can save time. First is that we can usually operate the global network(s) at a lower resolution, thus reducing the amount of data that must be processed. The other is that usually the job of the global network is easier, as it does not need to worry about false alarms. It just needs to catch every instance of the macro feature it is seeking. Catching a few extras here and there is no disaster. Thus, it can usually be made very fast and act as a quick screening device. The designer should not neglect to strive for both of these goals. Try to find macro features based on low resolution data. And do not design a complex, high performance network for global use. Go for simplicity and speed. Save the complexity for the micro-feature detector.

Finally, keep in mind that there is nothing magical about *two* networks. Sometimes an entire hierarchy of increasingly complex networks is the optimal design. One lightning-fast network may discard only half of the data. The remaining half goes to an intermediate network, which gets rid of three-quarters of what is left. The remaining small chunk goes to a fairly complex network, which finds all micro features plus just a few false alarms. The final network is extremely slow, but it can be counted on to separate correctly the sheep from the goats. Four or more levels in the hierarchy are not at all uncommon in practice.

Factorable Problems

Sometimes a large problem can be systematically broken down into several smaller problems. When this is so, it may be appropriate to use separate neural networks for each part. The decision of whether or not to do this should be based on practical considerations. If a huge training set is available and training time is not a problem, it is usually better to throw all of the data at one network and let it tackle the problem however it chooses. However, there may not be a sufficient amount of training data to cover as many combinations of input variables as we would wish. Or, a single network would be so large that training it would be impractical. In this case, we should attempt to break the problem into natural subproblems. Each would be solved separately and the solutions fed into a "master" network which makes the final decision.

One small example might come from medical diagnosis. Suppose we can perform a blood test that measures 8 factors, which we will call $Blood_1$ through $Blood_8$. We can also tap the patient here and there, measuring the strength of 6 different reflexes, which we will call $Reflex_1$ through $Reflex_6$. The final diagnosis will be based on these 14 measurements. A training sample is available. It consists of the 14 measurements, plus a correct diagnosis, for each of many patients.

The basic solution would involve designing a single 14-input network, having as many outputs as there are diagnoses. In a problem this small, such a network would almost always be the best choice. But if there were a dozen or more families of tests instead of the two used here, and if each family contained many tests, the network might be too large to be trainable in a reasonable period of time. An intuitive way to split the problem is shown in Figure 14.5.

We can use such a splitting method if it is possible to make separate diagnoses for each test family. Maybe the eight blood factors can be used to classify the patient's blood into one of three categories, $Blood_A$, $Blood_B$, and $Blood_C$. The reflex tests can be used the same way. We train network 1 to classify the blood, and train network 2 to classify the reflexes. Finally, network 3 is trained by applying the training set data to the already trained networks 1 and 2, and using their outputs as input to network 3.

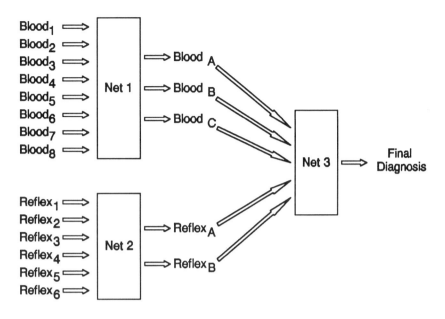

Fig. 14.5: A factorable medical diagnosis problem

Training the Data Reduction Networks

There are two radically different approaches to training the networks that accept the original data and reduce it for the final decision network. The most common is *supervised* training. We decide in advance what each network's output classes will be. For each member of the training set, we must know the correct class decision of each network. The networks are individually trained as ordinary classifiers. In the above example, we would need physically meaningful classes for the three blood classes and two reflex classes.

The other approach is *unsupervised* training (page 327). In this method, we do not need to name classes. In some versions, we do not even need to specify how many classes we want. The network can make that decision on its own. Unsupervised training is valuable if it is difficult to designate classes. Perhaps we do not wish to presume ourselves capable of naming medical conditions. Perhaps there isn't even any rational basis for such classification. We are willing to let the network find its own classes. If we cannot specify physically meaningful classes, the network will probably do a better job than we could do ad hoc.

These two approaches can be mixed. It is permissible to train some of the data reduction networks with supervision and let others find their own classes.

Splitting Is Not Always Effective

Before getting carried away with the beauty and logic of splitting large problems into many smaller ones, be warned that there is a hidden danger in it. Examining Figure 14.5 again, we see that the eight blood test numbers have been reduced to three intermediate diagnosis numbers. Furthermore, the relatively high resolution data of the test results has been reduced to practically binary numbers as a result of the training for classification. *Information has been thrown away.* Unfortunately, we cannot be quite sure whether or not that which was discarded would be of value in making the final diagnosis. We hope that the classes selected for data reduction are the source of the information that is ultimately needed, but we probably do not know that for sure.

> *A fundamental assumption when a problem is split is*
> *that all information necessary to the final decision is*
> *embodied in the intermediate variables.*

The reason why a single, large network can perform better than a split model is that there may be some important information that does not make it through the splitting process. Referring to the previous example, it may be that the relationship of $Blood_1$ relative to $Blood_2$ is a crucial bit of knowledge for the final decision. If that relationship does not affect the decision that network 1 makes as to an intermediate diagnosis of $Blood_A$, $Blood_B$ or $Blood_C$, we are in trouble.

15

Designing the Training Set

The best tool is worthless if it is applied to inferior material. This chapter discusses some issues involved with putting together an effective collection of training samples.

Children of English-speaking families growing up in America generally learn to speak English. Yet a child raised in Louisiana will sound very different from a child raised in the Bronx. The same is true of neural networks. Two different researchers may train their networks to learn the same thing, yet the networks may perform quite differently in some ways. The subtle prejudices inherent in an experimental design can creep into the network's mind, influencing it in ways that, for better or for worse, may be apparent only to outside observers. This chapter assumes that the researcher is capable of handling the gross aspects of designing the training set and collecting the data. The focus here will be on subtlety: how we take a good design and make it excellent.

Number of Samples

The most obvious decision to be made by the training set designer is the size of the collection. There is a definite tradeoff in speed versus performance. Iterative training algorithms that use the full set on each epoch generally respond linearly to training set size. Double the size, and twice as much training time is required. (This assumes, of course, that all other factors are held constant. In practice, the time will often more than double.) Probabilistic neural networks have a run-time speed proportional to the training set size. So, if speed were the only consideration, we would want the training set to be as small as possible. As will be seen, speed is not by any means the only consideration.

If the neural network is going to be effective at its ultimate task, the training set must be complete enough to satisfy two goals:

1) **Every class must be represented.** Usually, the training data will consist of several possible subgroups, each having its own central tendency toward a particular pattern. All of these patterns must be represented.

2) **Within each class, statistical variation must be adequately represented.** It is the presence of random noise imposed onto pure patterns which makes most of our work necessary. The training set designer must insure that an adequate variety of noise effects is included.

The necessity of the first goal is apparent. If a neural network will be used to shut down a potato chip factory line when it detects defective chips emerging, it must be trained on more than just normal and burned chips. Uncooked chips and any other type of defect must play a part in the training procedure.

It is the second goal that may not be so obviously important. Is it true that if you've seen one burned potato chip, you've seen them all? Of course not. A uniform moderate brown may be considered burned. One small black spot may also be burned. If the oven thermostat has expired and the oven is overheated, that condition may manifest itself in any number of ways. If all burned chip samples that went into the training set have black spots only near their perimeter, later chips with black spots in their center may not be recognized as burned.

Communal Random Errors

Do not let the facetious tone of the above description lead to a callous attitude regarding adequate sampling for nullifying random effects. Unlikely random events have an unpleasant habit of occurring too often. When all samples of a particular subclass are contaminated by roughly the same noise pattern, purely by chance, that noise pattern will be blindly learned by the network. When that erroneously learned noise pattern does not appear along with the true pattern when the network is used later, the network may fail to detect the true pattern.

The problem of confusion of random patterns with important patterns becomes more serious for cases near decision boundaries. As long as patterns belonging to subclasses leading to different decisions are very different, we can get away with using relatively few training samples. But when a subclass lies near a decision boundary, it is important to use a large number of samples in order to avoid learning patterns of noise which are in common among a large fraction of the representatives of that subclass. This is because when near a boundary, the communal random noise problem is far more likely to lead to an incorrect decision.

Overfitting

Another reason to use a large training set is to avoid *overfitting*. Every experienced user of linear regression is familiar with that phenomenon. Except in degenerate cases, we can always perfectly fit n sample points if we use $n - 1$ independent variables plus a constant. How wonderful to have a model that explains our experimental results with no error whatsoever. Unfortunately, that is probably all it will explain. If the experiment is repeated, the new data will not fit the model derived from the old data. As a result of using so many free parameters (weights for variables), the model has been overfitted. Rather than being satisfied with using a few variables to provide a relatively simple explanation for the majority of the experimental results, an explanation which likely has universal application, we have zeroed in on characteristics of the data which are unique to that data set. In doing so, the more universal truths have diminished in relative importance.

Because of their large number of parameters, neural networks are far more sensitive to overfitting than most traditional statistical methods. Suppose that we have a three-layer feedforward network with 25 input neurons and 10 hidden neurons. That's 260 free parameters, not counting output weights! The author would feel uncomfortable training this network with any less than 500 training samples, and preferably many more.

Network Size Affects Training Set Size

Larger networks require larger training sets. When there are more input neurons, there is more opportunity for false random patterns to be learned. If there are only two inputs, a dozen or so training samples will probably cover every possible *error* pattern, at least for all practical purposes. There are only so many unusual patterns possible. But if there are 100 inputs, the chance of some pattern being repeated many times in the training set is much higher. For example, the probability of any *specified* input being unusually high throughout a large fraction of the training set is very small. If we don't specify which input, though, and there are many, the probability that *some* one of them is unusually high throughout much of the training set is much larger. If that happens, the trained network will expect that particular input to be high when it has no just cause for doing so.

Overfitting is also more likely when the model is large. Weights connecting the inputs to the hidden layer usually comprise the majority of the free parameters. If there are n inputs and m hidden neurons, there will be $(n + 1) * m$ weights. For networks that solve real world problems, n is often in the hundreds, and m is nearly always at least 5, and perhaps as much as 20 or more. That's a lot of free parameters. The only way to prevent the network from learning unique characteristics of the training set, to the detriment of learning universal characteristics, is to flood it with so many examples that it cannot possibly learn all of their idiosyncracies. As a rule of thumb, compute the number of weights in the network and double it to get the *minimum* number of training samples required. Double it again to get a better sample size. And don't forget to save out a separate bunch for validation after the network is trained!

Stratified Training Data

There is one situation in which an especially large number of training samples should be used. This is when the data is highly stratified. The presence of many subclasses in the training data necessitates larger training sets because communal random patterns are much more likely. Suppose that the characteristics of a subclass place it in a position in data space that is fairly isolated from other subclasses. Then we must rely on many training samples *from this subclass* to swamp out random patterns *common to members of this subclass*. If we have only five samples from this subclass, and fate conspires to contaminate all five of them with approximately the same random error pattern, this subclass will not be properly learned. When the network is later called upon to perform its duty, it will probably fail to recognize members of that subclass unless, by some rare chance, they happen to be contaminated with the same error pattern. This is a far more common occurrence than most people like to admit.

Borderline Cases

The majority of the training set collector's energy should be devoted to borderline cases. These are training samples that are very close to a decision boundary. Only a few of the easily classified samples suffice to teach the network how to respond to easy cases. There is no point in consuming extra training time processing cases that are superfluous. Also, it is not just time that is wasted. Algorithms that minimize the mean error across the training set will not devote sufficient attention to the cases that need the most attention if they can smugly reduce their mean error by learning the easy ones. If the training set is focused on difficult cases, the algorithm will not be able to avoid them.

Payment of extra attention to borderline cases can be automated. In this way, the researcher can simply collect a large number of samples without worrying about which cases may be difficult and which easy, and without being concerned over duplication. [Strand and Jones, 1992] have a procedure in which the error of each training case is considered during training. Those cases that are handled well by the partially trained network are set aside in a holding queue, while the learning algorithm focuses on the problem areas. To prevent the network from forgetting what it already learned, cases are retrieved periodically from the holding queue. Not only does this improve the final performance of the network, but it also has the nice side effect of speeding training by reducing the workload involved in cumulating weight update information across the training set.

[Davis and Hwang, 1992] take a different route toward the same end. First they fully train the network using the entire training set. Then they determine which members of the training set are closest to decision boundaries. These potentially troublesome samples are used to continue training the network. They report that this two-tiered approach can significantly improve performance.

Hidden Bias

One of the most dangerous phenomena in training set construction is accidental incorporation of human biases. These are learned by the network just as easily as any other pattern. The problem is that we may not know that the bias was learned until it is too late — if we ever get to know it at all. The disaster will be all the worse if it turns out that it was the *bias*, and nothing else, that was responsible for the network's apparently good behavior.

The author is familiar with one infamous experiment in which a neural network was trained to recognize shapes displayed on a computer screen. The training set builder was required to manually position a rectangle around known shapes, pressing keys to identify each shape as belonging to one of two classes. Since the rectangle was slightly larger than the shape, he was instructed to center the shape inside the rectangle. This was done for hundreds of sample shapes from each of the two classes. Training went excellently, with the training set being able to be perfectly reclassified. The same person then tested the network with unknown samples. It performed excellently, and the research team was jubilant. The jubilation vanished when an independent agent tested the network and saw very mediocre performance. The original trainer was called back, and in front of all he demonstrated superb results. The independent agent tried again and failed again. The mystery was solved when the training sets were displayed on a grid and carefully studied. The trainer had been unconsciously biased when "centering" the rectangle over the shape. Some facet of the shape for one class had led him consistently to place the rectangle a little high over the shape samples from that class, and the opposite had happened for the other class. The misplacement was so small as to go unnoticed by everyone involved. But the network didn't miss it. It faithfully learned that if the shape was a little below the rectangle's center, it was from class A, and if it was a little high it was from class B. When the independent party failed to exhibit the same prejudice as the trainer, the network was stymied.

Balancing the Classes

At least some consideration should always be given to the choice of how many members of each class or natural group should be present in the training set. Some neural network models, such as the probabilistic neural net, can implicitly adjust for unbalanced training sets. But others, such as the multilayer feedforward net, cannot do so without special training procedures. When a network learns by minimizing the mean error across the entire training set, the proportional representation in the training set can have a profound influence on the network's performance. If a particular subclass is disproportionally represented, the network will strive to optimize its performance when presented with members of that subclass, at the expense of members of other subclasses. By the same token, classes that have only token membership in the training set may not be handled well when the network is used.

Sometimes we may want to take advantage of this training property. It is possible to introduce an almost "Bayesian prior" effect. If we know in advance that when the network is used class A is twice as likely to appear as class B, then it may be reasonable to use twice as many members of class A as class B in the training set in order to improve its average performance. The same would be done if we know that errors in responding to members of class A are twice as expensive as errors in responding to members of class B. By unbalancing the training set this way, we give double the weight to errors in class A, hence encouraging the network to learn to perform better on class A than class B.

Before deliberately unbalancing a training set, we should give careful consideration to the reason for doing so. Always remember that Bayes' Principle of Equidistribution of Ignorance [Kendall and Stuart, vol. II] states that unless we have firm reason for doing so, we should leave all priors equal.

Fudging Cases

It is sometimes legitimate, even desirable, to generate cases in the training set with the aid of a random number generator. There are two principal reasons for doing so.

1) When it is expensive or impractical to collect a large number of samples, but we can accurately simulate samples, it is reasonable to do so.

2) When the population can be expected to emulate the training set except for superimposed random error, robustness can sometimes be increased by supplementing the training set with noisy samples.

An example of the first reason can be had from OCR (optical character recognition) software. Naturally, a neural network being trained to recognize individual characters can expect some sort of standardization. Uniform rules for positioning the character in the network's sensory grid will be established and used for both training and testing. Every font that the network will be expected to handle should be represented. But there are many variations that are impractical to sample for training. Edges of characters may be blurred or misplaced due to mechanical error. Parts of characters may be missing. Extraneous smudges may be present. Examples of these flaws are far more easily generated artificially than sampled. As long as our generation method accurately reflects reality, this is a useful technique.

An example of the second reason for randomly generating training cases occurs when the training data arises from physical processes that allow only noisy and/or expensive sampling. Of necessity, the foundation training set is small, and its measured values may be contaminated by random error. In this case, it is sometimes effective to generate additional training samples by adding random noise to the measured set. This may improve the ability of the trained network to handle the noisy samples that will later be presented to it. And it will certainly decrease the likelihood of overfitting. The use of jittered training samples is rigorously discussed in [Reed, Oh, and Marks, 1992].

16

Preparing Input Data

Just because neural networks are more robust than most standard statistical techniques doesn't mean that we can abuse them with impunity. This chapter discusses the care and feeding of the input and output layers.

Different network models impose different constraints on their training data. Some recommendations are universal, though. Since restrictions peculiar to a single network model are discussed thoroughly in the chapters devoted to those models, they will be only briefly mentioned here. This chapter will focus primarily on aspects of data preparation that have more widespread application.

General Considerations

Neural network practitioners must remember that they are not competing with their networks; they are working together as a team. Neural networks can sometimes produce such startlingly excellent results that there is a tendency to regard them as miracle workers. Viewed in this light, we feel that we can throw anything at them and they'll handle it. We may even develop the perverse attitude of *trying* to stump the very network on which our salary depends, just to see if we can do it. This attitude is perpetuated by the fact that often they *can* handle seemingly impossible problems. But always remember that data preparation can make the difference between a network that trains in five days and performs quite well, versus a network that trains in five minutes and performs excellently.

It may sound facetious, but one of the most important questions to ask oneself before asking a neural network to learn a collection of data is, "Can this problem be solved when presented this way?" If our purpose is exploratory, then it may be reasonable to throw data quickly and carelessly at a network. But few professionals have that luxury. Time is money, and the clock is ticking. Seasoned programmers have an adage: every hour spent planning is two hours saved coding. The same can apply to the training of neural networks. Your time may be expensive, but time spent waiting for a solution can be more expensive. And asking your manager to wait a week while a network trains, then finding out that it has learned rubbish, is embarrassing at best. Therefore, before pushing the start button, ask yourself if you are making the network's job as easy as you can. Have you given it enough of the right information? Have you screened out as much of the confusing and irrelevant information as possible? Are there any transformations that would make the data more straightforward? Have you left out any important samples in the hope that somehow the network will infer their existence? Are you asking it to solve more than one problem when you could break things down into individual problems to be solved by individual networks? All of these issues are well worth exploring *before* paying for computer time.

Types of Measurements

Measured variables can be categorized according to the type and degree of information they contain. Thinking about the type of each variable in an experiment can help the researcher to present them correctly to the network. The principal categories will now be defined.

Nominal Variables

Nominal variables are sometimes thought of as naming things. They do not have any numerical value. Measured values of a nominal variable never have relationships like "greater than" or "less than." The only mathematical relationships germane to nominal variables are equality and inequality.

A variable called "fruit type" which can take on the values "apple", "peach", and "banana" is a nominal variable. Sex is the archetypical nominal variable. Numerical data can also be nominal. Zip codes and telephone area codes are classic examples.

The fundamental test of whether or not a variable is nominal is made by answering the question, "Do I want to imply an order relationship by means of the values of this variable?" If so, the variable belongs to a higher information category.

Nominal variables are almost always presented to a network by using as many neurons as there are values that the variable can take on. Exactly one of the neurons will be turned on according to the value of the variable. All of the other neurons will be turned off. This is called *one-of-n encoding*. The only exception to this rule is if the variable is binary, taking on one of only two possible values. In this case, one neuron is used. It is turned on for one value, and off for the other.

For many network models it is theoretically possible to encode nominal variables having few values into one neuron. For example, if a fruit variable can take on three values, we might code apples as fully off, peaches as half on, and bananas as fully on. Many networks are capable of reacting to inputs coded this way and can learn outputs coded this way. However, learning is usually slowed considerably when this is done. Also, it is aesthetically disquieting due to the fact that you are implicitly assigning an order relationship when none is deserved. When it comes time to submit your paper for publication, the reviewers will not be pleased.

Traditional one-of-n encoding does have a special problem, particularly when it is used for outputs. The problem stems from the fact that, especially when the number of categories is large, the data vectors are all similar to each other. For example, suppose that we have eight categories. The activation vector for a case belonging to the third category would be (0, 0, 1, 0, 0, 0, 0, 0), while another case's activation vector might be (0, 0, 0, 0, 0, 0, 1, 0). The coordinates in six of the eight dimensions are exactly the same for both cases. Now suppose that we are trying to teach a neural network to respond with such vectors as outputs. If it simply responds to each and every case by turning off all of its outputs, only one of them will be wrong! This will produce a relatively small mean square error. In practice, a weight configuration producing this result may be a strong local minimum, having a broad domain of attraction featuring nothing more than large negative biases. Not good. Even when such vectors are used as inputs, the small variation relative to dimensionality among cases can sometimes be a problem, though rarely as serious as when they are outputs.

The solution lies in projecting the basis vectors into a space of one less dimension, where they will form an equilateral figure. Not surprisingly, this operation is often called *equilateral coding*. Every possible vector endpoint will be equidistant from every other possible vector endpoint, and this distance will be the maximum possible. This is illustrated in Figure 16.1. We also gain the slight but significant advantage of having one less neuron. On the other hand, if we are constructing a classifier, we lose having an easy reject category (all neurons off).

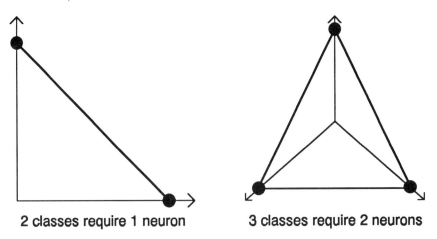

2 classes require 1 neuron   3 classes require 2 neurons

Fig. 16.1: Equilateral coding

We already know that if we have a strictly binary decision, we should use exactly one output neuron, coding the classes as minimum and maximum activation. This is the degenerate case of equilateral coding, as shown in the left half of Figure 16.1. The two-neuron approach produces the coordinate system shown as vertical and horizontal axes. The two classes, in which exactly one of the two output neurons is activated, are shown as black circles. Encoding this information into one neuron results in the new one-dimensional coordinate axis connecting the circles. The classes lie at opposite extremes of this axis, representing minimum and maximum activation.

The right half of that figure shows the case of three classes. Ordinary one-of-n coding results in three coordinate axes, with the corresponding neuron activations as shown. Observe that for any class, its neuron activations are all zero except for one that is fully activated. The three points in 3-space define a two-dimensional plane. The positions of the three points in this 2-space define the corresponding activations of the two output neurons.

If this method is used to train outputs, we need a way to decode test set outputs into classes. This is trivially done by computing the Euclidean distance between the output vector and each of the class basis vectors. That having the minimum distance is the output class.

Code for computing the equilateral activation vectors is shown below. The algorithm is from [Guiver and Klimasauskas, 1991]. The subroutine is given the number of categories and a range flag. If the range flag is nonzero, the activations are returned in the range -1 to 1. This is suitable for network inputs and some activation function outputs. If zero, the activations are from 0.1 to 0.9, which is suitable for logistic activation function outputs. It computes a matrix having as many rows as there are categories, and one less column. Each row contains the neuron activations for a single category.

```
void equilat (
    int n ,                    // Number of values, at least 2
    double *mat ,              // Output n by n-1 matrix of activations
    int range                  // 0 for .1 to .9, 1 for -1 to 1
    )


{
    int i, j, k, nm1 ;
    double r, f ;


/*
    Initialize mat[0,0]=-1 and mat[1,0]=1
*/

    nm1 = n - 1 ;
    mat[0] = -1.0 ;
    mat[nm1] = 1.0 ;
```

```
/*
   Recursively build rest of matrix
*/


   for (k=2 ; k<n ; k++) {

      // Scale matrix so far
      r = (double) k ;
      f = sqrt ( r * r - 1.0 ) / r ;    // Scaling factor
      for (i=0 ; i<k ; i++) {           // Rows of mat so far
         for (j=0 ; j<k-1 ; j++)        // And cols
            mat[i*nm1+j] *= f ;         // Scale it
         }

      // Append a column of all -1/k

      r = -1.0 / r ;                    // Value of new column
      for (i=0 ; i<k ; i++)             // Rows of mat so far
         mat[i*nm1+k-1] = r ;           // New column on right

      // Append new row of all 0's except 1 at end

      for (i=0 ; i<k-1 ; i++)
         mat[k*nm1+i] = 0.0 ;
      mat[k*nm1+k-1] = 1.0 ;
      }


/*
   The above algorithm left the values in -1 to 1.
   If they need to be rescaled .1 to .9, do it now.
*/

   if (range)
      return ;

   i = n * nm1 ;
   while (i--)
      mat[i] = 0.4 * mat[i] + 0.5 ;
}
```

The usefulness of the above recoding is problem dependent. It is almost certainly wasted effort if the number of categories is small. It is usually wasted on input data. However, it may help learning if used for an output variable having a large number of categories. It may also be helpful even for inputs with small numbers of categories if used repeatedly, thus saving a significant number of neurons.

Ordinal Variables

Next up from nominal variables in the "amount of information" hierarchy comes ordinal variables. Variables measured on an ordinal scale have order relationships. The values that can be taken on by an ordinal variable can be placed in a unique order. "Greater than" and "less than" have meaning. But the actual numerical values of ordinal variables *do not convey any information whatsoever beyond the order itself.* For example, suppose that we measure an ordinal variable for three subjects. The measured values are 3, 4, and 250, respectively. All we know is that the second subject measures greater than the first subject on this variable, and the third subject measures greater than both of the others. We cannot say that the third subject is greater than the second to a larger degree than the second is greater than the first. The ability to do so would imply a higher type of variable than just ordinal.

The classic example of an ordinal variable is ranking within a group. Let's say that the CIA wants to train a network to predict a person's propensity toward treasonous activity based on high school class rank, among other things. Perhaps they are hesitant about using numerical grade point averages because they suspect that a person's position *relative* to his or her peers is more important than his or her *absolute* position. Rank data within the class would be an appropriate way to measure this quantity.

When rank data is used, we cannot compare differences. In a class of 200, suppose person A ranks 20, person B ranks 25, and person C ranks 70. It might be that the grade point averages of persons B and C are very close, but their widely differing ranks are due to a cluster of people with approximately that average. We simply do not know. All we can say is that A is less than B, and B is less than C.

The usual way to prepare rank data for presentation to a neural network is by a percentile transformation. For each measured value in the ranked group, count the number of cases in the group whose values are less than or equal to the case being transformed. Divide by the total number of cases. This gives a fraction ranging from nearly zero to one. This fraction is usually expressed as a percentage. In this way, we remove the effect of the group size, standardizing the measurements to a uniform range of zero to one.

When we apply a percentile transformation, we must think carefully about the population on which we base the counting. There are two different approaches, and they produce different results. In the CIA task, the information desired was the student's position relative to those people with whom he or she worked and played. Therefore, the class was used for the counting. National scholarship examinations often report a person's percentile score based on national results. If the CIA converted a person's grade-point average to a rank based on averages of high school students across the country, information of a very different sort would be presented to the neural network. Something would have been lost, and something gained. The position of the student relative to his or her peers would be gone. The student might have a national ranking in the 80th percentile. If his or her classmates all ranked in the 80s, he or she is at the bottom of his or her class. If they all ranked in the 70s, he or she is at the top of his or her class. We do not know which is the case, given only national ranking. But we have gained a more global picture of the student's abilities. The effect of attending a good or poor school has been overcome by including so many schools in the count. Neither method is right or wrong in general. *The question of which to use revolves around what we want to measure.*

An additional complication ensues if we deliberately use a non-local ranking system. Now we must be sure that the same basis population is used for both training and testing the network. Some aspect of the information pertaining to rank within a class is probably valid for any school, as it conveys basic psychological facts. But suppose that we used all schools in the student's state for the basis population. In other words, the student's percentile rank is computed relative to all students in his or her state. Local information concerning the position is his or her own class has now vanished. We have a more globally oriented variable. What if we train the network with data from only one or a few states? If we attempt to use the network with data collected from other states, we must suspect its decisions. These states may have very different grade distributions than those used in training the network. This will have a confounding influence. Is the student's position relative to his or her home state the information we really want? Probably not. This is a very subtle way in which we can end up training the network using data not representative of that which it will be called upon to work with later.

Although rank data is one of the most common types of ordinal data, it is not the only type. Ordinal data can also arise out of categories that have an order relationship. Climatological plant-hardiness zones are one example. Food grades are another. Certainly, grade A eggs are "better" in some sense than grade B eggs, and those in turn are better than grade C. But how much better? We cannot say, so egg grade would be an ordinal variable.

Ordinal variables are often presented to neural network inputs as *thermometers*. We use as many neurons as there are values for the ordinal variable, minus one. If that is too many, as would be the case of percentiles which can take on a great number of values, we use an "appropriate" number of neurons and quantize the variable. We might, for instance, use 9 neurons, breaking the percentiles into "less than 10", "10 to 19", et cetera. Arbitrarily assign an order to the neurons and map each neuron to an ordinal value other than the smallest. Then, for a given input value, turn on the corresponding neuron *and all neurons less than it*. If the input is the smallest value, leave all the neurons off. In the above case of 10 neurons representing a percentile score, an input value of 35% would be represented by turning on the first 3 neurons.

A thermometer representation of egg grades is shown in Figure 16.2. The four egg grades require three neurons. The lowest grade, D, turns off all three neurons. Higher grades turn on successive neurons.

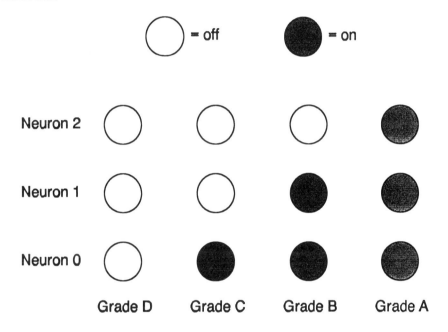

Fig. 16.2: Thermometer representation of ordinal data

There is no theoretical need for turning on neurons below the one designating the variable's value. The same information could be conveyed by turning on exactly one neuron. However, experience has shown that training is usually faster with this method. It more closely corresponds to the physical reality of ordinal data. Each neuron makes a contribution to a decision, and larger values retain the contributions of smaller values.

If there is a very large number of ordinal values, and keeping fine distinctions is necessary, it may make more sense to use just one neuron and set its activation proportional to the ordinal value. This is not usually done. In general, true ordinal data does not suffer when moderately quantized. Only higher-order data needs full precision. However, there is no compelling reason to avoid the one-neuron approach if it is deemed more satisfactory. It is just that the thermometer method fits the ordinal structure better, and its effectiveness has been proven by much experience. If the single-neuron method works in your application, use it.

Interval Variables

The second-highest order of measured data is achieved with *interval* scales. These measurements share the property of order relationships with ordinal variables. If we have three interval measurements, A, B, and C, it makes sense to rank them as A < B < C or some other ordering. But with interval data, we can go one step further: we can also rank *differences* between measurements. We can say things like (C - B) > (B - A). Now, if A = 4, B = 5, and C = 250, we can genuinely say that C is very much larger than B, while B is only a little larger than A. This was not possible with ordinal data.

Variables measured on an interval scale are almost always presented to a neural network using exactly one neuron. The variables must be scaled in such a way as to be commensurate with the model's neuron-activation limits. Care must be taken that the scaling is done so that the data used in training will be commensurate with that used in testing. It would not do, for example, to scale the training data based on the minimum and maximum values in the training set, then scale a batch of test data based on the extremes in the test set. The scaling must be done in a universally applicable way.

Probably the most common scaling method employed is simple linear mapping of the variable's practical extremes to the network's practical extremes. In the unusual case that a measured value goes beyond the limit, the value would be truncated to that limit. Let the variable's maximum and minimum values expected in normal use be designated V_{max} and V_{min} respectively. Let the network's practical limits be A_{max} and A_{min}. For a feedforward network with logistic activation functions, output activation limits would typically be 0.9 and 0.1, respectively. Inputs, of course, have no theoretical limits, but stability is usually improved by using comparable limits. We scale an observed value V to a presentable value A with a simple formula.

$$A = r \left(V - V_{min} \right) + A_{min}$$
$$= r V + \left(A_{min} - r V_{min} \right)$$
$$r = \frac{A_{max} - A_{min}}{V_{max} - V_{min}}$$

16-1

If the variable was used to train an output neuron, we need the ability to unscale activation levels to obtain meaningful values for the variable when the network is used. This is done by trivially inverting the preceding formula.

$$V = \frac{(A - A_{min})}{r} + V_{min}$$

$$= \frac{A}{r} + \left(V_{min} - \frac{A_{min}}{r} \right)$$

16-2

Measured variables often have an approximately normal distribution. If a variable is unimodal, nearly symmetrically distributed about its mean, and virtually never has significant values extremely far from its mean, we may want to employ a more sophisticated normalization based on its mean and standard deviation. In practice, this scaling will often turn out to be almost identical to that provided by Equation 16-1. However, if the data meets the above assumptions, this scaling has more theoretical (and perhaps even practical) appeal. A random variable is standardized to a *Z-score* by subtracting its mean and dividing by its standard deviation:

$$Z = \frac{x - \mu}{\sigma}$$

16-3

This removes all effects of offset and measurement scale. If two researchers conduct essentially the same experiment, but one measures the subjects' weight fully dressed and in units of kilograms, while the other measures weight naked and in units of pounds, their data would not be directly comparable. Scaling to a Z-score reduces the measurements to comparable units.

Sometimes we have a theoretical basis for knowing the mean and standard deviation of our variable. If not, they are easily estimated from a sample:

$$\hat{\mu} = \frac{1}{n} \sum_{i=0}^{n-1} x_i$$

$$\hat{\sigma} = \sqrt{\frac{1}{n-1} \sum_{i=0}^{n-1} (x_i - \hat{\mu})^2}$$

16-4

Recall that we divide by $n - 1$ rather than n in the above formula because we are estimating the standard deviation of the population from a sample. The exact sample standard deviation, obtained by dividing by n, would, on the average, slightly underestimate the true population standard deviation.

It is assumed that the sample is large enough that we can have faith in the quality of our estimators. Methods for dealing with that issue would take us too far from the subject at hand. Consult any standard statistics text for details.

Simply scaling to a Z-score is not generally sufficient for our purposes, as the scaled values would still exceed the activation limits implicit in many neural network models. We must first do the Z scaling, then apply Equation 16-1 to the practical limits of the Z-scores to bring things in line with what the network demands. Now we come to a somewhat thorny problem. Z-scores have no theoretical bounds. They can approach positive and negative infinity. Luckily, if the variable is approximately normally distributed, the Z-scores definitely have practical limits. The following table shows the probability of the absolute value of a Z-score exceeding some limits.

Z limit	P(exceeding)
1.28	0.20
1.64	0.10
1.96	0.05
2.58	0.01

Statisticians would call these "two-tailed" probabilities, since they are the probability that a Z-score will either be greater than the limit or be less than the negative of the limit. All we need to do is choose a probability that we are comfortable with, then consult this table to find corresponding practical limits. We would set V_{max} equal to the value shown, and V_{min} equal to the negative of it, using Equation 16-1 to do the final scaling from Z-score to neuron activation.

The choice of a comfortable limit from the above table involves a tradeoff between the usable range and the probability of having to truncate values. If we pick a large limit, there is only a very small probability that an observed value will exceed this limit and have to be truncated at the neuron's activation limit. On the other hand, the majority of observed values will be scaled into a relatively narrow range, limiting the diversity of values presented to the network. This can impede learning. Conversely, picking a small limit will allow the full range of activations to be attained for most observations. But a significant number of extreme values will have to be truncated, resulting in some loss of information. It has been the experience of the author that usually this is the lesser of the two evils when the variable is presented to neurons having firm activation limits. In this case, it is generally better to err on the side of a small limit. Of course, frequently the variable is presented to neurons having no firm activation limits. We may only want to scale the variables for reasons of conformity. This would be the case when applying it to the input layer of a feedforward network. Then, it is better to err on the side of larger limits. This will result in less loss of information, and the compressed range will be made up for by the network when its input weights are learned. In fact, if the network does not impose firm limits, we may wish to avoid the second scaling altogether, using Z-scores directly as inputs. The fact that Z-scores are balanced between negative and positive values slightly helps learning in many cases.

It is wasteful of computer time to do the Z-score scaling and neuron-limit scaling separately. They can be combined into one operation:

$$A = r(\frac{x-\mu}{\sigma} - V_{min}) + A_{min}$$

$$= \frac{r}{\sigma}x + (A_{min} - r(\frac{\mu}{\sigma} + V_{min})) \qquad 16\text{-}5$$

where r in the above equation is as defined in Equation 16-1, noting that V_{min} and V_{max} in that equation and the above equation are from the previous table of Z-score limits, not referring to the raw data itself. The above formula is inverted to convert output-neuron activations to original variable scales:

$$x = \frac{\sigma}{r}A + (\mu + \sigma(V_{min} - \frac{A_{min}}{r})) \qquad 16\text{-}6$$

In summary, it should be stated that this relatively complex procedure of scaling by both standard deviation and neuron limits will in practice usually give results that are nearly identical to those obtained with the much more straightforward procedure of scaling based on practical data limits. This is because the pragmatic limits will usually be close to the limits implied by the variable's mean and standard deviation, resulting in the same ultimate transformation constants. But there are two reasons for favoring the more complex method if the variable's distribution allows it.

1) It removes the arbitrary nature of picking limits for the variable. The limits are picked by a more objective criterion, although the choice of the probability limit is somewhat arbitrary.

2) Scaling of variables can be easily automated. Rather than requiring the user to choose limits, automatic scaling based on mean and standard deviation can be incorporated into the computer program.

Ratio Variables

Ratio data is the highest information scale. It is identical to interval data, except that the meaning of zero in an interval scale is arbitrary, whereas zero in a ratio scale is a true zero. The Fahrenheit and Celsius temperature scales are both interval, because zero is arbitrarily defined. The Kelvin scale, on the other hand, is a ratio scale. Zero degrees Kelvin is *absolute* zero; there is no molecular motion at that temperature. Weight is ratio data, since zero grams really means zero.

Only in ratio data are ratios meaningful. It makes no sense to say that a temperature of 40 degrees Fahrenheit is twice the temperature of 20 degrees. But a weight of 40 pounds *is* twice a weight of 20 pounds.

For neural networks, ratio data is usually treated identically to interval data. The only possible exception is that sometimes we may want to consider the possibility of using zero as the practical lower limit on ratio data, rather than some more arbitrarily chosen limit. This is because zero has real meaning for ratio data. But that decision is problem dependent.

Is Scaling Always Necessary?

The short answer to that question is, "No, but it's almost always recommended." This section will explore why this is so.

First, we must distinguish between when scaling MUST be done, as opposed to when we are able to choose. If a variable is being used to train output neurons, and the output neurons have an activation function with bounded range, we certainly must limit the target activations to values that can be comfortably learned. Some network models, such as the Kohonen, have strict limits on their input values. In these cases, there is no choice allowed. We scale.

Sometimes, though, we have the option of working with raw data. It is possible to design multiple-layer feedforward networks with the identity function as the activation function of the output neurons. (Of course, hidden neurons must still be nonlinear, or the network is reduced to linear regression!) Such networks can have unbounded outputs, so no scaling of output variables is theoretically needed. And feedforward networks have no implicit limits on their inputs, so no scaling of input variables is needed. Nevertheless, scaling to uniform ranges is still recommended.

One of the reasons for uniform scaling is to initially equalize the importance of variables. Theoretically, it should be possible for a network to learn the relative importance of variables by adjusting input weights. If one variable has an order of magnitude of 1,000,000, while another is about 0.000001, the network *should* be able to learn to use tiny input weights for the first variable and huge weights for the second. But that is a very iffy *should*. It is asking a lot of the learning algorithm to traverse such a range. In fact, many learning algorithms impose fixed limits on their weights to prevent getting stuck out in the far forty. These algorithms will simply not be able to learn such extreme data. We can make the network's life a lot easier by giving it data scaled in such a way that all weights can remain in small, predictable ranges.

This becomes even more important when the data is being learned by output neurons. Most training algorithms minimize the total error of all outputs. If the output variables are unequally scaled, those with larger variabilities will be favored, as they will dominate the error sum. This can have profound consequences and is a problem that should always be considered.

Another reason for scaling the data is to improve interpretability of network weights. We may want to look at the weights learned by our network, in hopes of making some sense of what the network uses to make its decisions. Under the best of conditions that can be a very difficult task. If we have to take input scaling into account simultaneously, our job becomes even more difficult.

Transformations

If the distribution of a variable is "unusual", it may be more difficult for the neural network to learn to use it, even if it is linearly scaled to a reasonable range. This is because the information content in the variable is too distorted. Small but important variation may be compressed into a relatively narrow area, while other variation is spread out in a wider range than its importance justifies. In this case, we should investigate nonlinear transformations.

There are primarily three properties that we would like our network's data to possess. If it is found lacking, the goal of nonlinear transformation is to endow the data with these properties as much as possible. Note that they overlap to some degree. Also, they cannot always be all satisfied. But it behooves us to do our best. These desirable properties are as follows:

Homoscedasticity - The variance of the data should be approximately the same for all values it takes on. It often happens that larger measured values of a variable will have larger variances. That is not good.

Normality - Strictly speaking, a normal distribution is not particularly important to a neural network. In fact, there is some evidence that flat distributions are learned most easily. What is important is that the distribution be approximately symmetrical and not have a heavy tail (frequent wild values).

Additivity - Most practical neural networks have more than one input variable. It helps the network to learn if the contributions of these variables are as additive as possible. When, for example, it is the product or quotient of two variables that is most important to the decision, we are burdening the network more than we need to. Multiplicative relationships can be changed to additive by taking logs.

Sometimes we must make difficult choices between these properties, finding that we cannot possess all three at once. In this instance, it may be worthwhile to do several different transformations, using the results of all of them as network inputs. With multiple regression and many other standard statistical techniques, this is a recipe for disaster due to the introduction of near singularity in matrices that must be inverted. But for neural networks, it can be immensely useful. On the other hand, we will often be pleasantly surprised when we find that a transformation that gives us one of these properties gives us the others as well.

We can get an excellent indication of the need to transform a variable if we plot its sample distribution. If the plot looks like Figure 16.3, it is a sure sign that we need to apply a compressing transformation to it.

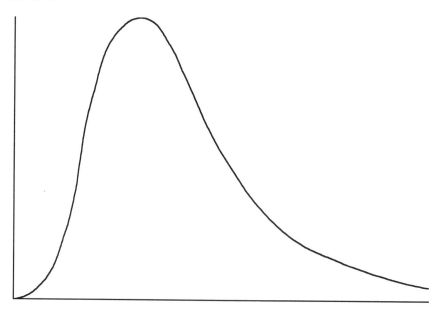

Fig. 16.3: A sure candidate for a compressing transformation

The most commonly employed compressing transformation is the logarithm. Don't forget to offset the variable if it can take on values of zero! Other common compressing transforms are the square root and cube root.

Sometimes we know without even examining a plot that we need to do a log transform. Data whose variation is more meaningful when defined relative to its value is one example. This would include most economic figures, such as stock price. A $5 variation in a stock price has one meaning for a $10 stock, and another meaning for a $100 stock. Data which are *counts* of large populations should nearly always be subjected to a logarithmic transformation. The truth of the matter is that a vast proportion of the data fed to neural networks should be so treated.

J. Tukey, cited in [Acton, 1959], suggests several special purpose transformations for count variables from small populations. Our measured variable may be a count of members of a population which meet some criterion. Perhaps we periodically remove 10 widgets from the assembly line and count the number of them whose oozle lies within 1 millimeter of their snoozle. This quantity is an input to a neural network that controls the factory's oozle positioner. Unfortunately, the variance of this count depends on the probability of a misplaced oozle, since it will follow a binomial distribution. The traditional approach to stabilizing the variance of a binomial variate is

$$y = \arcsin\left(\sqrt{\frac{x}{n}}\right) \qquad 16\text{-}7$$

Tukey's improved transformation is

$$y = \arcsin\left(\sqrt{\frac{x}{n+1}}\right) + \arcsin\left(\sqrt{\frac{x+1}{n+1}}\right) \qquad 16\text{-}8$$

A similar problem occurs when we are counting events that happen in a fixed-time interval. This might be persons arriving in a service queue, noise pulses in a communications line, or any other random variable arising from cumulations of random events. Such random variables often follow a Poisson distribution. The traditional remedy is to take the square root of the variable. Tukey proposed the following improved transformation:

$$y = \sqrt{x} + \sqrt{x+1} \qquad 16\text{-}9$$

We should develop the habit of always examining the distributions of variables that we intend to present to a neural network. Then, after applying supposedly appropriate transformations, examine the distributions again! Neural networks are not nearly as sensitive to "unusual" distributions as most traditional techniques are. Neural networks can work with variables having distributions that standard linear models could not possibly handle. Yet why ask them to do so when it may not be necessary? Time spent taking care of this detail can be paid back handsomely in improved performance and training time.

Circular Discontinuity

Sometimes the variables we present to neural networks are fundamentally circular. The position of a rotating shaft is an obvious example. The azimuth angle at which we are viewing a solid object is another. Even color, measured on many popular scales, is circular. These variables introduce a special problem due to the fact that they have a discontinuity. If we define the position of a rotating object as being an angle measured from 0 to 360 degrees, we have a serious problem when the object passes from 360 on to 0. If we use a single neuron to encode this value, we find that two extremely close values, 359 degrees and 1 degree, are represented by two extremely different activations, nearly off and nearly fully on. Neural networks are miracle workers sometimes, but this is asking too much of them. Variables with circular discontinuity are very difficult to learn.

One simple way to solve this problem is to discretize the variable into categories and assign one neuron for each category. For example, we may use eight neurons. One is on when the angle is from 0 to 45 degrees, the next for 45 to 90, et cetera. This has two disadvantages. Obviously, either we lose a lot of precision or we use a lot of neurons. The other problem is that this method is useful mainly for input neurons. When we train outputs this way, run-time interpretation can be difficult. After presenting an unknown sample to the network's inputs, we must choose the most-activated output neuron in this variable's group in order to make the decision. Often there will be no clear winner. This may force arbitrary decisions to be made, always an uncomfortable happening.

The best way to handle circular variables is to encode them using two or three neurons. Two are sufficient. Three are sometimes best in special cases. We find new variables, functions of the circular variable, which change smoothly as the circular variable changes, and whose values taken together are in a one-to-one relationship with the circular variable. Additionally, we would like the new variables, taken as a group, to convey as much detail as possible about the circular variable, no matter what that value may be. It would not do to have variables that changed only in the fifth significant digit in response to a 10 percent change in the circular variable for some value of that variable.

The most common choice for new variables is the (sine, cosine) pair.

$$f_1(x) = \sin(x)$$
$$f_2(x) = \cos(x)$$

16-10

Each new variable changes smoothly; they together uniquely define (and are uniquely defined by) the circular variable; and they convey good information at all values when taken together. At those values for the circular variable where the sine conveys little information (near 90 and 270 degrees), the cosine is very sensitive, and the converse is also true.

View Angles

There are at least two cases when it may be preferable to use three new variables to encode a single circular variable. One arises when some symmetry of other variables around the axis of rotation can be expected. This would happen, for example, if we are visually inspecting a three-dimensional solid and using its azimuth (radial position) as a variable. If we are looking at it downward from an elevated position, most objects will have a unique appearance at every rotation. (Of course, cylinders won't. And some shapes may have multiple symmetries. We ignore this possibility here.) But if we are looking at it from a direction nearly perpendicular to the axis of rotation, and the object has symmetry about a vertical plane, we may have trouble distinguishing between some views. See Figure 16.4 for an illustration of this phenomenon.

If the front edge is difficult for the network to "see", a common occurrence, then the two views shown will not be able to be separated well at low view angles. Assuming without loss of generality that the object's principal plane of symmetry is aligned with one of the horizontal coordinate axes, then the sign of one of the new functions (sine, cosine) will be of little use. Thus, we are inspired to use the absolute value of that function, rather than its actual value. The third variable would then be the sign of the variable whose absolute value was used. We obviously lose no information. But we have just made the network's life a lot easier by separating the information that is always useful from that which is largely rubbish.

The separation just described is particularly worthwhile when the variable is being learned by outputs. Suppose that we are training the network with views at plus and minus 20 degrees (among others). The new (sine, cosine) variables would be (0.342, 0.940) and (-0.342, 0.940) respectively. If the two views are nearly indistinguishable by the network, but we are asking an output neuron to learn 0.342 for one view and -0.342 for the other, we can drive it to the brink of insanity. The end result is that it will not learn to do either well. Mathematicians would say that we are trying to teach it something that is not a function, since a single input (the view that is identical for both positions) results in different outputs. If, on the

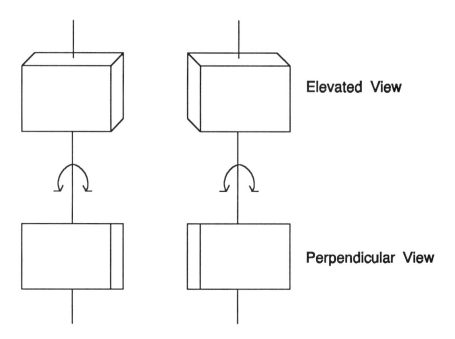

Fig. 16.4: Symmetry problem for low view angles

other hand, we use three neurons and train them to respond with (0.342, 0.940, 1.0) and (0.342, 0.940, -1.0), respectively, at least the network should be able to get the important information learned. It may not always do well with the third neuron. But when it doesn't get it right, it will be because the information is fundamentally missing rather than because of any weakness in the network itself.

Hue

Another case in which it may be preferable to use three neurons to encode a circular variable, rather than the two that are sufficient, is when there is a physical reason for doing so. A classic example of this is when the variable is color, expressed as a hue. Raster displays, printers, television broadcasters, and people who regularly work with color almost always do so in a three-variable system. One common one is RGB: red, green, blue. A hue, such as "light mauve", might be expressed as so many parts red, so many green, and so many blue. Colors are often represented cyclically, as in the hexagram shown in Figure 16.5. If the variable being presented to the network is limited to a few discrete colors, it is usually best to treat it as a nominal variable. Use one neuron for each color, turning on exactly one neuron according to the color value. If many colors are possible, we are better off treating it as interval data. In this case, it would be suicide in many applications to use one neuron, encoding it according to

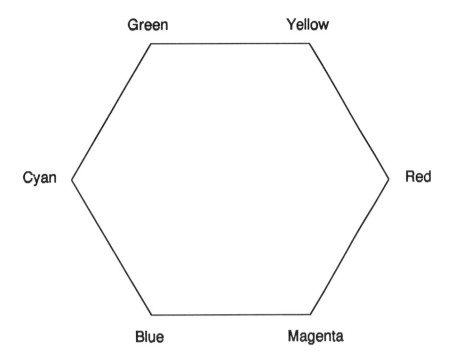

Fig. 16.5: Cyclic color representation

wavelength. Granted, some applications that are physically sensitive to the actual wavelength may do well if we code red as low activation, increasing until we get to violet being fully activated. But many other applications are grounded in a reality much closer to the cyclic relationship illustrated in Figure 16.5. We could, of course, get away with using just two neurons. Transform the red-to-violet range to 0–360 degrees, then activate the neurons according to the sine and cosine of that angle. It would often be more pleasing and physically meaningful, though, to transform the color to RBG levels and activate three neurons according to those levels. The transformation algorithms are very simple, but too tediously repetitive to show here. They can be found in any good computer graphics text. One of the best is [Foley et al., 1990].

Outliers

A previous section dealt with data having outlying values that are correct, being a natural product of the variable's distribution. This section tackles the problem of what to do about outlying values that very well may not be correct. Data collection instruments occasionally hiccough. Noise creeps into communication lines. Keyboard operators may even make data entry errors. How serious are these problems? How can we detect them? How can we correct them? Detailed answers to these questions must be found in appropriate statistics and data analysis textbooks. This section will briefly review aspects of the problem which are particularly relevant to neural networks.

We must lead off with a stern warning against being overly zealous in rejection of nonconformist data. Unless we have firm a priori reason to believe that our data may be tainted, we must restrain our desire to make things pretty. There are two principles to keep in mind when facing the data rejection dilemma.

First, remember that some abnormality is normal. By definition of the task, we are examining the outliers of our data collection. In any group, there *will be* outliers. Nearly 90 percent of a normal distribution lies within 1.5 standard deviations of its mean. Yet even a pristine normally distributed collection of 100 samples can be expected to have at least one data point 2.5 standard deviations away. On a scatter plot, that point may glare out at us. And it doesn't take much departure from normality to increase this effect dramatically. So one rule of thumb is that we usually shouldn't reject a point unless it is *really* wild.

The other important principle of data rejection is that we *must* completely sample the possibilities inherent in the data distribution. If our training set is not representative of the data on which the network will be tested, we will be wasting our time. Even if a suspicious sample is so wild that it cannot possibly be an expected outlier from the same distribution as the rest of the data, consider the possibility that it is from another, perfectly valid, distribution. Perhaps more is going on in the experiment than we realize. To perform an out-of-hand rejection of an observed value is to bury our heads in the sand. Unless we can satisfy ourselves beyond a reasonable doubt that the observed value is erroneous, we should endeavor to find an explanation for the value and perhaps modify our collection procedure so as to include its relatives.

Another argument in favor of keeping questionable outliers is the innate robustness of most neural network models. Researchers accustomed to traditional linear techniques are rightfully frightened of outliers. A formula based on squared terms derived from raw data, such as linear regression, can be tossed asunder by a single point out in the boondocks. But most neural networks accommodate such points far better. Layer networks having sigmoid activation functions have "data normalizers" built right into them. For example, if a neuron having a logistic activation function has a net input of 2.5, its output will be 0.92, a reasonable value. If a wild data point drives the net input to that neuron up to 1,000,000, its output will only increase to slightly less than 1.0, having absorbed the shock quite well. Naturally, we still face the problem of asking it to learn an incorrect piece of information, assuming, of course, that the information *is* incorrect. If the training set is reasonably large, though, this is no problem. For networks that learn by minimizing the mean error across the training set, rare outliers will have a comparatively small impact on the learned weights, being first tamed by the squashing function, then swamped out by the masses of correct data.

Some networks even have an implicit ability to process wild data without its having an effect on learning of the "normal" data. The probabilistic neural network (page 201) stands out in that category. Unless the smoothing parameter is unusually large, unique data points will be so separated from the rest of the data that they will make essentially no contribution to the potential functions that determine the network's response. That is, of course, unless the unusual sample point was meaningful, and a relative is encountered when the network is used. In that case, the wayward point will make a most valuable contribution! If the goal is classification, and "unusual" data is expected, this is often the network of choice.

Discarding Data

Now that the reader has hopefully been convinced that discarding data is a last resort, we will give a few hints as to how the decision to discard may and may not be made. The most obvious (and generally least desirable) method is to estimate the mean and standard deviation of the sample, assume that it is normally distributed, and decide based on Z-scores. Recall that the Z-score of a sample point is computed by subtracting the population mean, then dividing by the standard deviation (Equation 16-3). Under the assumption of normality, we can easily find in standard statistics texts the probability of getting random samples with Z-scores as extreme as any attained value. Knowing, for example, that there is only about a one-quarter of one percent chance of getting a sample with an absolute Z-score of 3 or more might lead us to reject all data points whose absolute Z-scores exceed 3. This, though, would be foolhardy, as even trivial departures from the assumption of normality can greatly increase the probability of Z-scores this large.

A more sensible approach is to drop, or at least relax, the assumption of normality. Unfortunately, this is quite difficult. Nonparametric outlier tests are discussed slightly in [Acton, 1959] and in [Kendall and Stuart, vol. 2]. A more in-depth treatment of outlier rejection can be found in [Hald, 1952]. One of the thorniest issues involved in these tests is the decision of how many data points are suspicious. What if, as is often the case, there is a continuum of "outliers?" The test of those that are farthest out can depend on whether or not we include the marginal cases in the reference set.

It is the strong opinion of the author that automated rejection of neural network training variable outliers should *never* be done. The recommended method is to plot a sample histogram. Careful scrutiny and experienced judgment will invariably triumph over blind application of statistics. The recently graduated, new researcher may be surprised at how many times histograms similar to that shown in Figure 16.6 will appear.

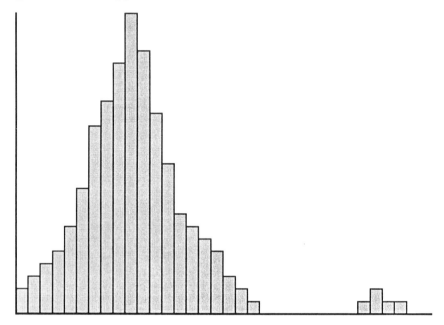

Fig. 16.6: Why we avoid automated outlier rejection

When we see histograms like that one, it immediately becomes apparent that a new look at our sampling procedure is required. Automated rejection based on statistical tests might blindly dispose of representatives of an enigmatic population.

Missing Data

Gaps in the sample are the bane of statisticians. They can lead to countless lost hours trying to recover the data, making difficult decisions on how to proceed without it, and recovering from errors that resulted from incorrect decisions. Two initial steps should always be taken.

First, *try to find the missing data!* This seemingly obvious step is all too often overlooked. If it was worth taking the trouble to collect the data, it's probably worth taking a little more trouble to find it.

Dealing with the consequences of its lack may prove more expensive than finding it. If a search of all relevant desktops is fruitless, perhaps the experiment is still set up. It may just be a matter of pressing a few switches again before a structure is disassembled. Do it now, so you can skip reading the rest of this section.

If the data is truly missing, and there is nothing to be done about it, the next vital question to be answered is, "Why is it missing?" The answer may be useless, as would be the case if it was simply misplaced, or there was an ill-timed power outage. On the other hand, the answer may be highly informative. Is there a pattern? Perhaps every time a set of control variables is in the same configuration, one of the experimental variables becomes unmeasurable. Never neglect the possibility of unsuspected interactions within an experiment. Data that is missing without a solid explanation may be some of the most valuable data of all.

Sometimes there are hard physical reasons why certain pieces of data *must* occasionally be missing. Maybe some values for a set of control variables render the values of other control variables meaningless, so we do not bother recording them. Or, maybe we know that the fact that a variable *is* missing is significant. In this case, consider the possibility of dedicating a neuron-activation pattern to the "missing" condition. If an occasionally missing value is a nominal variable (page 255), we can turn off all of its associated neurons for missing values. We may also want to dedicate one more neuron to the task of being a "missing value" indicator.

If the variable is a higher scale than nominal, we may want to dedicate an extra neuron to signify "missing" or "present". In theory, the network should be able to learn to ignore the neuron(s) dedicated to values of the variable when the "missing" neuron is turned on. We can help it by following the procedures of the next paragraph to set values for the missing variable, even though we have turned on the dedicated "missing value" neuron.

Whether or not we dedicate a neuron to signify missing values, we obviously must give the network *something* for a value. It's not like analysis of variance, where we can simply exclude missing values from sums. The traditional choice is to use a value that is somehow representative of the collection. If the variable is nominal, and we do not have a dedicated "missing value" code, we would use the mode (most common value). If the data is ordinal, the median is most appropriate. For interval or ratio data, the mean is probably best unless the distribution has heavy tails (expected wild points). The exact value is not critical. What is important is that we do not give it an oddball value that can be a misguided teacher.

In summary, missing values of nominal variables are usually best handled in one of two ways. If one-of-n coding is used, all of the n neurons dedicated to this variable would be turned off. Otherwise, a special "missing value" pattern should be defined and used.

For *any* type of variable, including nominal, an alternative is to dedicate a special neuron to signify "missing value." Normally, this neuron would be turned off. But for missing values it would be turned on. The other neuron(s) dedicated to this variable would be activated to some reasonable representative value.

17

Fuzzy Data and Processing

The data input to neural networks is not always hard physical measurements. It may include subjective responses, or membership in ill-defined categories. Similarly, the response required may not be a hard number. Some techniques for handling this sort of data are discussed. Most importantly, this chapter shows how fuzzy processors may be integrated with neural networks to improve performance relative to what either could do alone.

When a neural network is fed with physically measured exact data, there are straightforward rules for handling that data. Some of these are discussed beginning on page 253. But suppose the data is inexact or subjective in nature. Perhaps a potato chip factory employs a person to sample regularly from the assembly line and rate a chip as being undercooked, perfectly cooked, overcooked, or very overcooked. Or maybe we are doing a market analysis of a newly introduced product. Our input data includes customer reactions as reported by sales clerks. These reactions may be indifferent, curious, excited, or ecstatic. Special procedures may be required when presenting such data to neural networks.

Compounding the problem is the fact that we may often want to take more measurements of subjective or imprecise data to compensate for its lack of precision. This increased number of measurements may overwhelm a neural network, making some sort of data reduction necessary. For example, we may be working for a winery that employs trained tasters who can answer questions regarding various aspects of a wine's flavor. Early in the fermentation process, the wine is given to a small group of tasters, who file a report. Then the batch is split into several smaller batches, each of which is treated differently. One has some sugar added, another has its temperature changed, et cetera. When the wine is finished, it is tasted again, and the best treatment identified. This *pre-taste, treat, post-taste* process is repeated for many different production runs. A neural network is trained using the first-round taste tests as inputs and the ultimately selected best treatment as the target output. The goal is to develop a network that can be given the results of early taste tests and predict which treatment will produce the best final taste. How should the taste test results be presented to the network?

One approach would be to treat each taster as a single case. If each of the m experts answered n questions, the network would have n inputs (or groups of inputs if the data is treated as nominal or ordinal), and there would be m cases in the training set contributed by this batch test. Responsible experimental designers would be uncomfortable with this approach, though. Since different people are involved, the exact meaning of each of the n variables could conceivably change when the taster changed for a new case. This error variation due to interpersonal differences would be a confounding factor, making it more difficult for the network to learn. This problem could be eliminated by using different input neurons dedicated to each taster. Then, a single batch test would contribute one case to the training set, and each case would have mn variables. Provided that we could run enough such batch tests to build a reasonable training set, this would be the better approach. But what if mn is so large that the neural network becomes unwieldy? We can alleviate this difficulty by combining the opinions of all of the experts into one composite opinion. Thus, the number of variables is once again down to n, and each is presumably more precise due to being a composite derived from many people. Fuzzy set theory gives us ways of consolidating subjective data in this way.

It is not only input values that sometimes need fuzzy processing. It may be that the ultimate goal of our network is to provide results stated in apparently subjective terms. Perhaps we have a network that has been trained to predict economic performance figures given various strategies. Upper management wants to say to us, "What if we raise prices 10 percent and shift 30 percent of our advertising budget to the midwest region?" Our network can tell us what the predicted sales will be in each region as a result of that strategy change. However, our boss may not be interested in all of the details. All that is wanted is something like, "That's good," or "That's great," or "That stinks." How can we reduce the set of exact numbers that are output by our neural network into a vague categorization? Fuzzy set theory can help.

Treating Fuzzy Values as Nominal and Ordinal

Before one launches into fuzzy set techniques, the more straightforward approach should be addressed. After reading Chapter 16, *Preparing Input Data* (page 253), most people would automatically treat all of the variables in the examples of the previous section as nominal or ordinal. If the responses have no definite order relation, we would use one input neuron for each possible response and present the variable to the network as a one-of-n coding. If, as is usually the case, the responses are ordered, we would likely treat the variable as ordinal. A thermometer encoding would generally be appropriate. However, two disadvantages to this approach should be considered.

The primary problem with nominal or ordinal treatment is that the number of neurons required is increased. A thermometer code for a variable that has n possible responses requires $n - 1$ neurons. If there are few variables and each has few responses, this is no problem. Multiplication can inflate the number of neurons quickly, though. Training time is strongly impacted by the number of neurons. And in layer models, more input or output neurons usually mean more hidden neurons, further aggravating the situation.

The other problem with nominal or ordinal treatment is that we may be throwing away useful information. Granted, we may often legitimately be uncomfortable trying to coax interval information out of "big, medium, small" responses. On the other hand, we may be readily willing to do so. If we have confidence in the skill of our judges, we may consider their response to possess numerical significance at the interval level. This is all the more true if the response presented to the network is an aggregate compiled from the responses of a team of experts. Of course, we could even then avoid the fuzzy route by assigning arbitrary numbers to the responses. We might say that big = 90, medium = 50, and small = 10. But fuzzy set theory can help us to understand the assignment better and guide us in more objective criteria for combining opinions to generate hard numbers.

Advantages of Fuzzy Set Processing

Now that we have seen why more conventional treatment of neural network variables is not always excellent, let us explore briefly why fuzzy set methods can be valuable.

First, it must be emphasized that fuzzy set operations are grounded on a solid theoretical foundation. Although they deal with imprecise quantities, they do so in a most precise, well-defined way. Despite the fact that the user-defined membership functions may be disturbingly arbitrary, and hence provide a path to erroneous results, at least we know that the fuzzy operations that act on the membership functions lead to consistent, logical conclusions. And we know that if we use appropriate membership function definitions and rules, we can achieve useful results.

It might be argued that pre- and/or postprocessing of neural network data is reasonable, but a more straightforward rule-based approach should be used. That, of course, is a possibility. However, especially for the sorts of problems neural networks often are called upon to solve, fuzzy set methods are usually better. There are several advantages.

One of the most useful properties of the fuzzy set approach is that contradictions in the data need not cause problems. If one piece of evidence says, "This potato chip is burned," while another says, "This potato chip is underdone," conventional rule-based methods require special arbitration procedures. Fuzzy set processors, on the other hand, accept such data as part of their normal diet, having no problems with it at all.

A related property of fuzzy set logic is that memberships need not sum to one. Many strict rule-based algorithms would return a result saying that there is a 70 percent chance that option A would be the best choice, and a 30 percent chance that option B would be best. The probabilities are constrained to sum to 100 percent. A fuzzy set approach, on the other hand, might return results of 60 percent and 20 percent, respectively. It might superficially seem better to have the results sum to one. Yet, not enforcing that constraint can have advantages. The absolute numbers can have more meaning. That will become clearer later, as basic fuzzy operations are described.

One final advantage of the fuzzy set approach as opposed to strict rule-based approaches is simplicity. Expert-system designers generally find that fuzzy rule bases require 50–80 percent fewer rules than strict rule bases to accomplish the same task. Since economy is always an admirable goal, we can work toward that goal by choosing fuzzy operations whenever possible.

The Neural Network – Fuzzy Set Interface

The introductory remarks for this chapter gave a few specific illustrations of why knowledge of basic fuzzy set theory could be useful to neural network practitioners. We will now demonstrate in a general manner how fuzzy processors and neural networks can be interconnected effectively.

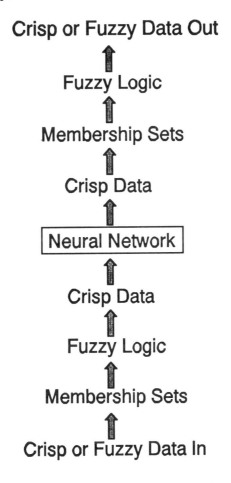

Fig. 17.1: Interconnecting fuzzy processors and a neural network

Figure 17.1 shows the most general arrangement of fuzzy processors and a neural network. The inputs may be *crisp numbers* (hard measurements) and/or fuzzy measurements (big, small, tall, et cetera). First, they are converted to or operated on by fuzzy set *membership functions*, defined later. All desired fuzzy operations are performed on these membership functions to generate a resultant set of membership functions. Those are *defuzzified* to produce crisp numbers, which make up the inputs to the neural network. The network may also have other, direct inputs that do not need fuzzy processing. The network outputs, which are crisp numbers, undergo the same sequence of operations.

All of these operations are not always used. Maybe only the input side needs fuzzy processing, or only the output side. Sometimes defuzzification is not needed. The entire sequence is shown here for generality. In most practical applications, the organization is far more modest.

Membership Functions

A fundamental tenet of fuzzy set theory is that observations can *partially* belong to predefined sets. This is in sharp contrast to traditional Boolean logic, in which membership in a set is an all-or-nothing proposition. Suppose that we measure a person's weight and have sets called Light and Heavy. Boolean logic would dictate that we determine set membership by means of a fixed cutoff point of, say, 150 pounds. Persons whose weight is at least equal to that cutoff would be a member of the Heavy set, while all others would be in the Light set. This is illustrated in the upper half of Figure 17.2. Fuzzy definitions of these sets, on the other hand, allow for partial membership.

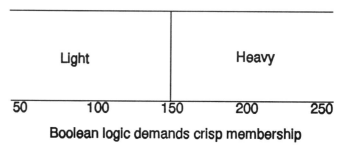

Boolean logic demands crisp membership

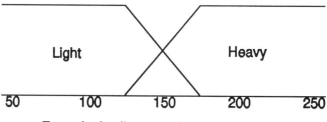

Fuzzy logic allows partial membership

Fig. 17.2: Boolean sets and fuzzy sets

A person weighing slightly over 125 pounds would be almost a full member of the Light set and only trivially a member of the Heavy set. Someone weighing 150 pounds would be a half-member of each set. As can be seen from that figure, larger weights correspond to increasing membership in the Heavy fuzzy set and decreasing membership in the Light fuzzy set.

When practical fuzzy-set processors are designed, the rules that guide their logical behavior are usually simple to formulate. In a great many cases, they are little more than common sense. The difficult part of the design is defining the membership functions (sometimes also called *belief functions*). The characteristics of the membership functions can make or break a fuzzy processor. Therefore, some guidelines are in order.

A membership function is a function that maps one or more variables to a degree of membership (zero to one) in a fuzzy set. Usually, the domain variables are crisp numeric values, but this need not be the case. A wine taster may be asked to rate a wine as falling into one of five categories: very dry, dry, average, sweet, very sweet. We may want to define two fuzzy sets, Dry Wine and Sweet Wine. The membership functions for each of these two sets may be discrete, consisting of five points. For simplicity, the majority of the discussion that follows will focus on the case of the domain variable being a single real number. Extensions to discrete and vector-valued inputs should be clear.

It should be pointed out that in the most general case, the range of membership functions need not be zero to one. It can be any set that is at least partially ordered. However, since the zero-to-one convention is most commonly used in practice, all membership functions discussed in this text will assume that range.

Membership functions are usually written with the Greek letter mu, μ, subscripted by a designator of the set. For example, a crisp membership function is

$$\mu_A(x) = \begin{cases} 1 & \text{if } x \in A \\ 0 & \text{if } x \notin A \end{cases} \qquad 17\text{-}1$$

Most designers like to use simple shapes for membership functions. Triangles and trapezoids are particularly popular. These are illustrated for Light, Medium, and Heavy fuzzy sets in Figure 17.3.

The Gaussian function is popular for implementing fuzzy representations of single numbers:

$$\mu_a(x) = e^{-K(x-a)^2} \qquad 17\text{-}2$$

The constant K in the equation above controls the width of the fuzzy set. That function has a relatively wide main body, which drops rapidly to zero as the distance from the center increases. To produce

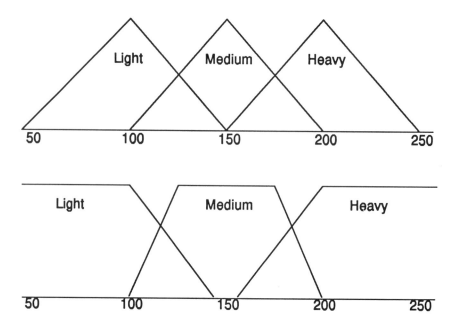

Fig. 17.3: Triangular and trapezoidal membership functions

a narrower body with comparatively heavy tails, a function suggested in [Klir and Folger, 1988] may be more appropriate:

$$\mu_a(x) = \frac{1}{1 + K(x-a)^2} \qquad\qquad 17\text{-}3$$

These two membership functions are graphed as overlays in Figure 17.4.

      There are a few definitions that should be given. The *support* of a fuzzy set is the domain over which its membership function is not zero. So, for example, the Gaussian function above has theoretical support over the entire set of real numbers, although in practice its support is nonexistent outside of plus or minus three standard deviations. The `Medium` weight fuzzy set of Figure 17.3 has support from 100 to 200 pounds. Knowledge of the support of a fuzzy set can speed computation by avoiding operations in null areas.

      The *height* of a fuzzy set is the maximum value attained by its membership function. In all of the examples above, the height of each fuzzy set is one. This quantity will be important at the end of fuzzy processing when it helps us to judge the quality of our procedure. That topic will be discussed later.

      A fuzzy set is said to be *normalized* if its height is one. It is usually best to use membership functions that allow this for all of the basic fuzzy sets.

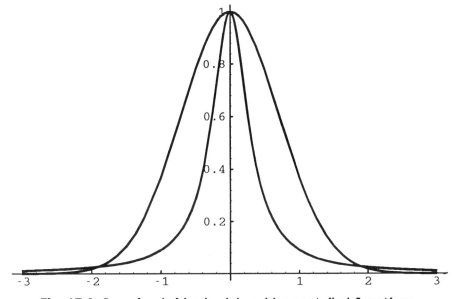

Fig. 17.4: Gaussian (wider body) and heavy tailed functions

Continuous Variables

The most common implementation of fuzzy sets involves mapping a continuous real variable to a small collection of fuzzy sets. The previous illustration of mapping a person's weight to the three fuzzy sets Light, Medium, and Heavy is one such example. The traditional approach is to use overlapping trapezoids. Bart Kosko [Kosko, 1992] is particularly fond of using seven fuzzy sets to represent the practical range of a real variable. He uses two-letter abbreviations for each, defined by the first letters of the following phrases: Large Negative, Medium Negative, Small Negative, Zero, Small Positive, Medium Positive, Large Positive. A typical mapping is shown in Figure 17.5.

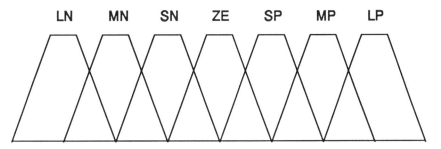

Fig. 17.5: Typical mapping of a real number to 7 fuzzy sets

We may optionally want to extend the support of the left- and right-most fuzzy sets so that all real numbers are included.

The shape of the trapezoids in that mapping can obviously affect the performance of the fuzzy system. The only rule of thumb that Kosko claims to have observed is that the areas of adjacent trapezoids should overlap by about 25 percent. Traditionally, overlap does not extend to neighbors beyond the adjacent neighbor, though it is, of course, permissible to do so. It is the lengths of the top and bottom of the trapezoids which are most problem-dependent. The best approach is to try different lengths with actual problem data and select the size that gives the best performance.

Multivariate Domains

There is no reason to restrict the domain of a fuzzy set's membership function to being univariate. We may, for example, measure the height and weight of a person, using these two variables to define a Thin fuzzy set:

$$\mu_{thin}(h,w) = \begin{cases} 1 & \text{if } w/h < c \\ \dfrac{1}{e^{K(\frac{w}{h} - c)}} & \text{if } w/h \ge c \end{cases} \qquad 17\text{-}4$$

This membership function, generally useful when ratios are involved, is depicted in Figure 17.6.

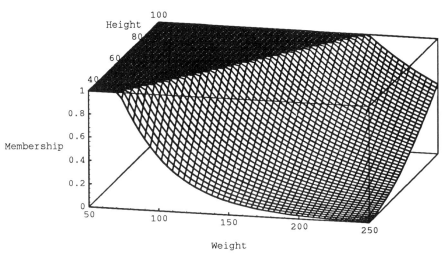

Fig. 17.6: "Thin" membership as a function of height and weight

Discrete Variables

The domain of a fuzzy set's membership function need not be continuous. Suppose that we have a fuzzy set called Well Liked, which represents critical acclaim of a movie. We may compute a membership in this set by means of the number of stars that a critic gave to the movie. This function may resemble that shown in Figure 17.7

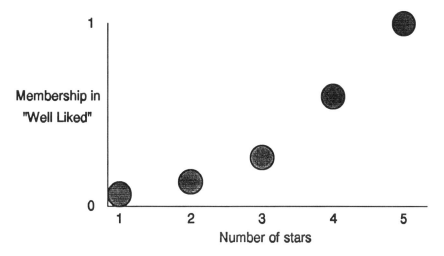

Fig. 17.7: A membership function can have a discrete domain

Hedges

It is frequently convenient to define several fuzzy sets based on a fundamental model. For example, we may have a fuzzy set called Sweet Wine whose membership function is based on sugar content. We may also want to have two other related sets: Very Sweet Wine and Somewhat Sweet Wine. When we modify the membership function of a fuzzy set based on a linguistic modification (such as the adverbs *very* and *somewhat*), we are applying a *hedge*.

Naturally, we could just start from scratch to develop a new membership function for Very Sweet Wine. But a tradition has been established that certain linguistic hedges are implemented by modifying the unhedged version in specific ways. The hedge *very* is usually effected by squaring the membership function at every point. The hedge *somewhat* is accomplished by taking the square root. This is illustrated in Figure 17.8.

These are the two most common hedges. Others are somewhat specialized and are not discussed here. See the relevant literature, such as [Cox, 1992a] and his bibliography, for more examples.

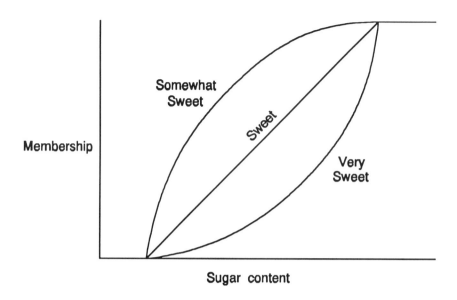

Membership

Sugar content

Fig. 17.8: Common linguistic hedges

Negation, Conjunction, and Disjunction

The most basic logical operations are NOT (negation), AND (conjunction), and OR (disjunction). In Boolean logic, NOT X is true if and only if X is false. X AND Y is true if and only if both X and Y are true. X OR Y is true if and only if at least one of X or Y is true. We need a means of evaluating the results of these operations when dealing with fuzzy sets.

There is actually a fantastic array of choices for computing fuzzy logical operations. Many of them even have practical use. For an extensive list of the possibilities, along with bibliographic references, see [Klir and Folger, 1988]. For our purposes, we will stick with Zadeh's original rules, still the most commonly used because of their simplicity and their robust behavior in the presence of noise.

The negation of a fuzzy membership is found by subtracting it from 1. Fuzzy conjunction is done by taking the minimum of the two values. Fuzzy disjunction is found by taking the maximum.

$$\mu_{\bar{A}}(x) = 1 - \mu_A(x)$$
$$\mu_{A \cap B}(x) = \min[\mu_A(x), \mu_B(x)]$$
$$\mu_{A \cup B}(x) = \max[\mu_A(x), \mu_B(x)]$$

17-5

This is best illustrated with an example. Suppose that we have a pair of fuzzy sets related to the performance of a new drug. One, called Safe, concerns the appearance of dangerous side effects. The other fuzzy set, called Effective, is indicative of the ability of the drug to do what it is intended to do. The membership functions of both of these fuzzy sets have the same domain variable, dose. Using the same domain variable makes it easy to graph logical relations. Figure 17.9 shows their conjunction and disjunction.

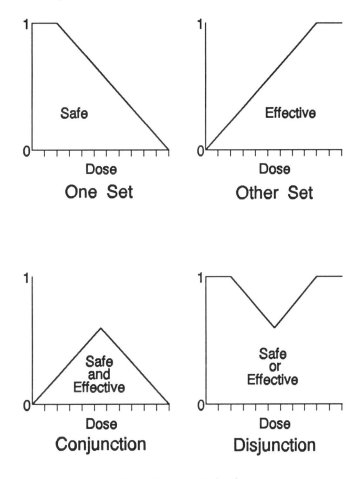

Fig. 17.9: Basic logic

The upper-left graph in Figure 17.9 is the membership function of the Safe fuzzy set. The upper-right is the Effective fuzzy set. As would be expected, increasing the dose results in less membership in the Safe set and more membership in the Effective set. The lower-left graph is the membership function of a new fuzzy set called Safe and Effective. This set is defined to be the conjunction of Safe and Effective. Its membership function would be useful in practice, as it clearly depicts the dose that maximizes membership in this most important set. The lower-right is the membership function of a rather useless fuzzy set, Safe or Effective. Observe that the conjunction is computed by taking the pointwise minimum of the two parent sets, while the disjunction is the pointwise maximum.

It is often the case that the pair of functions entering into the logical relationship have different domain variables. Visualizing this requires a three-dimensional graph. Let us consider a military application. We may have an infrared sensor pointed at a distant vehicle. If the vehicle's engine is running (or has recently been running), the IR return will be high. We may define a fuzzy set called Engine whose membership depends on the relative return of the IR sensor. We may also have a neural network examining the shape or other characteristics of the vehicle. One of the output neurons of this network has been trained to activate highly for vehicles known to be of a type employed by the enemy. This inspires us to define another fuzzy set called Enemy whose membership is based on the activation of that output neuron. These functions are graphed in Figure 17.10.

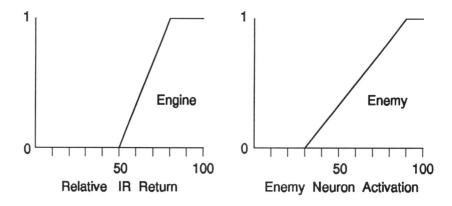

Fig. 17.10: Membership functions for parent fuzzy sets

Military planners would likely be interested in a new fuzzy set, perhaps called Active Enemy, which is the conjunction of the Engine and Enemy fuzzy sets. An observed vehicle is a member of the Active Enemy set if it is a member of both the Engine and Enemy sets. Membership in this new fuzzy set is a function of both relative IR return and Enemy neuron activation. This membership function is shown in Figure 17.11.

Modus Ponens

The logical operations of negation, conjunction and disjunction discussed above are the foundation upon which much of rule-based processing rests. But the processor structure itself is primarily based on inference. The most fundamental inference rule is *modus ponens*

$$(A \wedge (A \to B)) \to B \qquad\qquad 17\text{-}6$$

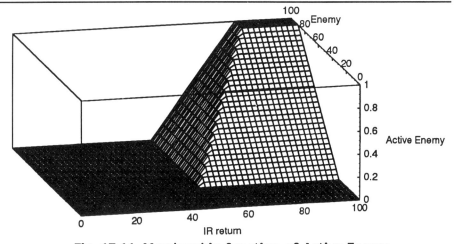

Fig. 17.11: Membership function of Active Enemy

It is *modus ponens* that allows the following type of reasoning:

1) RULE: If an animal is a dog, then it has four legs.
2) PREMISE: This animal is a dog.
3) CONCLUSION: This animal has four legs.

We use a *rule* to infer a *conclusion* from a *premise*. That is very straightforward in Boolean logic. But here, the premise and conclusion are not simple yes–no decisions. They are fuzzy sets. This section will discuss fuzzy inference.

It should be pointed out that there is little agreement on some basic vocabulary. The term *premise* is sometimes called the *antecedent* or even, incorrectly, the *proposition*. The term *conclusion* is sometimes called the *consequent*. Since premise and conclusion are easily understood linguistically, they will be used here.

At the beginning of the previous section, it was noted that there is a large number of methods for computing fuzzy negation, conjunction, and disjunction, but that common practice has settled on essentially just one method for each. That is not quite so for fuzzy inference. Again, there is a large number of methods. Unfortunately, common practice embraces several possibilities. The two most common will be focused upon.

It is probably easiest to understand fuzzy inference by picturing the fuzzy conclusion reached as being the basic, hypothetical-conclusion fuzzy set, except that its membership function is modified by the truth of the premise. In other words, the new fuzzy set created by an application of *modus ponens* is essentially nothing more than the original-conclusion fuzzy set. The only difference is that making membership in the conclusion fuzzy set conditional on membership in the premise fuzzy set results in altering the membership function of the conclusion fuzzy set based on the truth of the premise.

This can be clarified with the aid of an example from structural engineering. We have two fuzzy sets. One, called Overloaded, refers to a structure being subjected to excessive load. Its membership function variable is weight. The other fuzzy set is called Deformed. It membership function variable is distance. As happens so often in fuzzy set processors, the basic rule is nothing more than common sense:

If X is Overloaded, then X is Deformed.

When we apply this rule to a specific instance of *X*, we end up with *X* being a member of a new fuzzy set whose membership function is a modified version of the membership function of Deformed.

The question begging to be answered is, "How do we modify the membership function of the conclusion to accommodate the premise?" There are two popular methods. One is called *correlation-minimum inference*. It says that we truncate the membership function of the conclusion at the membership value of the premise. In other words, as long as the membership function of the conclusion is less than or equal to the truth of the premise, leave it unchanged. At any point that it exceeds the membership value of the premise, set it equal to the membership value of the premise.

$$\mu_{\hat{B},A}(x) = \min[\mu_A, \mu_B(x)] \qquad\qquad \text{17-7}$$

This method has some nice theoretical properties, which in practice sometimes translate into worthwhile attributes. However, it has one serious drawback. It totally discards all information about the conclusion's membership function when that function exceeds the truth of the premise. This is a dreadful loss. (Inquisitive readers should ponder the relationship between correlation-minimum inference and the conjunction operator applied to both the premise and the conclusion.)

A very popular alternative to correlation-minimum inference is *correlation-product inference*. It says that in order to compute the inference membership function, we multiply the membership function of the conclusion by the truth of the premise.

$$\mu_{\hat{B},A}(x) = \mu_A \cdot \mu_B(x) \qquad\qquad \text{17-8}$$

Thus, the resulting membership function is a scaled version of the original conclusion's membership function. This has the significant advantage of preserving all of the information in the conclusion's membership function. Many practitioners value this so much that correlation-product inference is their only choice. Resultant membership functions for both popular inference procedures are shown in Figure 17.12.

Both graphs use the same conclusion membership function, a trapezoid shown as the tallest function. The two intermediate shaded

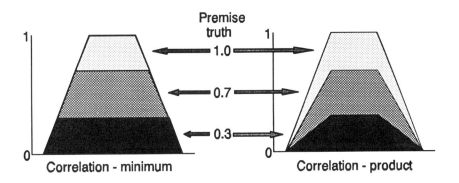

Fig. 17.12: Two popular fuzzy inference methods

areas outline the resultant membership functions for premise truths of 0.7 and 0.3.

Combining Operations

The operations described thus far are almost never used in isolation. A practical fuzzy-processing system combines them in useful ways. This section demonstrates a simple combination of operations which can serve as a basic building block for larger systems.

Let us take a simplified example from chemical manufacturing. A reaction is taking place in a vessel. There are two exit valves: the normal outlet and the emergency relief. As the reaction progresses, pressure is generated. The higher the temperature, the more rapidly the pressure increases. Once the reaction is complete, pressure no longer increases. Our fuzzy system's task is to control the opening of the emergency relief valve. The rules given here will be restricted to this one task. Rules related to other aspects of the operation are ignored.

The first rule governs the relief valve based on the state of having excessive pressure in the vessel and the state of the normal exit valve. If the pressure is excessive and the normal exit valve is already open, we are in trouble. Open the relief valve to supplement the normal valve.

The second rule is based on temperature and completeness of the reaction. If the temperature is excessive and the reaction is not yet complete, that means that pressure will be building too rapidly. Take preventative measures and open the relief valve.

The third rule gets slipped in by a greedy vice-president. Knowing that anything flowing out of the relief valve represents lost profits, this rule states that the relief valve is not open. No ifs, ands, or buts. That valve stays closed. Let us now examine the interaction of these three rules.

The first step is to define appropriate fuzzy sets. One is Pressure Excessive, and its membership is a function of a pressure sensor's reading. Another is Outlet Open, and it is determined by the degree of opening of the normal outlet valve. Another is Temperature Excessive, obviously determined by a temperature sensor. One more is Reaction Complete. The membership function of this fuzzy set is dependent on the problem. Let us say for now that its domain variable is the concentration of some chemical product in the mix. Finally, the most important fuzzy set is Relief Open. This is determined by the degree of opening of the emergency relief valve. The three rules can now be formally stated in terms of fuzzy set membership:

1) If Pressure Excessive and Outlet Open, then Relief Open
2) If Temperature Excessive and not Reaction Complete, then Relief Open
3) Not Relief Open

One of the strengths of fuzzy set methods can be seen immediately from the above rules. Rule 3 obviously conflicts with the other two rules. The ability of fuzzy set methods to resolve conflicts between rules in an intelligent manner is one of their principal advantages.

It should be pointed out that the above rules are very incomplete as regards a practical fuzzy controller. The most serious problem is that they are strongly one-sided. With the exception of the last, they are all geared toward degree of opening of the relief valve. Worse, their domain is based on varying degrees of opening of the valve. A workable fuzzy controller would be more balanced. It would be based on forces working toward opening *and* toward closing the valve. There would be rules that apply forces to close the valve. The final valve position would be determined by the ultimate balance of the opposing forces. However, the above rules clearly demonstrate basic fuzzy logic. On page 299 we will see how the incompleteness of this rule base could be detected. On page 320 a balanced example will be shown.

One aspect of fuzzy rule processing which often confuses beginners is the implicit use of conjunction and disjunction when rules are combined. These uses are very standardized and follow common sense. But because they are not explicitly stated in the rule base, they may not be obvious. One such implicit procedure is that the results of implications into the same fuzzy set are combined by disjunction to produce one grand resultant fuzzy set. Thus, the first two rules above are both implications into the same fuzzy set, Relief Open. Therefore, after evaluating each of the two implications, we OR the results together. This certainly makes intuitive sense. If either rule says that we should open the emergency relief valve, then by all means open the valve! This implicit ORing of implications generally applies to all fuzzy rule bases.

The other implicit logical operation is that after combining all implications as above, all rules are ANDed together. In other words, all rules are assumed to be true simultaneously. So in the above example, after combining the first two rules by ORing them, we AND the result with rule 3. Again, this makes intuitive sense. We want to base our action on the results of the safety rules AND the rule of the greedy vice-president. This, too, is generally applicable to all fuzzy rule bases.

The combination of all of these rules and principles can be made more clear with a numerical example. Refer to Figure 17.13 during the following discussion. Each of the nine graphs in that figure represents the membership function of a fuzzy set.

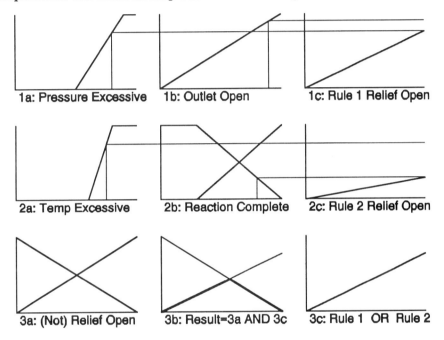

Fig. 17.13: Combining multiple fuzzy rules

Suppose that the pressure is quite high. Graph 1a shows that membership in the Pressure Excessive fuzzy set is high. Also, the main outlet valve is nearly fully open. Graph 1b shows that membership in the Outlet Open fuzzy set is very high. Rule 1 above states that if both of those conditions are true, then we have membership in the Relief Open fuzzy set. Since the two premises are combined by conjunction, we take the minimum of their truths as the combined truth of the rule's premise. The method of correlation-product implication says that a rule's resultant membership function is the membership function of the conclusion multiplied by the truth of the premise. The membership function of Relief Open is not graphed here to avoid clutter. It is simply a straight diagonal line identical to that in graph 1b for the main valve. Thus, when we scale that function by the truth of the combined premise, we arrive at the function shown in graph 1c. This is the membership function of the fuzzy set produced by rule 1 for the given pressure and main outlet valve values.

We do the same thing for rule 2. Suppose that the temperature is moderately high and that the reaction is nearly complete. The latter is slightly complicated by the fact that the rule's premise says Not Reaction Complete. The membership function for Reaction Complete is shown slanting upward in graph 2b. The membership function for Not Reaction Complete, obtained by subtracting from 1, is shown slanting downward. Again, we take the minimum of the two premises and multiply by the membership function of the conclusion set, Relief Open. The resultant membership function for rule 2 is shown in graph 2c.

As discussed above, the resultants of implications into the same fuzzy set are combined by disjunction to produce one grand result. When we take the pointwise maximum of 1c and 2c, we arrive at the grand resultant shown in graph 3c. With the data as given here, rule 1 indicates more danger. Thus, it should not be surprising that rule 1 determines the combined membership function. Rule 2 did not portend any threat because the reaction was nearly complete.

If it weren't for that greedy vice-president, we would now be done combining rules. Graph 3c would be the final result. But we still have to deal with rule 3, which states that the relief valve is closed. The membership function for Relief Open is shown slanting upward in graph 3a. We get the membership function for Not Relief Open, shown slanting downward in graph 3a, by subtracting from 1. When that membership function is combined with that in graph 3c by conjunction, we are left with the final result shown darkly in graph 3b. The light lines in that graph are the membership functions from graphs 3a and 3c. The conjunction of them is their pointwise minimum.

We have finally arrived at a membership function for a fuzzy set produced by the application of three fuzzy rules onto some measured data. The domain of this fuzzy set's membership function is the degree of opening of the emergency relief value. We can proudly stare at our result in graph 3b. But aside from that, what good is the result? How does it help us to determine how wide the relief valve should be open? This brings us to the next topic.

Defuzzification

Sometimes fuzziness just is not good enough. We need a crisp number. A valve actuator cannot be expected to understand a fuzzy membership function such as that in graph 3b of Figure 17.13. It needs to know in numerical terms how much to open the valve. The process of selecting a single optimal point from the domain of a fuzzy membership function is called *defuzzification*.

Before attempting to defuzzify or otherwise use a fuzzy resultant, we should try to ascertain its validity. Perhaps the rule base and/or primitive membership functions are less than excellent. A good quick-and-dirty indicator is the height of the fuzzy set. This maximum value of the membership function, sometimes called the *compatibility index*, should be reasonably large. If the resultant set's membership function is uniformly small, it indicates that the fuzzy domains may be incompatible with the data. There may be too many conjunctive rules or too few disjunctive rules. In any case, a low height usually means that some redesign of the fuzzy system is needed.

In the relief valve controller example of the previous section, it should be apparent that when the pressure and temperature are normal, the resultant membership function for relief valve opening will have a very low compatibility index. It was pointed out early in that section that the example was incomplete in that it lacked counterbalancing rules for closing the valve. That deficiency is reflected in the low height. On page 320 we will see an example of a balanced rule base that exhibits uniformly large height.

In some cases, very large heights (over 0.9) can be indicative of problems in the rules. Also, the membership function can usually be expected to vary by a considerable amount over the domain. If it does not vary much, that can be a sign of poor rules. But these trouble indicators are generally not as significant as having a low height.

As might be expected, defuzzification is not a straightforward task. For every method that might be proposed, a membership function can be constructed for which that proposed method is abominable, leading to erroneous results. It is an unfortunate fact that the choice of the best method is highly problem dependent and can only be made by careful study of the rules and likely data. The two simplest, and hence most common, methods will be described here.

Maximum Height Method

The most straightforward way to choose an optimal point from the domain of a fuzzy set membership function is to choose the point whose membership function value is maximum. This has the advantage of speed, an important consideration in real-time processors. It also has an obvious flaw: the maximum may not be unique. One solution to that problem is to average all ties. But multiple maxima may not even be close to each other. If the membership function was created by the disjunction of several distant peaked functions, as shown in Figure 17.14, averaging the maxima is obviously not a good approach.

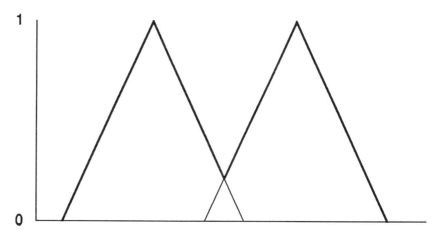

Fig. 17.14: Distant disjunction makes difficult defuzzification

A modification of the maximum height method which avoids problems with U-shaped membership functions is to employ a secondary tie-breaking algorithm. We still pick only one point, which is one of the tied maximum height points. This avoids the problem of nonsense points obtained from averages. But we break a tie between multiple maxima by computing some measure of local membership. This might, for example, be the mean membership over some small fraction of the total practical domain width. The maximum membership point that has maximum local mean membership is chosen. Backup rules for breaking stubborn ties, such as by expanding the local area, are often necessary. If worse comes to worse, a random number generator can always come to the rescue!

Centroid Method

Luckily, membership functions shaped like that in Figure 17.14 are unusual in practice. In fact, for most real-life problems, the membership function is fairly convex. Nonetheless, simply choosing the point having maximum membership is not a good defuzzification method. That method discards all information about the shape of the membership function other than the location of the highest point. Figure 17.15 shows two functions that are very different but have the same maximum point.

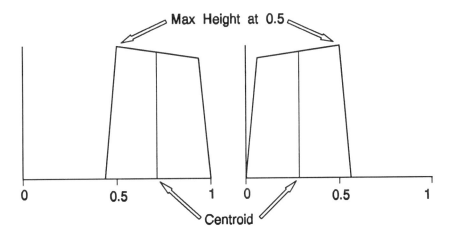

Fig. 17.15: Maximum height method discards valuable information

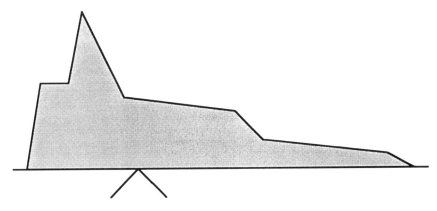

Fig. 17.16: Physical interpretation of the centroid

A defuzzification method that makes good use of all of the information in the membership function is to compute the centroid of the function. This is the point in the domain at which the function would balance if it were a physical object. Figure 17.16 depicts this.

The centroid is defined mathematically in terms of integrals over the domain D of the fuzzy set's membership function $\mu(x)$:

$$\bar{x} = \frac{\int_D x\, \mu(x)\, dx}{\int_D \mu(x)\, dx} \qquad\qquad 17\text{-}9$$

In practice, it would nearly always be overkill to estimate those integrals numerically using sophisticated general methods. Rather, one of two methods will be appropriate. The quick-and-dirty method is to store the membership function of each component fuzzy set as an array of equally spaced function values between specified endpoints for the domain. The basic processes of negation, conjunction, disjunction, and inference are then trivial pointwise operations. The final defuzzification can be done with simple discrete approximation:

$$\bar{x} = \frac{\sum_i x_i\, \mu(x_i)}{\sum_i \mu(x_i)} \qquad\qquad 17\text{-}10$$

That method has the advantage of computational simplicity. Also, it will usually have sufficient accuracy for most applications. However, long, straight lines in the function, which require storage of only their two ends in order to be defined, will waste memory and time by unnecessarily storing many interior points. Also, areas of rapid change may not be followed unless resolution is high. Last but certainly not least, it's just plain klutzy. No programmer with real pride would ever stoop to this method for anything but the crudest personal applications.

The superior method requires less memory, is faster to compute, and is mathematically exact when the fuzzy set's membership function is piecewise linear. It is based on the fact that the integrals in Equation 17-9 can be explicitly computed for piecewise linear functions. Obviously, the standard workhorse trapezoid can be easily represented as a piecewise linear function. Even more complex functions, such as the Gaussian, can be satisfactorily approximated this way. All of the logical operations discussed in this chapter result in piecewise linear functions when they are applied to such functions. Negation and inference by multiplication are still trivial pointwise operations. Conjunction and disjunction involve passing along both parent functions, looking for places where they intersect. As long as no intersection occurs, computation is trivial. When the functions for the two parents do cross, new line segments are generated. Selecting which one to pass on to the resultant set is a simple min–max choice. This method is detailed in the next section.

Code for Fuzzy Set Operations

This section provides a set of routines for basic fuzzy set operations. They all use piecewise linear approximations to the membership function. Declarations for the FuzzySet class are as follows:

```
class FuzzySet {

public:
    FuzzySet () ;
    FuzzySet ( int npts , double *xpts , double *ypts ) ;
    FuzzySet ( double x0 , double y0 , double x1 , double y1 ,
            double x2 , double y2 , double x3 , double y3 ) ;
    FuzzySet ( const FuzzySet& s ) ;
    void operator= ( const FuzzySet& s ) ;
    ~FuzzySet () ;
    double centroid () ;
    void cj ( const FuzzySet& s , int conj ) ;
    int invalid() ;
    double membership ( double pt ) ;
    void negate () ;
    void print () ;
    void scale ( double fac ) ;

private:
    int n ;                   // N of points in membership function def
    double *x ;               // Domain points
    double *y ;               // Corresponding function values
} ;
```

Constructors

Three constructors are supplied. The first takes no arguments and simply initializes a null set. The second takes the membership function and initializes a true fuzzy set. The third avoids use of arrays for simple functions like triangles and trapezoids. For completeness, copy and assignment constructors are also included, as well as the destructor. Two trivial auxiliary routines, invalid and print, are given. The former returns 1 if the fuzzy set is null. This facilitates tracking down memory-allocation problems. The latter just lists the membership function. Membership evaluates the membership function at a point.

Negate and scale provide negation and correlation-product inference, respectively. Centroid computes the centroid of the fuzzy set.

The real workhorse is cj. It computes the conjunction or disjunction of a pair of fuzzy sets.

The constructors and destructor are as follows:

```
FuzzySet::FuzzySet ()
{
   n = 0 ;
}


FuzzySet::FuzzySet ( int npts , double *xpts , double *ypts )
{
   if (npts < 1) {
      n = 0 ;    // Flag as invalid
      return ;
      }

   x = (double *) malloc ( 2 * npts * sizeof(double) ) ;
   if (x == NULL) {
      n = 0 ;    // Flag as invalid
      return ;
      }

   y = x + npts ;  // This saves a call to malloc

   memcpy ( x , xpts , npts * sizeof(double) ) ;
   memcpy ( y , ypts , npts * sizeof(double) ) ;
   n = npts ;
}


FuzzySet::FuzzySet ( double x0 , double y0 , double x1 , double y1 ,
               double x2 , double y2 , double x3 , double y3 )
{
   double xx[4], yy[4] ;

   xx[0] = x0 ;
   yy[0] = y0 ;
   n = 1 ;

   if ((x1 != x0)  ||  (y1 != y0)) {
      xx[n] = x1 ;
      yy[n] = y1 ;
      ++n ;
      }

   if ((x2 != x1)  ||  (y2 != y1)) {
      xx[n] = x2 ;
      yy[n] = y2 ;
      ++n ;
      }
```

```
            if ((x3 != x2)  ||  (y3 != y2)) {
              xx[n] = x3 ;
              yy[n] = y3 ;
              ++n ;
              }

          x = (double *) malloc ( 2 * n * sizeof(double) ) ;
          if (x == NULL) {
            n = 0 ;    // Flag as invalid
            return ;
            }

          y = x + n ;  // This saves a call to malloc

          memcpy ( x , xx , n * sizeof(double) ) ;
          memcpy ( y , yy , n * sizeof(double) ) ;
        }


FuzzySet::~FuzzySet ()
{
   if (n)
      free ( x ) ;  // Recall malloc'd only once
}
```

The only unusual aspect of the above code is that we do not allocate memory for x and y separately. Rather, we allocate double length for x, then store y in the second half. This saves unnecessary calls to malloc, realloc and free.

The copy and assignment constructors are equally straightforward:

```
FuzzySet::FuzzySet ( const FuzzySet& s )
{
   n = s.n ;
   if (!n)
     return ;

   x = (double *) malloc ( 2 * n * sizeof(double) ) ;
   if (x == NULL) {
     n = 0 ;
     return ;
     }

   y = x + n ;
   memcpy ( x , s.x , n * sizeof(double) ) ;
   memcpy ( y , s.y , n * sizeof(double) ) ;
}
```

```
void FuzzySet::operator= ( const FuzzySet& s )
{
  if (this == &s)  //  Handles s=s correctly
    return ;

  if (n)
    free ( x ) ;

  n = s.n ;
  if (!n)
    return ;

  x = (double *) malloc ( 2 * n * sizeof(double) ) ;
  if (x == NULL) {
    n = 0 ;
    return ;
    }
  y = x + n ;

  memcpy ( x , s.x , n * sizeof(double) ) ;
  memcpy ( y , s.y , n * sizeof(double) ) ;
}
```

Keep in mind that the first *if* in the assignment constructor is not just optimization. It is necessary to prevent deletion of our data if a careless user invokes it with s=s.

We often need to evaluate the membership function at a point. The following uses binary search and linear interpolation to do this.

```
double FuzzySet::membership ( double pt )
{
  int lo, mid, hi ;
  double yy ;

  if (! n)
    return 0.0 ;

  if (pt <= x[0])
    return y[0] ;

  if (pt >= x[n-1])
    return y[n-1] ;

  lo = 0 ;                      // We will keep x[lo] strictly less than pt
  hi = n-1 ;                    // and x[hi] greater or equal to pt
```

```
      for (;;) {                    // Cuts interval in half each time
        mid = (lo + hi) / 2 ;       // Center of interval
        if (mid == lo)              // Happens when lo and hi adjacent
          break ;                   // So then we are done
        if (x[mid] < pt)            // Replace appropriate end with mid
          lo = mid ;
        else
          hi = mid ;
        }

      yy = (pt - x[hi-1]) / (x[hi] - x[hi-1]) * (y[hi] - y[hi-1]) ;
      return yy + y[hi-1] ;
}
```

Two trivial utility routines are shown here:

```
FuzzySet::invalid()
{
  return !n ;
}

void FuzzySet::print()
{
  int i ;
  for (i=0 ; i<n ; i++)
    printf ( "\n%8.3lf %8.3lf", x[i], y[i] ) ;
}
```

Negation and Scaling

Negation and scaling of the membership function (for correlation-product inference) are trivial pointwise operations:

```
void FuzzySet::negate ()
{
  int i ;

  i = n ;
  while (i--)
    y[i] = 1.0 - y[i] ;
}

void FuzzySet::scale ( double fac )
{
  int i ;

  i = n ;
  while (i--)
    y[i] = fac * y[i] ;
}
```

Conjunction and Disjunction

The most computationally complex routine is the following, which performs conjunction and disjunction. It follows both parent functions from left to right. For each domain point, the values of both functions are compared, with the smaller (conjunction) or larger (disjunction) being output. Interpolation is used when necessary. If the functions cross, their intersection point is also output. This is illustrated in Figure 17.17.

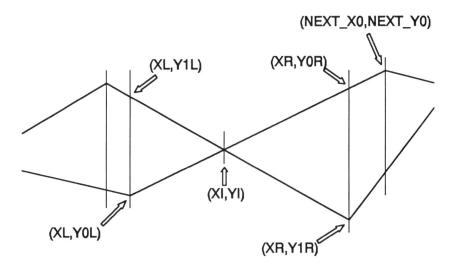

Fig. 17.17: Crawling along membership functions

This figure shows part of two fuzzy-set membership functions. Computation and generation of an output point will occur at each of the five vertical lines. Points are labeled according to variable names in the upcoming program. Let us now examine how the central section of these functions would be processed.

Suppose that we have finished through the second dotted line from the left, at X coordinate XL. The value of parent function 0 at XL is Y0L. That of parent function 1 is Y1L. The next point to the right happens to occur in function 1, and it is (XR,Y1R).

The first step is to compute the value of function 0 at XR. This is done by interpolation based on the next point in function 0:

$$YOR = YOL + (NEXT\,YO - YOL)\ \frac{XR - XL}{NEXT\,XO - XL} \qquad \text{17-11}$$

Now we determine whether or not the parents cross in this interval. This is trivially done by comparing the signs of (Y0L-Y1L) and (Y0R-

Y1R). They cross if and only if the signs differ. If they do not cross, we are done with this section. Output the appropriate function value for the right point, make it the left point for the next step, and go on.

If the lines cross, we need to generate a new point for the intersection before outputting the right point. This is computed as

$$XI = \frac{XR\ Y1L - XL\ Y1R - XR\ Y0L + XL\ Y0R}{Y1L - Y1R - Y0L + Y0R} \qquad \text{17-12}$$

$$YI = \frac{Y1L\ Y0R - Y1R\ Y0L}{Y1L - Y1R - Y0L + Y0R} \qquad \text{17-13}$$

The code for implementing that algorithm now follows.

```
void cj_out ( double x , double y , double *xn , double *yn , int *nn ) ;
void intsec ( double x1 , double y1 , double x2 , double y2 ,
          double y3 , double y4 , double *xint , double *yint ) ;

void FuzzySet::cj (
   const FuzzySet& s,          // Modifying set
   int conj                    // conjunction if 1, disjunction if 0
   )

{
   int i, nn, vertex0, vertex1, use_func_0 ;
   double *xn, *yn, xl, xr, y0l, y0r, y1l, y1r, xint, yint ;
   double next_x0, next_y0, next_x1, next_y1, rightmost_x, frac ;

   if (!n)        // Cannot operate on an invalid set
      return ;

   if (!s.n) {    // Propagate invalidity
      free ( x ) ;
      n = 0 ;
      return ;
      }

   xn = (double *) malloc ( 4 * (n + s.n) * sizeof(double) ) ;
   if (xn == NULL) {
      n = 0 ;
      free ( x ) ;
      return ;
      }
   yn = xn + 2 * (n + s.n) ;

   conj = (conj != 0) ;  // Sloppy user may not restrict to 0/1
```

```
/*
    In the following, the suffix '0' refers to the current set,
    being modified.  '1' means the external, modifying set.
    The domain endpoints are always xl and xr.  The corresponding
    function values are y0l, y0r, y1l, y1r.
*/


/*
    Initialize the leftmost point.  If one of the domains starts
    lower than the other, imply a continued function value for the
    other so they can start together.
*/

    if (x[0] < s.x[0]) {              // Start result at leftmost x
      xl = x[0] ;                     // Which is this one
      vertex0 = 1 ;                   // Subscript of next point
      vertex1 = 0 ;                   // Other was an implicit point
      }

    else if (x[0] > s.x[0]) {         // Same thing, other set
      xl = s.x[0] ;
      vertex0 = 0 ;
      vertex1 = 1 ;
      }

    else {
      xl = x[0] ;
      vertex0 = vertex1 = 1 ;
      }

    y0l = y[0] ;
    y1l = s.y[0] ;

    nn = 0 ;
    cj_out ( xl , (conj ^ (y0l>y1l)) ? y0l : y1l , xn , yn , &nn ) ;

/*
    Also initialize the rightmost point so we end together.
*/

    if (x[n-1] >= s.x[s.n-1])
      rightmost_x = x[n-1] ;
    else
      rightmost_x = s.x[s.n-1] ;

/*
    At any time from now on, next_?? will be the next point in
    each function.  We will advance by choosing the closest.
*/
```

```
        if (vertex0 < n) {
          next_x0 = x[vertex0] ;
          next_y0 = y[vertex0] ;
          }
        else {
          next_x0 = rightmost_x ;
          next_y0 = y[vertex0-1] ;
          }

        if (vertex1 < s.n) {
          next_x1 = s.x[vertex1] ;
          next_y1 = s.y[vertex1] ;
          }
        else {
          next_x1 = rightmost_x ;
          next_y1 = s.y[vertex1-1] ;
          }

  /*
    Main loop is here
  */

        while ((vertex0 < n) || (vertex1 < s.n)) {

          if (next_x0 < next_x1)                // Func 0 has closest next x
            use_func_0 = 1 ;
          else if (next_x1 < next_x0)           // Func 1 has closest next x
            use_func_0 = 0 ;
          else
            use_func_0 = (vertex0 < n) ;        // Whoever can advance

          if (use_func_0) {

            xr = next_x0 ;
            y0r = next_y0 ;

            if (next_x1 == xl)        // Interpolate to corresponding y
              frac = 0.0 ;
            else
              frac = (xr - xl) / (next_x1 - xl) ;
            y1r = y1l + frac * (next_y1 - y1l) ;

            if (++vertex0 < n) {      // Advance in this function
              next_x0 = x[vertex0] ;
              next_y0 = y[vertex0] ;
              }
            else
              next_x0 = rightmost_x ;
            }

          else {                     // Function 1 has closest next x

            xr = next_x1 ;
            y1r = next_y1 ;
```

```
            if (next_x0 == xl)  // Interpolate to corresponding y
               frac = 0.0 ;
            else
               frac = (xr - xl) / (next_x0 - xl) ;
            y0r = y0l + frac * (next_y0 - y0l) ;

            if (++vertex1 < s.n) {        // Advance in this function
               next_x1 = s.x[vertex1] ;
               next_y1 = s.y[vertex1] ;
               }
            else
               next_x1 = rightmost_x ;
            }
/*
   If the functions cross, generate new point at intersection
*/

         if ((xr > xl)  &&  ((y0l-y1l) * (y0r-y1r) < 0.0)) {
            intsec ( xl , y0l , xr , y0r , y1l , y1r , &xint , &yint ) ;
            cj_out ( xint , yint , xn , yn , &nn ) ;
            }

         cj_out ( xr , (conj ^ (y0r>y1r)) ? y0r : y1r , xn , yn , &nn ) ;

         xl = xr ;
         y0l = y0r ;
         y1l = y1r ;

         } // Main loop
/*
   The logic is done.  Save the results.
*/

      free ( x ) ;
      for (i=0 ; i<nn ; i++)
         xn[nn+i] = yn[i] ;

      x = (double *) realloc ( xn , 2 * nn * sizeof(double) ) ;
      y = x + nn ;
      n = nn ;
   }
/*
--------------------------------------------------------------------------

   cj_out - Local routine to output a point
   intsec - Local routine to intersect two line segments

--------------------------------------------------------------------------
*/
```

```
static void cj_out (              // save a resultant point
  double x ,                      // x value of new point
  double y ,                      // and y
  double *xn ,                    // Array of x's
  double *yn ,                    // and y's
  int *nn                         // Number in above
  )

{
  double d ;

/*
  Do not store identical points
*/

  if ((*nn > 0)  &&
     (fabs(x-xn[*nn-1]) < 1.e-20)  &&  (fabs(y-yn[*nn-1]) < 1.e-20))
     return ;

/*
  Do not store collinear points
*/

  if (*nn > 1) {
     d = xn[*nn-1] * (y - yn[*nn-2]) +
         yn[*nn-1] * (xn[*nn-2] - x) +
         x * yn[*nn-2] - y * xn[*nn-2] ;
     if (fabs(d) < 1.e-10)
        --*nn ; // Collinear, so replace midpoint
     }

  xn[*nn] = x ;
  yn[*nn] = y ;
  ++*nn ;

}


static void intsec ( double x1 , double y1 , double x2 , double y2 ,
              double y3 , double y4 , double *xint , double *yint )
{
  double den ;

  den = y1 - y2 - y3 + y4 ; // Guaranteed >0 if they cross
  *xint = (x2 * y1 - x1 * y2 - x2 * y3 + x1 * y4) / den ;
  *yint = (y1 * y4 - y2 * y3) / den ;
}
```

Most of the above routine was explained earlier. The only remaining comments concern output of the points of the resultant membership function. The local subroutine cj_out does not output every point with which it is called. First it checks to see if the new point would duplicate the previous point. This can happen because of careless users, identical points in the parents, or even occasionally as part of the normal functioning of the algorithm. Then it checks to see if the point it is about to output is collinear with the most recent two points. In this case, the middle point (last one output) is superfluous, so it is replaced with the current point. Collinearity can happen when the output is being determined by one function while the other function passes through defining points. Of course, neither duplication nor collinearity presents any serious hazard. They are eliminated simply for the sake of cleanliness and efficiency.

Centroid

Computation of the centroid of a fuzzy set is based on the definition given by Equation 17-9. When the membership function is piecewise linear, the numerator and denominator integrals can each be broken up into a sum of integrals, one for each line segment:

$$\bar{x} = \frac{\sum_i \int_{a_i}^{b_i} x f_i(x)\, dx}{\sum_i \int_{a_i}^{b_i} f_i(x)\, dx} \qquad\qquad 17\text{-}14$$

Each line segment defines a trapezoid, as shown in Figure 17.18.

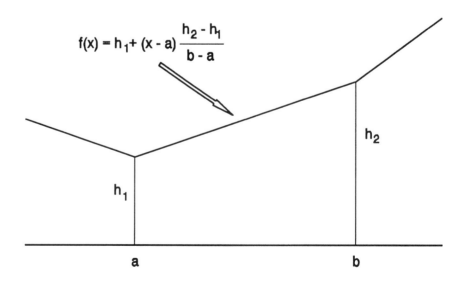

$$f(x) = h_1 + (x - a)\frac{h_2 - h_1}{b - a}$$

Fig. 17.18: Piecewise linear function defines trapezoids

Observe that the equation of a line from (a, h_1) to (b, h_2) can be written as

$$f(x) = h_1 + (x-a) \frac{h_2 - h_1}{b-a} \qquad \text{17-15}$$

The integral in the denominator of Equation 17-14 is simply the area of the trapezoid:

$$\int_a^b f(x)\, dx = (b-a) \frac{h_1 + h_2}{2} \qquad \text{17-16}$$

The integral in the numerator is slightly more complicated, but can still be written explicitly:

$$\int_a^b x f(x)\, dx = \frac{b-a}{6} (h_1 (2a+b) + h_2 (a+2b)) \qquad \text{17-17}$$

The routine for computing the centroid is a straightforward implementation of the above formulas.

```
double FuzzySet::centroid ()
{
    int i ;
    double t, numer, denom ;

    if (n < 2)
        return 0.0 ;

    numer = denom = 0.0 ;

    for (i=1 ; i<n ; i++) {
        t = y[i-1] * (2.0 * x[i-1] + x[i]) + y[i] * (x[i-1] + 2.0 * x[i]) ;
        numer += t * (x[i] - x[i-1]) ;
        denom += (x[i] - x[i-1]) * (y[i-1] + y[i]) ;
    }

    return numer / (3.0 * denom) ;
}
```

Examples of Neural Network Fuzzy Preprocessing

When a neural network solution is being proposed as a solution to a problem, one of the many design options for consideration is the appropriateness of the network's inputs. Certainly, the points discussed in Chapter 16, *Preparing Input Data*, (page 253) should be reviewed. Ideally, though, one should look beyond simple properties of variables taken individually. What about the possibility of important properties of individual variables in subranges of their range? How about interactions of input variables which are easily seen by the designer, but may be difficult for a network to learn? This section will provide two examples of fuzzy preprocessing of neural network inputs.

Simplifying Interactions

Let us consider an industrial quality-control situation. We have two identical sensors examining products on an assembly line. If either one of them indicates a problem, we want to turn on a neural network input. There is a slight complication, though. If a third sensor is in a particular state, we can safely ignore the values of the first two sensors. Their indications will be random garbage. Thus, we should address two issues:

1) There are two sensors whose indications are interchangeable. The value of one relative to the other conveys no useful information.

2) The utility of those two sensors is gated by a third sensor. We sometimes need to ignore the first two sensors.

The simple-minded approach would be to design a neural network with three inputs, one for each sensor. Training this network would be impeded in two ways, though. One small but significant obstacle is that we are unnecessarily burdening the network by having it examine inputs from both identical problem sensors when either one of them alone conveys sufficient information for making the decision. Neural networks are very adept at learning such OR operations. But why make the network learn something that we can handle for it?

A far more serious impediment to learning is the gating action of the third sensor. First of all, whoever is responsible for training the network is burdened with the task of constructing a needlessly large training set. The network cannot be expected to learn to ignore inputs according to the value of other inputs unless it is given a wide variety of values to ignore. Although the values of the first two inputs are irrelevant for some values of the third input, the network being trained must be provided with a representative variety of inputs to the first two neurons *even when the third neuron is in its "ignore" state*. What a waste of training time. Second, this gating is a logical AND operation. Multiple-layer feedforward networks often have more difficulty learning multiplicative operations than additive operations. It can involve learning weights and biases sufficiently large that a neuron can be driven into saturation. Probabilistic neural networks have even more difficulty with this task, unless the training set is very thorough.

Thus, we are led to fuzzy preprocessing of the input data. We would define a fuzzy set called `Problem_a`, whose membership is determined by the value reported by the first problem sensor. A second fuzzy set, `Problem_b`, would be similarly defined for the second problem sensor. Finally, the third sensor would determine membership in a fuzzy set called `Believable`. The ultimate goal is a fuzzy set called `Problem`, whose membership function value will be the single input to the neural network. We employ two rules:

1. If `Problem_a` or `Problem_b` then `Potential Problem`
2. If `Potential Problem` and `Believable` then `Problem`

By intelligently designing the three primitive membership functions, we can reduce three variables having a complex relationship into one variable having a simple meaning.

Fuzzy One-of-*n* Coding

When an input variable conveys interval information, we usually want to dedicate one input neuron to that variable. At most, a nonlinear transformation would be applied before presenting the value to the network. But there is a situation in which a more complex approach is in order. Suppose that the value of the variable is especially influential around one area of its domain. For example, it may be that when the variable is in the interval 0.4 to 0.5, it has a particularly significant interaction with one or more other variables. For other values, it is not very important. But in that one area of its domain, it exerts a profound influence. Neural networks are certainly *capable* of discovering that fact and capitalizing on it. The necessary weights may be hidden off in some secluded corner of weight space though. An effective network may be difficult to find.

We can simplify the learning task by providing the network with some specialized neurons. Each neuron focuses on one region of the variable's domain. This is called *fuzzy one-of-n coding* and is illustrated in Figure 17.19.

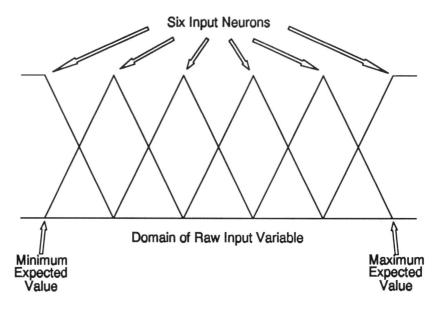

Fig. 17.19: Fuzzy one-of-n coding

The domain is divided into several regions. Each region is assigned a fuzzy set having a triangular membership function. The lowest and highest sets could have their membership functions extended as shown to accommodate unexpectedly small or large measurements. The membership value in each fuzzy set determines the activation level of its associated input neuron. Thus, one original input variable covering the entire domain is expanded into multiple network inputs, each covering a fraction of the domain. The resulting specialization often facilitates learning. The obvious disadvantage is that the number of neurons is increased. This, of course, acts to slow learning by increasing the number of weights. Whether or not the tradeoff is worthwhile is problem-dependent. As a general rule, this type of coding is effective if and only if the importance of the variable varies significantly across its domain.

[Klimasauskas, 1992b] describes a useful modification of the above technique. Rather than equally spacing the membership function triangles, they are positioned to capture fractions of the data equally. The training sample is sorted and divided into as many equal-size (count) groups as desired. The minimum and maximum values in each group define the 50-percent membership point for that group's triangle. This approach can more equitably distribute the variable's information across network inputs.

Examples of Neural Network Fuzzy Postprocessing

A neural network can be trained to produce results directly in a form that is the final goal. But it is frequently the case that it is better to train the network to produce intermediate, more detailed results that are then processed to yield final solutions. There are two advantages to this approach. First, it may be easier to train the network to learn the intermediate variables than to learn the final results. Second, it provides long-term versatility. If management decides that it wants to see a different but related result, the network may not need retraining. Only the postprocessor would need to be changed. This section provides two examples of fuzzy postprocessing of neural network outputs.

Simple Membership Output

The most basic fuzzy processors avoid defuzzification and its attendant concerns by using fuzzy membership directly as the output variable. This can be illustrated with a simple business investment example. Suppose that we have a neural network trained to guide investors. Its inputs include current and historical economic data for a company. It has two outputs. One estimates the profit potential to be realized by purchasing shares in the company. The other estimates the probability of the company going bankrupt. These details are important, but we would also like a single number to guide us as to whether or not to invest in the company. The obvious solution is to look for companies with high profit potential and low risk. This can be done methodically with the aid of fuzzy sets. The basic flowchart is shown in Figure 17.20.

The first step is to define membership functions for two fuzzy sets. One, `Profitable`, is based on the activation of one output neuron. The other, `Risky`, has its membership function based on the other output neuron. The conclusion fuzzy set, `Good Investment`, does not need a membership function defined. We have one simple rule to evaluate:

> If `Profitable` and not `Risky` then `Good Investment`

Investment Decision

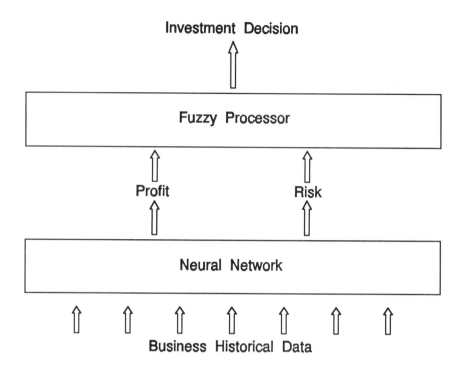

Fig. 17.20: Fuzzy postprocessing for investment advising

Postprocessing is now easy. Use the neuron outputs to compute the memberships in the first two fuzzy sets. Subtract the second from 1 to get the membership in Not Risky. The minimum of the two memberships is the membership in Good Investment, which is our final goal. Obviously, a practical model would be far more complex. But this example illustrates a very common structure.

Postprocessing with Defuzzification

This section presents a more complex example of fuzzy postprocessing in that defuzzification will be required. On page 295 we examined a simplified fuzzy control problem involving defuzzification. To facilitate learning about fuzzy logic, many important rules were ignored. Later, on page 299, we saw that the incompleteness of the rule base could be detected by observing a low compatibility index under some normal conditions. Now we will demonstrate a more balanced, practical rule base. Naturally, to keep things manageable, we must employ other simplifications. Hopefully, between this example and the one on page

295, the reader will gain a satisfactory understanding of the basics of fuzzy rule-base processing.

The problem to be addressed here concerns hydroelectric generation. A large reservoir feeds a generator under the control of a valve. We normally want the valve to be sufficiently open to meet the needs of the power grid. Rules governing the valve relative to electricity demand are omitted for clarity. Rather, we will be interested in budgeting water levels. Understand that if an excess of electricity is generated, it can most likely be sold to other producers. Conversely, if the station cannot meet its demand, electricity can be purchased. Thus, there is flexibility on the electricity side of the problem. On the other hand, the water side is at the mercy of the weather. Our basic approach is shown in Figure 17.21.

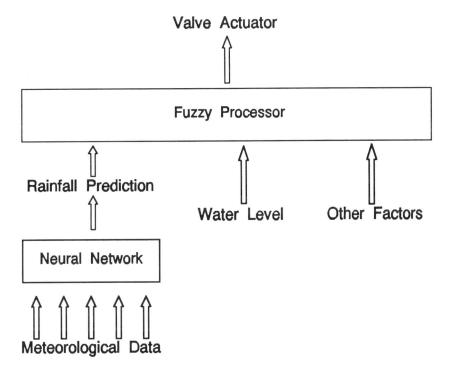

Fig. 17.21: Fuzzy postprocessing for hydroelectric generation

We have a neural network trained to predict the expected quantity of rainfall in the near future, based upon current and historical meteorological data. We also have a sensor that indicates the level of water in the reservoir. Finally, we have other input data, such as current and anticipated electricity demand, which will be ignored here. It would be possible to train a single neural network to digest all of this data, then output a judgment on the valve status. But in many cases it is easier to train a specialized network for a difficult part of the problem, then use a fuzzy logic processor to fuse the network's output(s) with other relevant data.

In the earlier fuzzy controller example (page 295), the ultimate goal was the degree of opening of a valve. That approach was used for simplicity. It is more common for fuzzy controllers to work with *change* variables rather than with final status variables. That is what will be done here. The valve connecting the reservoir to the generator is operated by an actuator motor that can open or close the valve in varying amounts. The goal of the fuzzy processor will be to determine the amount, if any, that the valve opening is to be adjusted. We define four fuzzy sets whose membership is dependent on the valve actuator. These sets are Strong Close, Close, Open, and Strong Open. The *Strong* sets correspond to more extreme valve adjustment. These membership functions are graphed in Figure 17.22.

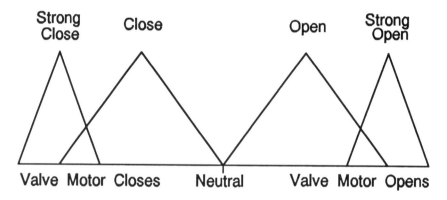

Fig. 17.22: Valve actuator fuzzy sets

The horizontal axis of that figure is valve adjustment by the actuator. The center corresponds to no adjustment. Positions further to the left mean greater closing action, while positions to the right mean greater opening action.

The neural network's output is a rainfall prediction. Based on that output, we define a fuzzy set called Predicted Rain. For simplicity, we make its membership function a straight line. It can be seen in the upper-left section of Figure 17.23. The fuzzy set Not Predicted Rain is understood to be the negation of Predicted Rain. Its name is abbreviated to Not Rain in the illustration.

The height of the water in the reservoir determines membership in two more fuzzy sets. The first, Level High, implies that the reservoir is extremely full. Its membership function is shown toward the lower left of Figure 17.23. As would be expected, the membership does not become nonzero until the water height (horizontal axis) becomes very high. Then the membership increases rapidly. We similarly define Level Low to indicate seriously low water levels. Its membership function is also graphed in that Figure.

The rule base governing the valve actuator consists of four simple rules:

- If Predicted Rain then Open
- If Not Predicted Rain then Close
- If Level High then Strong Open
- If Level Low then Strong Close

Figure 17.23 illustrates fuzzy processing for one particular situation. The conditions shown are that the neural network is predicting a considerable amount of rain and the water level is quite low. Since the earlier fuzzy controller example (page 295) employed correlation-product inference, we will use correlation-minimum inference here for variety. The logic flow is now described.

First, examine the Predicted Rain and Not Predicted Rain membership functions at the top left of Figure 17.23. The vertical light line represents the output of the neural network, indicating a high activation level (much predicted rain). The horizontal light lines extending from the intersection of the vertical line with the membership functions indicate the degree of membership in each of these two fuzzy sets. Following them to the right brings us to membership functions graphed along the valve-actuator axis (see Figure 17.22 for these functions). The top right graph corresponds to the first rule: if Predicted Rain then Open. It is the membership function for Open, truncated at the truth of the antecedent. If correlation-product inference were being used, we would have here the membership function *scaled* by the truth, rather than truncated at the truth. Below this, we have the same thing for the second rule: if not Predicted Rain then Close.

The other two rules appear below the first two. Again, the vertical light line shows the reservoir water level, which is quite low. The horizontal light line indicates the degree of membership in Level Low. The Level High fuzzy set has zero membership because the water is so low. Thus, one rule — If Level High then Strong Open — has no contribution to the final outcome. The remaining rule — If Level Low then Strong Close — makes a significant contribution, though.

The bottom right of the figure shows the final resultant membership function, derived by combining the above rules. A numerical value for the valve-actuator command would be found by applying a defuzzification procedure to the resultant function. The centroid method, described on page 314, would be most appropriate.

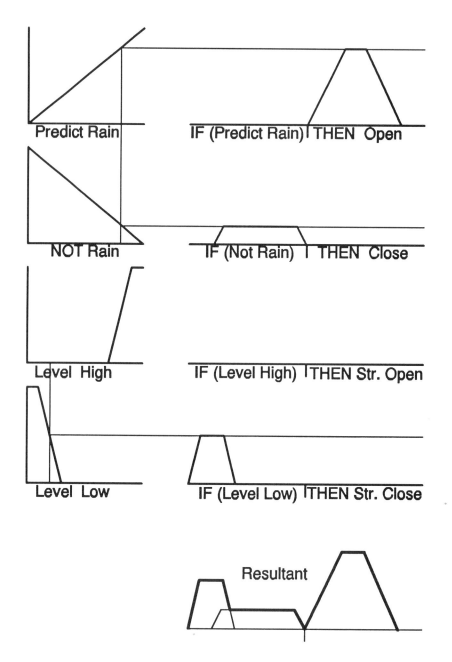

Fig. 17.23: Fuzzy postprocessing for valve adjustment

Several comments need to be made regarding the combination of the four fuzzy rules to produce the resultant function. First, it was noted on page 296 that we combine inferences into the same fuzzy set by a fuzzy OR, which is just what was done in that fuzzy controller example. In this example, we have gone a step further. We have used fuzzy OR to combine membership functions of *different* fuzzy sets. This is a traditional procedure when the membership functions all have the same domain variable, and our final goal will be defuzzification of the resultant function. We can no longer easily hang a name on the resultant, but we certainly can defuzzify it.

The other important comment is that there is a very popular alternative to the fuzzy OR for combining inference-rule conclusions in preparation for defuzzification. Examination of the resultant function in Figure 17.23 shows that the portions of the individual contributions which lie below the pointwise maximum will be ignored in the defuzzification procedure. The obvious remedy is to *add* the contributions, rather than taking maximum values as is done when we OR them. We can no longer consider the resultant to be a membership function, unless we scale it in some way. But that is no real loss. Furthermore, we gain a very useful practical advantage. Computation of the centroid can be done much faster, as will now be described.

[Kosko, 1992] proves the following theorem. Suppose that we have a collection of fuzzy inference rules governed by *correlation-product* inference. (This will not work for correlation-minimum inference, but most people prefer the correlation-product method anyway.) Let I_i be the area of the conclusion fuzzy set for the ith rule. This is the original, raw set before it is scaled by the inference. In the example of this section, we would be referring here to the functions shown in Figure 17.22. Let c_i be the centroid of that set. Note that these values can be precomputed and stored before the fuzzy processor is called into play. Let w_i be the truth of the antecedent for that rule. Then, if we compute the grand resultant by *adding* (not ORing) the individual conclusions, the centroid of that resultant can be computed as

$$c = \frac{\sum_i w_i c_i I_i}{\sum_i w_i I_i} \qquad \text{17-18}$$

Physicists, and others who understand that the centroid of a mass can represent the entire mass, will not be surprised by that formula. Its practical implication is that we can precompute all of the areas and centroids, then rapidly defuzzify later.

In the same reference, Kosko proves another more powerful but somewhat restrictive theorem. It requires that the individual conclusion fuzzy sets be symmetric and unimodal in the broad sense of being trapezoids. It then provides an even simpler way to compute the grand centroid. Since its applications are less broad-based, being principally useful for real-time fuzzy controllers, the reader is referred to [Kosko, 1992] for details.

18

Unsupervised Training

Most networks of practical interest are trained by presentation of cases for which the desired network outputs are known. Sometimes, though, neural networks can be used to discover patterns in data without relying on other information. This chapter discusses the most popular such network, along with a few variations.

The majority of neural network applications call for supervised training. For each sample input contained in the training set, the desired outputs are also known. The inputs and outputs are both presented to the network, and the network learns to associate them. There are some applications, though, for which "correct" outputs are not known. Or sometimes we may know the outputs that we would like the network to learn, but we want to see if the network can learn them on its own. Finally, we may be most interested in the patterns that the network discovers in the data. As has already been seen, it can be extremely difficult to understand the means by which many neural networks perform their duties. Usually, networks trained by unsupervised methods can be much more easily persuaded to reveal their secrets. For such applications, unsupervised training is the appropriate choice.

The most famous neural network model geared toward unsupervised training is the Kohonen network, named after its inventor, Teuvo Kohonen. It relies on a type of learning called *competitive learning*. In most other network models, all neurons adjust their weights in response to a training presentation. In competitive learning, the neurons compete for the privilege of learning. Only one, or at most, a few neurons are allowed to adjust their weights in response to a presentation.

The Kohonen network is essentially a two-layer network. Because special input normalization is required, some people call it a three-layer network, with the layer following the input layer being a normalization layer. But most people consider the normalization step nothing more than input preprocessing, not deserving designation as a dedicated layer.

Some types of input normalization result in generation of an additional input, referred to here as a *synthetic* input. Thus, if each observed sample is a vector of n components, the network's input layer will actually consist of $n + 1$ neurons. The activations of input neurons 0 through $n - 1$ will be equal to the n actual inputs times a scaling factor. The activation of input neuron n, corresponding to the synthetic input, will be a function of all of the actual inputs. For normalizations not requiring a synthetic input, we will still use $n + 1$ input neurons to keep the notation consistent. It will simply be understood that the synthetic input in this case will be identically zero. The basic structure of a Kohonen network is shown in Figure 18.1.

There are n actual inputs to the network. However, since normalization in its most general form produces an extra input, we say that the network has $n + 1$ input neurons. It has m output neurons, each of which is called a Kohonen neuron. Each of these neurons operates in a very simple manner. Its output is equal to its net input.

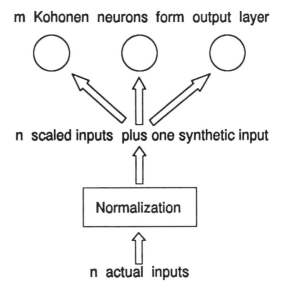

n scaled inputs plus one synthetic input

Fig. 18.1: Kohonen network

In other words, the output of a Kohonen neuron is a weighted sum of its inputs. There is no activation function applied. There is not even a bias term. In particular, let the n actual inputs be x_i, $i = 0, ..., n\text{-}1$. Let s be the synthetic input. Then, the output is computed as:

$$out = \sum_{i=0}^{n-1} x_i w_i + s w_n \qquad \text{18-1}$$

If the input normalization does not produce a synthetic input, the second term in the above equation is ignored.

A Kohonen network is virtually always used as a classifier. After the weights in the above equation are computed by training, an unknown case is presented to the network. All output activations are found. The output neuron having maximum activation is declared the winner, thus determining the class to which the case belongs.

Readers familiar with the theory presented in the multiple-layer feedforward network chapter will immediately see that the Kohonen network is a relatively weak classifier. It has no hidden layer, and it is strictly linear in its response. Thus, it must rely on brute force. Most practical Kohonen networks have a very large number of output neurons, each of which focuses on a single pattern. As we will see, the utility of the Kohonen network lies mainly in its fairly rapid training and its easy interpretability. Also, theoreticians like its apparent similarity to biological models. Some variations of the Kohonen network, not presented in detail here, learn in ways that exhibit a striking resemblance to creature learning.

Input Normalization

One of the most serious impediments to widespread use of the Kohonen network is the fact that its inputs are subject to serious restrictions. Ideally, they should lie within symmetric bounds, usually taken to be [-1, 1]. The length of the input vector must be the same for all training and test cases. This length is typically chosen to be 1. Finally, for best performance, each input should be able to cover the majority of its range. For example, if some of the input variables are physically restricted to the domain [0, 1], while the network expects inputs in [-1, 1], performance will suffer.

The first step in input normalization is to insure that all variables match the network's domain, here assumed to be [-1, 1]. For each variable, determine its practical minimum and maximum. Devise a transformation, usually but not necessarily linear, which maps the minimum to -1 and the maximum to 1. Transformations are discussed in Chapter 16, *Preparing Input Data* (page 253). This transformation must be applied to every training and test case. Some normalizations, such as simple length adjustment discussed later, do not mathematically require this step. However, performance is almost always improved by mapping to [-1, 1]. Other normalizations, such as the Z-axis method discussed later, do require bounded inputs. For the remainder of this chapter, it will be assumed that transformation to [-1, 1] has been done, and the resulting values will be referred to as the *raw inputs*.

Once all variables have been mapped to [-1, 1], we must devise a way of presenting a unit length vector to the network. The most obvious solution is to compute the length of the raw vector, then divide each component by that length:

$$l = \sqrt{\sum_{i=0}^{n-1} x_i^2}$$

$$\hat{x}_i = \frac{x_i}{l} \qquad i = 0, ..., n-1$$

18-2

This method certainly meets the mathematical criteria for acceptability and is commonly used. On the other hand, it has a grave deficiency in many applications. It discards absolute-magnitude information, preserving only relative values of variables. Input cases of (-2, 1, 3) and (-10, 5, 15) will both be transformed to the same network input vector. Sometimes this is no problem. If the raw data is binary, every variable can be coded as plus or minus one, and there will be no absolute variation. But the reader should have no trouble imagining situations in which absolute information is crucial. The solution lies in a more sophisticated normalization scheme.

Z-Axis Normalization

The most common alternative to simple length adjustment is Z-axis normalization. (Note that this has nothing to do with either statistical Z-scores or the Z-transform of signal theory.) The term comes from analogy with computer graphics, where an extra axis, called the Z-axis, is imagined as emanating from the (X, Y) coordinate display screen to the viewer's eyes. What we do is create an extra dimension in the data. The raw inputs are augmented by a synthetic variable whose value is a function of the actual inputs. This value is chosen so that the length of the augmented vector is constant. Here, that constant length is chosen to be 1. In particular, let l be the length of the input vector as defined by Equation 18-2, and let s be the synthetic input value. Then Z-axis normalization is performed as follows:

$$
\begin{aligned}
f &= \frac{1}{\sqrt{n}} \\
\hat{x}_i &= f x_i \qquad i = 0, ..., n-1 \\
s &= f \sqrt{n - l^2}
\end{aligned}
$$

$$18\text{-}3$$

As can be seen, the scaling factor applied to the raw inputs does not depend on the data itself. It is a constant. Therefore, absolute-magnitude information is preserved. Because we almost always need that information, the Z-axis method is popular. Understand, however, that there is a small but significant price to pay. If most input values are near zero most of the time, the synthetic component of the input vector will dominate. Numerical stability will be less than excellent, and successful convergence of the learning algorithm may be questionable. This is rarely a serious problem, though, and is a price definitely worth paying if absolute variation is important.

Code for implementing both simple length normalization and Z-axis normalization is shown below. This subroutine can be found in context in the KOHNET.CPP listing on page 451 of the Appendix.

```
void KohNet::in_norm (
   double *input ,                    // Input vector
   double *normfac ,                  // Output: multiply input by this
   double *synth                      // Output: synthetic last input
   )

{
   double length, d ;

   length = veclen ( nin , input ) ;           // Squared length

   if (normalization == 0) {                    // Multiplicative
      *normfac = 1.0 / sqrt ( length ) ;
      *synth = 0.0 ;
      }

   else if (normalization == 1) {  // Z
      *normfac = 1.0 / sqrt ( nin ) ;
      d = (double) nin - length ;
      if (d > 0.0)
         *synth = sqrt ( d ) * *normfac ;
      else                           // If the inputs are all -1 to 1
         *synth = 0.0 ;              // this error never occurs
      }
}
```

The variable nin is a KohNet class variable which is the number of inputs (n in the above equations). Similarly, normalization is a class variable that specifies which of the normalization methods to use. The subroutine veclen actually computes the squared length. Note that the above routine does not change any inputs. It simply computes a normalizing factor by which the inputs should be multiplied. Also, it assumes that all inputs are in [-1, 1].

Training the Kohonen Network

The Kohonen network is trained in a manner quite different from most other networks. It employs competitive learning. For each training presentation, output neurons compete with each other, and only the winner (and its neighbors in some variations) is allowed to learn. The form of competition is very straightforward. Each output neuron is connected to the normalized inputs by a vector of $n + 1$ weights. There is one weight for each of the n actual inputs, plus a weight for the synthetic input. That extra weight is identically zero if the input normalization does not generate a synthetic input. These weight vectors are normalized to unit length, as are the inputs. The activation of a neuron is the dot product of the weight vector with the normalized input vector. (See Equation 18-1.) The neuron having maximum activation for a given presentation is declared the winner.

Its weights are updated in such a way that it will react to this particular presentation even more strongly the next time it appears, thus strengthening its winning position. If all goes well, the weight vectors will eventually converge to a point of stability, after which further training presentations do not significantly change them. Once this point is reached, training is said to be complete. Unknown cases can now be presented to the network, and classification of the unknown can be performed by finding the maximally activated neuron.

The training process is easily visualized when the input vector is two-dimensional. When we say that the inputs and weights are normalized to unit length, we are saying that these vectors all lie on a unit sphere. In two dimensions, this is a circle.

Data Points Are Light Arrows
Weights Are Dark Arrows

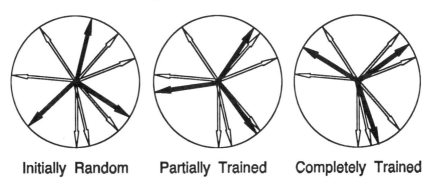

Initially Random   Partially Trained   Completely Trained

Fig. 18.2: Kohonen training in two dimensions

Figure 18.2 shows three stages of typical training. The seven light arrows in each drawing represent samples in the small training set. The user has specified that three output neurons be used. Their weights are represented by the dark arrows. In the leftmost chart, training has not yet begun. The weights are random. In the center chart, some training has been done. The weights have gravitated toward natural clusters in the data. In the rightmost chart, training is complete. Each of the weight vectors has stabilized in a position near the centroid of a cluster.

Updating the Weights

There are two popular methods for updating a neuron's weight vector in response to a training presentation. One, sometimes called the *additive* method, is the algorithm proposed in [Kohonen, 1982]. In this method, a fraction of the input vector is added to the weight vector; then the sum is renormalized to unit length. This slightly pushes the weight vector in the direction of the data vector. In particular, let x be the input training vector presented to the network, and let w^t be the weight vector of the winning neuron at time t. We then compute the updated weight vector, w^{t+1}, with a simple formula.

$$w^{t+1} = \frac{w^t + \alpha x}{\|w^t + \alpha x\|} \qquad \text{18-4}$$

The double vertical lines in the denominator of the above equation mean the length (usually, but not necessarily, the Euclidean norm) of the vector. The constant α is called the *learning rate*. It is discussed more fully in the next section.

Although the above learning algorithm usually works quite well, it can sometimes exhibit excessive instability. Therefore, an alternative, sometimes called the *subtractive* method, has become popular. It is actually basic Widrow-Hoff learning, discussed in most standard neural network textbooks. It relies on the fact that one way to nudge a weight vector toward a data vector is to subtract them, finding the error difference between them. If a fraction of this difference is then added to the weight vector, it will be pulled toward the data vector. Using the same variable definitions as were used in the additive method, we have the following update formula:

$$e = x - w^t \qquad \text{18-5}$$
$$w^{t+1} = w^t + \alpha e$$

Many traditionalists adjust the weights after presenting each training case. The author dislikes the fact that much jumping about occurs as the training set is traversed, and so prefers to cumulate theoretical corrections across the entire training set. The mean correction, derived from all training cases, is then applied to the weights. This prevents the weights from being pulled one way by one case, then pulled back again by another case. A beneficial side effect of this method is that convergence is much easier to ascertain. This is discussed in a later section.

It was already stated that the weight vectors, like the input vectors, are normalized to unit length. There is a great temptation to use brute force to keep them normalized throughout the training process. After each correction, each vector could be rescaled so that its length equals 1. *This is not recommended.* First, it is not necessary. Although exact normalization will be lost after the first correction, the weight vectors will always remain approximately normalized as long as the inputs are normalized. This is because the updating process constantly pulls the vectors toward inputs. Second, convergence is usually hindered if the vectors are renormalized during training. This can be understood by examining Figure 18.3.

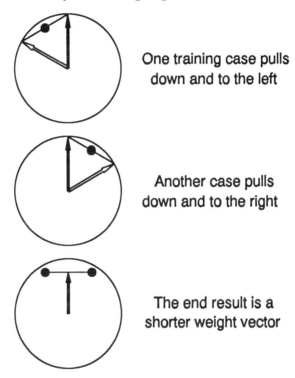

One training case pulls down and to the left

Another case pulls down and to the right

The end result is a shorter weight vector

Fig. 18.3: Normalization impedes convergence

The top section of Figure 18.3 shows a weight vector as a dark arrow and a training case as a light arrow. The line connecting them represents their difference. Assuming a learning rate of approximately 0.5, the black circle shows the result of adding the learning rate times the error vector to the weight vector. The correction based on this case alone would produce an updated weight vector terminating at the center of the black circle.

The middle section of that figure shows the same thing for a different training case. This time, the corrected weight vector would move down and to the right. When averaged in with the first case's correction, the net correction vector will be straight down. Thus, the updated weight vector will be a shortened version of the original vector. It is no longer normalized to unit length. As iterations continue, the weight vector will become shorter and shorter, until it reaches an equilibrium point determined by the training cases.

Consider now what would happen if the weight vector were renormalized after each epoch. The updated vector would be lengthened back to its original size, and the epoch would have been worthless. Convergence will never occur. We will become trapped in an endless loop of shortening by correction, then lengthening by renormalization.

Superficially, it may seem that the above problem is an artifact of using the entire training set to determine the correction. The illustrative figure can give that impression. However, careful thought and experimentation will show that the same effect occurs with single-case updating. It is just as critical to avoid renormalizing when that method is used. It is important to understand that the above example greatly exaggerates the problem. Even with such widely spaced data points, the shortening was not severe. And in practice, the cases will form much more compact clusters around each neuron, reducing this effect to trivial levels.

Finally, it should be noted that there is not uniform consensus as to whether or not the weight vectors should be normalized at the end of training or left in their shortened condition. An unscientific survey by the author concludes that most practitioners leave them alone. However, the author rebels, choosing to normalize them before the network is put to work. This seems to improve generalization to the unknown population. On the other hand, the difference is so slight that no firm conclusion can be reached.

Complete code for the above algorithms can be found in KOHNET.CPP, listed on page 451 of the Appendix. The specific routines are KohNet::epoch1 for computing the correction, and KohNet::epoch2 for updating the weights. Learning is supervised by KohNet::learn.

Learning Rate

The constant α in the learning equations of the previous section is called the *learning rate*. It must always be much less than 1, typically at most 0.4 or so. Best results are usually obtained by slowly decreasing it as training progresses, although this is not as important when corrections are cumulated across the entire training set as it is when weights are updated for each case. Up to a point, larger learning rates will make training progress faster. If the learning rate is too large, though, convergence may never occur. The weight vectors may oscillate wildly. A good way to determine if the learning rate is acceptable is to watch the maximum (across all neurons) length of the mean correction vector. (This quantity is discussed in the *Convergence* section.) The maximum correction should quickly and steadily decrease. If it only slowly decreases, the learning rate is too small. If it occasionally (or regularly) increases, the learning rate is dangerously high, leading to instability. Note that the above advice applies only if the corrections are averaged across the entire training set, which is generally recommended. If weights are corrected in response to each training case, the correction vectors can be expected to vary considerably.

Measuring Network Error

There is no official way of defining the error of a Kohonen network. This is partially due to the fact that since training is unsupervised, there are by definition no right or wrong answers. Also, no single method naturally complements the training algorithm, as for example, mean square error complements gradient learning for multiple-layer feedforward networks. However, there are several possibilities.

Remember that the ultimate goal of training is that each neuron's weight vector should in some way represent the natural tendency of a cluster of data points. Thus, we are led to examine the error vectors between training set vectors and their nearest weight vectors. Certainly, the length of those error vectors would tell us something about how well the network is performing. One common approach is to define the network error as the mean error vector length across the entire training set. However, there is reason to consider an alternative to the mean error.

An excellent error measure should provide an indication of whether or not a network's performance can be improved. The mean error vector length does not do this well. It may be that most of the training set cases differ from their closest neuron weight vectors by a moderate amount, leading to moderate mean error. On the other hand, the vast majority may be very close to their neuron's weights, while just a few outliers are present. This, too, would lead to moderate average error. In the first case, adding more neurons would do little good. In the second case, though, adding one or several neurons to accommodate the training cases not well represented by the existing neurons could work wonders. Averaging the error across the entire training set does not allow us to distinguish between these two situations. What we need to examine is the *maximum* error across the training set. A large maximum error indicates the need for more neurons. Thus, it may be argued that the maximum error is a better error measure than is the mean error.

Determining Convergence

How do we know when to stop training the Kohonen network? The answer is actually quite simple. We stop training when the changes to the weight vectors become insignificant. Assume that the corrections are cumulated across the entire training set. We simply examine the length of the grand correction vector applied to each neuron. When the maximum length for all neurons becomes tiny, we can be assured that convergence is at hand.

Things are not so simple when corrections are made in response to each case. Even when convergence is satisfactory, one case may pull the weights one way, while the next pulls them back again. A low learning rate may alleviate this but may also mask lack of convergence. Basing a convergence decision on such corrections is difficult. This is one of the many reasons that full epoch training is recommended over individual case training.

Note that the network error is nearly worthless as an indicator of convergence. We have no idea in advance of what its final value should be, so we obviously cannot judge when it is getting close. It is possible for the error to remain nearly constant for many iterations, even as the weight vectors rearrange themselves significantly. Sometimes the error will even increase as training progresses! Thus, the error should be ignored when ascertaining convergence.

Care should be exercised in judging convergence when small learning rates are in use. It may be that convergence is still far away, but corrections are getting small due to small learning rates. An effective remedy is to divide the maximum correction vector length by the learning rate, using the quotient as the convergence indicator. This is an excellent approach for both the additive and subtractive learning formulas.

There is some disagreement as to what to do when the network error at the time of convergence exceeds its minimum value during training. This phenomenon has received very little attention, probably because it is not worthy of much attention. It is rare that there is much difference in the error. And whatever difference there is, it is most likely due to trivial departures from normalization in the weights. The author prefers to keep track of the minimum error weights, using those to define the trained network. However, there is no firm reason to believe that method preferable to using the final weights. In any case, it is the experience of the author that any difference is probably insignificant. Further experimentation is invited.

Neurons That Refuse to Learn

Recall that only those neurons that win the activation competition are allowed to adjust their weights. And that adjustment is such that they tend to win by ever greater margins as training progresses. It is not only possible, but highly likely, that one or more neurons will start out so unlike any training case that they will never win. Thus, these neurons are dead weight. They take up memory and require execution time, yet they do not share the burden of representing input patterns. Worse, the neurons that do learn are overburdened. They are forced to represent a wider variety of input patterns than would otherwise be necessary, and hence cannot do a good job of specializing. Thus, we need a way of transferring some training patterns from neurons that are too heavily laden to those carrying no load at all.

There is a wide variety of ways to do this, none of which is an agreed-upon standard. Some of the most popular methods involve a *conscience* mechanism. The learning algorithm keeps a tally of the number of times each neuron wins. It sets a goal of having each neuron win an equal number of times. Those that win more than their share of times develop a guilty conscience, effected by penalizing their activation levels by an amount related to their excesses. Those that fail to win often enough have their activations increased, making it more likely that they win. This method has some nice theoretical properties involving the final distribution of information. A detailed description of a quite sophisticated implementation of conscience is described in [Hecht-Nielsen, 1991]. That algorithm appears to perform excellently when the goal is equidistribution of weights.

The author prefers an approach that often has more practical utility in real-life classification problems. It differs from most conscience methods in that it does not try to enforce equality in wins. Rather, it tries to optimize specialization. This may conflict with equal winning when different patterns do not appear with equal frequency. The algorithm looks for neurons that are attempting to represent too wide a variety of patterns. Some of the load is transferred to unused neurons. Also, unlike conscience methods, this method stops interfering when all neurons are established learners. This means that it is possible for some trained neurons to respond to only a tiny fraction of the training set. In some applications, this may be a problem. However, in many practical situations, this increased specialization is an advantage.

There are three steps to be performed when we want to force an orphan neuron to learn a pattern. In the first step, we pass through the entire training set. For each case, find the winning (maximally activated) neuron. Keep track of the *minimum* winning activation across the training set. This enables us to locate the training case least represented in the network. It is reasonable to assume that this training pattern deserves a neuron of its very own, rather than being forced to share a neuron with patterns dissimilar to it.

The second step is to present the network with the outlying case found in the first step. Examine the activation level of all neurons *that did not win for any training case.* Select the neuron from among these that has maximum activation. This is the neuron that we will choose to represent that case.

The final step is to use that case to set the weight vector for that neuron. This is trivial, in that we simply copy the normalized input vector, including the synthetic input, to the weight vector.

Complete code for the above algorithm can be found in KOHNET.CPP, listed on page 451 of the Appendix. The specific routine is KohNet::force_win.

Self-Organization

In the interest of completeness, a variation on basic Kohonen learning should be briefly mentioned. Self-organization of the weight vectors was a fundamental part of Kohonen's original work. See, for example, [Kohonen, 1982]. It also has plausibility in creature learning. Because of this historical and biological importance, and because witnessing it is almost like seeing magic performed, many implementations of Kohonen learning use it. It is not presented in detail here because the author has found it to be of mainly academic interest, often even being deleterious to practical performance. For those who are especially interested, [Freeman and Skapura, 1992] describe it in considerable depth.

The fundamental tenet of self-organization is that knowledge is not concentrated in single neurons. Rather, it resides in localized areas. If a particular neuron represents a given pattern, then its neighbors represent similar patterns. This is implemented by allowing more than one neuron to learn from each presentation. A training case is presented to the network, and the winning neuron found. That winner has its weights updated as already described, using the current learning rate. In addition, its neighbors have their weights updated also. The learning rate for neighbors is less than that for the winner, so their weights change less. Nevertheless, they do gravitate slightly toward the case, tending to localize knowledge of that pattern in the area of the winner.

The simplest implementations use a one-dimensional layout, conceptually stringing all neurons together in a single line. The most common structure, though, is two-dimensional. The neurons are arranged in a rectangular grid, so that winners have neighbors on all sides. Even higher orders such as cubes are possible.

Most often, only immediately adjacent neighbors are updated. Some more sophisticated algorithms extend the updating to several neighbors away. It is important in this case that the learning rate rapidly decrease with distance. Some of the most complex algorithms include *inhibition*. One or several adjacent neighbors are updated as already described. Then, the next most distant set of neighbors is also updated, but at a very low learning rate in the *opposite* direction from the training case. This strengthens the localization of knowledge.

It is fascinating watching self-organization take place. Networks are able to learn patterns of patterns in ways that are almost unbelievable. Unfortunately, the extra updating of weights tremendously slows learning. Worse, neurons whose learning is influenced by their neighbors are less able to specialize. More neurons are typically required in order to attain a fixed level of performance. These two facts make self-organized learning impractical in most situations. However, sometimes we are as interested in the pattern of learning as we are in the learned patterns. In this case, a self-organizing model may be appropriate.

Evaluating Performance
of Neural Networks

Several measures of network performance are described in this chapter.

Overview

When a neural network is trained, the measure of performance that is optimized is usually the mean square error of the outputs. There are many theoretical and practical advantages to using it, and it will be briefly reviewed here. However, the mean square error has little intuitive meaning to most people. More pragmatic measures of performance are needed if the ability of a network actually to perform its job is to be evaluated. Naturally, the best measure for a particular network depends on the job duties of that network. Therefore, the topics of this chapter may each be specific to a particular task and be independent of the network model employed.

It should go without saying that the performance of a network must be evaluated by testing it on a different data set than the one on which it was trained. Statistical techniques that estimate only a few parameters relative to the number of training samples can often be exempted from this restriction. Although the strictest rules dictate that performance measures based on the training set are unfairly biased toward false optimism, in practice this is often not a serious problem for many traditional statistical techniques. Such is not the case with neural networks, though. The relatively large number of parameters involved (many weights) means that it is all too easy for the network to capitalize on unique characteristics of the training samples, rather than generalizing on properties of the population. Experienced applied statisticians accustomed to safely judging the ability of a discriminant function based on its performance reclassifying several hundred training samples must be warned that such casual violation of the rules can lead to disaster with neural networks.

Mean Square Error

Many statistical techniques use mean square error as their basic measure of performance. It is easily computed by summing the squared differences between what a predicted variable should be versus what it actually is, then dividing by the number of components that went into that sum. Such a measurement has great intuitive appeal. It also emphasizes large errors more than smaller errors, a frequently valuable property. More importantly, for models (statistical, neural, or otherwise) that are mathematically defined, the derivative of the mean square error can often be far more easily computed than most other performance measures. This means that direct methods of optimizing performance, such as linear regression, can often be easily done when the optimization criterion is mean square error. Even in nonlinear cases, such as feedforward networks with nonlinear activation functions, indirect methods are feasible. Optimization of performance measures for which a derivative cannot be found is a far more expensive proposition. Finally, the mean square error lies close to the heart of the normal distribution. If errors can be assumed to be normally distributed, minimizing the mean square error often corresponds to other very desirable optimizations. For these reasons, nearly all training algorithms for feedforward networks (and many other models as well) rely solely on the mean square error as the object of their optimization efforts.

Let us review the definition of mean square error for neural networks in general. We are concerned only with the output neurons. For any input, the output neurons take on an activation level determined by the input and by the network. For that input, there is a desired set of output activations. Suppose that we are processing case p. Let the correct (target) activation of output neuron j be designated as t_{pj}, and let the observed activation be o_{pj}. If there are n output neurons, the error for that single presentation is

$$E_p = \frac{1}{n} \sum_{j=0}^{n-1} (t_{pj} - o_{pj})^2 \qquad \text{19-1}$$

If there are m presentations in the epoch, the error for that epoch is

$$E = \frac{1}{m} \sum_{p=0}^{m-1} E_p \qquad \text{19-2}$$

Problems with Mean Square Error

The most obvious disadvantage of mean square error is that it is a purely mathematical construct. It has little meaning with respect to the task performed by the network. If the network is attempting to determine the presence of a particular signal pattern in a time series, the mean square error says nothing about the likelihood of missing the pattern if it is present, or falsely detecting it when it is not present. If the task is to classify a pattern into one of several categories, the mean square error tells us nothing about expected frequency of misclassification, let alone the nature of potential misclassifications.

A more subtle but important problem with using mean square error as a guide to performance is that it fails to distinguish between minor and serious errors. Suppose that the purpose of our network is to make us rich by predicting a stock market average one day, one week, and one month in the future, based on daily averages over the previous year. Thus, the network has 365 inputs and 3 outputs. In practice, the month-ahead prediction will have so much more error than the day-ahead figure that its error will dominate the mean square error. The learning algorithm will expend considerable effort reducing the month-ahead error to moderate levels, while neglecting to fine tune the day-ahead predictions. As a practical matter, the month-ahead prediction may not be this much more important than the day-ahead prediction and does not deserve such heavy weighting. Of course, this particular problem is easily solved by using three networks of one output each. In some cases, though, such separation is not practical.

Another example of this failure to weight errors per their severity may be found in medical diagnosis. Suppose a network has been trained to examine characteristics of a blood sample in a screening process. Falsely reporting that a patient has leukemia would lead to more medical tests and some needless worry. But failing to report a case of leukemia could be a fatal error. Mean square error does nothing to address this issue.

Relatives of Mean Square Error

There are some error measures closely related to the mean square error which are especially suitable for some problems. The mean *absolute* error is the average magnitude of the error. It is identical to the mean square error except that the individual errors are not squared. Only their absolute value is taken. This eliminates the emphasis given to large errors. Sometimes this is desirable. If the network is being used to compute negative feedback in a control situation, we would often be most interested in minimizing the mean absolute error. Sacrificing this to reduce large errors can increase the chance of oscillations.

Maximum absolute error is the most intuitively informative error measure in this family. It can be useful to have an upper bound on the error.

Finally, the *median* error, whether it be absolute or squared, is more robust than measures based on the mean. A few exceptionally large individual errors will not influence it like they would influence the mean.

Cost Functions

Suppose that our network is testing for the presence or absence of a condition. Perhaps it is analyzing a biological sample for the purpose of detecting disease. Perhaps it is monitoring a passive sonar signal for engine noise from another submarine. We will probably want to measure the network's performance based on one or both of two considerations:

1) It may be known a priori that the probability of the presence of the condition being sought is very different from the probability of its absence. In the above examples, health is more likely than disease, and enemy submarines are uncommon (it is hoped).

2) Falsely detecting the condition in its absence may be more or less serious than failing to detect it if present. Confusing a belching whale with an enemy submarine may result in loss of a whale. Failing to detect an enemy submarine may result in loss of our submarine. The reader may judge which is the worse loss.

Let q be the prior probability that the condition is present. Let p_1 be the measured probability that our network will falsely detect the condition when it is absent, and p_2 be the probability that it will not be detected when it is in fact present. Let c_1 be the cost of incorrectly detecting the condition, and c_2 be the cost of failing to detect it. In practice, q will be known from experience, and c_1 and c_2 set by a committee. A presumably representative test set (not the training set!) containing many samples with and without the condition will be evaluated by the network to estimate p_1 and p_2. Given these numbers, the cost of using the tested network is computed as

$$\text{COST} = (1-q)\,p_1\,c_1 \;+\; q\,p_2\,c_2 \qquad\qquad 19\text{-}3$$

The above cost formula is easily generalized to the case of multiple classes. Each class will have its own prior probability, which naturally sum to one. A test set will be used to estimate the probability of failing to detect members of each class. Each type of failure will have its own cost. The overall cost of using the network is then computed as the sum for all classes of that class's prior probability, times its misclassification probability, times its cost. In particular, let q_i be the prior probability that our application will encounter a member of class i. Of course, $\Sigma q_i = 1$. Let p_i be the measured probability of failing to detect a member of class i. Let c_i be the cost of failing to detect a member of class i. The total cost of using this network is

$$\text{COST} = \sum_i q_i p_i c_i \qquad \text{19-4}$$

Even more generalization is possible if cost can be defined for particular types of misclassification. Computation of a confusion matrix will be discussed in a later section. This matrix exhibits every possible type of misclassification error. The cost associated with the network would then be computed as the sum of the cost times probability for each element of the confusion matrix. This is discussed more fully on page 349.

The astute reader may wonder why, in case of disparate costs and/or prior probabilities, the network is not simply trained in the first place to minimize expected cost rather than mean square error. There are several considerations here. First, note that there is a (usually) simple way of approximately doing this by correctly designing the training set. See page 251 for details. Second, be warned against attempting to modify the error function by weighting output-neuron errors differently. Skewing the mean square error to favor different neurons is possible and requires only trivial changes in the computation of derivatives. But that is very different from what has been discussed in this section and is generally of little practical value. Finally, note that there is a method for adjusting the classification rules of a trained network so as to minimize expected cost. This is discussed on page 389.

Confusion Matrix

If the task of a neural network is to classify cases into one of several categories, the traditional technique of examining a confusion matrix can be highly informative. A reject category, reserved for cases which do not clearly fall into one of the possible classes, can also be included.

A confusion matrix is a matrix containing as many rows (and columns) as there are classes, plus an optional additional column (but not row) if there is to be a reject category. If a reject category is used, a threshold is chosen in advance. Cases that fail to activate any output neuron to at least this threshold are banished to the reject pile. For every other case, its class is chosen to be that corresponding to the output neuron that has maximum activation (assuming, of course, that the network has been trained to respond in this way). The content of row i and column j of the confusion matrix is the number of test cases that truly belong to class i but which were classified into class j.

Ideally we would want to obtain a strictly diagonal matrix, with the reject column entirely zero. Quantities in off-diagonal positions represent misclassifications.

The elements of the basic confusion matrix are case counts. It is desirable also to examine the relative confusion for each class. This is obtained by dividing each element of the confusion matrix by the sum of the elements in its row. This figure represents the fraction of cases in a given class which were classified into each class. It may be easier to interpret this number if it is multiplied by 100 so that it expresses a percentage.

The principal strength of the confusion matrix is that it clearly identifies the *nature* of the errors, as well as their quantity. The experimenter is then free to evaluate the performance of the network in terms of relative severity of misclassifications.

The cost measure of the previous section can be generalized to multiple classes with the aid of a confusion matrix. Costs for every type of misclassification (including into a reject category if used) must be provided. The first step is to compute relative confusion by dividing each element of the confusion matrix by the sum of the elements in its row. Then each element of the relative confusion matrix is multiplied by the prior probability of the class corresponding to that element's row. This gives us the proportion of each possible classification pattern. Finally, multiply each element of that matrix by the cost constant associated with that particular misclassification. (Presumably, the cost along the diagonal would be zero.) The general cost associated with the neural network is found by summing all of these products.

An example may make this more clear. Suppose our network must examine a microscopic tissue sample and decide whether it is normal, from a benign tumor, or from a malignant tumor. Laboratory experience indicates that the prior probabilities of these three categories are 0.6, 0.3, and 0.1, respectively. Since this laboratory is operated by a for-profit hospital, costs associated with each possible misdiagnosis are based on monetary considerations (additional tests, lawsuits, et cetera) rather than subjective estimates of human pain and suffering. Let us say that the cost of misdiagnosing normal tissue as a benign tumor is 1 unit, and 10 units if it is misdiagnosed as malignant. The cost of misclassifying a benign tumor as normal is 2, and misclassifying it as malignant is 8. Finally, calling a malignant tumor normal will cost 100 units (possible lawsuit), while calling it benign will cost 50. The following table illustrates the computations for a hypothetical neural network. The rows correspond to actual category, and the columns are the classified category. Within each cell of this matrix, the top number is the number of test cases that fell into the given category pair. Thus, 96 in the upper left corner means that there were 96 samples of normal tissue that were diagnosed as being normal. The second row in each cell is the normalized confusion computed by dividing that cell by the row sum. So 0.96 in the upper-left cell means that 96 percent of the normal tissue samples were correctly classified. The third row in a cell is the expected quantity, obtained by multiplying by the prior probability for that row. Again looking at the upper-left cell, we multiply 0.96 by 0.6 to get 0.576. In other words, for a typical laboratory collection, we would expect that 57.6 percent of the samples would be normal tissue that is correctly classified. The fourth row in a cell is obtained by multiplying the expected quantity by the cost. This is the expected cost of the samples that fall into that cell. The total cost is obtained by summing all of these expected costs.

	Normal	Benign	Malignant
Normal	96	3	1
	0.960	0.030	0.010
	0.576	0.018	0.006
	0	0.018	0.060
Benign	2	47	1
	0.040	0.940	0.020
	0.012	0.282	0.006
	0.024	0	0.048
Malignant	1	2	27
	0.033	0.067	0.900
	0.003	0.007	0.090
	0.333	0.333	0

Total cost = 0.018 + 0.060 + 0.024 + 0.048 + 0.333 + 0.333 = 0.816.

Users of this performance measure should take careful note of its extreme sensitivity to prior probabilities and cost constants. In an industrial quality control situation, where prior probabilities are a matter of design, and costs are known to the penny, this can be a superb method for measuring the competence of a neural network. But when these quantities are subjective in nature, or even undefinable like human suffering, it may be worthless. Minuscule changes in the prior probabilities or costs can produce huge changes in the performance measure.

ROC (Receiver Operating Characteristic) Curves

A common use for neural networks is detecting the presence of a condition. The network is trained to produce a low activation level if the condition is absent, and a high level if it is present. Often, for lack of any apparently better choice, a threshold of half-activation is chosen for making the decision. If an unknown case activates the output neuron to at least half of full activation, it is decided that the condition is present. Otherwise, conclude that it is absent. Some of the techniques previously described in this chapter can be used to evaluate the performance of the network.

A broader performance measure can be obtained if we break down errors into two types and do not limit ourselves to a single decision threshold. One possible error, called a *type I error*, is to decide that the condition is present when indeed it is not. The other, not surprisingly called a *type II error*, is made if we conclude that the condition is not present when it is in fact present. It should be clear that the probability of making each of these errors depends on the decision threshold. If we set the threshold very high, we will conclude that the condition is present only when there is overwhelming evidence supporting that conclusion. Thus, the probability that we commit a type I error will be very small. However, we can expect to commit many type II errors. Setting the threshold very low will have the opposite effect. The optimum choice for the threshold depends on the relative severity of each of the possible errors. But that is another problem, discussed later (page 389). For now, we are concerned only with evaluating the network's performance based on the total picture of error types and thresholds.

The ensuing discussion can be followed more easily with an example. Suppose our trained network has been tested on a collection of samples both with and without the condition that is to be detected. For the remainder of this section, absence of the condition will be termed the *null* hypothesis, and presence of the condition will be called the *alternative* hypothesis. Assume that the probability distributions of the output-neuron activations are as shown in Figure 19.1. The left distribution is, of course, under the null hypothesis (lower activations achieved), while the right distribution is under the alternative hypothesis. As is usually the case in real life problems, there is significant overlap, so perfect performance cannot be expected.

Suppose that a decision threshold has been set. When an unknown is classified, we will decide that the condition is present (alternative hypothesis) if and only if the achieved activation level is at least as large as our threshold. A type I error is committed if we conclude that the condition is present when it is not. We can see that the probability of this occurring is equal to the area under the left

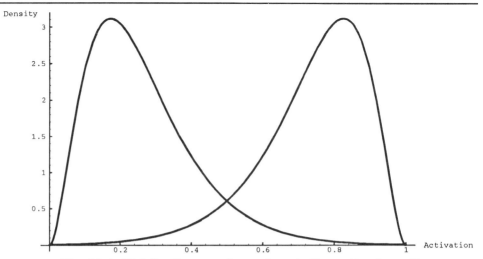

Fig. 19.1: Distributions under null and alternative hypotheses

curve to the right of the threshold. This *false positive* probability is also frequently called the *false alarm rate*. A type II error is committed if we conclude that the condition is absent (null hypothesis is true) when it is really present. The probability of this error is the area under the right curve to the left of the threshold. One minus this error is the *true positive rate*. In military applications it is frequently called the *hit rate*, since it is the probability that we will detect the condition when it is present.

If we plot the hit rate against the threshold, we get the graph shown in Figure 19.2. If hit rate were the only consideration, we would obviously want to set the threshold as low as possible in order to have high probability of detecting the condition when it is present. Unfortunately, there is another consideration.

The false alarm rate, plotted against the threshold, is shown in Figure 19.3. Not surprisingly, better performance in terms of false alarms is achieved by setting the threshold higher.

There is another graph that can help us to understand the relationship between these two curves. If we evaluate the hit rate and false alarm rate for all possible thresholds, we can make a parametric plot of these quantities. Traditionally, the x-axis is the false alarm rate and the y-axis is the hit rate. This plot, shown in Figure 19.4, is called the ROC (Receiver Operating Characteristic) curve of the network.

The lower-left corner (0, 0) of the ROC curve will always be one endpoint of this curve. It corresponds to a threshold infinitesimally larger than the maximum obtainable at the network's output. At this threshold, a decision in favor of the null hypothesis will always be made, so both the hit rate and the false alarm rate will be zero. The

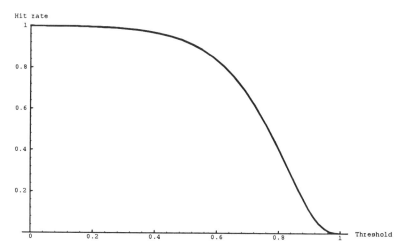

Fig. 19.2: Hit rate versus activation threshold

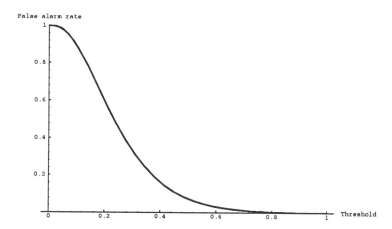

Fig. 19.3: False alarm rate versus activation threshold

upper-right corner (1, 1) will be the other endpoint of the ROC curve. This corresponds to a threshold of zero, which results in all decisions being in favor of the alternative hypothesis. The hit rate and the false alarm rate will both be 100 percent.

If the network were worthless, the curve would be a straight line along the diagonal. This can be seen by realizing that when we say the network is worthless, we mean that the distribution of its activation levels is the same under both the null and alternative hypotheses. Thus, the hit rate and the false alarm rate will be the same for all thresholds.

If there were some threshold at which the network could perfectly discriminate, the ROC curve would be a right angle. At that

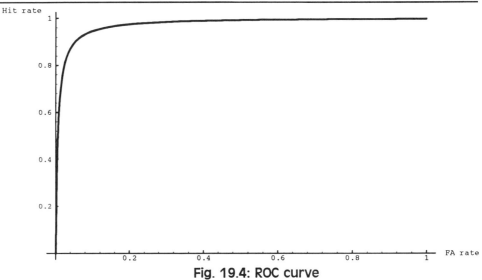

Fig. 19.4: ROC curve

magic threshold, the hit rate would be 1 and the false alarm rate
would be 0. This point would be plotted at (0, 1), the upper-left corner.
For all lesser thresholds, the hit rate would remain at 1, while the
false alarm rate would increase to 1 also. For greater thresholds, the
false alarm rate would remain at 0, while the hit rate would drop to
0. The ROC curve would be two straight lines that intersect at (0, 1).

The quality of performance of the network is demonstrated by
the degree to which the ROC curve pushes upward and to the left.
This can be quantified by the area under the curve. The area will
range from 0.5 for a worthless network to 1.0 for a perfect discriminator. This is a commonly used performance measure. The next section
presents a method for computing the approximate area under the ROC
curve if we have collections of representative samples from both
hypotheses.

Computing the ROC Curve Area

There is no single preferred method for computing the area under the
ROC curve from a collection of samples. It is the opinion of the author
that the error due to random sampling is much larger than that due
to inadequacies in any reasonable method. Thus, we can safely avoid
exotic integration algorithms based on density approximations or
smoothed curves. The good old trapezoidal rule is quite sufficient.

The trapezoidal rule states that the area of a trapezoid is equal
to the product of its width times the average of its two heights. We
sort the null-hypothesis collection, then evaluate the ROC curve for
thresholds equal to each sample activation level. The hit rate is the

proportion of the alternative-hypothesis collection whose activation level is at least as large as the threshold. The false alarm rate is the proportion of the null-hypothesis collection whose activation level equals or exceeds the threshold. Each adjacent pair of such points defines a trapezoid based on the x-axis. The width of its base is the difference between the false alarm rates, and its two heights are the hit rates for the two thresholds. Summing the areas of all trapezoids gives the area under the ROC curve.

There is no special reason for evaluating the performance at thresholds equal to those obtained from the null-hypothesis collection, thereby using vertical trapezoids. We could just as well use the alternative samples and base our calculation on horizontal trapezoids. The results should in general be very close relative to sampling error.

The rightmost and leftmost trapezoids need special attention. The parametric plot starts at the upper-right corner of the ROC curve, which corresponds to a threshold of 0. At this point, 100 percent of both collections are greater than or equal to the threshold. Thus, the rightmost trapezoid has its right base point at (1, 0) and its upper right corner at (1, 1). The left side of this trapezoid is defined from a threshold equal to the minimum value in the null-hypothesis collection. But 100 percent of this collection is greater than or equal to its minimum value, so the left base of the first trapezoid has an x coordinate of 1, just like the right base. Since our "first" trapezoid will always have zero area, skip it. Start summing trapezoid areas with the threshold equal to the minimum value in the null hypothesis sample.

The leftmost trapezoid is slightly trickier. Its left base is, of course (0, 0). But what about its left height? Its right height is the hit rate corresponding to the largest activation in the null-hypothesis collection. The fair procedure is to use as this final threshold the smallest activation in the alternative-hypothesis collection which is strictly larger than the largest activation in the null-hypothesis collection. This is the threshold that provides the highest hit rate possible with no false alarms.

Code for implementing the trapezoid method for computing ROC curve area now follows. The sorting routine shellsort can be found on page 372. The remainder of this program should be clear from its comments and the preceding discussion.

```
double roc_area (
    int n0 ,                    // Number of samples under null hypoth
    int n1 ,                    // And under alternative
    double *s0 ,                // Null hypothesis samples
    double *s1                  // And alternative
    )
```

```
{
  int i0, i1 ;
  double xl, yl, xr, yr, thresh, sum ;

  shellsort ( n0 , s0 ) ;          // Sort ascending
  shellsort ( n1 , s1 ) ;

/*
   We start at the upper right corner (1,1) which corresponds to a thresh-
   old of 0 (100 percent of both collections are greater than or equal to 0).
   Thus, the first trapezoid has right base xr=1 and upper right corner
   yr=1. The left base of this trapezoid corresponds to the minimum value
   in s0. But... 100 percent of s0 is greater than or equal to its minimum
   value, so the left base of the first trapezoid is xl=1 also!  Since our 'first'
   trapezoid will always have zero area, skip it.  We really start with thresh
   equal to the minimum value in s0, and yr the fraction of s1 which
   equals or exceeds this quantity.
*/

  i0 = i1 = 0 ;                    // Subscripts in x0 and x1
  thresh = s0[0] ;                 // Start at lowest and work up
  xr = 1.0 ;                       // R base of trap 1 (100% of s0 >= thresh)

  while ((i1 < n1)  &&  (s1[i1] < thresh))
     ++i1 ;
  yr = (double) (n1 - i1) / (double) n1 ;       // Fraction of s1 >= thresh

/*
   Main loop does all trapezoids
*/

  sum = 0.0 ;
  for (;;) {

     while ((i0 < n0)  &&  (s0[i0] == thresh)) // Advance to next threshold
        ++i0 ;

     if (i0 == n0)                 // Did all of them?
        break ;

     thresh = s0[i0] ;
     xl = (double) (n0 - i0) / (double) n0 ;   // Fraction of s0 >= thresh

     while ((i1 < n1)  &&  (s1[i1] < thresh))
        ++i1 ;
     yl = (double) (n1 - i1) / (double) n1 ;   // Fraction of s1 >= thresh

     sum += (xr - xl) * (yr + yl) / 2. ;       // Area of this trapezoid
     xr = xl ;                                 // Left point of this
     yr = yl ;                                 // becomes right of next
     }
```

```
/*
    Do the leftmost trapezoid.  Its left base is of course zero, but its left top
    is the hit rate just past the final threshold.
*/

    xl = 0. ;
    while ((i1 < n1)  &&  (s1[i1] == thresh))
        ++i1 ;

    yl = (double) (n1 - i1) / (double) n1 ;      // Fraction of s1 > thresh

    sum += (xr - xl) * (yr + yl) / 2. ;          // Area of this trapezoid
    return sum ;
}
```

Cost Functions and ROC Curves

The area under the ROC curve can be a deceptive indicator of performance. It is frequently the case that one type of error (usually type II)
is particularly costly. ROC curves emphasize the central portions of
the area of confusion. This is true both visually and in terms of the
area under the curve. If we are primarily interested in the network's
performance at thresholds in which there is great disparity in the
occurrence of the two types of error, we should be wary of placing
undue emphasis on ROC curves. This is further complicated by the
fact that two competing networks may have ROC curves that cross.
Thus, their areas may be almost the same, while their actual performance may be dramatically different. Examine Figure 19.5. That
figure shows the ROC curves of two neural networks whose perfor-
mances are being compared. Observe that although the curves are
very different, their areas are essentially equal.

     Now let us consider the cost function associated with each
network. Look back at Equation 19-3. Recall that q, c_1, and c_2 are
fixed constants, while p_1 and p_2 are dependent on the chosen threshold.
Apply simple algebraic manipulation to that equation.

$$\frac{\text{COST}}{(1-q)\,c_1} = p_1 + \frac{q\,c_2}{(1-q)\,c_1}\,p_2 \qquad\qquad 19\text{-}5$$

We see that for any fixed cost, the relationship between the two types
of error probability will be linear. The slope of the line depends only
on the predefined error costs and prior probabilities. The error
probabilities will define a straight line parameterized by the threshold,
just like an ROC curve. Allowing the fixed cost to vary generates a
family of parallel lines, each of which corresponds to a particular fixed
cost. We can graphically locate the threshold that gives us the

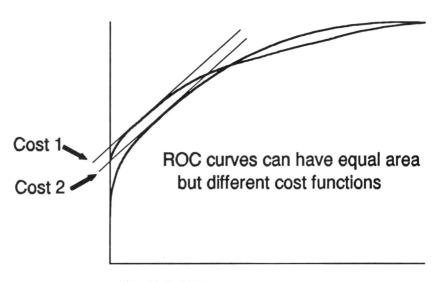

Fig. 19.5: ROC curves can cross

minimum cost decision by selecting the line from this family that lies tangent to the ROC curve. Lines above and to the left of the curve represent levels of performance that are unobtainable by the network. Lower lines are inferior. The two intersection points of that lower line with the ROC curve represent two thresholds having equal and excessive cost, with one or the other of the two types of error dominating. The line that lies as far up and to the left as possible, while still touching the ROC curve, is the smallest cost line obtainable by the network.

Figure 19.5 shows the minimum cost lines for the two competing networks. They assume some particular values for prior probabilities and error costs. Note that although the areas under the ROC curves are equal, the costs of using the networks *when the minimum cost threshold is employed* are quite different. More importantly, notice that the relative performance of the networks depends on the cost function through the slope of the line of fixed cost. If different values for the error costs were used, the slope might become more horizontal. In that case, the relative performance of the networks would reverse!

The moral of the story is that we should not blindly judge performance by the ROC curve area. Examine the curves. They might have an interesting story to tell.

Signal-to-Noise Ratio

One application of neural networks is filtering noisy signals. Some aspects of this problem are discussed in Chapter 3, *Autoassociation*, especially on page 24 and following. This section will present a popular means of assessing the effectiveness of filters that are designed to separate a signal from noise. Note that this generalizes beyond the autoassociative filters discussed earlier. Other applications will be discussed at the end of this section.

We often are faced with a problem in which a message signal, $v(t)$, is contaminated with random noise, $n(t)$. In the simplest case, considered here, the contamination is additive. Thus, we are given a composite signal:

$$f(t) = v(t) + n(t) \qquad\qquad \text{19-6}$$

The mean power in this composite signal, over a time period extending from time 0 to time T, is given by:

$$P = \frac{1}{T}\int_0^T v(t)^2\, dt \ + \ \frac{1}{T}\int_0^T n(t)^2\, dt \ + \ \frac{1}{T}\int_0^T 2v(t)\,n(t)\, dt \quad \text{19-7}$$

In nearly all cases of practical interest, we can make the simplifying assumption that the noise is uncorrelated with the signal. When this is true, the rightmost term in the above equation vanishes. We can now say that the power in the composite signal is equal to the sum of the powers in the message and noise signals.

$$P = S + N$$
$$S = \frac{1}{T}\int_0^T v(t)^2\, dt \qquad\qquad \text{19-8}$$
$$N = \frac{1}{T}\int_0^T n(t)^2\, dt$$

We will, of course, be dealing with signal samples measured at discrete time intervals. In this case, the power is approximated by the discrete analog of the above integrals:

$$S = \frac{1}{m}\sum_{i=0}^{m-1} v_i^2 \qquad\qquad \text{19-9}$$

The noise power is similarly defined.

The *decibel* is an extremely common unit for measuring the ratio of two powers. It is defined as 10 times the base 10 logarithm of the ratio. Thus, the signal-to-noise ratio, often abbreviated S/N, is defined in decibels as

$$\text{S/N} = 10 \, \log_{10}\left(\frac{S}{N}\right)$$
19-10

So, for example, a signal-to-noise ratio of 10 db means that the signal is 10 times as powerful as the noise, while an S/N of 20 db means that it is 100 times more powerful.

Since the uses of signal-to-noise ratio measurement are obvious when filtering, let us consider two very different neural network applications where this might be useful. First, suppose that we are doing event detection. The network's input is a set of samples from a time series, and its output is a single neuron that serves to signal the occurrence of an event. The network is trained to turn on its output if and only if the event is present in the input. A very useful indicator of the power of the network to detect the event is to determine how much noise can be tolerated. Contaminate the event with a fixed amount of random noise, then apply it to the network and record the decision. Do this many times, using the same level of noise each time. This will give us a probability of detection with that degree of contamination. By trying a variety of different noise levels, we can plot a graph showing how the network's performance deteriorates as noise increases. In many instances, the most descriptive measurement for degree of contamination, the horizontal axis of that graph, is the signal-to-noise ratio.

Another use for S/N is in time-series prediction. Suppose that we have trained a neural network to predict a future value of a time series given historical values. On page 64 we presented several ways of measuring prediction error. Here we provide one more alternative. Make a prediction and check it against its known true value. Repeat this many times. Consider the true values to be the message signal. Define the error signal to be the difference between the true and predicted values. When the ratio of variances is expressed as a signal-to-noise ratio in decibels, this figure can be very meaningful. In particular, let t_i be the true value of sample i, and p_i be the value predicted by the network. The signal-to-noise ratio achieved by the network, measured in decibels, is computed as

$$\text{S/N} = 10 \, \log_{10}\left(\frac{\sum_i t_i^2}{\sum_i (t_i - p_i)^2}\right)$$
19-11

20

Confidence Measures

This chapter discusses the generally difficult task of assigning confidence levels to a neural network's decisions.

Some applications cannot be adequately served by providing nothing more than an ambiguous output-neuron activation level. Suppose that we must design a neural network that resides in a fighter plane, examining the radar return signature of distant objects. The purpose of our network is to help the pilot judge whether or not a blip on the screen is an aircraft. She would be dismayed if the network simply reported that a blip that just appeared had activated the network's output neuron to a 73-percent activation level! It would be far more informative for the network to report that there is a 92-percent chance that the blip is from an aircraft. How do we go about converting that 73-percent activation to 92-percent probability? In practice, the answer is generally discouraging, possibly even dangerous due to overconfidence in our abilities. However, this topic certainly merits discussion, if for no other reason than to force developers to think long and hard about testing procedures and validation.

This chapter will take two quite different approaches to the confidence problem. They involve radically different computations, frequently result in significantly different confidence figures, and provide the user with different types of information. The first is based on the standard statistical concept of *hypothesis testing* and will deal primarily with the negative task of rebutting decisions. The second is based on *Bayes inference*. That approach typically requires more assumptions and more information, but can provide the user with more informative results.

Testing Individual Hypotheses

This section draws on the standard statistical technique of hypothesis testing. The definition of confidence given here is very different from that which will be given in a later section when Bayesian methods are presented. The methods of this section are predicated on our possession of distribution information under one or more individual hypotheses. The decisions reached will involve rebuttal of those individual hypotheses. We will show how, under some circumstances, rebuttal of one hypothesis can lead to confidence in its alternative. We will also explore some dangerous pitfalls. Later in this chapter we will demonstrate how knowledge of distributions under all possible hypotheses allows us to use Bayesian inference to make very different types of confidence statements.

In this section, we will often refer to a hypothetical network whose purpose is to decide whether or not a radar blip is from an aircraft. We possess a neural network that has been trained to produce high activation for aircraft, and low activation for nonaircraft. Assume that our network has received a blip, and that after processing, it has activated its output neuron to a level of 73 percent of the maximum possible. Also suppose that the 73-percent activation has been mapped to a 92-percent confidence that the blip represents an aircraft. This mapping was based on our knowledge of the network's behavior with regard to typical nonaircraft blips. For the beginning of this section, we will assume that we know nothing about the network's behavior with typical aircraft; only its behavior with typical nonaircraft. Interpretation of these numbers from a hypothesis-testing point of view will be discussed, then a means of mapping activation to confidence will be given.

First, we must describe the concept of *confidence*, which here we will interpret in the strictest sense of being *probability of making a correct decision*. (This is opposed to other common views of confidence as being little more than ill-defined, vague feelings.) When we say that our network has 92-percent confidence that a radar blip is an aircraft, exactly what do we mean? If we follow standard hypothesis-testing theory, the answer may not be obvious and is worth careful thought. We mean that *if the blip is not an aircraft, then there is only an 8-percent chance (100 minus 92) that the neuron would have achieved an activation level at least as high as the 73 it reached.* From another perspective, we mean that there is a 92-percent probability that a nonaircraft would have activated the neuron to a lesser degree (less than 73). The crux of the matter is the *order* of things. We are not talking about probabilities of aircraft or nonaircraft, given the observation. That will be discussed later. Rather, we are talking about the probability of such an observation, given the hypothesis that it is a nonaircraft. In much of the following discussion, we will speak as if we are considering probabilities of aircraft or nonaircraft, as that is more straightforward. Remember, though, that it is really the probability of the observation that is the basis of it all.

It is often reasonable to equate low probability of the observation under the nonaircraft hypothesis with high probability in the alternative that it is an aircraft. That, in fact, is exactly what we are doing when we translate a high activation, having only an 8-percent chance of being a product of a nonaircraft, into a 92-percent probability of having come from an aircraft. In practice, we can usually get away with this as long as there are no other possibilities. If the network has been trained and tested with representative examples of every possible blip, with no types of blip ignored, it is reasonable to equate rejection of the nonaircraft hypothesis with acceptance of the alternative. Statisticians do this all the time. On the other hand, truly cautious practitioners will always remember that doing so is treading on thin philosophical ice. Remember that we are testing the assumption that the nonaircraft hypothesis is true, and calculating the probability of having achieved an activation level as high as the one we obtained, given that the assumption is true. If the probability of such a high activation is low, we may legitimately doubt that nonaircraft hypothesis. But when, on the basis of doubting that hypothesis, we then accept the alternative hypothesis that it is an aircraft, we are taking a leap of faith whose justification should be subject to careful scrutiny. The reasoning goes like this:

1) Either it is or it is not an aircraft.
2) If it is not an aircraft, there is only a small probability that we would have attained such high activation.
3) Therefore it is probably an aircraft.

In the absence of any information about expected activations if it *is* an aircraft, this is the best we can do, so for the remainder of this section we will allow ourselves that leap of faith.

Notice that nothing has been said yet about the operation of the network when the object *is* an aircraft. The possibility of failing to detect an actual aircraft is another issue. Even more important, *nothing has been said about the probability that this IS a nonaircraft.* We have only inferred the probability that it is an aircraft by virtue of the rareness of such a high activation level from a nonaircraft. This definition of confidence is crucial to understanding the remainder of this chapter.

The most common error made in inferences of this kind is interpreting lack of rejection of a hypothesis as acceptance of it. For example, when we have such a high activation level that there is only an 8-percent chance that the blip is a nonaircraft (92-percent confidence that it is an aircraft), interpretation of this figure is straightforward. We conclude that the blip is quite likely an aircraft. Suppose, though, that the activation is so low that we have only 10-percent confidence that the object is an aircraft (90-percent chance that under our assumed nonaircraft hypothesis we could obtain an activation level this high or higher). Does that mean that we are safe in concluding that the blip is probably *not* an aircraft? The answer is an emphatic NO! If nothing else is remembered from this chapter, remember that *failure to reject an assumed hypothesis does not imply that it may be legitimately accepted.* Hopefully this will all become clear as the details for computing confidences are set forth.

A statistician would approach these concepts in the following way. We have two hypotheses. One is called the *null* hypothesis. For this problem, the null hypothesis is that the blip is not an aircraft. The other, the *alternative* hypothesis, is that the blip is an aircraft. Either one or the other of these two hypotheses is true. We can err in one of two ways. We may falsely reject the null hypothesis by asserting that the blip is an aircraft when, in fact, it is not. This is called a *type I error*. The probability of making this error in the above example would be 100 - 92 = 8 percent, because we have already agreed that we know there is an 8-percent chance that a nonaircraft could activate the neuron to a level of 73 or more. Or we may commit a *type II error* by falsely accepting the null hypothesis, concluding that the blip is not an aircraft when, in fact, it is. The 92-percent confidence of it being an aircraft *tells us <u>nothing</u> about the probability of making a type II error*. As we will see, it is often more difficult to find the probability of making this error. In other words, if we know that we have very low probability of making a type I error (high confidence that it is an aircraft), then we know something worthwhile. But if we have a high probability of making a type I error (low confidence that it is an aircraft), then *we know nothing truly useful!* The only way we will ever be able to assert the null hypothesis with any confidence (conclude that it is not an aircraft) is if we also know the behavior of the network when confronted with aircraft. That will be discussed later.

How do we go about converting activation levels to confidences? Recall that the confidence level in the alternative hypothesis is 1 (100 percent) minus the probability of making a type I error. If we know the probability distribution function of the activation level under the null hypothesis, we can easily find the type I error probability. For example, suppose we know that random nonaircraft blips encountered in real life produce activations in our network which are distributed as shown in Figure 20.1.

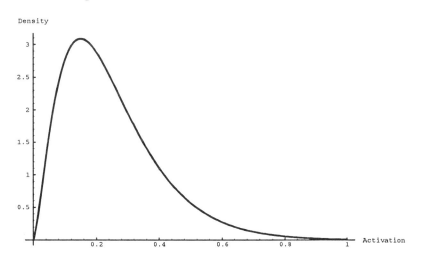

Fig. 20.1: Typical activations under null hypothesis

Then, for any given network activation level, the probability that a nonaircraft could have been responsible for a level this high (or higher) is equal to the area under this curve to the right of the activation level. As can be seen, activation levels approaching 1 have vanishing area to their right, hence have alternative-hypothesis confidence approaching 1.

At the risk of boring those familiar with testing statistical hypotheses, a repeated warning is appropriate. Suppose that the activation level in response to a blip is 0.2 or so. It is tempting to look at this distribution of nonaircraft blips, observe that activations around 0.2 are extremely common for nonaircraft, and conclude that there is a high probability that this is a nonaircraft. NO! In order to reach such a conclusion, we need to know the distribution of activations for aircraft. For all we know, the network may be incompetent and may readily produce activations of 0.2 for aircraft. Determining the competency of our network in this regard can only be done by measuring its behavior under the alternative hypothesis, a task discussed later.

We now know how to convert activation levels to confidences in the alternative hypothesis if we know the probability distribution of the activation function under the null hypothesis. Therein lies the root of the problem. Finding an estimate of that distribution is far more difficult than most researchers like to admit. In nearly all real-life problems, the only way is to estimate it by random sampling. However, the following caveat is necessary. *Correctly sampling the activation levels under a hypothesis is difficult at best, and impossible under many circumstances.* This is because two vitally important conditions must be satisfied:

1)   All possible cases must be represented in the sample.

2)   These cases must be represented in the sample in quantities proportional to their expected occurrence in the application.

Take the aircraft radar problem as an example. In order to produce a reliable function for mapping activation levels to confidences, we must sample every possible blip that is not an aircraft. As if that is not bad enough, suppose that both sparrows and hawks can produce blips of different characteristics. If in our application we assume that sparrows are twice as likely to appear as hawks, then our sample should contain twice as many sparrows as hawks. Of course we might be able to cheat by replicating sparrow samples. Yet hopefully the reader can see the problem. If even one type of nonaircraft blip is omitted from the sample, and that blip happens to be significantly different from any in the training sample, then that object may well produce a false alarm if it appears in the application. The same thing can happen if some nonaircraft objects are present in the sample, but under-represented in number. With that dire warning firmly entrenched, let us proceed.

Computing Confidence

In Chapter 12, *Probabilistic Neural Networks*, we saw how probability distributions could be estimated from samples by means of Parzen windows. We will use that technique later in this chapter. For now, though, a much more straightforward method is preferable in that it does not require arbitrary choice of a smoothing parameter or a particular window function. Also, note that for computing confidence measures as described above, we do not really need density functions, which are computed by Parzen estimators. We need cumulative distribution functions (CDFs), since what we want are areas under the probability density curve.

It is easy to estimate the CDF from a sample. Simply sort the sample and count! For example, suppose that our (ridiculously small) collection of nonaircraft blip activation levels consists of 0.1, 0.2, 0.2, 0.4, and 0.7, for a total of five samples. Then we see that two out of five (40 percent) of our sample achieved an activation level of at least 0.4, four out of five (80 percent) were at 0.2 or more, et cetera. This percentage gives the probability of a type I error. The confidence level in the alternative hypothesis is computed by subtracting the type I error probability from 100 percent. Thus, if our application achieved an activation level of 0.7, the confidence in the alternative hypothesis would be 80 percent.

Notice that we counted activations *greater than or equal to* rather than *less than or equal to* as is traditionally done in statistical estimation of CDFs. This is because we are estimating inclusive right-tail probabilities. In practice this is insignificant, as the sample will be much larger and duplicated activations will be essentially nonexistent. However, to be strictly correct (and to allow for the possibility of discrete measurements), we must adhere to this, despite tradition.

If the application generates an activation level that did not occur in the sample used to estimate the CDF, simple linear interpolation is sufficient. More sophisticated methods, such as cubic splines, produce voodoo precision. Given the random error inherent in any sampling scheme, not to mention user errors in designing the collecting operation, even linear interpolation probably provides more accuracy than the data justifies. The only hint of a problem arises if the application produces an activation in excess of the largest obtained in the sample. For this reason, more than any other, we must collect a sample large enough that, should this happen, we can be satisfied with asserting a confidence equal to that of the highest in the collection. For example, if our collection contained only the 5 samples listed above, but our application produced an activation level of 0.99, we could only assert a confidence of 80 percent. We would have to treat the 0.99 as if it were 0.7, the largest in our collection, because we know nothing of the probability distribution beyond that point. Do not be tempted into thinking that 100 percent of our sample was less than 0.99, so we can assert a confidence of 100 percent. What if the observed activation were 0.700001?

Confidence in the Null Hypothesis

Now that we have taken the first daring step down the road to ruin by having the audacity to believe ourselves capable of adequately sampling under the null hypothesis, we might as well take a second step. It has already been beaten into the reader that although large confidences mean something, small confidences mean nothing. It would be nice to do better. When a radar blip comes out with a 20-percent confidence of being an aircraft, the pilot would be more comfortable if she could also see a confidence of, say, 70 percent that it is *not* an aircraft. As has been seen, knowledge of the distribution of nonaircraft activations is not sufficient to give us such a figure. We need to know the distribution of activations produced by aircraft. Unfortunately, this is sometimes even more difficult than sampling under the null hypothesis. Superficially, this would not seem to be the case. Surely it is far easier to collect a variety of aircraft samples than it is to collect sparrows, hawks, hot air balloons, et cetera. That may be true. The problem lies rather in *consequences*. In nearly all practical applications, type II errors are far more severe than type I errors. Falsely identifying a hawk as a plane may cause some momentary panic, as will falsely diagnosing a patient as having leukemia. However, erring in the other direction is far worse. And it is precisely this type of error that is most likely to result from inadequate sampling under the alternative hypothesis. If we accidentally omit one particular pattern that happens to produce low activation (probably due to also being omitted from the training set), then when the network receives this signal in real use, a false high level of confidence in being a nonaircraft will be produced. Do not take this warning lightly.

Computation of the function that maps activation to confidence in the null hypothesis is nearly identical to what has already been presented. However, one slight difference should be mentioned. Since cases arising from the null hypothesis will produce small activations, we now calculate the probability of erroneously rejecting the alternative hypothesis (in favor of the null hypothesis) by counting samples from the alternative collection which are *less than or equal to* the attained activation. Thus, suppose our collection of aircraft consists of activations of 0.5, 0.7, 0.7, 0.8, and 0.9. If an activation of 0.7 were attained, 3 out of the 5 samples are less than or equal to it, so it then maps to a confidence of 40 percent (1.0 - 0.6) in the null (nonaircraft) hypothesis. Activations less than or equal to 0.5 map to a confidence of 80 percent.

One trivial point should be made to mollify readers who may be disturbed by counting samples that are less than *or equal to*, rather than strictly less than, a particular activation level. They may be concerned that since the rule is to reject the null hypothesis when the achieved activation equals or exceeds a threshold, and since we did just that in computing the type I error from a null-hypothesis sample, we should compute this supposed type II error by counting samples that are strictly less than the threshold. The answer is that although in one sense we are computing a type II error, our actual use for this confidence will be closer to being a type I error with the roles of the hypotheses reversed. For example, if our radar network were to achieve a very low activation level, we would want to reject the hypothesis that it is an aircraft by finding the probability that an activation level this low or lower could be obtained by an aircraft. Of course, in practice, when we have a large collection with essentially zero probability of repeats, this is a nonissue. But the subtle distinction may be of some academic interest.

Multiple Classes

The above discussion focused on the case of a simple decision: either the null hypothesis is true, or the alternative hypothesis is true. Confidence computation can be generalized to the case of multiple alternative hypotheses. A radar blip may be a nonaircraft, fighter, or passenger plane. Things get so much more difficult, though, that it is rarely worth the effort. The Bayes method for probabilistic neural networks is usually better if there is more than one alternative. See page 219.

The problem is that the confidence methods described so far apply only to rejecting the particular hypothesis whose distribution was sampled. When there are only two possibilities, null and one alternative, rejection of one generally constitutes acceptance of the other. But when there are multiple alternatives, rejection of one has less clear implications. For example, suppose we know the distributions of nonaircraft, fighters, and passenger planes. We can compute the three confidences that a blip is not a nonaircraft, not a fighter, and not a passenger plane. Pity the poor pilot in a combat situation who must sort out the meaning of these three numbers in a fraction of a second. And this is with only two alternative hypotheses. In general, we wish to avoid confidences computed this way when there are multiple alternatives.

Confidence in the Confidence

There are two sources of error in our computed confidence. In practice, the worst is nearly always design flaws in the collection procedure. Certain cases are under-represented, or missed entirely. And of course human nature dictates that it is precisely these same cases that failed to appear in the training set, a recipe for disaster. However, should we be smug enough to believe that we have devised a collection procedure capable of completely and fairly representing all possible cases, we should consider the other source of error: random-sampling error.

The activation levels under a given hypothesis have an unknown distribution. We are attempting to estimate this distribution by presumably fair random sampling from the population. It is reasonable to assume that the randomness (not design errors, mind you) inherent in the collection process will cause some activation levels to be attained in greater or lesser frequency than would be expected if the true distribution were followed exactly. It should also be intuitively obvious that the larger our collection, the more accurately it will reflect the true distribution. How accurately does our random sample reflect the true distribution? This can be quantified.

Suppose we collect n cases using fair random sampling. Define $S_n(x)$ to be the proportion of cases in that collection whose activations are less than or equal to x. In other words, if there are k cases in the sample whose activations are less than or equal to x, then $S_n(x) = k/n$. Let $F(x)$ be the true cumulative distribution function, which we are attempting to approximate with our sample. The maximum difference between the true CDF and that implied by the sample can be written:

$$D_n = \max_x |S_n(x) - F(x)| \qquad\qquad \text{20-1}$$

It is rather remarkable that the distribution of D_n, commonly called the Kolmogorov statistic, does not depend on $S_n(x)$ or $F(x)$. See [Kendall and Stuart, vol. II] for details. Thus, for some (typically small) significance level α, we can find a constant d_α such that:

$$P\{D_n = \max_x |S_n(x) - F(x)| > d_\alpha\} = \alpha \qquad \text{20-2}$$

regardless of the actual distribution function. The above formula may be inverted to provide the following immensely useful result:

$$P\{S_n(x) - d_\alpha \le F(x) \le S_n(x) + d_\alpha\} = 1 - \alpha \qquad \text{20-3}$$

In other words, we can find confidence bounds on the entire distribution function. Tables of d_α for various values of n and α can be found in nonparametric statistics textbooks that discuss the Kolmogorov-Smirnov test. Since, in our case, sample sizes are likely to be large, we can use the asymptotic formula:

$$d_\alpha \approx \sqrt{\frac{-\ln\left(\frac{\alpha}{2}\right)}{2n}} \qquad \text{20-4}$$

This formula is always conservative and is acceptably close for values of n greater than 35. When n exceeds 100 or so, the formula is nearly exact. For example, suppose that our sample size is 100 and we desire 95-percent confidence in our CDF estimates. α is then 0.05, so d_α = 0.136. In other words, we know with 95-percent certainty that the true distribution function lies everywhere within a band of plus or minus 13.6 percent of that implied by our sample. So even if we assume that our sampling method is fair, and even if we collect 100 samples, there is a 5-percent chance that a computed confidence of, say, 85 percent could actually be as low as 85 - 13.6 = 71.4 percent, or as high as 85 + 13.6 = 98.6 percent, with that degree of error due to nothing more than random collection error. Hmmm...

Example Programs

This section presents a subroutine for estimating a distribution function from a collection of activation function values. Also given are a pair of routines for computing left- and right-tail confidences for rejecting hypotheses.

Sorting

The world is overflowing with books that discuss sorting algorithms and that provide sample code for sorting routines. Therefore, no great amount of space will be wasted here with a lengthy exposition on the topic. However, for the sake of completeness, a sorting routine favored by the author for this type of problem is provided, along with a mercifully short discourse.

The sorting algorithm chosen is a version of the shellsort. Every graduate of computer science 101 knows that if a long array is to be sorted, some member of the quicksort family is nearly always the fastest. So why choose a shellsort? First, realize that top speed is not really needed here, as the sorting is done only once, offline. No sorting is needed during application of the network. Still, speed is nice. But there are two problems with the quicksort relative to the shellsort. First, the quicksort only runs away with the speed race for very long arrays. With moderate length arrays, the high overhead of the quicksort places it in the same ballpark as the quite respectable shellsort. Second, quicksorts suffer from the need of a stack whose length is data-dependent and hence difficult to predict in advance. The simplest versions use recursive calls, which can exhaust the run-time program stack, causing system crashes. More complex versions use internal stacks, but managing these stacks is more trouble than it is worth unless the amount of data to be sorted is very large and speed is critical.

For those who want to understand basically the sorting code shown below, the shellsort works by sorting equispaced subsets of the array. For example, on one pass it may act on the subset consisting of elements 1, 11, 21, 31, and so on. It will leave this subset sorted. It will similarly act on elements 2, 12, 22, 32, et cetera. At the end of a "width 10" pass, all subsets consisting of elements separated by 10 positions will be sorted. Then another pass is made, using narrower width. Obviously, when the width gets to one, the entire array will be sorted. By doing wider shells first, unusually large or small elements can be quickly transported nearly to their destination, rather than having to be moved there one position at a time. The sequence of shell widths can have a profound effect on performance. With those sketchy details dispatched, let us proceed to the code. Readers wanting more detail can see [Sedgewick, 1988], or any of a number of similar texts.

```
void shellsort (
    int n ,                    // Length of x array
    double *x                  // Data to be sorted ascending
    )
```

```
{
  int i, j, width, other ;
  double sentinel ;

/*
  Generate (in reverse order) a good sequence of sorting widths
*/

  for (width=1 ; width<n ;)        // Until we get large enough
    width = 3 * width + 1 ;        // avoid common factors in widths

  do { // Outer loop does each of a diminishing sequence of widths
    width /= 3 ;                   // Next shell width

    for (i=width ; i<n ; i++) {    // Do each of the shells

      sentinel = x[i] ;
      j = i ;

      for (;;) {
        other = j - width ;
        if ((other < 0) ||  (x[other] <= sentinel))
          break ;
        x[j] = x[other] ;
        j = other ;
        }

      x[j] = sentinel ;
      } // For each shell of this width

    } while (width > 1) ; // Outer loop does diminishing seq of widths
}
```

Estimating the Distribution

This subroutine performs the trivial task of counting sorted sample
values. It is given an unsorted array containing the collection of
samples under a given hypothesis. It calls the above shellsort routine
to sort the sample into ascending order. Duplicate values are removed
from the data array, and tail probabilities are computed. The output
array lprob is such that lprob[i] is the fraction (0 – 1) of the sample
which was less than or equal to x[i]. Similarly, rprob[i] is the fraction
greater than or equal to x[i]. It also uses the Kolmogorov-Smirnov test
to compute the estimated width of a confidence band around these
probabilities. The user inputs in ks_alpha an alpha level, such as 0.05
or 0.01. The value returned in ks_err is the amount which, if added to
and subtracted from any value in lprob (or rprob), would give a range
having 1 - ks_alpha probability of including the true population value
of lprob (or rprob). The estimated ks_err is always conservative (larger

than the true value). Its accuracy is quite good if the sample size is at least 35, and excellent for samples larger than 100.

```
void tailprob (
    int n ,                          // Length of data array as input
    double *x ,                      // In of data, out sorted with reps removed
    int *new_n ,                     // Output length of x after reps removed
    double *lprob ,                  // Output new_n long of left tail probs
    double *rprob ,                  // Ditto for right tail
    double ks_alpha ,                // Inp (often .05) of type I error for KS test
    double *ks_err                   // Out of corresponding error in l(r)prob   )

{
    int i, j ;

    shellsort ( n , x ) ;            // Sort ascending

    i = j = 0 ;                      // i indexes source, j dest
    while (i < n) {                  // Pass through entire array
        x[j] = x[i] ;                // Copy first occurrence of val
        rprob[j] = (double) (n-i) / (double) n ;    // Number greater or equal
        while ((++i < n)  &&  (x[i] == x[j])) ;      // Bypass repeats
        lprob[j++] = (double) i / (double) n ;       // Number less than or equal
        }

    *new_n = j ;

// Following is good if n>35, excellent if n>100, and always conservative

    *ks_err = sqrt ( -0.5 * log ( 0.5 * ks_alpha ) / (double) n ) ;
}
```

Estimating Confidences

After the above routine, tailprob, has been applied to the collection of samples made under some hypothesis, we need to be able to convert activation levels obtained in use to confidence levels for rejecting that hypothesis. The following two routines do this. They are essentially identical in operation. The first, leftconf, uses the left tail of the distribution. It would be used when the alternative to the sampled hypothesis involves low activation levels. Thus, if applied to the aircraft versus nonaircraft example presented several pages back, the leftconf routine would be used on a collection sampled from the aircraft category. Its computed confidences would be used to reject the hypothesis that the blip is an aircraft in favor of the hypothesis that it is a nonaircraft. The other routine, rightconf, would be used on nonaircraft samples to reject the hypothesis that the blip is a non-aircraft.

Both routines are given the sorted data array and appropriate tail probability array as returned by the tailprob subroutine. Of course, the n given to these routines would be the new_n returned by tailprob. They are also given an observed activation level. They simply scan the sorted array until the location is found such that the observed value is bounded between two adjacent elements of the data array. Linear interpolation is used to generate an approximate tail probability. The confidence is 1 minus the tail probability, and it is multiplied by 100 to express it as a percent. If the observed value lies outside the data array, the appropriate extreme value is returned.

```
double leftconf (
   int n ,                       // Length of x and lprob arrays
   double *x ,                   // Input of data, sorted with reps removed
   double *lprob ,               // Input of left tail probs from tailprob
   double observed               // Observed data value to be tested
   )

{
   int lo, mid, hi ;
   double p ;

   if (observed > x[n-1])
      return 0. ;

   if (observed <= x[0])
      return 100. * (1.0 - lprob[0]) ;

   lo = 0 ;                      // At all times we keep x[lo] < observed
   hi = n-1 ;                    // and x[hi] >= observed

   for (;;)                      // This loop cuts interval in half each time
      mid = (lo + hi) / 2 ;      // Center of interval
      if (mid == lo)             // Happens when lo and hi adjacent
         break ;                 // So then we are done
      if (x[mid] < observed)     // Replace appropriate intval end with mid
         lo = mid ;
      else
         hi = mid ;
      }

   p = (observed - x[hi-1]) / (x[hi] - x[hi-1]) * (lprob[hi] - lprob[hi-1]) ;
   p += lprob[hi-1] ;
   return 100. * (1.0 - p) ;
}


double rightconf (
   int n ,                       // Length of x and rprob arrays
   double *x ,                   // Input of data, sorted with reps removed
   double *rprob ,               // Input of right tail probs from tailprob
   double observed               // Observed data value to be tested
   )
```

```
{
  int lo, mid, hi ;
  double p ;

  if (observed > x[n-1])
    return 100. * (1.0 - rprob[n-1]) ;

  if (observed <= x[0])
    return 0. ;

  lo = 0 ;                    // At all times we keep x[lo] < observed
  hi = n-1 ;                  // and x[hi] >= observed

  for (;;) {                  // This loop cuts interval in half each time
    mid = (lo + hi) / 2 ;     // Center of interval
    if (mid == lo)            // Happens when lo and hi adjacent
      break ;                 // So then we are done
    if (x[mid] < observed)    // Replace appropriate intval end with mid
      lo = mid ;
    else
      hi = mid ;
  }

  p = (observed - x[hi-1]) / (x[hi] - x[hi-1]) * (rprob[hi] - rprob[hi-1]) ;
  p += rprob[hi-1] ;
  return 100. * (1.0 - p) ;
}
```

Bayesian Methods

The method for computing confidence discussed thus far has many advantages. It is straightforward, easy to compute, and relatively intuitive in meaning once its foundation is understood. There are no arbitrary decisions to be made in implementation (apart from sample collection details), and the Kolmogorov statistic provides at least a rough estimate of its accuracy. On the other hand, it is disturbing, especially to users not accustomed to dealing with statistics, that failure to reject a hypothesis does not imply its acceptance. And if we do happen to know the distributions of activation levels under both the null and alternative hypotheses, it would probably be preferable to have only one number to deal with rather than two. If we are willing to sacrifice some of that method's advantages, we can devise a method for computing confidence which gives us just one number having the property that high values imply high confidence in the alternative hypothesis, while low values imply high confidence in the null hypothesis. The dramatic improvement in interpretability of such a confidence measure may offset the fact that much more complex and somewhat arbitrary computations are involved, and that no method for statistically bounding potential errors is known (at least to the author).

An important prerequisite to using the method described here is that the null and alternative hypotheses (and of course the samples used to estimate their distributions) must be mutually exclusive and exhaustive. In other words, between them they should comprise every possible case, and neither of them should include cases that may fall into the other hypothesis. Furthermore, the random samples collected to estimate the distribution of activation levels for each hypothesis should fairly represent the full range of possibilities in each hypothesis. This is somewhat stronger than what is required for the straightforward method previously described. That method demanded that the hypotheses not overlap (no blip could be both aircraft and nonaircraft) and that the collection of samples should fairly represent the expected proportions of each case. But it did not necessarily demand that all possibilities be covered. It only demanded that sampling be correct for any hypothesis that was going to be tested for rejection. For example, suppose that we had three classes: nonaircraft, propelled aircraft, and hot air balloons. Hot air balloons are totally excluded from the study. If we want to find confidence levels for rejecting the null hypothesis that a blip is a nonaircraft, we need to sample completely all possible nonaircraft. Of course, now we can no longer equate rejecting the null hypothesis with confidence in the blip being a propelled aircraft; it may be a hot air balloon! But at least our confidence in rejecting the null hypothesis is valid. This is no longer true for the Bayes technique presented now. All possible cases must be covered and representative samples of each obtained. Failure to do so will result in falsely high confidence figures. Proceed with extreme caution in critical applications.

A formal statement of the procedure begins with Bayes' theorem. (Actually, Bayes' theorem is slightly more complex. See [Kendall and Stuart, vol. I] for details.) Suppose that we have K different hypotheses, which we will label $\{H_k, k = 1, ..., K\}$. These hypotheses are mutually exclusive and exhaustive. Let the likelihood of a random variable X under hypothesis H_k be written $L(x \mid H_k)$. This likelihood would be a probability in the case of a discrete distribution, and the value of the density function in the case of a continuous distribution. We know that exactly one of these hypotheses holds true, and the *prior* probability of H_k being in control is p_k, where $\Sigma p_k = 1$. If a sample of the random variable is obtained, we can use Bayes' theorem to compute the *posterior* probability that hypothesis H_k was in effect when the random variable was sampled:

$$P(H_k|x) = \frac{p_k L(x|H_k)}{\sum_i (p_i L(x|H_i))}$$ 20-5

We need to know two things in order to apply this formula for confidences. We must have a notion of the prior probabilities, and we need a reasonable estimate of the likelihood function of the neuron activation levels under every hypothesis.

The concept of prior probabilities is a major source of conflict among statisticians and researchers. Sometimes there are valid reasons for imposing unequal prior probabilities, and there may even be ways of estimating them. However, in case of doubt, it is nearly always best to follow the advice given by Bayes himself. In what is generally known as *Bayes' Postulate* (occasionally also referred to as the *Principle of Equidistribution of Ignorance*), he states that the prior probabilities should be assumed equal when nothing is known to the contrary. A large body of practical experience indicates that unless there is a compelling reason to assign unequal priors, it is best to leave them equal. A lively discussion of this topic, along with theoretical support, can be found in Chapter 8 of [Kendall and Stuart, vol. I].

The second piece of information needed, likelihood functions for neuron activations, is unfortunately much more difficult to obtain. Some possibilities are as follows:

1)   The network input data may be discrete, in which case the activations will also be discrete. If there is not a large number of possible values, the best approach may be to count occurrences of each value and treat the likelihood function as probabilities. In practice this will rarely arise. Also, unless the number of possible values is small relative to the number of samples obtained, the category counts are subject to unacceptably large statistical variation due to sampling error. Use this method only with great caution.

2)   If the data is continuous, the activation levels may still be counted in categories. For example, we may count the number of cases that produce an activation in the range 0–0.05, 0.05–0.1, et cetera. If a smoothing function, even something as simple as linear interpolation, is applied to the counts, this method may provide acceptable results. The category width is an arbitrary decision, and this method is uncomfortably susceptible to sampling error. But it is intuitive and easy to implement. If the sample is very large, this may be a good choice.

3) The method preferred by the author is the Parzen window approximation described in Chapter 12, *Probabilistic Neural Networks*. It does have the disadvantage of requiring an arbitrary choice of σ, the window width. But this is really no different than choosing the category width for the method above and is probably even less critical if the Parzen window function is smooth.

A class of density estimators was proposed by [Parzen, 1962]. This text describes it in some detail on page 205, so it will be only briefly reviewed here. Let $\{x_i, i = 1, ..., n\}$ be a random sample of size n from a population having unknown density function $f(x)$. He shows that we can construct from this sample an estimate of the density function:

$$g(x) = \frac{1}{n\sigma} \sum_i W\left(\frac{x - x_i}{\sigma}\right) \qquad \text{20-6}$$

Under very loose conditions on the underlying distribution and the choice of the window function W and constant σ, this estimator asymptotically approaches the true density function as the sample size increases.

It should be noted that for our purposes, $g(x)$ does not need to be strictly a probability density function. If it is a fixed multiple of the true density function, with the multiplier being the same for all alternative hypothesis populations, the constant multiplier will cancel in the Bayes formula for posterior probabilities. This means that we can simplify the ensuing discussion by eliminating constants like π and σ (assuming that the same σ is used for all populations). We should keep constants involving the sample size, though, as we would not like to impose the harsh restriction of sampling all populations equally.

Although there is an infinite number of choices for the window function, extensive experience has indicated that the Gaussian function performs well.

$$W(d) = e^{-d^2} \qquad \text{20-7}$$

It meets the intuitive criteria of being at a maximum at zero, then smoothly tapering to essentially zero as the difference increases.

Choosing the window width σ is slightly more difficult. We cannot simply optimize some criterion as we did with the jackknife procedure in the case of the probabilistic neural network. On the other hand, we do have a few advantages here. Since there is only one variable, the neuron activation level, we do not need to be concerned with interaction between σ and the number of variables in a sample vector. Also, the domain of the random variable is zero to one, since it is a neuron activation level expressed as a fraction of the maximum possible. This eliminates scaling problems. Also, we have the same rule of thumb that smaller values of σ should be used when the sample size is larger. In all cases of practical interest, the sample size would be quite large, as small samples have so much sampling error that our computed confidences would be useless. Thus, it appears that all we need to do is find a value of σ which works well for a sample of size 100 or so. Smaller samples, which would require larger values of σ for adequate smoothing, would never be encountered. And although larger samples might dictate smaller values of σ in order to squeeze out the last bit of accuracy in the estimate, we do not need to worry about this. Errors in the design of the sampling procedure will surely swamp out inadequacies in the density estimate due to excessive values of σ. So how do we choose this universal σ? A few pictures and an heuristic formula can help.

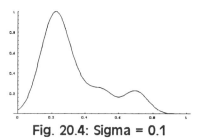

Fig. 20.2: Sigma = 0.004

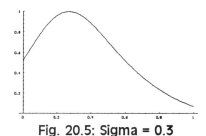

Fig. 20.3: Sigma = 0.05

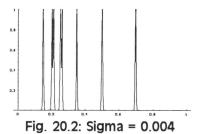

Fig. 20.4: Sigma = 0.1

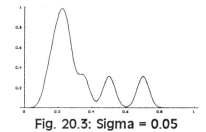

Fig. 20.5: Sigma = 0.3

A simulated collection of eight samples was created. The activation levels in this artificial collection are {0.15, 0.20, 0.21, 0.25, 0.26, 0.35, 0.50, 0.70}. This might resemble data collected under the null hypothesis for an application in which low activations are expected. The above four graphs show the estimated density function of this collection for sigmas of 0.004, 0.05, 0.1, and 0.3. It is the opinion of the author that σ should always be chosen so as to err on the side of being too large. This helps to smooth out the effects of sampling error. Even more importantly, it tends to broaden the rejection tail, resulting in more conservative confidence measures. Examination of the above graphs shows that blurring is very significant at $\sigma = 0.1$, so this should probably be an upper limit.

More definitive statements can be made, though. If we include σ in the definition of the Gaussian window function:

$$W(d) = e^{-(\frac{d}{\sigma})^2}$$
20-8

we can rewrite this formula to tell us the difference in activation levels needed to reduce the influence of a sample point to a given fraction of the maximum (which is 1.0). If we let a be that fraction and d be the difference in activations, we can solve for d.

$$d = \sigma\sqrt{-\ln(a)}$$
20-9

If we use $\sigma = 0.05$, an excellent general-purpose choice, then plugging $a = 0.5$ in the above formula gives $d = 0.04$. So, if we were estimating the density function at an activation level of, say, 0.3, then sample points having activation levels of 0.34 and 0.26 would have only half the influence on the density contribution as a point right at 0.3. Letting $a = 0.1$ gives $d = 0.076$, so we see that sample points greater than 0.376 or less than 0.224 would have almost no influence on the density estimate at 0.3. If for some reason more accuracy is deemed justifiable and important, values for σ as low as 0.02 may be acceptable. Only in the most special cases, involving huge, reliable collections, should smaller values be considered.

Example Program

A subroutine for computing the confidence in the alternative hypothesis given an attained activation level and samples collected under both hypotheses is shown below. Of course, the confidence in the null hypothesis is one minus that in the alternative (delightful!). This program simply passes through the data for each hypothesis, computing the distance between the observed and each sample point. The distance is weighted by σ, then plugged into the Gaussian function. The mean of the Gaussian function is computed for each sample. If the sum rather than the mean were used, the effect would be to bias the computed confidence with prior probabilities proportional to the size of the collections. The user could easily incorporate the effect of arbitrary prior probabilities and/or misclassification costs by multiply-

ing sum0 and sum1 by the prior probability and/or cost before returning the ratio of sum1 to their sum.

```
double parzconf (            // Returns conf in alternative hypothesis
   int n0 ,                  // N of samples in null hypoth collection
   int n1 ,                  // And alternative
   double *h0 ,              // Null hypothesis samples
   double *h1 ,              // And alternative
   double sigma ,            // Scale parameter (0.02 to 0.05 best)
   double observed           // Observed value to be classified
   )

{
   int i ;
   double d, sum0, sum1 ;

   sum0 = 1.e-30 ;                    // Insurance against dividing by 0 later
   for (i=0 ; i<n0 ; i++) {
      d = (observed - h0[i]) / sigma ;
      sum0 += exp ( - d * d ) ;
      }
   sum0 /= (double) n0 ;

   sum1 = 1.e-30 ;
   for (i=0 ; i<n1 ; i++) {
      d = (observed - h1[i]) / sigma ;
      sum1 += exp ( - d * d ) ;
      }
   sum1 /= (double) n1 ;

   return 100. * sum1 / (sum0 + sum1) ;
}
```

Multiple Classes

The author knows of no simple, direct way of generalizing the Bayes
method for activation levels of a single output neuron to the problem
of more than one alternative hypothesis. Although the Bayes theorem
cited earlier was stated in its full, multiple-class generality, the sample
program was written for the two-hypothesis problem. There are three
possible solutions to consider, though.

It may be feasible, in some rare circumstances, to train the
network to achieve different activation levels for different classes. For
example, we may train it to achieve minimum activation for nonaircraft, half-activation (0.5) for hot air balloons, and full activation for
propelled aircraft. In this case, the Bayes method could be used.
Three means would be computed, each based on a collection from one
of the three hypotheses. The confidence in each hypothesis would be
the mean for that hypothesis divided by the sum of all three means.
This method is not generally recommended, though, as training a

network to respond in this manner is often difficult. Some researchers would say that it is impossible unless there is some ordinality in the classes; a propelled aircraft must be "more" of something than a hot air balloon is. They would be wrong. It is quite possible to train a network to respond with 0.1 activation for apples, 0.5 for oranges, and 0.9 for bananas. It is just difficult in many cases, as well as ugly.

The second possibility is that Bayesian confidences can be easily and legitimately computed for multiple-class problems if a probabilistic neural network is used. The problem we have with the method of this chapter is that rather than using the original data, we are using achieved activation levels of a single output neuron. But if Bayesian confidences are important, strong consideration should be given to using a probabilistic neural network. Multiple-class confidences are discussed on page 219.

The third possible approach involves using multiple output neurons from an arbitrary network as inputs to a probabilistic neural network. This would most likely be one neuron for each class, though that is not strictly necessary. More compact coding schemes are possible (though generally less effective). The network would be trained to activate fully exactly one neuron according to the class to which the training sample belongs. No neurons would be activated for the "reject" class (null hypothesis). Bayesian confidences could then be computed by treating the output neurons' activations as a multivariate sample vector. The probabilistic neural network model would be applied to this vector. This is, of course, a rather silly, roundabout route. It would nearly always be better to use the probabilistic neural network on the raw data directly, rather than going through what is essentially a data-reduction process, which is likely to cause information loss. However, there are several scenarios under which this method may be appropriate:

1) There may be a very large number of input neurons, and rapid classification may be vital. If the relatively slow performance of the probabilistic neural network precludes its direct use, it may be necessary to train a feedforward network (or some other model) in order to take advantage of its fast classification. After reducing the amount of data to the number of output neurons, the probabilistic neural network will run much faster.

2) A network may already exist which has proven competence or sentimental value. It might be impossible to convince the powers-that-be to switch to a probabilistic neural network. This method allows us to compute confidences from an existing network.

3) We must reluctantly admit at least the *possibility* that a probabilistic neural network may have performance that is inferior to that of some other model. This is rare, but it can happen. In this case, a hybrid model may be appropriate.

The hybrid scheme just described is presented in more detail on page 235.

Hypothesis Testing versus Bayes' Method

The reader may be thoroughly confused at this point, wondering about the relative merits of the two confidence computation methods discussed in this chapter. They frequently give very different results, so which one is right? The answer lies in the fact that they are telling us different types of information. This section will attempt to clarify their similarities and differences.

First, it must be remembered that sometimes we do not have the luxury of choosing between these two methods. We can use the Bayes method only when two conditions are satisfied:

1) The hypotheses must be mutually exclusive (usually easy) and exhaustive (not so easy). If any possibilities are not covered by one of the hypotheses, then individual hypothesis testing is our only choice.

2) Fair and representative samples must be available under all hypotheses. If, as is often the case, we cannot sample under one or more hypotheses, the Bayes method cannot be used. We can only compute confidence in rejecting hypotheses that can be sampled.

The meanings of these two types of confidence measures can be better understood with the aid of an example. Suppose that we plot (Figure 20.6) in one chart the distribution of activation levels under the null hypothesis (left curve) and the alternative hypothesis (right curve). This degree of separation is an unrealistic dream, but it will

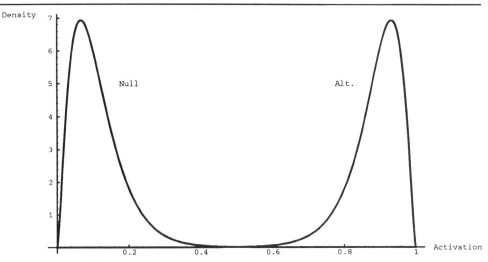

Fig. 20.6: Response distributions of a dream network

help to clarify some points of confusion.

If the network achieves an activation level of 0.1, the two competing confidence measures will be numerically different, but identical in meaning. The confidence in rejecting the null hypothesis is about 50 percent (just eyeballing the left curve), which tells us nothing useful. However, the confidence in rejecting the alternative hypothesis is essentially 100 percent, because virtually all of the area under the right curve lies to the right of 0.1. This tells all. Finally, the confidence in the alternative hypothesis as computed with the Bayes method, which is the height of the right curve at 0.1 divided by the sum of the heights of the left and right curves at that point, is clearly 0. Hence the Bayes confidence in the null hypothesis is 100 percent. No conflict between the two methods there. Similarly, there would be no problem for activations near 1.

Now let us examine the case of an activation level of 0.3. The confidence in rejecting the alternative hypothesis, and the Bayes confidence in the null hypothesis, will still both be 100 percent. But now the confidence in rejecting the null hypothesis is greater than 95 percent, for less than 5 percent of the area under the left curve lies to the right of 0.3 as the author's eye sees it. Very strange. Bayes' theorem tells us that the confidence in the null hypothesis is 100 percent, while hypothesis testing tells us that we can have better than a 95-percent confidence in *rejecting* the null hypothesis! What's going on?

One more example is needed. If our network achieves an activation level of 0.5, things get really confusing. Hypothesis testing will give us virtually 100-percent confidence in rejecting *both* the null and alternative hypotheses. Yet, if we can take the liberty of supposing that the minuscule heights of both curves are equal at the 0.5 activation level point, Bayes' method tells us that we have 50-percent confidence in both hypotheses!

The answer to this confusion lies in understanding that the Bayes method treats the hypotheses themselves as random events, one of which *must* have occurred (so their confidences *must* sum to one). A radar blip appears. Whether it was created by an aircraft or a nonaircraft is random, but certainly one of those two things created it. Given that fact, and its resultant neuron activation level, Bayes' method assigns probabilities to the random hypotheses. It cares nothing about the probability of having received a particular form of blip. It takes the blip as given and treats the hypotheses as random events.

Hypothesis testing works in the reverse direction. One of the two hypotheses is given to be true. It is not a random event. It is the blip that is the random event. The question answered concerns the probability of getting the attained neuron activation level under the assumption of a particular hypothesis. *This probability is not addressed in Bayes' method.* So in the final example above, in which a 50-percent activation level was attained, Bayes' method ignores the fact that this is a practical impossibility. It just says that there is a 50–50 chance that either hypothesis could be true. Hypothesis testing, on the other hand, recognizes the rareness of that event and tells us to reject both hypotheses.

This difference in information has immense practical implications. It is tempting to say that Bayes' method, when it can be used, is always superior to hypothesis testing. The fact that it gives one number instead of two is compelling, as is the fact that low confidences as well as high confidences have meaning. However, its greatest strength is also its greatest weakness. What if, despite our best efforts, we failed to sample adequately one or both of our hypotheses? When that unexpected event occurs in use, the network may attain an intermediate activation level unlike that expected under either hypothesis. *Bayes' method will fail to warn us.* Examining the above distributions again, suppose that an activation of 0.6 is attained. The height of the right curve at that point is hundreds of times that of the left curve there. Bayes' method will give us a confidence of 100 percent in the alternative hypothesis. But that confidence may be unwarranted in view of the fact that there would be only the tiniest probability under the alternative hypothesis of getting an activation so low. Hypothesis testing would inform us of this.

One solution to the dilemma of which method to choose is to use both to generate two confidences. The primary confidence would be the Bayes figure, as it is the most interpretable for most users. However, the probability of being wrong under the hypothesis *that has maximum Bayes probability* could also be provided. Thus, in the example above in which an activation of 0.6 was obtained, we would present the user with both the 100-percent Bayesian confidence in the alternative, and the nearly zero probability of attaining this activation. This figure would be the area under the right curve to the left of 0.6. If we attained an activation of 0.4, we would return a Bayesian confidence in the alternative hypothesis of 0, and also supply the area under the left curve to the right of 0.4. Whether or not this secondary confidence should be implemented in the final product is debatable. However, it can be a lifesaver during the validation phase.

21

Optimizing the
Decision Threshold

When a neural network is used to make a decision, a threshold of half-activation is traditionally used. If it is possible to estimate reliably the distribution of activation levels under both the null and alternative hypotheses, we can often choose the threshold more intelligently.

One of the most common uses for a neural network is to make a yes–no decision. Does this blood sample test positive for leukemia? Is that radar blip an aircraft? Does this person's financial history justify issuing a credit card? Is this bolt flawed? These and similar questions are answered every day by neural networks. One important aspect of the decision process, that of choosing an appropriate neuron-activation threshold, is the topic of this chapter.

Much of the material here is related to material in Chapter 20, *Confidence Measures* (page 361). It is strongly suggested that the reader be familiar with that material before reading this chapter. In fact, as will be made clear later, the methods of this chapter are largely unnecessary if the Bayesian confidence is computed as described in Chapter 20, and decisions are based on that confidence. However, the approach taken here is somewhat different, and certainly instructive in that it approaches the same fundamental problem from a radically different angle.

The traditional method for creating a neural network capable of making a simple yes–no decision is to collect a training set consisting of samples from both categories. One of these categories will be called the null hypothesis, and the other will be called the alternative hypothesis. There is no strict rule that states which of the question's answers is to be called the null hypothesis and which the alternative. As far as the mathematics of this chapter goes, they are interchangeable. However, in many other statistical procedures, it does matter. For now, we will simply agree to abide by the convention that the null hypothesis is generally the simpler, or perhaps more "normal" state. If the question is one of disease, usually we would make health the null hypothesis. If the question regards the presence of a certain pattern in a signal, we make the null hypothesis correspond to the lack of the pattern.

Once suitable training samples have been collected, a neural network is trained to have a relatively small activation (typically 10 percent or so) for members of the null hypothesis collection, and large activation (90 percent) for members of the alternative collection. When it comes time for the network actually to make a useful decision, that decision is based on the achieved activation relative to a predefined threshold. Since 50-percent activation is halfway between the trained levels, it is intuitively obvious that we should decide that the alternative hypothesis is in effect if and only if the achieved activation is at least 50 percent. But as we all know, intuition is not foolproof. We will now investigate how to choose a threshold that may be better.

First, we must define precisely what we mean by a "better" threshold. How do we judge the merit of one threshold versus another? One commonly used, excellent criterion is the *expected misclassification cost*. This was presented in detail on page 347. To review briefly, suppose we know that when the network is used, there will be a certain probability q that the alternative hypothesis is true. By implication, the null hypothesis will be true with probability $1 - q$. Let c_1 be the cost of incorrectly deciding that the alternative is true (often called a type I error), and c_2 be the cost of failing to detect it (a type II error). Note that if we are unable to provide at least rough approximations to q, c_1, and c_2, there is no point in trying to improve on the 50-percent threshold tradition. As a last resort, try setting $q = 0.5$ and assign equal costs to both types of error. Suppose also that we have some threshold whose performance we wish to evaluate. Using this threshold, let p_1 be the probability that our network will falsely detect the condition when it is not present, and p_2 be the probability that it will fail to detect it when it is present. The two probabilities would be measured from large random samples. Given these numbers, the cost of using this threshold is computed as

$$\text{COST} = (1 - q)p_1 c_1 + q p_2 c_2 \qquad \text{21-1}$$

Basically what we do then is to try many thresholds, and choose the one that minimizes this cost.

There is one subtle but important difference between evaluating the cost here and evaluating it with the same formula in the *Cost Functions* section of Chapter 19 (page 347). In that section, we evaluate the performance of an existing network, using a fixed threshold. For that purpose, it is vital that a test set independent of the training set be used. Basing a performance evaluation on the same data on which the network was trained would be grossly unfair. However, here we are not rigorously demanding such fairness. Our goal is simply to choose a threshold optimally. In a sense, this is actually part of the training. Therefore, *as long as each training set (null and alternative hypotheses) fairly represents the underlying populations*, it is somewhat legitimate to use the training set if it is impossible to collect new samples. It is certainly preferable to use independent collections if possible. The training set may well generate distributions that are overly optimistic in their clustering about the target activations. The effect of this bias on the computed optimal threshold is data dependent and cannot be generally predicted. However, using the training set here would not be the monstrous sin that it would be in the case of evaluating the network's performance.

The size of the two collections need not reflect the relative frequency (prior probability) of each hypothesis. The algorithms that follow will normalize for the collection size. All that is important is that within each of the two hypotheses the sampling is done randomly and fairly. If some component of the population is over or under-represented, the calculated optimal threshold may be in error.

Once we have our collections of sample activations obtained under the null and alternative hypotheses, and have the prior probabilities and cost constants, it is trivial to compute the cost due to a given threshold. Count the number of samples from the null hypothesis which equal or exceed the threshold and divide by the number of samples in that collection. This gives the probability of a type I error. Multiply by the prior probability of the null hypothesis, and by the cost of a type I error. This is the expected cost due to type I errors. Then we count the number of samples from the alternative hypothesis whose activations are strictly less than the threshold, and divide by the total number to get the probability of a type II error. Multiply this by the prior probability of the alternative hypothesis and the cost of a type II error to get the expected cost due to type II errors. Adding the two expected costs gives us the total expected cost due to this threshold.

An example will clarify the above discussion and also make another important point. Figure 21.1 shows the probability density functions of hypothetical samples under the null hypothesis (left curve, having smaller activations) and the alternative hypothesis.

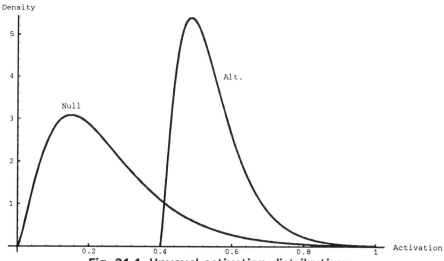

Fig. 21.1: Unusual activation distributions

For simplicity, assume that the prior probabilities are both 0.5 and the misclassification costs are equal. Thus, the total expected cost due to a given threshold is proportional to the area under the left curve to the right of the threshold plus the area under the right curve to the left of the threshold. The optimal threshold that we seek is that which minimizes the sum of these areas. Clearly, the traditional choice of 0.5 would produce a dreadful number of type II errors; we must use something lower. But what?

This unusual pair of distributions was chosen to illustrate an extremely common error made by inexperienced practitioners. It is commonly thought that the correct choice is made by sliding the threshold until the probabilities of each type of error are equal. Obviously, the probabilities are related to the threshold in opposite directions. Changing the threshold raises the probability of one type of error while lowering the probability of the other. Suppose that some threshold can be found such that both errors have a probability of, say, 0.1. Raising the threshold increases the probability of a type II error and lowers the probability of a type I error, and vice versa. It is tempting to think that the balance point is the optimal criterion. It may *not* be so! This can be easily seen from the above figure. The optimal threshold is actually the point at which the densities intersect. In the above case, the probability of a type II error is practically zero at that point; virtually all of the misclassification cost is coming from type I errors. Yet increasing the threshold for a more equitable balance will increase the type II error probability far faster than the type I error is decreased, raising the total cost. Thus, we must consider the sum of the errors in choosing the optimal threshold.

There are two very different approaches to finding the minimum cost threshold. One directly uses the distributions of the samples in each collection. The cost due to any given threshold can be explicitly computed by counting as previously described. The other approach involves estimating the density function under each hypothesis by means of the samples, then seeking the intersection of the two densities. In practice, both methods will usually give very nearly the same optimal threshold. The direct method has several advantages. It is easily understood, fast to compute, and does not require any arbitrary decisions to be made. The density estimation method is much slower and more complex, and requires that several arbitrary decisions be made as to how the sample is smoothed to yield a density function. On the other hand, it is the opinion of the author that the density estimation method is superior because it makes more efficient use of the sample to reduce the effects of random sampling errors. And remember that speed is not essential for this operation, as it is done only once, offline, as part of the training procedure.

For practical reasons, and for the education of the reader, both methods will be presented. The fast, crude, direct method will be used to make an initial guess as to the location of the optimum threshold. Then the slower but more accurate density estimation method will be used to refine the threshold.

Code for computing the cost by means of the direct method is shown next. The prior probabilities and misclassification costs are combined into wt0 and wt1. The count subroutine uses binary search to count the number of samples which equal or exceed the supplied threshold. The direct_crit subroutine divides these counts by the number of samples to get the error probability, then multiplies by the prior probability times the misclassification cost, summing to get the total cost.

```
static int count (
   int n ,
   double *array ,
   double value
   )

{
   int lo, mid, hi ;

   if (value > array[n-1])
     return 0 ;

   if (value <= array[0])
     return n ;

   lo = 0 ;                      // At all times we keep array[lo] < value
   hi = n-1 ;                    // and array[hi] >= value

   for (;;) {                    // This loop cuts interval in half each time
     mid = (lo + hi) / 2 ;       // Center of interval
     if (mid == lo)              // Happens when lo and hi adjacent
       return n - hi ;           // This is the number >= value
     if (array[mid] < value)     // Replace appropriate intval end with mid
       lo = mid ;
     else
       hi = mid ;
     }
}

double direct_crit (
   int n0 ,                      // Number of samples under null hypoth
   int n1 ,                      // And under alternative
   double *s0 ,                  // Null hypoth samples (sorted ascending)
   double *s1 ,                  // And alternative (sorted ascending)
   double wt0 ,                  // Null prior times cost of type I error
   double wt1 ,                  // Alt prior times type II error cost
   double thresh                 // Threshold to evaluate cost criterion
   )

{
   double type_I, type_II ;

   type_I = (double) count ( n0 , s0 , thresh ) / (double) n0 ;
   type_II = 1.0 - ((double) count ( n1 , s1 , thresh ) / (double) n1) ;

   return wt0 * type_I + wt1 * type_II ;
}
```

We will estimate the density function from the collection of samples by means of the Parzen window approach, described on page 205. As was done there, the Gaussian function is used for the Parzen window. Also, constant factors common to both hypotheses can be ignored, so we need not normalize our estimator to produce a true density (which integrates to 1). Thus, our (modified) density estimator is

$$g(x) = \frac{1}{n\sigma} \sum_i W\left(\frac{x-x_i}{\sigma}\right)$$ 21-2

where the window function W is the Gaussian function:

$$W(d) = e^{-d^2}$$ 21-3

Choosing an effective value for σ will be discussed later.

Code for computing the difference between the null and alternative densities is shown here. Each hypothesis is treated identically. The trial threshold is subtracted from each sample and weighted by σ. This difference is acted upon by the Gaussian function, and the mean across the collection found. This gives us a constant multiple of the estimated density function at that threshold. These are multiplied by the prior probability times the misclassification cost, and subtracted. Finally, the difference in weighted densities is divided by their sum. This normalization, while not strictly necessary, makes the function more sensitive in areas of low density. Note that sum0 and sum1 are initialized to a tiny number, rather than zero. This harmless insurance guarantees that we won't divide by zero when returning the final criterion.

```
double parzen_crit (
   int n0 ,                    // Number of samples under null hypoth
   int n1 ,                    // And under alternative
   double *s0 ,                // Null hypoth samples (sorted ascending)
   double *s1 ,                // And alternative (sorted ascending)
   double wt0 ,                // Null prior times cost of type I error
   double wt1 ,                // Alternative prior times type II error cost
   double sigma ,              // Scale parameter (0.05 - 0.1 best)
   double thresh               // Threshold at which to evaluate criterion
   )

{
   int i ;
   double d, sum0, sum1 ;
```

```
sum0 = 1.e-30 ;                    // Insurance against dividing by 0 later
for (i=0 ; i<n0 ; i++) {
   d = (thresh - s0[i]) / sigma ;
   sum0 += exp ( - d * d ) ;
   }
sum0 /= (double) n0 ;              // Multiple of density under null hypothesis

sum1 = 1.e-30 ;
for (i=0 ; i<n1 ; i++) {
   d = (thresh - s1[i]) / sigma ;
   sum1 += exp ( - d * d ) ;
   }
sum1 /= (double) n1 ;              // Multiple of density under alternative

return (wt0 * sum0  - wt1 * sum1) / (wt0 * sum0 + wt1 * sum1) ;
}
```

The routine that controls computation of the optimal threshold is shown here. It starts by calling a sort routine (page 372) for both collections. This allows the count routine to use a fast binary search, rather than brute force counting. Then a search across the entire range of thresholds, zero to one, is done. The number of equally spaced trial thresholds, nfirst, would typically be at least 20, perhaps 50 or more. Occasionally, false minima can appear, and fine spacing makes it less likely that they will be a problem. Once the best threshold has been found with this quick and crude method, we are ready to refine it with the more sophisticated method.

The first step in the refinement phase is to replace our direct-method criterion with one computed by the Parzen method. Then we evaluate the criterion at a second point very near the best. This second point is chosen so that it is closer to the center of the legal threshold range than the first. The criterion is evaluated at the second point. The two points are swapped if necessary, so that the one designated (xnew, ynew) has a smaller (better) criterion. This is because the upcoming refinement loop will always discard the oldest point, and we certainly want to discard the worse one.

The iterative refinement is the basic secant method, with a few specialized enhancements. The old and new points are used to compute an estimate, by linear interpolation or extrapolation, of where the criterion is expected to be equal to zero. One of our special enhancements is that the computed change, diff, is limited in absolute value. This prevents wild jumps, which are all too common. Then, the new values become old, and we compute new new values by adding the computed difference to xnew and evaluating the criterion there. Again, we enhance the traditional secant method by limiting the threshold to its legal domain of zero to one. In the vast majority of cases, this will very quickly converge to the threshold at which the Parzen criterion is zero.

The parameter tol is provided to insure timely escape from the optimization loop. Setting it to 0.001 or so will provide more than enough accuracy, while still not requiring an excessive number of iterations. The maxits parameter gives us an insurance policy against (rare) lack of convergence. Since in the vast majority of problems, convergence is obtained after fewer than 5 iterations, setting this to 20 or so is reasonable.

Additional insurance against lack of convergence is obtained by keeping track of the best criterion (the absolute value of the signed criterion) throughout the entire process. In the unusual event that the secant method fails, we will at least be left with the value obtained by scanning the domain with the direct method. In practice, this is generally a perfectly acceptable figure and in fact rarely differs much from the refined figure.

```
double conf_opt (
    int n0 ,                        // Number of samples under null hypoth
    int n1 ,                        // And under alternative
    double *s0 ,                    // Null hypothesis samples
    double *s1 ,                    // And alternative
    double wt0 ,                    // Null prior times type I error cost
    double wt1 ,                    // Alternative prior times type II error cost
    double sigma ,                  // Scale parameter (0.05 - 0.1 best)
    int nfirst ,                    // Number of trials for first approx (20-50)
    int maxits ,                    // Max number of secant iterations (0-20)
    double tol                      // Quit if this rel error (.001 good)
    )

{
    int i ;
    double thresh, crit, bestcrit, bestthresh, xold, yold, xnew, ynew ;
    double diff, temp ;

    shellsort ( n0 , s0 ) ;                 // Sort ascending
    shellsort ( n1 , s1 ) ;

/*
    Find a first approximation by trying nfirst equispaced intervals in 0-1.
    Use the direct distribution method as the criterion.
*/

    bestcrit = 1.e30 ;  // Will keep best criterion here

    for (i=0 ; i<nfirst ; i++) {
        thresh = (double) i / (double) (nfirst-1) ;
        crit = direct_crit ( n0 , n1 , s0 , s1 , wt0 , wt1 , thresh ) ;
        if (crit < bestcrit) {
            bestcrit = crit ;
            bestthresh = thresh ;
            }
        }
```

```
/*
    We have found a threshold 'bestthresh' whose direct method criterion
    'bestcrit' is the best of all of our initial search tries. Now switch to the
    Parzen criterion. Evaluate it at bestthresh and replace bestcrit with the
    Parzen criterion. Then iterate with the secant method, keeping track of
    the best for safety.
*/

    if (! maxits)                      // User may not want use of Parzen
      return bestthresh ;

    xold = bestthresh ;                // This is first secant point
    yold = parzen_crit ( n0 , n1 , s0 , s1 , wt0 , wt1 , sigma , xold ) ;
    bestcrit = fabs(yold) ;            // Going to new (Parzen) criterion now

    if (xold >= 0.5)                   // Choose second secant pt slightly away
      xnew = xold - 0.02 ;             // from the first, in the direction of
    else                               // the larger interval
      xnew = xold + 0.02 ;

    ynew = parzen_crit ( n0 , n1 , s0 , s1 , wt0 , wt1 , sigma , xnew ) ;

    if (fabs(ynew) < fabs(yold)) { // Make the newest point be one which
      bestthresh = xnew ;          // has the best criterion, so that we
      bestcrit = fabs(ynew) ;      // later throw out the worse point
      }

    else {
      temp = xold ;
      xold = xnew ;
      xnew = temp ;
      temp = yold ;
      yold = ynew ;
      ynew = temp ;
      }

    while ((maxits--)  &&  (bestcrit > tol)) {   // Secant method loop
      diff = ynew - yold ;                       // This term will be in denom
      if (fabs(diff) < 1.e-30) {                 // so avoid dividing by zero
        if (diff > 0)
          diff = 1.e-30 ;
        else
          diff = -1.e-30 ;
        }

      diff = (xold - xnew) * ynew / diff ;       // Offset to next root guess
      if (diff > 0.05)                           // Do not allow wild jumps
        diff = 0.05 ;                            // Recall that we should
      if (diff < -0.05)                          // already be near the root
        diff = -0.05 ;

      xold = xnew ;                              // Last iteration's new point
      yold = ynew ;                              // becomes old for this iter
      xnew += diff ;                             // This is the next guess
```

```
        if (xnew > 1.0)                          // Bound to legal domain
           xnew = 1.0 ;
        if (xnew < 0.0)
           xnew = 0.0 ;

        ynew = parzen_crit ( n0 , n1 , s0 , s1 , wt0 , wt1 , sigma , xnew ) ;
        if (fabs(ynew) < bestcrit) {             // Keep track of best
           bestthresh = xnew ;                   // as secant method may
           bestcrit = fabs(ynew) ;               // not necessarily converge!
           }
        }

     return bestthresh ;
}
```

Little has been said regarding the choice of σ, the window-width parameter. Larger values result in loss of detail but more immunity to sampling error. On page 379, where the subject was confidences, it was suggested that σ be somewhere around 0.02 to 0.05. This is good when important multiple modes may be present and we want to squeeze as much accuracy as possible out of the sample (though we are in danger from sampling error). When our goal is simply to choose one optimal threshold, it is in our better interest to smooth the collections more. The author would tend to use 0.05 as a lower limit, and perhaps go as high as 0.1 or so.

This chapter should end with several warnings. The first is that random sampling error, even in collections containing several hundred samples, can be surprisingly large. This is especially true around thresholds where the probability density is small. The densities will often be at their smallest in the vicinity of the optimal threshold, so we can expect the most instability there. The net effect is that unless the collections consist of many hundreds of samples (which they really should for important applications), it is to be expected that considerable variation in the chosen threshold could occur if the collection process is repeated.

On the other hand, the same mechanism that makes such variation likely also reduces its importance. By definition, if the probability density is low in an area, it is unlikely that many cases will fall into that area in application. Conversely, if there is consider-able overlap in the null and alternative distributions, meaning that a significant number of samples can be expected to appear near the chosen threshold, then the estimated optimal threshold will be much more stable due to the large number of training samples in its vicinity.

This entire chapter has implicitly assumed that fair and representative random sampling could be done. The most dire warning of this chapter must be that *such sampling is far more difficult than most people realize*. In fact, for many applications, it may be nearly impossible. It is easy to overlook one or more possibilities, which may later appear when the finished network is used, with disastrous consequences. Even more difficult and complex is the issue of fair representation. Sometimes this may not be too difficult. If, for example, we are seeking the presence of a particular signal among background noise, we may be able to collect thousands of samples of background noise and be satisfied that we have a reasonable represen-tation of all significant noise patterns in proportions close to what may be expected in practice. What if our task is sonar identification of underwater military targets, though? Probably we would want boulders to be among the null-hypothesis collection. But how can we be sure that we have a representative set of boulders of all sizes and shapes? And how many do we include, relative to other members of the null-hypothesis collection? These questions are frequently perplexing. We must not fall into a false sense of security from using a sophisticated optimization algorithm when we have fed garbage to that algorithm.

The final warning concerns the possibility of multimodal distri-butions. This is not at all unlikely. It is quite possible that certain subpopulations may produce their own little groups of activation levels. Figure 21.2 shows activation distributions under the two hypotheses.

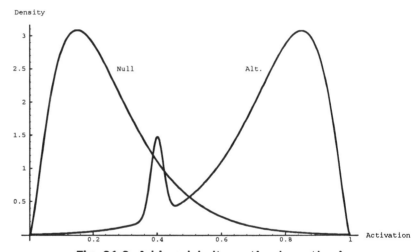

Fig. 21.2: A bimodal alternative hypothesis

The alternative hypothesis has such a subpopulation. The methods of this chapter will zero in on one of the three intersection points. Unfortunately, that would not be satisfactory. Recall that for optimal performance we want to choose the hypothesis that has the larger density function at the achieved activation level. Clearly, the null hypothesis should be chosen for activation lower than the leftmost intersection point, and the alternative chosen for activations exceeding the rightmost. However, the situation reverses between these points. No single threshold will do.

There is a poor solution to this dilemma, and a good solution. The poor but sometimes reasonable solution is to choose σ so large that the subpopulation gets blurred into the main population. Examination of a graph of the estimated density function will help. The only instance in which this may be valid is if there is reason to believe that the secondary hump may be due to sampling error, an unlikely event if a large collection was obtained.

The good solution is to abandon entirely the single threshold methods of this chapter. Use the Bayes technique describe on page 376. By choosing the hypothesis having the larger posterior confidence, we guarantee optimal performance regardless of the number of modes and intersection points.

Using the NEURAL Program

This chapter is a user's manual for the NEURAL program partially listed in the Appendix and completely supplied on disk.

The NEURAL program is a general purpose, neural network training and testing program. Three- and four-layer feedforward models trained by the conjugate gradient algorithm are supported. Weight initialization can be done by genetic optimization or simulated annealing (with or without regression enhancement). Simulated annealing is used to escape from local minima. Unsupervised training is also implemented with a basic Kohonen network. Learned weights can be saved to a disk file for later retrieval. This allows training to be interrupted, then resumed.

Three output models are possible. CLASSIFY mode implements a classifier, using one output neuron for each class. AUTO mode uses an autoassociative model. GENERAL mode allows arbitrary input–output mappings to be learned. When in CLASSIFY mode, confusion matrices can be computed and optionally written to ASCII disk files. In any mode, output responses to data in an input file can be written to disk.

The program is controlled by commands having a simple syntax. Each command occupies a single line. Case (upper/lower) is ignored, as are leading blanks. The first word (or several words) defines the command. Most commands also require a parameter, which is separated from the main command by a colon (:). Spaces before and after the colon are optional. If a semicolon (;) appears, all text that follows on the line is ignored. This facilitates comments.

Commands may be typed in interactively, or they may be stored in an ASCII text file. A command control file is processed with the command:

CONTROL : filename

Control files may be nested. In other words, CONTROL commands may appear inside control files.

The command **QUIT:** is used to exit the program and return to the operating system.

The command line parameter **/DEBUG d**, where d is the letter of a disk drive, may appear after the program name. For example:

NEURAL /DEBUG C

This causes a file called MEM.LOG to be written to that drive. This file contains detailed memory allocation–deallocation information, making it easier to fine-tune performance on a system with limited memory. Naturally, considerable programming experience and familiarity with the program source code are prerequisites to effective use of this option.

Output Models

The *output model* refers to the way in which outputs are related to inputs. It has nothing to do with the *network model*. The NEURAL program supports three different output models, which should cover the majority of all practical problems.

CLASSIFY Model

This model is specified with the command **OUTPUT MODEL:CLASSIFY**. It assumes that there will be exactly as many output neurons as there are possible classes. When the training set is built, the class for each case (or collection of cases) will be specified with the **CLASSIFY OUTPUT** command described later. The network will be trained so that only the output neuron corresponding to that class will be activated. This output model allows the network to be tested with confusion matrices. This model must be used if the KOHONEN network model is used.

AUTO Model

This model is autoassociative. It is specified with the command **OUTPUT MODEL:AUTO**. The network will be trained so that its outputs reproduce its inputs. The user must specify an equal number of input and output neurons when this architecture is defined. Remember to consider range restrictions for the data. For example, the LAYER model should not be presented with data less than 0.1 or greater than 0.9 or so. The limits for the KOHONEN model are strictly -1 to 1 if Z-axis normalization is used.

GENERAL Model

This is a fully general $\Re^n$ to $\Re^m$ mapping model. It is specified with the command **OUTPUT MODEL:GENERAL**. Remember to consider range restrictions for the output data to be learned. For example, the LAYER model should not be asked to learn data having values less than 0.1 or greater than 0.9 or so. The limits for the KOHONEN model are strictly -1 to 1 if Z-axis normalization is used.

Building the Training Set

The training set is built by means of one or more **TRAIN:filename** commands. Each time this command is encountered, any existing training set will be augmented with additional data from the named file. To erase the entire training set, use the **CLEAR TRAINING** command.

The training file is in ASCII format, with one line per case. Each line contains one or more real numbers with an optional sign and decimal point. The number of numbers per line depends on the output model. The CLASSIFY and AUTO models will have one number for each input. The GENERAL model will have that, plus one number for each output. The inputs come first on the line.

If the CLASSIFY output model is in effect, and the LAYER network model is being used, a class number must be specified before a TRAIN command is issued. This is done with the **CLASSI-FY OUTPUT:integer** command. The integer is the class number, from 1 through the number of outputs. A value of zero can also be specified. This says that the upcoming cases are in a reject category. The network will be trained to turn off all output neurons for such cases. A CLASSIFY OUTPUT command must appear before the first TRAIN command. It will remain in effect for all subsequent TRAIN commands until another CLASSIFY OUTPUT command appears. Thus, they do not need to be repeated for each TRAIN command if those TRAIN commands refer to the same class.

The LAYER Network Model

This is a classical multiple-layer feedforward network. It can contain zero, one, or two hidden layers. It must have at least one input neuron and one output neuron. This model is defined by specifying the LAYER model and giving the number of input, hidden, and output neurons. Five commands are required:

> NETWORK MODEL : LAYER
> N INPUTS : integer
> N HIDDEN1 : integer
> N HIDDEN2 : integer
> N OUTPUTS : integer

Set N HIDDEN1 to zero for no hidden layers. It is illegal to specify a positive number for N HIDDEN2 if N HIDDEN1 is zero. The number of outputs must be equal to the number of inputs if AUTO output mode will be used. In CLASSIFY output mode, the number of outputs will be set equal to the number of classes.

Initialization by Simulated Annealing

The weight vectors are initialized by simulated annealing if the command LAYER INIT:ANNEAL (optionally followed by NOREGRESS to suppress regression enhancement) is used before the LEARN command. The annealing parameters can be specified as follows:

ANNEAL INIT TEMPS : integer - The number of temperatures.

ANNEAL INIT ITERS : integer - The number of trials at each temperature.

ANNEAL INIT SETBACK : integer - Amount to set back the iteration counter each time improvement is had.

ANNEAL INIT START : number - Starting temperature. This is the standard deviation of the weight perturbation.

ANNEAL INIT STOP : number - Final temperature.

Reasonable defaults are provided for all of these values. See NEU-RAL.CPP in the program listing on disk for a complete listing of all defaults.

Initialization by Genetic Optimization

The weight vectors are initialized by genetic optimization if the command LAYER INIT:GENETIC is used before the LEARN command. The genetic parameters are fully described in Chapter 8. They can be specified as follows:

GENETIC INIT POOL : integer - The size of the gene pool.

GENETIC INIT GENS : integer - The number of generations.

GENETIC INIT CLIMB - Specifies that hill climbing is to be used.

GENETIC INIT NOCLIMB - Specifies that hill climbing is not to be used.

GENETIC INIT CROSS : number - Probability (0–1) of crossover.

GENETIC INIT MUTATE : number - Probability (0–1) of mutation.

GENETIC INIT OVERINIT : number - Overinitialization factor, at least 1.0 (which provides no overinitialization).

Reasonable defaults are provided for all of these values. See NEURAL.CPP in the program listing on disk for a complete listing of all defaults.

Learning

After the training set has been built, the network is trained by issuing one of the following initialization commands, followed (not necessarily immediately) by the LEARN: command. Note that the LAYER INIT commands do not initiate learning. That is done with the LEARN command. These only specify how weight initialization is to be done. One of these commands *must* be issued after the model is set or saved weights are retrieved.

LAYER INIT : NOINIT - No weight initialization is done. Learning picks up at the current weight values. This would most likely be used after retrieving a saved weight file which was a product of incomplete training. This must never be used for initial training, as the conjugate gradient algorithm will stall when confronted with an all-zero weight set.

LAYER INIT : ANNEAL - Simulated annealing is used to initialize the hidden layer weights. Regression is then used to initialize the output weights.

LAYER INIT : ANNEAL NOREGRESS - Simulated annealing is used to initialize all weights. This requires less memory than the regression method, but usually gives inferior results.

LAYER INIT : GENETIC - Genetic optimization is used to initialize the weights.

LAYER INIT : REGRESS - This is valid only when there are no hidden layers. Regression is used to initialize the output weights.

After initialization, the conjugate gradient algorithm is used to minimize the mean-squared output error. When the minimum is found, simulated annealing is used to attempt to break out of what may be a local minimum. The parameters for this annealing can be set with commands that are identical to those for annealing initialization, as listed earlier, except that the INIT is omitted from the command. For example, **ANNEAL TEMPS:4** would set the number of temperatures to 4. If annealing reduces the error, the conjugate gradient method is used again. This repeats infinitely, unless several iterations in a row produce only trivial improvement. If that happens, or if annealing causes no improvement at all, annealing around a center of zero is used to find an entirely new set of starting weights, and the conjugate gradient algorithm is tried again. This is illustrated as a flowchart in Figure 22.1.

The command **QUIT ERROR:number** can be used to specify a stopping criterion. The number is a percent, 0–100, of the maximum possible output error. If the learning progresses to the point that the error becomes that small, it is halted. Usually, we would set the error equal to zero, then press ESCape to halt training when patience expires. But setting it to larger, realistic values can be useful when running multiple experiments in a control-file batch.

The number of times simulated annealing about a center of zero is used for retries can be limited with the command **QUIT RETRIES:number**. After the initial try, at most this many retries will be done if the error never drops to the quitting error level. This provides an alternative method of escape when running in batch mode. The QUIT ERROR could be set equal to zero, and the QUIT RETRIES set to a reasonably small number.

The KOHONEN Network Model

This is a classical Kohonen network with single neuron learning. It has no hidden layers. It must have at least one input neuron and one output neuron. This model is defined by specifying the KOHONEN model and an input normalization, and giving the number of input and output neurons. Four commands are required:

> NETWORK MODEL : KOHONEN
> KOHONEN NORMALIZATION : MULTIPLICATIVE/Z
> N INPUTS : integer
> N OUTPUTS : integer

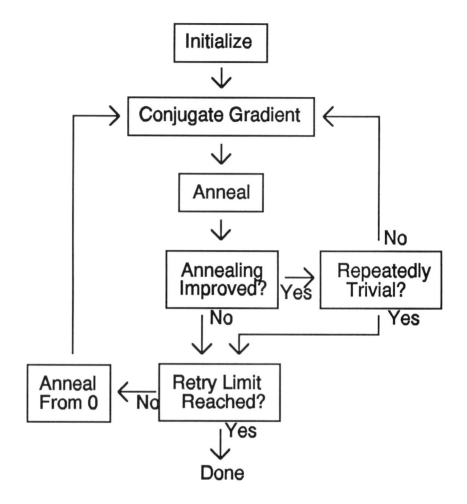

Fig. 22.1: LAYER network learning

Initialization and Learning

After the training set has been built, the network is trained by issuing one of the following initialization commands, followed (not necessarily immediately) by the LEARN: command. Note that the KOHONEN INIT commands do not initiate learning. That is done with the LEARN command. These only specify how weight initialization is to be done. One of these commands *must* be issued after the model is set or saved weights are retrieved.

KOHONEN INIT : NOINIT - No weight initialization is done. Learning picks up at the current weight values. This would most likely be used after retrieving a saved weight file that was a product of incomplete training. This must never be used for initial training, as the Kohonen algorithm behaves poorly when confronted with an all-zero weight set. The starting error will often slightly exceed the previous final error due to the weights being normalized to unit length.

KOHONEN INIT : RANDOM - The weights are initialized randomly. This is the traditional approach.

The type of input normalization must be specified as either MULTIPLICATIVE or Z. The learning algorithm should also be specified:

KOHONEN LEARN:ADDITIVE or
KOHONEN LEARN:SUBTRACTIVE

The learning rate and rate reduction may be specified with the commands:

KOHONEN LEARNING RATE : number
KOHONEN LEARNING REDUCTION : number

Typical values are 0.4 and 0.99, respectively. These topics are discussed in Chapter 8.

After initialization, the Kohonen algorithm is used to minimize the error. When the minimum is found, a new set of random weights is generated, and the learning process restarted. The command **QUIT ERROR:number** can be used to specify a stopping criterion. The number is a percent, 0–100, of the maximum possible output error. If the learning progresses to the point that the error becomes that small, it is halted. Usually, we would set the error equal to zero, then press ESCape to halt training when patience expires. But setting it to larger, realistic values can be useful when running multiple experiments in a control-file batch.

The number of times random weight retries are done can be limited with the command **QUIT RETRIES:number**. After the initial try, at most this many retries will be done if the error never drops to the quitting error level. This provides an alternative method of escape when running in batch mode. The QUIT ERROR could be set equal to zero, and the QUIT RETRIES set to a reasonably small number.

Confusion Matrices

After a neural network (LAYER or KOHONEN) has been trained as a classifier (in CLASSIFY mode), its performance can be evaluated with the aid of a confusion matrix (page 348). This matrix is evaluated one row at a time. A row consists of as many elements as there are output neurons, plus one for the reject category.

The first step is to zero the counters in the row. This is done with the command **RESET CONFUSION:**. We must also set the classification threshold. This command is **CONFUSION THRESH-OLD:number**, where the number is a percent (0–100) of full activation. Once set, it will remain at that value unless explicitly set again.

The confusion is cumulated by means of one or more **CLASSI-FY:filename** commands. The format of the input data file is identical to that of training files. It is an ASCII text file, having one line per case. Each line contains as many real numbers, with optional sign and decimal point, as there are network inputs. Each case will be presented to the network, and the maximally activated output neuron located. If that activation is at least as large as the confusion threshold, the element of the confusion row corresponding to that neuron will be incremented. Otherwise, the last element of the row, the reject counter, will be incremented.

When a row has been completely cumulated, the results can be made available in one of two ways. The command **SHOW CONFUSION:** lists the vector on the computer screen. The command **SAVE CONFUSION:filename** appends the vector as a new line at the end of an ASCII text file. If the file does not exist, it will be created.

Saving Weights and Execution Results

After a network (any model, any output mode) has been trained, its weights can be saved to a disk file with the command **SAVE WEIGHTS:filename**. This is not an ASCII text file. Rather, it is a more compact form. The file header format can be found in WT_SAVE.CPP, while the weight format can be found in the wt_save member function of the specific network class. The weights are retrieved with the **RESTORE WEIGHTS:filename** command. The learning parameters are not saved with the file. If a LEARN: command is issued to continue training, the user must make sure that NOINIT is specified for initialization, and all important learning parameters are set as desired. The appropriate NOINIT command must be issued *after* the network model is set (either explicitly or by RESTORE WEIGHTS), as setting the model voids previous initialization methods. Note that if KOHONEN model weights are restored and LEARN restarted, the error may exceed that listed as the previous final result due to the fact that weights were normalized before being saved.

The execution results of a trained network can be saved to disk also. The first step is to provide the name of the ASCII text file to which the results will be written. The command is **OUTPUT FILE:filename**. That command does not actually do anything. It simply tells the program that from now on (until another OUTPUT FILE command appears), all execution results are to be appended to that file. Then, one or more EXECUTE:filename commands appear. The format of the named input data file is identical to that of the TRAIN file, noting that only inputs are present on each line. In GENERAL output mode, we would not specify outputs! For each case read, a row will be appended to the output file. This row will contain as many real numbers, each in the range 0–1, as there are output neurons. Each number in the line will be the fraction activation of each output neuron in response to a case in the input data file named on the EXECUTE statement.

Alphabetical Glossary of Commands

ANNEAL INIT ITERS : integer - The number of trials at each temperature (for LAYER model simulated annealing weight initialization).

ANNEAL INIT SETBACK : integer - Amount to set back the iteration counter each time improvement is had (for LAYER model simulated annealing weight initialization).

ANNEAL INIT START : number - Starting temperature. This is the standard deviation of the weight perturbation (for LAYER model simulated annealing weight initialization).

ANNEAL INIT STOP: number - Final temperature (for LAYER model simulated annealing weight initialization).

ANNEAL INIT TEMPS : integer - The number of temperatures (for LAYER model simulated annealing weight initialization).

ANNEAL ITERS : integer - The number of trials at each temperature (for LAYER model simulated annealing local minimum escape).

ANNEAL SETBACK : integer - Amount to set back the iteration counter each time improvement is had (for LAYER model simulated annealing local minimum escape).

ANNEAL START : number - Starting temperature. This is the standard deviation of the weight perturbation (for LAYER model simulated annealing local minimum escape).

ANNEAL STOP : number - Final temperature (for LAYER model simulated annealing local minimum escape).

ANNEAL TEMPS : integer - The number of temperatures (for LAYER model simulated annealing local minimum escape).

CLASSIFY:filename - Read an ASCII text file of input data and cumulate confusion. Valid only in CLASSIFY output mode.

CLASSIFY OUTPUT:integer - Set the class number (0 for reject) for subsequent TRAIN commands. Valid only in CLASSIFY output mode.

CLEAR TRAINING: - Erase the entire training set.

CLEAR WEIGHTS: - Erase learned weights.

CONFUSION THRESHOLD:number - Specify the minimum percent activation (0–100) necessary to avoid being tossed into the reject category. Valid only in CLASSIFY output mode.

CONTROL:filename - Read and execute an ASCII text file of commands.

EXECUTE:filename - Read a file of input data, and write results to the current output file.

GENETIC INIT CLIMB - Specifies that hill climbing is to be used for LAYER model genetic weight initialization.

GENETIC INIT CROSS : number - Probability (0–1) of crossover for LAYER model genetic weight initialization.

GENETIC INIT GENS : integer - The number of generations for LAYER model genetic weight initialization.

GENETIC INIT MUTATE : number - Probability (0–1) of mutation for LAYER model genetic weight initialization.

GENETIC INIT NOCLIMB - Specifies that hill climbing is not to be used for LAYER model genetic weight initialization.

GENETIC INIT OVERINIT : number - Overinitialization factor, at least 1.0 (which provides no overinitialization). For LAYER model genetic weight initialization.

GENETIC INIT POOL : integer - The size of the gene pool for LAYER model genetic weight initialization.

KOHONEN INIT:NOINIT - Train a KOHONEN network with no weight initialization being done. Learning picks up at the current weight values. This would most likely be used after retrieving a saved weight file that was a product of incomplete training. This must never be used for initial training, as the Kohonen algorithm may stall.

KOHONEN INIT:RANDOM - Train a KOHONEN network with random weight initialization being done. This is the usual method.

KOHONEN LEARN:ADDITIVE - Kohonen's original learning formula is used during training.

KOHONEN LEARN:SUBTRACTIVE - The more modern learning formula is used during training.

KOHONEN LEARNING RATE:number - Specifies the learning rate (0–1).

KOHONEN LEARNING REDUCTION:number - Specifies the learning rate reduction per epoch (0–1).

KOHONEN NORMALIZATION:MULTIPLICATIVE - Specifies that multiplicative input normalization is to be used. Input vectors that are identically zero are prohibited.

KOHONEN NORMALIZATION:Z - Specifies that Z-axis input normalization is to be used. Inputs must strictly lie in [-1, 1].

LAYER INIT:ANNEAL - Train a LAYER network using simulated annealing to initialize the hidden layer weights. Regression is then used to initialize the output weights.

LAYER INIT:ANNEAL NOREGRESS - Train a LAYER network using simulated annealing to initialize all weights. This requires less memory than the regression method, but gives inferior results.

LAYER INIT:GENETIC - Train a LAYER network using genetic optimization to initialize the weights.

LAYER INIT:NOINIT - Train a LAYER network with no weight initialization being done. Learning picks up at the current weight values. This would most likely be used after retrieving a saved weight file that was a product of incomplete training. This must never be used for initial training, as the algorithm will stall when confronted with an all-zero weight set.

LAYER INIT:REGRESS - Train a LAYER network having no hidden layers. Regression is used to initialize the output weights.

LEARN: - Train the network.

NETWORK MODEL:KOHONEN - Set the network to be a Kohonen model.

NETWORK MODEL:LAYER - Set the network to be a multiple-layer feedforward model.

N HIDDEN1:integer - Set the number of neurons in the first hidden layer. May be zero for no hidden layer.

N HIDDEN2:integer - Set the number of neurons in the second hidden layer. Must be zero if N HIDDEN1 is zero.

N INPUTS:integer - Set the number of input neurons.

N OUTPUTS:integer - Set the number of output neurons.

OUTPUT FILE:filename - Name the ASCII text file to which subsequent EXECUTE results will be written.

OUTPUT MODEL:AUTO - Set the outputs to autoassociative mode.

OUTPUT MODEL:CLASSIFY - Set the outputs to CLASSIFY mode.

OUTPUT MODEL:GENERAL - Set the outputs to general function mapping.

QUIT: - Terminate the NEURAL program and return to the operating system.

QUIT ERROR:number - Specify a percent (0–100) error at which learning will terminate.

QUIT RETRIES:integer - Specify the number of times learning will restart at a new point after convergence is obtained, but the error is larger than the QUIT ERROR.

RESET CONFUSION: - Zero all elements in the confusion vector.

RESTORE WEIGHTS:filename - Retrieve learned weights from a disk file.

SAVE CONFUSION:filename - Append the confusion vector to a disk file.

SAVE WEIGHTS:filename - Write learned weights to a disk file.

SHOW CONFUSION: - Write the confusion vector on the computer screen.

TRAIN:filename - Read an ASCII text file of training data, appending it to any existing training set.

Verification of Program Operation

Several files are included on the supplementary disk for testing the program. They exercise all network and output models. Since the control files are also illustrative of typical program operation, they are listed here. They reference the following data files, which for the sake of space are not listed:

AUTO.DAT - Twenty equally spaced phases of a sine wave sampled at 20 points from minus π to π. There are 20 cases (lines), each containing 20 points (a complete sine wave at some phase). This is used for autoassociative learning of a sine wave. They are, of course, scaled to lie in 0.1 to 0.9.

GENERAL.DAT - Two-hundred one cases for learning the sine and cosine functions from minus π to π. Each case (line in the file) contains three points: x, $\sin(x)$ and $\cos(x)$. The sine and cosine are, of course, scaled to lie in 0.1 to 0.9.

KOHONEN.DAT - One hundred cases, each of which is three random numbers ranging from -1 to 1.

M5.DAT - Six cases of 5 bit binary numbers (1–31) that are divisible by 5. Each case (line) consists of 5 binary digits ordered from most to least significant.

M7.DAT - Four cases as above, but divisible by 7.

REJECT.DAT - Twenty-one cases as above. These are the numbers from 1 through 31 that are not divisible by 5 or 7.

Overall control is provided with the VERIFY.CON control file. It runs five different tests using a relatively high error limit. The weights are saved after each task is learned. Then the error limit is reduced to a tiny value and all of the tests are repeated, restoring the previously saved weight files. For the three tests that operate in CLASSIFY output mode, the confusion matrix is displayed. The VERIFY.CON file is as follows:

```
QUIT ERROR: 0.5
QUIT RETRIES: 2
CONFUSION THRESHOLD: 50

CONTROL: AUTO.CON
LEARN:
SAVE WEIGHTS: auto.wts
CLEAR WEIGHTS:
CLEAR TRAINING:

KOHONEN NORMALIZATION MULTIPLICATIVE:
CONTROL: KOHONEN.CON
LEARN:
SAVE WEIGHTS: koh1.wts
RESET CONFUSION:
CLASSIFY: kohonen.dat
SHOW CONFUSION:
CLEAR WEIGHTS:
CLEAR TRAINING:

CONTROL: CLASSIFY.CON
LEARN:
SAVE WEIGHTS: classify.wts
RESET CONFUSION:
```

```
CLASSIFY: reject.dat
SHOW CONFUSION:
RESET CONFUSION:
CLASSIFY: m5.dat
SHOW CONFUSION:
RESET CONFUSION:
CLASSIFY: m7.dat
SHOW CONFUSION:
CLEAR WEIGHTS:
CLEAR TRAINING:

KOHONEN NORMALIZATION Z:
CONTROL: KOHONEN.CON
LEARN:
SAVE WEIGHTS: koh2.wts
RESET CONFUSION:
CLASSIFY: kohonen.dat
SHOW CONFUSION:
CLEAR WEIGHTS:
CLEAR TRAINING:

CONTROL : GENERAL.CON
LEARN:
SAVE WEIGHTS: general.wts
CLEAR WEIGHTS:
CLEAR TRAINING:

; Read back all weight files, continue training

QUIT ERROR: 0.01
QUIT RETRIES: 5

CONTROL: AUTO.CON
RESTORE WEIGHTS: auto.wts
LAYER INIT: NOINIT
LEARN:
CLEAR WEIGHTS:
CLEAR TRAINING:

CONTROL: KOHONEN.CON
RESTORE WEIGHTS: koh1.wts
KOHONEN INIT: NOINIT
LEARN:
RESET CONFUSION:
CLASSIFY: kohonen.dat
SHOW CONFUSION:
CLEAR WEIGHTS:
CLEAR TRAINING:

CONTROL: CLASSIFY.CON
RESTORE WEIGHTS: classify.wts
LAYER INIT: NOINIT
LEARN:
RESET CONFUSION:
CLASSIFY: reject.dat
```

```
SHOW CONFUSION:
RESET CONFUSION:
CLASSIFY: m5.dat
SHOW CONFUSION:
RESET CONFUSION:
CLASSIFY: m7.dat
SHOW CONFUSION:
CLEAR WEIGHTS:
CLEAR TRAINING:

CONTROL: KOHONEN.CON
RESTORE WEIGHTS: koh2.wts
KOHONEN INIT: NOINIT
LEARN:
RESET CONFUSION:
CLASSIFY: kohonen.dat
SHOW CONFUSION:
CLEAR WEIGHTS:
CLEAR TRAINING:

CONTROL : GENERAL.CON
RESTORE WEIGHTS: general.wts
LAYER INIT: NOINIT
LEARN:
CLEAR WEIGHTS:
CLEAR TRAINING:
```

The first test is of a three-layer network learning all phases of a sine wave in autoassociative mode. Its control file, AUTO.CON, is as follows:

```
NETWORK MODEL: LAYER
LAYER INIT: GENETIC
OUTPUT MODEL: AUTO
N INPUTS: 20
N OUTPUTS: 20
N HIDDEN1: 5
N HIDDEN2: 0
TRAIN: auto.dat
```

The second test is of the Kohonen model. The training set consists of 100 cases, each containing 3 random numbers. Its control file, KOHONEN.CON, is as follows:

```
NETWORK MODEL: KOHONEN
KOHONEN INIT : RANDOM
OUTPUT MODEL: CLASSIFY
N INPUTS: 3
N OUTPUTS: 10
TRAIN: kohonen.dat
```

The third test uses a three-layer feedforward network as a classifier. There are two classes. One consists of the integers from 1 to 31 that are divisible by 5. The other class is those divisible by 7. Each integer is represented by a five-bit binary number, each of whose bits is used as an input to the network. CLASSIFY.CON is as follows:

```
NETWORK MODEL: LAYER
LAYER INIT : GENETIC
OUTPUT MODEL: CLASSIFY
N INPUTS: 5
N OUTPUTS: 2
N HIDDEN1: 6
N HIDDEN2: 0
CLASSIFY OUTPUT: 0
TRAIN: reject.dat
CLASSIFY OUTPUT: 1
TRAIN: m5.dat
CLASSIFY OUTPUT: 2
TRAIN: m7.dat
```

The fourth test is identical to the second, except that a different input normalization is used. This is specified in the VERIFY.CON file. The same control file is used as in the second test.

The final test is of a three-layer feedforward network simultaneously learning the sine and cosine functions. GENERAL.CON is as follows:

```
NETWORK MODEL: LAYER
LAYER INIT: GENETIC
OUTPUT MODEL: GENERAL
N INPUTS: 1
N OUTPUTS: 2
N HIDDEN1: 5
N HIDDEN2: 0
TRAIN: general.dat
```

The prospective user of the NEURAL program would do well to study the above examples. Examining the .DAT data files on disk would also be informative.

Appendix

This appendix contains source code listings of the most important routines in the NEURAL program. Complete code can be found on the accompanying disk.

This appendix contains a listing of the most important parts of the NEURAL program. This includes class headers and all neural computation. The main driver and most support routines are omitted, but may be found in the accompanying disk. The subroutines are arranged alphabetically by the name of the module file. All header files appear together first, followed by all program files. Within each file, the various subroutines are in no particular order, although some attempt at systematic ordering is made.

The following is a list of all source code modules that comprise the NEURAL propgram. They may be found in the \NEURAL subdirectory on the accompanying disk. An asterisk (*) next to the name here indicates that the module is listed in this appendix.

*CLASSES.H - Headers for all classes
*CONST.H - Constants and other declarations. This also contains comments important to compiling the program, so should be read carefully.
FUNCDEFS.H - Function declarations
ACTIVITY.CPP - Compute the activation of a single neuron
ACT_FUNC.CPP - Activation function
*ANNEAL.CPP - Simulated annealing initialization of weights
CONFUSE.CPP - Compute and output confusion matrix
*CONJGRAD.CPP - Conjugate gradient optimization
CONTROL.CPP - Read ASCII CONTROL files
*DIRECMIN.CPP - Directional minimization routine used for conjugate gradient optimization
DOTPROD.CPP - Dot product of two vectors
EXECUTE.CPP - Handle most aspects of the EXECUTE statement
*GEN_INIT.CPP - Genetic initialization of weights
*KOHNET.CPP - Kohonen network routines
*LAYERNET.CPP - Feedforward layer network routines
LONGRAND.CPP - Special random number generator
MEM.CPP - Memory allocation / deallocation
MESSAGES.CPP - Write messages to user
*NETWORK.CPP - General Network class routines
NEURAL.CPP - Main program
PARSDUBL.CPP - Parse floating point vectors from a string
*REGRESS.CPP - Use regression to estimate output weights
SHAKE.CPP - Randomly perturb a weight vector
*SVDCMP.CPP - Singular value decomposition
TRAIN.CPP - Read and process training sets
VECLEN.CPP - Compute the squared length of a vector
WT_SAVE.CPP - Save weights to disk

```
/********************************************************************************/
/*                                                                            */
/*   CLASSES - Headers for all classes                                        */
/*                                                                            */
/********************************************************************************/

/*
--------------------------------------------------------------------------------

   TrainingSet - Collection of samples which will be used for training

   All training data is stored in 'data'.  If the output model is HETERO, the
   input for each sample is followed in 'data' by the number (1 through nout)
   of the output class to which that sample belongs.  If the output model is
   GENERAL, the output values follow the input values.  No output values are
   stored in AUTO mode, since the output is the input!

   The variable 'bufcnt' is the number of samples which could still fit in
   'data' without allocating more memory.  This allows us to allocate memory
   in large blocks, avoiding the overhead of often expensive operating system
   calls to malloc.

--------------------------------------------------------------------------------
*/

class TrainingSet {

public:

   TrainingSet ( int outmodel , int n inputs , int n outputs ) ;
   ~TrainingSet () ;
   void train ( char *file , int outclass ) ;

   unsigned ntrain ;  // Number of samples in 'data'
   double *data ;     // Actual training data here
   int outmod ;       // Output model (see OUTMOD ? in CONST.H)
   int nin ;          // Number of input neurons
   int nout ;         // Number of output neurons

private:

   unsigned bufcnt ;  // Sample areas remaining unused at end of 'data'
} ;

/*
--------------------------------------------------------------------------------

   SingularValueDecomp - Singular value decomposition of matrices

   Normally, the user would:
      1) Use 'new' to create a SingularValueDecomp object with all necessary
         memory (a, u?, w, v, work, b) allocated by the constructor.
      2) Fill in the public 'a' with the matrix to be decomposed.
      3) Call svdcmp to decompose a, replacing it with the U matrix if preserve
         is zero, else computing u.
         This will also compute w and v, which are normally not used but are
         public just in case the user wants to access them.
      4) Fill in the 'b' vector with the right hand side of the equations.
      5) Call backsub with a pointer to the cols vector which is where the
         solution will be placed.  This vector is NOT allocated by the
         constructor.  The outputs of svdcmp (a, u?, w, v) will not be disturbed.
      6) Repeat the above step as desired.
      7) Delete the SingularValueDecomp object, which frees all memory which
         was allocated by the constructor.

--------------------------------------------------------------------------------
*/

class SingularValueDecomp {

public:

   SingularValueDecomp ( int rows , int cols , int preserve ) ;
   ~SingularValueDecomp () ;
   void svdcmp () ;
   void backsub ( double thresh , double *x ) ;

   int ok ;           // Was memory allocation successful?

/*
   The following four input/output areas are allocated by the constructor
*/
```

```
      double *a ;         // Rows by cols input of 'A' matrix, output of U
      double *u ;         // unless preserve != 0, in which case U output here
      double *w ;         // Cols vector output of singular values, not sorted
      double *v ;         // Cols by cols output of 'V' matrix
      double *b ;         // Rows vector of RHS input to backsub

   private:

      int rows ;          // Number of rows in 'A' matrix
      int cols ;          // and number of columns
      double *work ;      // Cols work vector (allocated by constructor)
} ;

/*
--------------------------------------------------------------------------------

   Network - General parent of things common to all networks

   The constructors for the child classes set 'ok' to one if all memory
   allocation succeeded.  Otherwise they set it to zero.

--------------------------------------------------------------------------------
*/

class Network {

public:
   void classify from file ( char *name , double thresh ) ;
   void execute from file ( char *inname , char *outname ) ;
   virtual void learn ( TrainingSet *tptr ,
                        struct LearnParams *lptr ) = 0 ;
   void reset confusion () ;
   void save confusion ( char *name ) ;
   void show confusion () ;
   virtual void trial ( double *input ) = 0 ;
   virtual int wt save ( FILE *fp ) = 0 ;
   virtual void wt restore ( FILE *fp ) = 0 ;

#if BAD COMPILER
   virtual ~Network() ;
#else
   virtual ~Network() = 0 ;
#endif

   int ok ;            // Was all constructor memory allocation successful?
   double *out ;       // Output neuron activations here if exe nonzero
   double neterr ;     // Mean square error of the network if executed
   int outmod ;        // Output model (see OUTMOD ? in CONST.H)
   int nin ;           // Number of input neurons
   int nout ;          // Number of output neurons
   int *confusion ;    // Handy work area avoids malloc/free (see CONFUSE.CPP)

protected:

   double trial error ( TrainingSet *tptr ) ;   // Compute training set error

   int exe ;           // Are work areas allocated to allow executing it?
} ;

/*
--------------------------------------------------------------------------------

   LayerNet

   Nhid1 and nhid2 are the number of neurons in the first and second layers
   respectively.  Either or both may be zero.  If nhid1 is zero, it is assumed
   that nhid2 is also zero.

   Weights for a layer are stored as a two dimensional matrix strung out into
   a vector.  For example, the first element in hid1 coefs is the weight
   connecting the first input neuron to the first hidden neuron.  The second
   connects the second input to the first hidden.  The nin+1 element is the
   bias for the first hidden unit.  The nin+2 connects the first input to the
   second hidden, et cetera.

--------------------------------------------------------------------------------
*/

class LayerNet: public Network {

public:
```

```
        LayerNet ( int outmodel , int n inputs , int n hidden1 , int n hidden2 ,
                   int n outputs , int exe , int zero ) ;
        ~LayerNet () ;
        void learn ( TrainingSet *tptr , struct LearnParams *lptr ) ;
        void trial ( double *input ) ;
        int wt save ( FILE *fp ) ;
        void wt restore ( FILE *fp ) ;

        int nhid1 ;                // Number of neurons in hidden layer 1
        int nhid2 ;                // Ditto for hidden layer 2

private:

        void anneal ( TrainingSet *tptr , struct LearnParams *lptr ,
                      LayerNet *bestnet , int init ) ;
        double conjgrad ( TrainingSet *tptr , int maxits ,
                          double reltol , double errtol ) ;
           void check grad ( TrainingSet *tptr , double *grad ) ;
           double find grad ( TrainingSet *tptr , double *hid2delta ,
                              double *outdelta , double *grad ) ;
           void find new dir ( double gam , double *g , double *h , double *grad ) ;
           double gamma ( double *g , double *grad ) ;
        void copy weights ( LayerNet *dest , LayerNet *source ) ;
        double direcmin ( TrainingSet *tptr , double start err ,
                          int itmax , double eps , double tol ,
                          double *base , double *direc ) ;
           void negate dir ( double *direc ) ;
           void preserve ( double *base ) ;
           void step out ( double step , double *direc , double *base ) ;
           void update dir ( double step , double *direc ) ;
        void gen init ( TrainingSet *tptr , struct LearnParams *lptr ) ;
        void perturb ( LayerNet *cent , LayerNet *perturbed , double temp ,
                       int regress) ;
        double regress ( TrainingSet *tptr , SingularValueDecomp *sptr ) ;
        void zero weights () ;

        double *hid1 coefs ;       // nhid1 * (nin+1) weights (in changes fastest)
        double *hid2 coefs ;       // nhid2 * (nhid1+1) weights (hid1 changes fastest)
        double *out coefs ;        // nout * (nhid?+1) weights (hid? changes fastest)
        double *hid1 ;             // Hid 1 neuron activations here if exe nonzero
        double *hid2 ;             // Ditto hidden layer 2
} ;

/*
--------------------------------------------------------------------------------

   KohNet

   There are no hidden units and no bias terms.
   The output weights are stored as a two dimensional matrix
   strung out into a vector.
   For example, the first element in out coefs is the weight
   connecting the first input neuron to the first output neuron.
   The second connects the second input to the first output.
   Element nin+1 connects the first input to the second output, etc.

--------------------------------------------------------------------------------
*/

class KohNet: public Network {

public:

        KohNet ( int n inputs , int n outputs , KohParams *kp ,
                 int exe , int zero ) ;
        ~KohNet () ;
        void learn ( TrainingSet *tptr , struct LearnParams *lptr ) ;
        void trial ( double *input ) ;
        int wt save ( FILE *fp ) ;
        void wt restore ( FILE *fp ) ;

        int normalization ;       // 0-multiplicative, 1-Z

private:

        void copy weights ( KohNet *dest , KohNet *source ) ;
        void epoch1 ( TrainingSet *tptr , double rate , int learn method ,
                      int *won , double *bigerr , double *correc , double *work ) ;
        void epoch2 ( double rate , int learn method , int *won ,
                      double *bigcorr , double *correc ) ;
        void force win ( TrainingSet *tptr , int *won ) ;
        void initialize () ;
```

```
      void in norm ( double *input , double *normfac , double *synth ) ;
      int winner ( double *input , double *normfac , double *synth ) ;
      void wt norm ( double *w ) ;
      void zero weights () ;

      double *out coefs ;          // nout * (nin+1) weights
   } ;

/***********************************************************************************/
/*                                                                                */
/* CONST.H - System and program limitation constants                             */
/*              This also contains typedefs, structs, et cetera.                  */
/*                                                                                */
/* See the comment above BAD COMPILER.                                            */
/*                                                                                */
/* The #if above MALLOC controls whether or not the diagnostic memory             */
/* allocation routines are used.  They only slow things a tiny bit.               */
/*                                                                                */
/* RANDMAX may be system dependent.  See your documentation.                      */
/*                                                                                */
/* MAX INPUTS, MAX HIDDEN and MAX OUTPUTS are primarily to simplify the           */
/* code involved in memory allocation.  The defaults provided should be          */
/* adequate for any project done on a 16 bit machine.  Users of larger            */
/* machines will want to increase these a lot.                                    */
/* This is controlled with VERSION 16 BIT.                                        */
/*                                                                                */
/* TRAIN BUF SIZE makes training set memory allocation faster by avoiding         */
/* many calls to realloc.  Users of 32 bit machines with much memory may          */
/* want to increase this considerably.                                            */
/*                                                                                */
/***********************************************************************************/

/*
   The author is aware of at least one big-name C++ compiler which is unable
   to correctly handle pure virtual functions.  The following toggle causes
   the Network destructor to be impure.  It is always correct to do this, but
   bad style.  Purists will want to change this to 0, or maybe even remove
   its code from CLASSES.H and NETWORK.CPP.
*/

#define BAD COMPILER 1

/*
   These interpose memory allocation checking.
*/

#if 1
#define MALLOC memalloc
#define FREE memfree
#define REALLOC memrealloc
#define MEMTEXT memtext
#define MEMCLOSE memclose
#else
#define MALLOC malloc
#define FREE free
#define REALLOC realloc
#define MEMTEXT notext
#define MEMCLOSE nomemclose
#endif

#define VERSION 16 BIT 0

#if VERSION 16 BIT
#define TRAIN BUF SIZE 16384        /* Alloc this much tsets mem (max) at a time */
#define MAX INPUTS 64               /* Number of network inputs */
#define MAX HIDDEN 64               /* Number of hidden neurons */
#define MAX OUTPUTS 64              /* Number of network outputs */
#else
#define TRAIN BUF SIZE 65536
#define MAX INPUTS 1024
#define MAX HIDDEN 1024
#define MAX OUTPUTS 1024
#endif

#define RANDMAX 32767               /* rand() returns from 0 through this */
#define CONTROL LINE LENGTH 255     /* Max length of user's control input */
#define MAX CONTROL FILES 16        /* Nesting of control files */
#define LTAB LENGTH 100             /* Activation function table length */
#define LTAB MAX 10.0               /* Maximum in that table */

#define NEURON ON  0.9              /* Target output activation levels */
#define NEURON OFF 0.1              /* must not be forced to 0 and 1 */
```

```
/*
    These are network model codes.  If additional networks are defined, they
    should be appended, leaving existing ones with the same codes, in order
    to avoid disk file incompatibilites.  They must be positive (-1 = unset).
*/

#define NETMOD LAYER 1
#define NETMOD KOH 2


/*
    These are output model codes.  If additional outputs are defined, they
    should be appended, leaving existing ones with the same codes, in order
    to avoid disk file incompatibilites.  They must be positive (-1 = unset).
*/

#define OUTMOD CLASSIFY 1
#define OUTMOD AUTO 2
#define OUTMOD GENERAL 3

/*
    The annealing parameters have a zero suffix for the value used for finding
    starting weights.  The non-zero parameters are for when annealing is used
    to (hopefully) escape from local minima during learning.
*/

struct AnnealParams {
    int temps0 ;          // Number of temperatures
    int temps ;
    int iters0 ;          // Iterations per temperature
    int iters ;
    int setback0 ;        // Set back iteration counter if improvement
    int setback ;
    double start0 ;       // Starting temperature
    double start ;
    double stop0 ;        // Stopping temperature
    double stop ;
    } ;

struct GenInitParams {
    int pool ;            // Number of individuals in population pool
    int gens ;            // Number of generations after initial population
    int climb ;           // Use hill climbing (elitism)?
    double overinit ;     // Overinitialization factor (<= 1)
    double pcross ;       // Probability of crossover
    double pmutate ;      // Probability of mutation
    } ;

struct LearnParams {
    int init ;            // 0-no init, 1-ann noreg, 2-anneal, 3-genetic, 4-regress
    double quit err ;     // Quit if mean square error fraction of max this low
    int retries ;         // Quit after this many random retries
    struct AnnealParams *ap ;
    struct GenInitParams *gp ;
    struct KohParams *kp ;
    } ;

struct KohParams {        // Both network and learning params here
    int normalization ;   // 0-multiplicative, 1-Z
    int learn method  ;   // 0-additive, 1-subtractive
    double rate ;         // Learning rate (0-1)
    double reduction ;    // Learning rate reduction per pass (0-1)
    } ;
/**************************************************************************/
/*                                                                        */
/*   ANNEAL - Use simulated annealing to optimize LayerNet weights        */
/*                                                                        */
/**************************************************************************/
#include <stdio.h>
#include <string.h>
#include <math.h>
#include <conio.h>
#include <ctype.h>
#include <stdlib.h>
#include "const.h"        // System and limitation constants, typedefs, structs
#include "classes.h"      // Includes all class headers
#include "funcdefs.h"     // Function prototypes

void LayerNet::anneal (
    TrainingSet *tptr ,          // Training set to use
```

```
        struct LearnParams *lptr ,  // User's general learning parameters
        LayerNet *bestnet ,         // Work area used to keep best network
        int init                    // Use zero suffix (initialization) anneal parms?
        )
{
        int ntemps, niters, setback, reg, nvars, key, user quit ;
        int i, iter, improved, ever improved, itemp ;
        long seed, bestseed ;
        char msg[80] ;
        double tempmult, temp, fval, bestfval, starttemp, stoptemp, fquit ;
        SingularValueDecomp *sptr ;
        struct AnnealParams *aptr ; // User's annealing parameters

        aptr = lptr->ap ;

/*
   The parameter 'init' is nonzero if we are initializing
   weights for learning.  If zero we are attempting to break
   out of a local minimum.  The main effect  of this parameter
   is whether or not we use the zero suffix variables in the
   anneal parameters.
   A second effect is that regression is used only for
   initialization, not for escape.
*/

        if (init) {
           ntemps = aptr->temps0 ;
           niters = aptr->iters0 ;
           setback = aptr->setback0 ;
           starttemp = aptr->start0 ;
           stoptemp = aptr->stop0 ;
           }
        else {
           ntemps = aptr->temps ;
           niters = aptr->iters ;
           setback = aptr->setback ;
           starttemp = aptr->start ;
           stoptemp = aptr->stop ;
           }

/*
   Initialize other local parameters.  Note that there is no sense using
   regression if there are no hidden layers.  Also, regression is almost
   always counterproductive for local minimum escape.
*/

        fquit = lptr->quit err ;
        reg = init  &&  nhid1  &&  (lptr->init != 1) ;

/*
   Allocate the singular value decomposition object for REGRESS.
   Also allocate a work area for REGRESS to preserve matrix.
*/

        if (reg) {
           if (nhid1 == 0)          // No hidden layer
              nvars = nin + 1 ;
           else if (nhid2 == 0)     // One hidden layer
              nvars = nhid1 + 1 ;
           else                     // Two hidden layers
              nvars = nhid2 + 1 ;

           MEMTEXT ( "ANNEAL: new SingularValueDecomp" ) ;
           sptr = new SingularValueDecomp ( tptr->ntrain , nvars , 1 ) ;

           if ((sptr == NULL)  || ! sptr->ok) {
              memory message (
                 "for annealing with regression. Try ANNEAL NOREGRESS.");
              if (sptr != NULL)
                 delete sptr ;
              neterr = 1.0 ; // Flag failure to LayerNet::learn which called us
              return ;
              }
           }

/*
   For every temperature, the center around which we will perturb is the
   best point so far.  This is kept in 'bestnet', so initialize it to the
   user's starting estimate.   Also, initialize 'bestfval', the best
   function value so far, to be the function value at that starting point.
*/
```

```
      copy weights ( bestnet , this ) ; // Current weights are best so far
      if (init)
         bestfval = 1.e30 ;   // Force it to accept SOMETHING
      else
         bestfval = trial error ( tptr ) ;

/*
   This is the temperature reduction loop and the iteration within
   temperature loop.  We use a slick trick to keep track of the
   best point at a given temperature.  We certainly don't want to
   replace the best every time an improvement is had, as then we
   would be moving our center about, compromising the global nature
   of the algorithm.  We could, of course, have a second work area
   in which we save the 'best so far for this temperature' point.
   But if there are a lot of variables, the usual case, this wastes
   memory.  What we do is to save the seed of the random number
   generator which created the improvement.  Then later, when we
   need to retrieve the best, simply set the random seed and
   regenerate it.  This technique also saves a lot of copying time
   if many improvements are made for a single temperature.
*/

      temp = starttemp ;
      tempmult = exp( log( stoptemp / starttemp ) / (ntemps-1)) ;
      ever improved = 0 ;                    // Flags if improved at all
      user quit = 0 ;                        // Flags user pressed ESCape

      for (itemp=0 ; itemp<ntemps ; itemp++) {  // Temp reduction loop

         improved = 0 ;                      // Flags if this temp improved

         if (init) {
            sprintf ( msg , "\nANNEAL temp=%.2lf ", temp ) ;
            progress message ( msg ) ;
            }

         for (iter=0 ; iter<niters ; iter++) {  // Iters per temp loop

            seed = longrand () ;             // Get a random seed
            slongrand ( seed ) ;             // Brute force set it
            perturb (bestnet, this, temp, reg) ;// Randomly perturb about best

            if (reg)                         // If using regression, estimate
               fval = regress ( tptr , sptr ) ; // out weights now
            else                             // Otherwise just evaluate
               fval = trial error ( tptr ) ;

            if (fval < bestfval) {           // If this iteration improved
               bestfval = fval ;             // then update the best so far
               bestseed = seed ;             // and save seed to recreate it
               ever improved = improved = 1 ; // Flag that we improved

               if (bestfval <= fquit)        // If we reached the user's
                  break ;                    // limit, we can quit

               iter -= setback ;             // It often pays to keep going
               if (iter < 0)                 // at this temperature if we
                  iter = 0 ;                 // are still improving
               }
            }                                // Loop: for all iters at a temp

         if (improved) {                     // If this temp saw improvement
            slongrand ( bestseed ) ;         // set seed to what caused it
            perturb (bestnet, this, temp, reg) ;// and recreate that point
            copy weights ( bestnet , this ) ; // which will become next center
            slongrand ( bestseed / 2 + 999 ) ; // Jog seed away from best

            if (init) {
               sprintf ( msg , " err=%.3lf%% ", 100.0 * bestfval ) ;
               progress message ( msg ) ;
               }
            }

         if (bestfval <= fquit)  // If we reached the user's
            break ;              // limit, we can quit

         if (kbhit()) {          // Was a key pressed?
            key = getch () ;     // Read it if so
            while (kbhit())      // Flush key buffer in case function key
               getch () ;        // or key was held down
            if (key == 27) {     // ESCape
               user quit = 1 ;   // Flags user that ESCape was pressed
```

```
                  break ;
                  }
               }

           if (user quit)
              break ;

           temp *= tempmult ;          // Reduce temp for next pass
           }                           // through this temperature loop

/*
   The trials left this weight set and neterr in random condition.
   Make them equal to the best, which will be the original
   if we never improved.

   Also, if we improved and are using regression, recall that bestnet
   only contains the best hidden weights, as we did not bother to run
   regress when we updated bestnet.  Do that now before returning.
*/

   copy weights ( this , bestnet ) ; // Return best weights in this net
   neterr = bestfval ;                // Trials destroyed weights, err

   if (ever improved  &&  reg)
      neterr = regress ( tptr , sptr ) ; // regressed output weights

   if (reg) {
      MEMTEXT ( "ANNEAL: delete SingularValueDecomp" ) ;
      delete sptr ;
      }
}


/*
--------------------------------------------------------------------------------

   Local routine to perturb coefficients

--------------------------------------------------------------------------------
*/

void LayerNet::perturb ( LayerNet *cent , LayerNet *perturbed , double temp ,
                         int reg )
{
   int n ;

   if (nhid1 == 0) {                // No hidden layer
      n = nout * (nin+1) ;
      shake ( n , cent->out coefs , perturbed->out coefs , temp ) ;
      }

   else if (nhid2 == 0) {           // One hidden layer
      n = nhid1 * (nin+1) ;
      shake ( n , cent->hid1 coefs , perturbed->hid1 coefs , temp ) ;
      if (! reg) {
         n = nout * (nhid1+1) ;
         shake ( n , cent->out coefs , perturbed->out coefs , temp ) ;
         }
      }

   else {                           // Two hidden layers
      n = nhid1 * (nin+1) ;
      shake ( n , cent->hid1 coefs , perturbed->hid1 coefs , temp ) ;
      n = nhid2 * (nhid1+1) ;
      shake ( n , cent->hid2 coefs , perturbed->hid2 coefs , temp ) ;
      if (! reg) {
         n = nout * (nhid2+1) ;
         shake ( n , cent->out coefs , perturbed->out coefs , temp ) ;
         }
      }
}
```

```
/******************************************************************************/
/*                                                                            */
/*   conjgrad - Conjugate gradient learning                                   */
/*                                                                            */
/*   Normally this returns the mean square error, which will be 0-1.          */
/*   If the user interrupted, it returns the negative mean square error.      */
/*   Insufficient memory returns -2.                                          */
/*                                                                            */
/******************************************************************************/

#include <stdio.h>
#include <string.h>
#include <math.h>
#include <conio.h>
#include <ctype.h>
#include <stdlib.h>
#include "const.h"        // System and limitation constants, typedefs, structs
#include "classes.h"      // Includes all class headers
#include "funcdefs.h"     // Function prototypes

double LayerNet::conjgrad (
   TrainingSet *tptr ,  // Training set to use
   int maxits ,         // Maximum iterations allowed
   double reltol ,      // Relative error change tolerance
   double errtol        // Quit if error drops this low
   )
{
   int i, j, n, iter, pnum, key, retry, max retry ;
   double gam, *g, *h, *outdelta, *hid2delta, *grad, *base ;
   double corr, error, *cptr, *gptr, *pptr, maxgrad ;
   double prev err ;

   max retry = 5 ;

/*
   Allocate work memory
*/

   MEMTEXT ( "CONJGRAD work" ) ;
   if (nhid2) {
      hid2delta = (double *) MALLOC ( nhid2 * sizeof(double) ) ;
      if (hid2delta == NULL)
         return -2.0 ;
      }
   else
      hid2delta = NULL ;

   outdelta = (double *) MALLOC ( nout * sizeof(double) ) ;

   if (nhid1 == 0)                  // No hidden layer
      n = nout * (nin+1) ;
   else if (nhid2 == 0)             // One hidden layer
      n = nhid1 * (nin+1) + nout * (nhid1+1) ;
   else                             // Two hidden layers
      n = nhid1 * (nin+1) + nhid2 * (nhid1+1) + nout * (nhid2+1) ;

   grad = (double *) MALLOC ( n * sizeof(double) ) ;
   base = (double *) MALLOC ( n * sizeof(double) ) ;
   g = (double *) MALLOC ( n * sizeof(double) ) ;
   h = (double *) MALLOC ( n * sizeof(double) ) ;

   if ((outdelta == NULL) || (grad == NULL) ||
       (base == NULL) || (g == NULL) || (h == NULL)) {
      if (hid2delta != NULL)
         FREE ( hid2delta ) ;
      if (outdelta != NULL)
         FREE ( outdelta ) ;
      if (grad != NULL)
         FREE ( grad ) ;
      if (base != NULL)
         FREE ( base ) ;
      if (g != NULL)
         FREE ( g ) ;
      if (h != NULL)
         FREE ( h ) ;
      return -2.0 ;    // Flags error
      }

   prev err = 1.e30 ;
   error = find grad ( tptr , hid2delta , outdelta , grad ) ;

   memcpy ( g , grad , n * sizeof(double) ) ;
```

```
        memcpy ( h , grad , n * sizeof(double) ) ;

/*
   Main iteration loop is here
*/

    for (iter=0 ; iter<maxits ; iter++) {   // Each iter is an epoch

/*
   Check current error against user's max.  Abort if user pressed ESCape
*/

        if (error <= errtol)    // If our error is within user's limit
            break ;             // then we are done!

        if (error <= reltol)    // Generally not necessary: reltol<errtol in
            break ;             // practice, but help silly users

        if (kbhit()) {          // Was a key pressed?
            key = getch () ;    // Read it if so
            while (kbhit())     // Flush key buffer in case function key
                getch () ;      // or key was held down
            if (key == 27) {    // ESCape
                error = -error ; // Flags user that ESCape was pressed
                break ;
                }
            }

        prev err = error ;
        error = direcmin ( tptr , error , 10 , 1.e-10 ,
                           0.5 , base , grad ) ;
        if (error < 0.0)  // Indicates user pressed ESCape
            goto CGFINISH ;

        if ((2.0 * (prev err - error)) <=         // If this direc gave poor result
            (reltol * (prev err + error + 1.e-10))) { // will use random direc
            prev err = error ;                        // But first exhaust grad
            error = find grad ( tptr , hid2delta , outdelta , grad ) ;
            error = direcmin ( tptr , error , 15 , 1.e-10 ,
                               1.e-3 , base , grad ) ;
            for (retry=0 ; retry<max retry ; retry++) {
                for (i=0 ; i<n ; i++)
                    grad[i] = (double) (rand() - RANDMAX/2) / (RANDMAX * 10.0) ;
                error = direcmin ( tptr , error , 10 , 1.e-10 ,
                                   1.e-2 , base , grad ) ;
                if (error < 0.0)  // Indicates user pressed ESCape
                    goto CGFINISH ;
                if (retry < max retry/2)
                    continue ;
                if ((2.0 * (prev err - error)) >
                    (reltol * (prev err + error + 1.e-10)))
                    break ;    // Get out of retry loop if we improved enough
                } // For retry
            if (retry == max retry)    // If we exhausted all tries
                break ;                // probably hopeless
            memcpy ( g , grad , n * sizeof(double) ) ;
            memcpy ( h , grad , n * sizeof(double) ) ;
            } // If this dir gave poor result

        prev err = error ;

/*
   Setup for next iteration
*/

        error = find grad ( tptr , hid2delta , outdelta , grad ) ;
        gam = gamma ( g , grad ) ;
        if (gam < 0.0)
            gam = 0.0 ;
        if (gam > 1.0)
            gam = 1.0 ;

        find new dir ( gam , g , h , grad ) ;

        }   // This is the end of the main iteration loop

/*
   Free work memory
*/

CGFINISH:
    MEMTEXT ( "CONJGRAD work" ) ;
```

```
      if (hid2delta !- NULL)
         FREE ( hid2delta ) ;
      FREE ( outdelta ) ;
      FREE ( grad ) ;
      FREE ( base ) ;
      FREE ( g ) ;
      FREE ( h ) ;

      return error ;
}

/*
--------------------------------------------------------------------------------

   Local routine to compute gradient for a trial epoch

--------------------------------------------------------------------------------
*/

double LayerNet::find grad (
   TrainingSet *tptr ,
   double *hid2delta ,
   double *outdelta ,
   double *grad
   )
{
   int i, j, size, tset, tclass, n, nprev, nnext ;
   double error, *dptr, diff, delta, *hid1grad, *hid2grad, *outgrad ;
   double *outprev, *prevact, *nextcoefs, *nextdelta, *gradptr ;

/*
   Compute size of each training sample
*/

   if (outmod -- OUTMOD CLASSIFY)
      size - nin + 1 ;
   else if (outmod -- OUTMOD AUTO)
      size - nin ;
   else if (outmod -- OUTMOD GENERAL)
      size - nin + nout ;

/*
   Compute length of grad vector and gradient positions in it.
   Also point to layer previous to output and its size.
   Ditto for layer after hid1.
*/

   if (nhid1 -- 0) {         // No hidden layer
      n - nout * (nin+1) ;
      outgrad - grad ;
      nprev - nin ;
      }
   else if (nhid2 -- 0) { // One hidden layer
      n - nhid1 * (nin+1) + nout * (nhid1+1) ;
      hid1grad - grad ;
      outgrad - grad + nhid1 * (nin+1) ;
      outprev - hid1 ;
      nprev - nhid1 ;
      nnext - nout ;
      nextcoefs - out coefs ;
      nextdelta - outdelta ;
      }
   else {                    // Two hidden layers
      n - nhid1 * (nin+1) + nhid2 * (nhid1+1) + nout * (nhid2+1) ;
      hid1grad - grad ;
      hid2grad - grad + nhid1 * (nin+1) ;
      outgrad - hid2grad + nhid2 * (nhid1+1) ;
      outprev - hid2 ;
      nprev - nhid2 ;
      nnext - nhid2 ;
      nextcoefs - hid2 coefs ;
      nextdelta - hid2delta ;
      }

   for (i-0 ; i<n ; i++)  // Zero gradient for summing
      grad[i] - 0.0 ;

   error - 0.0 ;  // Will cumulate total error here
   for (tset-0 ; tset<tptr->ntrain ; tset++) { // Do all samples

      dptr - tptr->data + size * tset ;      // Point to this sample
      trial ( dptr ) ;                       // Evaluate network for it
```

```
      if (outmod -- OUTMOD AUTO) {              // If this is AUTOASSOCIATIVE
         for (i-0 ; i<nout ; i++) {             // then the expected outputs
            diff - *dptr++ - out[i] ;           // are just the inputs
            error +- diff * diff ;
            outdelta[i] - diff * actderiv ( out[i] ) ;
            }
         }

      else if (outmod -- OUTMOD CLASSIFY) {   // If this is Classification
         tclass - (int) dptr[nin] - 1 ;        // class is stored after inputs
         for (i-0 ; i<nout ; i++) {            // Recall that train added a
            if (tclass -- i)                    // fraction so that the above
               diff - NEURON ON - out[i] ;     // truncation to get tclass is
            else                                // always safe in any radix
               diff - NEURON OFF - out[i] ;
            error +- diff * diff ;
            outdelta[i] - diff * actderiv ( out[i] ) ;
            }
         }

      else if (outmod -- OUTMOD GENERAL) {   // If this is GENERAL output
         dptr +- nin ;                         // outputs stored after inputs
         for (i-0 ; i<nout ; i++) {
            diff - *dptr++ - out[i] ;
            error +- diff * diff ;
            outdelta[i] - diff * actderiv ( out[i] ) ;
            }
         }

/*
   Cumulate output gradient
*/

      if (nhid1 -- 0)          // No hidden layer
         prevact - tptr->data + size * tset ;
      else
         prevact - outprev ;  // Point to previous layer
      gradptr - outgrad ;
      for (i-0 ; i<nout ; i++) {
         delta - outdelta[i] ;
         for (j-0 ; j<nprev ; j++)
            *gradptr++ +- delta * prevact[j] ;
         *gradptr++ +- delta ;   // Bias activation is always 1
         }

/*
   Cumulate hid2 gradient (if it exists)
*/

      if (nhid2) {
         gradptr - hid2grad ;
         for (i-0 ; i<nhid2 ; i++) {
            delta - 0.0 ;
            for (j-0 ; j<nout ; j++)
               delta +- outdelta[j] * out coefs[j*(nhid2+1)+i] ;
            delta *- actderiv ( hid2[i] ) ;
            hid2delta[i] - delta ;
            for (j-0 ; j<nhid1 ; j++)
               *gradptr++ +- delta * hid1[j] ;
            *gradptr++ +- delta ;   // Bias activation is always 1
            }
         }

/*
   Cumulate hid1 gradient (if it exists)
*/

      if (nhid1) {
         prevact - tptr->data + size * tset ;
         gradptr - hid1grad ;
         for (i-0 ; i<nhid1 ; i++) {
            delta - 0.0 ;
            for (j-0 ; j<nnext ; j++)
               delta +- nextdelta[j] * nextcoefs[j*(nhid1+1)+i] ;
            delta *- actderiv ( hid1[i] ) ;
            for (j-0 ; j<nin ; j++)
               *gradptr++ +- delta * prevact[j] ;
            *gradptr++ +- delta ;   // Bias activation is always 1
            }
         }

      } // for all tsets
```

```
      return error / ((double) tptr->ntrain * (double) nout) ;
   }

/*
--------------------------------------------------------------------------------

   Local routine to find gamma

--------------------------------------------------------------------------------
*/

double LayerNet::gamma ( double *g , double *grad )
{
   int i, n ;
   double denom, numer ;

   if (nhid1 == 0)             // No hidden layer
      n = nout * (nin+1) ;
   else if (nhid2 == 0)     // One hidden layer
      n = nhid1 * (nin+1) + nout * (nhid1+1) ;
   else                       // Two hidden layers
      n = nhid1 * (nin+1) + nhid2 * (nhid1+1) + nout * (nhid2+1) ;

   numer = denom = 0. ;

   for (i=0 ; i<n ; i++) {
      denom += g[i] * g[i] ;
      numer += (grad[i] - g[i]) * grad[i] ;   // Grad is neg gradient
      }

   if (denom == 0.)    // Should never happen (means gradient is zero!)
      return 0. ;
   else
      return numer / denom ;
}

/*
--------------------------------------------------------------------------------

   Local routine to find correction for next iteration

--------------------------------------------------------------------------------
*/

void LayerNet::find new dir ( double gam , double *g ,
                              double *h , double *grad )
{
   int i, n ;
   double *gptr, *hptr, *cptr ;

   if (nhid1 == 0)             // No hidden layer
      n = nout * (nin+1) ;
   else if (nhid2 == 0)     // One hidden layer
      n = nhid1 * (nin+1) + nout * (nhid1+1) ;
   else                       // Two hidden layers
      n = nhid1 * (nin+1) + nhid2 * (nhid1+1) + nout * (nhid2+1) ;

   for (i=0 ; i<n ; i++) {
      g[i] = grad[i] ;
      grad[i] = h[i] = g[i] + gam * h[i] ;
      }
}


/****************************************************************************/
/*                                                                          */
/*   direcmin - Minimize along a direction                                  */
/*                                                                          */
/*   Normally this returns the mean square error, which will be 0-1.        */
/*   If the user interrupted, it returns the negative mean square error.    */
/*                                                                          */
/*   This is a two step process.  First we find three points whose center has */
/*   the smallest function value (we bound the minimum).                    */
/*   Then we use Brent's algorithm to refine the interval.                  */
/*                                                                          */
/*   We leave 'coefs' set at the point that produced the minimum and return */
/*   the error function at that point.  We change the direction 'dir' to    */
/*   be the actual distance moved.                                          */
/*                                                                          */
/****************************************************************************/
```

```c
#include <stdio.h>
#include <string.h>
#include <math.h>
#include <conio.h>
#include <ctype.h>
#include <stdlib.h>
#include "const.h"         // System and limitation constants, typedefs, structs
#include "classes.h"       // Includes all class headers
#include "funcdefs.h"      // Function prototypes

double LayerNet::direcmin (
   TrainingSet *tptr , // Training set to use
   double start err ,  // Error (function value) at starting coefficients
   int itmax ,         // Upper limit on number of iterations allowed
   double eps ,        // Small, but greater than machine precision
   double tol ,        // Brent's tolerance (>= sqrt machine precision)
   double *base ,      // Work area (stepping out point)
   double *direc )     // Work area (stepping out direction)
{
   int key, user quit, iter ;
   double step, x1, x2, x3, t1, t2, numer, denom, max step ;
   double xlow, xhigh, xbest, testdist ;
   double current err, err, previous err, step err ;
   double prevdist, etemp, frecent, fthirdbest, fsecbest, fbest ;
   double tol1, tol2, xrecent, xthirdbest, xsecbest, xmid;
   double  first step = 2.5 ; // Heuristically found best

   user quit = 0 ;

/*
   Take one step out in the gradient direction.  First preserve
   original weights for use as departure point parameterized by STEP.
*/

   preserve ( base ) ;    // Establishes a base for stepping out
   step out ( first step , direc , base ) ;
   err = trial error ( tptr ) ;

/*
   If it increased, we had numerical problems computing the direction or
   the direction itself is too large a step.
   Negate the direction and use -1, 0 and 1.618 as first three steps.
   Otherwise use 0, 1 and 2.618 as first three steps.
*/

   if (err > start err) {
      negate dir ( direc ) ;
      x1 = -first step ;
      x2 = 0. ;
      previous err = err ;
      current err = start err ;
      }
   else {
      x1 = 0. ;
      x2 = first step ;
      previous err = start err ;
      current err = err ;
      }

/*
   At this point we have taken a single step and the function decreased.
   Take one more step in the golden ratio.
   Also keep errors lined up as 'previous err', 'current err' and 'err'.
   The corresponding abscissae will be x1, x2 and x3.
*/

   if (kbhit()) {            // Was a key pressed?
      key = getch () ;       // Read it if so
      while (kbhit())        // Flush key buffer in case function key
         getch () ;          // or key was held down
      if (key == 27)         // ESCape
         return (- err) ;
      }

   x3 = x2 + 1.618034 * first step ;
   step out ( x3 , direc , base ) ;
   err = trial error ( tptr ) ;

/*
   We now have three points x1, x2 and x3 with corresponding errors
   of 'previous err', 'current err' and 'err'.
   Endlessly loop until we bracket the minimum with the outer two.
*/
```

```
*/
    while (err < current err) {   // As long as we are descending...

      if (kbhit()) {              // Was a key pressed?
        key = getch () ;          // Read it if so
        while (kbhit())           // Flush key buffer in case function key
          getch () ;              // or key was held down
        if (key == 27) {          // ESCape
          user quit = 1 ;
          break ;
          }
        }

/*
   Try a parabolic fit to estimate the location of the minimum.
*/

      t1 = (x2 - x1) * (current err - err) ;
      t2 = (x2 - x3) * (current err - previous err) ;
      denom = 2. * ( t2 - t1 ) ;
      if (fabs ( denom ) < eps) {
        if (denom > 0.)
          denom = eps ;
        else
          denom = -eps ;
        }
      step = x2 + ((x2 - x1) * t1  - (x2 - x3) * t2) / denom ;//Here if perfect
      max step = x2 + 200. * (x3 - x2) ; // Don't jump too far

      if ((x2 - step) * (step - x3)  >  0.) {            // It's between x2 and x3
        step out ( step , direc , base ) ;
        step err = trial error ( tptr ) ;

        if (step err < err) {   // It worked!  We found min between b and c.

          x1 = x2 ;
          x2 = step ;
          previous err = current err ;
          current err = step err ;
          goto BOUNDED ;
          }
        else if (step err > current err) { // Slight miscalc.  Min at x2.
          x3 = step ;
          err = step err ;
          goto BOUNDED ;
          }
        else {              // Parabolic fit was total waste.  Use default.
          step = x3 + 1.618034 * (x3 - x2) ;
          step out ( step , direc , base ) ;
          step err = trial error ( tptr ) ;
          }
        }

      else if ((x3 - step) * (step - max step) > 0.0) { // Between x3 and lim
        step out ( step , direc , base ) ;
        step err = trial error ( tptr ) ;
        if (step err < err) {  // Decreased, so advance by golden ratio
          x2 = x3 ;
          x3 = step ;
          step = x3 + 1.618034 * (x3 - x2) ;
          current err = err ;
          err = step err ;
          step out ( step , direc , base ) ;
          step err = trial error ( tptr ) ;
          }
        }

      else if ((step - max step) * (max step - x3)  >= 0.) {  // Beyond limit
        step = max step ;
        step out ( step , direc , base ) ;
        step err = trial error ( tptr ) ;
        if (step err < err) {  // Decreased, so advance by golden ratio
          x2 = x3 ;
          x3 = step ;
          step = x3 + 1.618034 * (x3 - x2) ;
          current err = err ;
          err = step err ;
          step out ( step , direc , base ) ;
          step err = trial error ( tptr ) ;
          }
        }
```

```
            else {  // Wild!  Reject parabolic and use golden ratio.
               step = x3 + 1.618034 * (x3 - x2) ;
               step out ( step , direc , base ) ;
               step err = trial error ( tptr ) ;
               }
/*
   Shift three points and continue endless loop
*/

      x1 = x2 ;
      x2 = x3 ;
      x3 = step ;
      previous err = current err ;
      current err = err ;
      err = step err ;
      } // Endless stepping out loop

BOUNDED:
   step out ( x2 , direc , base);//Leave coefs at min

   if (x1 > x3) {   // We may have switched direction at start.
      t1 = x1 ;     // Brent's method which follows assumes ordered parameter.
      x1 = x3 ;
      x3 = t1 ;
      }

   if (user quit) {
      update dir ( x2 , direc ) ;// Make it be the actual dist moved
      return -current err ;
      }
/*
--------------------------------------------------------------------------------

   At this point we have bounded the minimum between x1 and x3.

   Go to the refinement stage.  We use Brent's algorithm.

--------------------------------------------------------------------------------
*/
/*
   Initialize prevdist, the distance moved on the previous step, to 0 so that
   the 'if (fabs ( prevdist )  >  toll)' encountered on the first iteration
   below will fail, forcing a golden section the first time.  Also initialize
   step to 0 to avoid a zealous compiler from pointing out that it was
   referenced before being set.
*/

   prevdist = step = 0.0 ;
/*
   We always keep the minimum bracketed between xlow and xhigh.
   xbest has the min function so far (or latest if tie).
   xsecbest and xthirdbest are the second and third best.
*/

   xbest = xsecbest = xthirdbest = x2 ;
   xlow = x1 ;
   xhigh = x3 ;

   fbest = fsecbest = fthirdbest = current err ;

/*
   Main loop.  For safety we impose a limit on iterations.
*/

   for (iter=0 ; iter<itmax ; iter++) {

      xmid = 0.5 * (xlow + xhigh) ;
      toll = tol * (fabs ( xbest ) + eps) ;
      tol2 = 2. * toll ;

      if (kbhit()) {              // Was a key pressed?
         key = getch () ;         // Read it if so
         while (kbhit())          // Flush key buffer in case function key
            getch () ;            // or key was held down
         if (key == 27) {         // ESCape
            user quit = 1 ;
            break ;
```

```
            }
        }

/*
    The following convergence test simultaneously makes sure xhigh and
    xlow are close relative to tol2, and that xbest is near the midpoint.
*/
        if (fabs ( xbest - xmid ) <= (tol2 - 0.5 * (xhigh - xlow)))
            break ;

        if (fabs ( prevdist ) > tol1) {  // If we moved far enough try parabolic
fit
            t1 = (xbest - xsecbest) * (fbest - fthirdbest) ; // Temps for the
            t2 = (xbest - xthirdbest) * (fbest - fsecbest) ; // parabolic estimate
            numer = (xbest - xthirdbest) * t2  - (xbest - xsecbest) * t1 ;
            denom = 2. * (t1 - t2) ;  // Estimate will be numer / denom
            testdist = prevdist ;     // Will soon verify interval is shrinking
            prevdist = step ;         // Save for next iteration
            if (denom != 0.0)         // Avoid dividing by zero
                step = numer / denom ; // This is the parabolic estimate to min
            else
                step = 1.e30 ;        // Assures failure of next test

            if ((fabs ( step ) < fabs ( 0.5 * testdist ))// If shrinking
              && (step + xbest > xlow)                // and within known bounds
              && (step + xbest < xhigh)) {            // then we can use the
                xrecent = xbest + step ;             // parabolic estimate
                if ((xrecent - xlow  < tol2) ||       // If we are very close
                    (xhigh - xrecent < tol2)) {       // to known bounds
                    if (xbest < xmid)                 // then stabilize
                        step = tol1 ;
                    else
                        step = -tol1 ;
                }
            }
            else {  // Parabolic estimate poor, so use golden section
                prevdist = (xbest >= xmid) ? xlow - xbest : xhigh - xbest ;
                step = .3819660 * prevdist ;
            }
        }
        else { // prevdist did not exceed tol1: we did not move far enough
               // to justify a parabolic fit.  Use golden section.
            prevdist = (xbest >= xmid) ? xlow - xbest : xhigh - xbest ;
            step = .3819660 * prevdist ;
        }

        if (fabs (step) >= tol1)      // In order to numerically justify
            xrecent = xbest + step ;   // another trial we must move a
        else {                        // decent distance.
            if (step > 0.)
                xrecent = xbest + tol1 ;
            else
                xrecent = xbest - tol1 ;
        }

/*
    At long last we have a trial point 'xrecent'.  Evaluate the function.
*/
        step out ( xrecent , direc , base ) ;
        frecent = trial error ( tptr ) ;

        if (frecent <= fbest) {    // If we improved...
            if (xrecent >= xbest)  // Shrink the (xlow,xhigh) interval by
                xlow = xbest ;     // replacing the appropriate endpoint
            else
                xhigh = xbest ;
            xthirdbest = xsecbest ; // Update x and f values for best,
            xsecbest = xbest ;      // second and third best
            xbest = xrecent ;
            fthirdbest = fsecbest ;
            fsecbest = fbest ;
            fbest = frecent ;
        }

        else {                    // We did not improve
            if (xrecent < xbest)  // Shrink the (xlow,xhigh) interval by
                xlow = xrecent ;   // replacing the appropriate endpoint
            else
                xhigh = xrecent ;
```

```
            if ((frecent <= fsecbest)     // If we at least beat the second best
             || (xsecbest == xbest)) {    // or we had a duplication
                xthirdbest = xsecbest ;   // we can update the second and third
                xsecbest = xrecent ;      // best, though not the best.
                fthirdbest = fsecbest ;   // Recall that we started iters with
                fsecbest = frecent ;      // best, sec and third all equal.
                }
            else if ((frecent <= fthirdbest) // Oh well.  Maybe at least we can
             || (xthirdbest == xbest)       // beat the third best or rid
             || (xthirdbest == xsecbest)) { // ourselves of a duplication
                xthirdbest = xrecent ;      // (which is how we start the
                fthirdbest = frecent ;      // iterations)
                }
            }
        }

    step out ( xbest , direc , base );//Leave coefs at min
    update dir ( xbest , direc ) ;// Make it be the actual distance moved

    if (user quit)
        return -fbest ;
    else
        return fbest ;
}


/*
--------------------------------------------------------------------------------

    Local routine to preserve coefs in 'base'

--------------------------------------------------------------------------------
*/

void LayerNet::preserve ( double *base )
{
    int n ;

    if (nhid1 == 0) {                   // No hidden layer
        n = nout * (nin+1) ;
        memcpy ( base , out coefs , n * sizeof(double) ) ;
        }

    else if (nhid2 == 0) {              // One hidden layer
        n = nhid1 * (nin+1) ;
        memcpy ( base , hid1 coefs , n * sizeof(double) ) ;
        base += n ;
        n = nout * (nhid1+1) ;
        memcpy ( base , out coefs , n * sizeof(double) ) ;
        }

    else {                              // Two hidden layers
        n = nhid1 * (nin+1) ;
        memcpy ( base , hid1 coefs , n * sizeof(double) ) ;
        base += n ;
        n = nhid2 * (nhid1+1) ;
        memcpy ( base , hid2 coefs , n * sizeof(double) ) ;
        base += n ;
        n = nout * (nhid2+1) ;
        memcpy ( base , out coefs , n * sizeof(double) ) ;
        }
}


/*
--------------------------------------------------------------------------------

    Local routine to step out from base

--------------------------------------------------------------------------------
*/

void LayerNet::step out ( double step , double *direc , double *base )
{
    int i, n ;

    if (nhid1 == 0) {                   // No hidden layer
        n = nout * (nin+1) ;
        for (i=0 ; i<n ; i++)
            out coefs[i] = *(base++) + *(direc++) * step ;
        }
```

```
         else if (nhid2 == 0) {              // One hidden layer
            n = nhid1 * (nin+1) ;
            for (i=0 ; i<n ; i++)
               hid1 coefs[i] = *(base++) + *(direc++) * step ;
            n = nout * (nhid1+1) ;
            for (i=0 ; i<n ; i++)
               out coefs[i] = *(base++) + *(direc++) * step ;
            }

         else {                              // Two hidden layers
            n = nhid1 * (nin+1) ;
            for (i=0 ; i<n ; i++)
               hid1 coefs[i] = *(base++) + *(direc++) * step ;
            n = nhid2 * (nhid1+1) ;
            for (i=0 ; i<n ; i++)
               hid2 coefs[i] = *(base++) + *(direc++) * step ;
            n = nout * (nhid2+1) ;
            for (i=0 ; i<n ; i++)
               out coefs[i] = *(base++) + *(direc++) * step ;
            }
}

/*
--------------------------------------------------------------------------------

   Local routine to make 'dir' be the actual distance moved

--------------------------------------------------------------------------------
*/

void LayerNet::update dir ( double step , double *direc )
{
   int n ;

   if (nhid1 == 0)                   // No hidden layer
      n = nout * (nin+1) ;
   else if (nhid2 == 0)              // One hidden layer
      n = nhid1 * (nin+1) + nout * (nhid1+1) ;
   else                             // Two hidden layers
      n = nhid1 * (nin+1) + nhid2 * (nhid1+1) + nout * (nhid2+1) ;

   while (n--) {
      *direc *= step ;
      ++direc ;
      }
}

/*
--------------------------------------------------------------------------------

   Local routine to negate 'dir'

--------------------------------------------------------------------------------
*/

void LayerNet::negate dir ( double *direc )
{
   int n ;

   if (nhid1 == 0)                   // No hidden layer
      n = nout * (nin+1) ;
   else if (nhid2 == 0)              // One hidden layer
      n = nhid1 * (nin+1) + nout * (nhid1+1) ;
   else                             // Two hidden layers
      n = nhid1 * (nin+1) + nhid2 * (nhid1+1) + nout * (nhid2+1) ;

   while (n--) {
      *direc = -*direc ;
      ++direc ;
      }
}
/*****************************************************************************/
/*                                                                           */
/*  GEN INIT - Use genetic method to initialize LayerNet weights             */
/*                                                                           */
/*****************************************************************************/

#include <stdio.h>
#include <string.h>
#include <math.h>
#include <conio.h>
```

```
#include <ctype.h>
#include <stdlib.h>
#include "const.h"        // System and limitation constants, typedefs, structs
#include "classes.h"      // Includes all class headers
#include "funcdefs.h"     // Function prototypes

/*
   Declarations for local subroutines
*/

static void decode( char *popptr , int nin , int nh1 , int nh2 ,
                       double *w1 , double *w2);
static void error to fitness ( int popsize , double favor best ,
          double fitfac , double *errors , double *fitness ) ;
static void fitness to choices ( int popsize , double *fitness , int *choices );
static void fval to fitness ( int popsize , double favor best ,
                       double fitfac , double *fvals , double *fitness ) ;
static void mutate ( char *child , int nvars , double pmutate );
static void pick parents ( int *nchoices , int *choices ,
                       int *parent1 , int *parent2 ) ;
static void rand ind ( char *popptr , int chromsize ) ;
static void reproduce ( char *p1 , char *p2 , int first child ,
                       int nvars , char *child , int *crosspt , int *split ) ;

/*
   For translation speed we convert from gray codes to binary with a lookup
   table which is built in the first call.
*/

static unsigned char gray code table[256] ;   // Translation table
static int gray initialized = 0 ;              // Has it been built yet?

/*
   Entry point is here
*/

void LayerNet::gen init (
   TrainingSet *tptr ,        // Training set to use
   struct LearnParams *lptr   // User's general learning parameters
   )
{
   int i, istart, individual, best individual, generation, n cross ;
   int first child, parent1, parent2, improved, crosspt, nchoices, *choices ;
   int initpop, popsize, gens, climb, nvars, chromsize, split, ind ;
   double pcross, pmutate, error, besterror, *errors, *fitness, worst ;
   double fquit, favor best, fitfac, maxerr, minerr, avgerr, overinit ;
   SingularValueDecomp *sptr ;
   struct GenInitParams *gptr ;   // User's genetic initialization parameters
   char *pool1, *pool2, *oldpop, *newpop, *popptr, *temppop, *best ;
   char msg[80] ;

   gptr = lptr->gp ;

   popsize = gptr->pool ;
   gens = gptr->gens ;
   climb = gptr->climb ;
   overinit = gptr->overinit ;
   pcross = gptr->pcross ;
   pmutate = gptr->pmutate ;

   fquit = lptr->quit err ;

   favor best = 3.1 ;
   fitfac = -20.0 ;

/*
--------------------------------------------------------------------------------

   Do all scratch memory allocation.

--------------------------------------------------------------------------------
*/
/*
   Allocate the singular value decomposition object for REGRESS.
*/

   if (nhid2 == 0)            // One hidden layer
      nvars = nhid1 + 1 ;
   else                       // Two hidden layers
      nvars = nhid2 + 1 ;
```

```
      MEMTEXT ( "GEN INIT: new SingularValueDecomp" ) ;
      sptr = new SingularValueDecomp ( tptr->ntrain , nvars , 1 ) ;

      if ((sptr == NULL)  ||  ! sptr->ok) {
         memory message("for genetic initialization. Try ANNEAL NOREGRESS.");
         neterr = 1.0 ;      // Flag failure to LayerNet::learn which called us
         if (sptr != NULL)
            delete sptr ;
         return ;
         }

      chromsize = nhid1 * (nin+1) ;        // Length of an individual's chromosome
      if (nhid2)                           // is the number of hidden weights
         chromsize += nhid2 * (nhid1+1) ;

      errors = fitness = NULL ;
      choices = NULL ;
      pool1 = pool2 = NULL ;
      MEMTEXT ( "GEN INIT: errors, fitness, choices, best, pool1,pool2");
      if (((errors = (double*) MALLOC ( popsize * sizeof(double))) == NULL)
       || ((fitness = (double*) MALLOC ( popsize * sizeof(double))) == NULL)
       || ((best = (char*) MALLOC( chromsize )) == NULL)
       || ((choices = (int*) MALLOC ( popsize * sizeof(int))) == NULL)
       || ((pool1 = (char*) MALLOC( popsize * chromsize )) == NULL)
       || ((pool2 = (char*) MALLOC( popsize * chromsize )) == NULL)) {
         if (errors != NULL)
            FREE ( errors ) ;
         if (fitness != NULL)
            FREE ( fitness ) ;
         if (choices != NULL)
            FREE ( choices ) ;
         if (pool1 != NULL)
            FREE ( pool1 ) ;
         if (pool2 != NULL)
            FREE ( pool2 ) ;
         delete sptr ;
         memory message("for genetic initialization.  Try ANNEAL NOREGRESS." ) ;
         neterr = 1.0 ;  // Flag failure to LayerNet::learn which called us
         return ;
         }

/*
   Generate initial population pool.

   We also preserve the best weights across all generations,
   as this is what we will ultimately return to the user.
   Its mean square error is besterror.
*/

      besterror = 1.e30 ;      // For saving best (across all individuals and gens)
      maxerr = avgerr = 0.0 ;  // For progress display only
      best individual = 0 ;    // Safety only
      initpop = popsize * overinit ; // Overinitialization of initial population
      progress message ( "\nGenerating initial population" ) ;

      for (ind=0 ; ind<initpop ; ind++) { // Try overinitialization times

         if (ind<popsize)                 // If still in pop size limit
            individual = ind ;            // just use next avail space
         else {                           // Else we search entire pop
            worst = -1. ;                 // for the worst member
            for (i=0 ; i<popsize ; i++) { // which we will then replace
               if (errors[i] > worst) {
                  worst = errors[i] ;
                  individual = i ;
                  }
               }
            avgerr -= worst ;             // Exclude discards from average
            }

         popptr = pool1 + individual * chromsize ; // Build init pop in pool1
         rand ind ( popptr , chromsize ) ;         // Randomly generate individual
         decode ( popptr , nin , nhid1 , nhid2 ,   // Convert genotype (chromosome)
                  hid1 coefs , hid2 coefs );       // to phenotype (weights)
         error = regress ( tptr , sptr ) ;         // Evaluate network error
         errors[individual] = error ;              // and keep all errors

         if (error < besterror) {                  // Keep track of best
            besterror = error ;                    // as it is returned to user
            best individual = individual ;         // This is its index in pool1
            }
```

```
      if (error > maxerr)                        // Max and average error are
         maxerr = error ;                        // for progress display only
      avgerr += error ;

      if (error <= fquit)
         break ;

      progress message ( "." ) ;
      }
   sprintf (msg , "\nInitial pop:    Min err=%7.4lf   Max=%7.4lf    Avg=%7.4lf",
            100. * besterror, 100. * maxerr, 100.0 * avgerr / (double) popsize);
   progress message ( msg ) ;


/*
   The initial population has been built in pool1.
   Copy its best member to 'best' in case it never gets beat (unlikely
   but possible!).
   Also, we will need best if the climb option is true.
*/

   popptr = pool1 + best individual * chromsize ; // Point to best
   memcpy ( best , popptr , chromsize ) ;         // and save it

/*
   This is the main generation loop.  There are two areas for population pool
   storage: pool1 and pool2.  At any given time, oldpop will be set to one of
   them, and newpop to the other.  This avoids a lot of copying.
*/

   oldpop = pool1 ;       // This is the initial population
   newpop = pool2 ;       // The next generation is created here

   for (generation=0 ; generation<gens ; generation++) {

      if (error <= fquit) // We may have satisfied this in init pop
         break ;          // So we test at start of generation loop

      error to fitness ( popsize , favor best , fitfac , errors , fitness ) ;

      fitness to choices ( popsize , fitness , choices ) ;

      nchoices = popsize ;          // Will count down as choices array emptied
      n cross = pcross * popsize ;  // Number crossing over
      first child = 1 ;             // Generating first of parent's 2 children?
      improved = 0 ;                // Flags if we beat best

      if (climb) {                  // If we are to hill climb
         memcpy ( newpop , best , chromsize ) ; // start with best
         errors[0] = besterror ;    // Record its error
         istart = 1 ;               // and start children past it
         }
      else
         istart = 0 ;

/*
   Generate the children
*/

      maxerr = avgerr = 0.0 ;    // For progress display only
      minerr = 1.0 ;             // Ditto

      for (individual=istart ; individual<popsize ; individual++) {

         popptr = newpop + individual * chromsize ; // Will put this child here

         if (first child)  // If this is the first of 2 children, pick parents
            pick parents ( &nchoices , choices , &parent1 , &parent2 ) ;

         if (n cross-- > 0)     // Do crossovers first
            reproduce ( oldpop + parent1 * chromsize , oldpop + parent2 *
chromsize ,
                        first child , chromsize , popptr , &crosspt , &split ) ;
         else if (first child) // No more crossovers, so just copy parent
            memcpy ( popptr , oldpop + parent1 * chromsize , chromsize ) ;
         else
            memcpy ( popptr , oldpop + parent2 * chromsize , chromsize );

         if (pmutate > 0.0)
            mutate ( popptr , chromsize , pmutate ) ;
```

```
               decode ( popptr , nin , nhid1 , nhid2 , hid1 coefs , hid2 coefs ) ;
               error - regress ( tptr , sptr ) ; // Evaluate child's error
               errors[individual] - error ;       // and keep each

               if (error < besterror) {           // Keep track of best
                  besterror - error ;             // It will be returned to user
                  best individual - individual ;  // This is its index in newpop
                  improved - 1 ;                  // Flag so we copy it later
                  }

               if (error > maxerr)                // Min, max and average error
                  maxerr - error ;                // for progress display only
               if (error < minerr)
                  minerr - error ;
               avgerr += error ;

               if (error <= fquit)
                  break ;

               first child - ! first child ;
               } // For all genes in population
      /*
         We finished generating all children.  If we improved (one of these
         children beat the best so far) then copy that child to the best.
         Swap oldpop and newpop for the next generation.
      */

            if (improved) {
               popptr - newpop + best individual * chromsize ; // Point to best
               memcpy ( best , popptr , chromsize ) ;          // and save it
               }

            temppop - oldpop ;   // Switch old and new pops for next generation
            oldpop - newpop ;
            newpop - temppop ;

            sprintf(msg, "\nGeneration %3d: Min err-%7.41f   Max-%7.41f   Avg-%7.41f",
                 generation+1, 100. * minerr, 100. * maxerr,
                 100.0 * avgerr / (double) popsize ) ;
            progress message ( msg ) ;
            }
      /*
         We are all done.
      */

         decode ( best , nin , nhid1 , nhid2 , hid1 coefs , hid2 coefs ) ;
         besterror - regress ( tptr , sptr ) ;              // Evaluate network error

         MEMTEXT ( "GEN INIT: errors, fitness, choices, best, pool1,pool2");
         FREE ( errors ) ;
         FREE ( fitness ) ;
         FREE ( choices ) ;
         FREE ( best ) ;
         FREE ( pool1 ) ;
         FREE ( pool2 ) ;
         MEMTEXT ( "GEN INIT: delete sptr" ) ;
         delete sptr ;
      }

      /*
      --------------------------------------------------------------------------
         error to fitness - Convert the objective function value of each individual
                     to a scaled fitness value.  The scaled fitness may be
                     considered an expected frequency of choice.
      --------------------------------------------------------------------------
      */

      static void error to fitness (
         int popsize ,        // Length of errors, fitness vectors
         double favor best ,  // Factor for favoring best over average (2-3 is good)
         double fitfac ,      // Factor for converting error to raw fitness (-20 good)
         double *errors ,     // Input popsize vector of values of objective function
         double *fitness      // Output popsize vector of scaled fitnesses
         )
      {
         int individual ;
         double fit, avgfitness, minfitness, maxfitness, ftemp, tmult, tconst ;

         avgfitness - 0.0 ;
         maxfitness - -1.e30 ;
```

```
         minfitness - 1.e30 ;

         for (individual-0 ; individual<popsize ; individual++) {
            fitness[individual] - fit - exp ( fitfac * errors[individual] ) ;
            avgfitness +- fit ;
            if (fit > maxfitness)
               maxfitness - fit ;
            if (fit < minfitness)
               minfitness - fit ;
            }

         avgfitness /- (double) popsize ;

         ftemp - maxfitness - avgfitness ;
         if (ftemp > 1.e-20) {  // Insurance: average may equal max!
            tmult - (favor best - 1.0) * avgfitness / ftemp ;
            tconst - avgfitness * (maxfitness - favor best * avgfitness) / ftemp ;
            }
         else {
            tmult - 1.0 ;
            tconst - 0.0 ;
            }

         if (tmult * minfitness + tconst < 0.0) { // Do not allow negative fitness
            ftemp - avgfitness - minfitness ;
            if (ftemp > 1.e-20) {
               tmult - avgfitness / ftemp ;
               tconst - -minfitness * avgfitness / ftemp ;
               }
            else {
               tmult - 1.0 ;
               tconst - 0.0 ;
               }
            }

         avgfitness - 0.0 ;
         for (individual-0 ; individual<popsize ; individual++) {
            fit - tmult * fitness[individual] + tconst ;
            if (fit < 0.0)
               fit - 0.0 ;
            fitness[individual] - fit ;
            avgfitness +- fit ;
            }

         avgfitness /- (double) popsize ;

         for (individual-0 ; individual<popsize ; individual++)
            fitness[individual] /- avgfitness ;
}

/*
--------------------------------------------------------------------------------

   fitness to choices - Convert the array of fitnesses (which contain
                 expected frequency of selection) into the array of parent
                 choices.  This will allow random selection of parents
                 without replacement later, while still insuring that
                 we select (to within one) the expected number of each.

--------------------------------------------------------------------------------
*/

static void fitness to choices (
   int popsize ,      // Length of fitness, choices vectors
   double *fitness ,  // Input array of expected selection frequencies
   int *choices       // Output array of parents
   )
{
   int individual, expected, k ;
   double rn ;

/*
   We build the choices array in two steps.  This, the first step, assigns
   parents according to the integer part of their expected frequencies.
*/

   k - 0 ;  // Will index choices array
   for (individual-0 ; individual<popsize ; individual++) {
      expected - (int) fitness[individual] ;     // Assign this many now
      fitness[individual] -- expected ;          // Save fractional remainder
      while (expected--)                         // Forcibly use the int expected
         choices[k++] - individual ;             // quantity of this individual
```

```
      }
/*
      The second step is to take care of the remaining fractional expected
      frequencies.  Pass through the population, randomly selecting members
      with probability equal to their remaining fractional expectation.
      It is tempting to think that the algorithm below could loop excessively
      due to a very small fitness.  But recall that the sum of the fitnesses will
      be AT LEAST as large as the number remaining tis is in the range 0-7,
      and is the bit number where the split takes place.  Like crosspt
      it is output for the first child and input for the second.

----------------------------------------------------------------------------
*/
static void reproduce (
      char *p1 ,         // Pointer to one parent
      char *p2 ,         // and the other
      int first child ,  // Is this the first of their 2 children?
      int chromsize ,    // Number of genes in chromosome
      char *child ,      // Output of a child
      int *crosspt ,     // If first child, output of xover pt, else input it.
      int *split         // In/out of within byte splitting point
      )

{
      int i, n1, n2, n3, n4 ;
      char left, right, *pa, *pb ;

      if (first child) {

          *split - longrand() % 8 ; // We will split boundary bytes here
          *crosspt - 1 + unifrand() * chromsize ;   // Randomly select cross pt

          if ((chromsize >- 16)  && (unifrand() < 0.33333)) // Two point?
              *crosspt - -*crosspt ; // flag this for second child

          pa - p1 ;
          pb - p2 ;
          } // If first child

      else {                        // Second child
          pa - p2 ;                 // so parents reverse roles
          pb - p1 ;
          } // If second child

/*
   Prepare for reproduction
*/

      if (*split) {               // Create left and right splitting masks
          right - 1 ;
          i - *split ;
          while (--i)
              right - (right << 1) | 1 ;
          left - 255 ^ right ;
          }

      if (*crosspt > 0) {         // Use one point crossover
          n1 - chromsize / 2 ;    // This many genes in first half of child
          n2 - chromsize - n1 ;   // and this many in second half
          n3 - n4 - 0 ;           // We are using one point crossover
          i - *crosspt - 1 ;      // We will start building child here
          }
      else {                              // Use two point crossover
          n1 - n2 - n3 - chromsize / 4 ;  // This many in first three quarters
          n4 - chromsize - n1 - n2 - n3 ; // And the last quarter gets the rest
          i - -*crosspt - 1 ;             // 2 point method was flagged by neg
          }

/*
   Do reproduction here
*/

      if (*split) {
          i - (i+1) % chromsize ;
          child[i] - (left & pa[i])  | (right & pb[i]) ;
          --n1 ;
          }

      while (n1--) {
          i - (i+1) % chromsize ;
```

```
         child[i] = pb[i] ;
         }

   if (*split) {
      i = (i+1) % chromsize ;
      child[i] = (left & pb[i]) | (right & pa[i]) ;
      --n2 ;
      }

   while (n2--) {
      i = (i+1) % chromsize ;
      child[i] = pa[i] ;
      }

   if (n4) {                     // Two point crossover?

      if (*split) {
         i = (i+1) % chromsize ;
         child[i] = (left & pa[i]) | (right & pb[i]) ;
         --n3 ;
         }

      while (n3--) {
         i = (i+1) % chromsize ;
         child[i] = pb[i] ;
         }

      if (*split) {
         i = (i+1) % chromsize ;
         child[i] = (left & pb[i]) | (right & pa[i]) ;
         --n4 ;
         }

      while (n4--) {
         i = (i+1) % chromsize ;
         child[i] = pa[i] ;
         }

      } // If two point crossover
}
/*
--------------------------------------------------------------------------------

   mutate - apply the mutation operator to a single child

--------------------------------------------------------------------------------
*/
static void mutate (
   char *child ,    // Input/Output of the child
   int chromsize ,  // Number of variables in objective function
   double pmutate   // Probability of mutation
   )
{
   while (chromsize--) {
      if (unifrand() < pmutate)                              // Mutate this gene?
         child[chromsize] ^= (char) 1 << (longrand() % 8) ;  // Flip random bit
      }
}
/*
--------------------------------------------------------------------------------

   rand_ind - Randomly generate an individual's chromosome

--------------------------------------------------------------------------------
*/
static void rand_ind ( char *popptr , int chromsize )
{
   while (chromsize--)
      *popptr++ = 255 & longrand() ;
}
/*
--------------------------------------------------------------------------------

   decode - Decode the genes in this chromosome to the network weights.
            In genetic parlance, convert the genotype to the phenotype.

--------------------------------------------------------------------------------
*/
```

```
static void decode ( char *popptr , int nin , int nh1 , int nh2 ,
                     double *w1 , double *w2 )
{
   int n ;
   unsigned char gray, bit, parity, sum ;
   double *wptr ;

   if (! gray initialized) {        // If the translation table has not yet
      gray initialized - 1 ;        // been built, do it now (but just once!)
      for (n-0 ; n<256 ; n++) {     // Each gene is a one byte gray code
         gray - (unsigned char) n ;
         sum - 0 ;
         bit - 128 ;
         parity - 0 ;
         while (bit) {
            if (bit & gray)
               parity - ! parity ;
            if (parity)
               sum |- bit ;
            bit - bit >> 1 ;
            }
         gray code table[n] - sum ;
         }
      }

   n - nh1 * (nin+1) ; // Do hid layer 1 first.  It has this many weights.
   wptr - w1 ;         // Point to its weights

   while (n--) {
      gray - (unsigned char) *popptr++ ;  // The gene is a one byte gray code
      *wptr++ - ((double) gray code table[gray] - 127.5) * .0392 ; // -5 to 5
      }

   if (nh2) {                     // Do second hidden layer if any
      n - nh2 * (nh1+1) ;
      wptr - w2 ;
      while (n--) {
         gray - (unsigned char) *popptr++ ;
         *wptr++ - ((double) gray code table[gray] - 127.5) * .0392 ;
         }
      }
}

/****************************************************************************/
/*                                                                        */
/*   KOHNET - All principal routines for KohNet processing                */
/*                                                                        */
/****************************************************************************/

#include <stdio.h>
#include <string.h>
#include <math.h>
#include <conio.h>
#include <ctype.h>
#include <stdlib.h>
#include "const.h"       // System and limitation constants, typedefs, structs
#include "classes.h"     // Includes all class headers
#include "funcdefs.h"    // Function prototypes

static void free non null ( void **p ) ;

/*
--------------------------------------------------------------------------

   Constructor

   Note that some normalization methods generate an extra input.
   Therefore we always allocate nin+1 length vectors, even though
   we may not need the extra weight.

   The parameter 'executable' determines whether work areas for
   output neuron activations are also allocated. These are needed
   if we will ever apply inputs and want to compute outputs.

   In case of malloc failure, we set 'ok' to zero so the user knows about it.
   Also, we always leave unallocated pointers set to NULL.  There is no
   hard reason for doing this; calling programs should always know enough not
   to reference them.  However, it is simply good style.  Most compilers are
   much better at producing code that intercepts NULL pointer references than
   just wild pointers.  An ounce of prevention...

--------------------------------------------------------------------------
```

```
*/

KohNet::KohNet (
   int n inputs ,
   int n outputs ,
   KohParams *kp ,   // Specialized parameters
   int executable ,  // Also allocate hidden and output neurons?
   int zero          // Zero all weights?
   )
{
   int i, n ;

   outmod = OUTMOD CLASSIFY ;
   nin = n inputs ;
   nout = n outputs ;
   normalization = kp->normalization ;
   exe = executable ;
   neterr = 1.0 ;

   confusion = NULL ;
   out coefs = out = NULL ;

   ok = 0 ;    // Indicates failure of malloc (What a pessimist!)

   if (exe && (confusion=(int *) MALLOC((nout+1) * sizeof(int))) == NULL)
      return ;

   n = nout * (nin+1) ; // Some normalizations generate extra input
   if (((out coefs = (double *) MALLOC ( n * sizeof(double) )) == NULL)
    || (exe && (out = (double *) MALLOC ( nout * sizeof(double) )) == NULL)){
      free non null ( (void **) &out coefs ) ;
      free non null ( (void **) &confusion ) ;
      return ;
      }

   if (zero) {
      while (n--)
         out coefs[n] = 0.0 ;
      }

   if (exe)
      memset ( confusion , 0 , (nout+1) * sizeof(int) ) ;

   ok = 1 ;                // Indicate to caller that all mallocs succeeded
}
/*
   Local routine to free non-null pointers
*/

static void free non null ( void **p )
{
   if (*p != NULL) {
      FREE ( *p ) ;
      *p = NULL ;
      }
}


/*
--------------------------------------------------------------------------------

   Destructor

--------------------------------------------------------------------------------
*/

KohNet::~KohNet()
{
   if (! ok)    // If constructor's mallocs failed
      return ;  // there is nothing to free

   FREE ( out coefs ) ;
   if (exe) {
      FREE ( out ) ;
      FREE ( confusion ) ;
      }
}
/*
--------------------------------------------------------------------------------
```

```
    copy weights - Copy the weights from one network to another
                   Note that this is NOT like a copy or assignment,
                   as it does not copy other parameters.  In fact,
                   it gets sizes from the calling instance!
*/

void KohNet::copy weights ( KohNet *dest , KohNet *source )
{
   int n ;

   dest->neterr = source->neterr ;
   if (source->exe  &&  dest->exe) // These may be important too!
      memcpy ( dest->confusion , source->confusion , (nout+1) * sizeof(int) ) ;

   n = nout * (nin+1) ;
   memcpy ( dest->out coefs , source->out coefs , n * sizeof(double) ) ;
}


/*
-------------------------------------------------------------------------------

   zero weights - Zero all weights in a network

-------------------------------------------------------------------------------
*/

void KohNet::zero weights ()
{
   int n ;

   neterr = 1.0 ;

   n = nout * (nin+1) ;
   while (n--)
      out coefs[n] = 0.0 ;
}

/*
-------------------------------------------------------------------------------

   KOH NORM - Routines for normalizing Kohonen vectors to unit length

   in norm - Normalize an input vector by computing a normalizing
             factor and the synthetic last input.
             The input vector itself is not touched.
             It is assumed that all inputs are in the range -1 to 1.
             The end result is that if the inputs are multiplied by
             normfac, that vector with synth appended has unit length.

   wt norm - Normalize a weight vector in place.  The synthetic last
             component is NOT computed.

-------------------------------------------------------------------------------
*/
void KohNet::in norm (
   double *input ,    // Input vector
   double *normfac ,  // Output: multiply input by this
   double *synth      // Output: synthetic last input
   )

{
   double length, d ;

   length = veclen ( nin , input ) ; // Squared length
   if (length < 1.e-30)              // Safety
      length = 1.e-30 ;

   if (normalization == 0) {        // Multiplicative
      *normfac = 1.0 / sqrt ( length ) ;
      *synth = 0.0 ;
      }

   else if (normalization == 1) { // Z
      *normfac = 1.0 / sqrt ( nin ) ;
      d = (double) nin - length ;
      if (d > 0.0)
         *synth = sqrt ( d ) * *normfac ;
      else                    // If the inputs are all -1 to 1
```

```
                *synth = 0.0 ;    // this error never occurs
         }
}

void KohNet::wt norm ( double *w )
{
    int i ;
    double len, norm ;

    len = veclen ( nin , w ) ;        // Ignore last weight
    if (len < 1.e-30)                 // Safety
        len = 1.e-30 ;

    if (normalization == 0) {         // Multiplicative
        len = 1.0 / sqrt ( len ) ;
        for (i=0 ; i<nin ; i++)
            w[i] *= len ;
        w[nin] = 0. ;
        }

    else if (normalization == 1) { // Z
        len += w[nin] * w[nin] ;
        len = 1.0 / sqrt ( len ) ;
        for (i=0 ; i<=nin ; i++)
            w[i] *= len ;
        }
}

/*
--------------------------------------------------------------------------------

    trial - Compute the outputs for a given input by evaluating the network.
            It is assumed that all inputs are from -1 to 1, but not
            necessarily normalized (that is done here).

--------------------------------------------------------------------------------
*/

void KohNet::trial ( double *input )
{
    int i ;
    double normfac, synth, *optr ;

    in norm ( input , &normfac , &synth ) ;  // Normalize input

    for (i=0 ; i<nout ; i++) {
        optr = out coefs + i * (nin+1) ;  // i'th weight vector
        out[i] = dotprod ( nin , input , optr ) * normfac
                 + synth * optr[nin] ;
        out[i] = 0.5 * (out[i] + 1.0) ;    // Remap -1,1 to 0,1
        if (out[i] > 1.0)    // Only trivially happens due to rounding
            out[i] = 1.0 ;
        if (out[i] < 0.0)
            out[i] = 0.0 ;
        }
}


/*
--------------------------------------------------------------------------------

    winner - Return the subscript of the winning neuron.
             This is identical to 'trial' above except that
             it also returns the normalization info and winner.

--------------------------------------------------------------------------------
*/

int KohNet::winner (
    double *input ,   // Input vector
    double *normfac , // Output: multiply input by this
    double *synth     // Output: synthetic last input
    )
{
    int i, win ;
    double biggest, *optr ;

    in norm ( input , normfac , synth ) ;   // Normalize input

    biggest = -1.e30 ;
    for (i=0 ; i<nout ; i++) {
        optr = out coefs + i * (nin+1) ;  // i'th weight vector
```

```
                    out[i] = dotprod ( nin , input , optr ) * *normfac
                             + *synth * optr[nin] ;
                    out[i] = 0.5 * (out[i] + 1.0) ;     // Remap -1,1 to 0,1
                    if (out[i] > biggest) {
                       biggest = out[i] ;
                       win = i ;
                       }
                    if (out[i] > 1.0)     // Only trivially happens due to rounding
                       out[i] = 1.0 ;
                    if (out[i] < 0.0)
                       out[i] = 0.0 ;
                    }

        return win ;
   }


/* -------------------------------------------------------------------------------
   ---------------------------------------------------------------------------------

   learn

   ---------------------------------------------------------------------------------
   ---------------------------------------------------------------------------------
*/

void KohNet::learn (
     TrainingSet *tptr ,          // Training set
     struct LearnParams *lptr     // Learning parameters
     )

{
    int i, key, tset ;
    int iter ;            // Iterations (epochs)
    int n retry ;         // Number of random retries
    int nwts ;            // Total number of weights
    int *won ;            // Counts how many times each neuron won
    int winners ;         // How many neurons won per epoch
    char msg[80] ;        // For messages to user
    double *work ;        // Scratch for additive learning
    double *correc ;      // Scratch for cumulative correction vector
    double rate ;         // Current learning rate
    double bigerr ;       // Biggest single error in epoch
    double bigcorr ;      // Biggest cumulative correction in epoch
    double best err ;     // Minimum error so far
    double *dptr ;        // Points to a training case
    KohNet *bestnet ;     // Preserve best here
    KohParams *kp ;       // User's parameters here

    if (! exe) {    // Should NEVER happen, but good style to aid debugging
       error message ( "Internal error in KohNet::learn" ) ;
       exit ( 1 ) ;
       }

    kp = lptr->kp ;  // Simplify pointing to parameters
    neterr = 1.0 ;

/*
   If this is multiplicative normalization, make sure all training
   cases are non-null.
*/

    if (normalization == 0) {        // Multiplicative
       for (tset=0 ; tset<tptr->ntrain ; tset++) {
          dptr = tptr->data + (nin+1) * tset ;
          if (veclen ( nin , dptr ) < 1.e-30) {
             error message (
                     "Multiplicative normalization has null training case" ) ;
             return ;
             }
          }
       }

/*
   Allocate scratch memory, then initialize weights
*/

    MEMTEXT ( "KOHNET::learn new bestnet" ) ;
    bestnet = new KohNet ( nin , nout , kp , 0 , 1 ) ;

    if ((bestnet == NULL)  ||  (! bestnet->ok)) {
       memory message ( "to learn" ) ;
       if (bestnet != NULL)
```

```
            delete bestnet ;
         return ;
         }

   nwts - nout * (nin+1) ;
   MEMTEXT ( "KOHNET: Learn scratch" ) ;
   won - (int *) MALLOC ( nout * sizeof(int) ) ;
   correc - (double *) MALLOC ( nwts * sizeof(double) ) ;
   if (! kp->learn method)  // Needed only for additive method
      work - (double *) MALLOC ( (nin+1) * sizeof(double)) ;
   else
      work - NULL ;

   if ((won -- NULL) || (correc -- NULL) ||
       ((! kp->learn method)  && (work -- NULL))) {
      if (won !- NULL)
         FREE ( won ) ;
      if (correc !- NULL)
         FREE ( correc ) ;
      if (work !- NULL)
         FREE ( work ) ;
      delete bestnet ;
      memory message ( "to learn" ) ;
      return ;
      }

   rate - kp->rate ;

/*
   If the user specified NOINIT, they are continuing to learn from
   existing weights.  Call epoch1 to find the error associated with
   those weights, and save the weights as best so far.
   Then don't waste that call to epoch1.  Call epoch2 to update
   the weights.
*/

   if (lptr->init -- 0) {        // NOINIT (continue learning)
      epoch1 ( tptr , rate , 1 , won , &bigerr , correc , work ) ;
      best err - neterr - bigerr ;
      copy weights ( bestnet , this ) ;
      epoch2 ( rate , kp->learn method , won , &bigcorr , correc ) ;
      }
   else if (lptr->init -- 1) { // RANDOM Initialize weights
      initialize () ;
      best err - 1.e30 ;
      }

/*
   Main loop is here.  Each iter is a complete epoch.
*/

   n retry - 0 ;
   for (iter-0 ; ; iter++) {

      epoch1 ( tptr , rate , kp->learn method , won ,
               &bigerr , correc , work ) ;

      neterr - bigerr ;

      if (neterr < best err) {  // Keep track of best
         best err - neterr ;
         copy weights ( bestnet , this ) ;
         }

      winners - 0 ;      // Count how many neurons won this iter
      i - nout ;
      while (i--) {
         if (won[i])
            ++winners ;
         }

      sprintf( msg ,
         "Iter %d err-%.2lf (best-%.2lf)  %d won",
         iter, 100.0 * neterr, 100.0 * best err, winners ) ;
      normal message ( msg ) ;

      if (kbhit()) {            // Was a key pressed?
         key - getch () ;       // Read it if so
         while (kbhit())        // Flush key buffer in case function key
            getch () ;          // or key was held down
         if (key -- 27)         // ESCape
            break ;
```

```
          }

        if (bigerr < lptr->quit err) // Are we done?
          break ;

/*
   If one or more neurons failed to ever win, make it a winner.
   Note that this has a theoretical flaw.
   If the training set has duplication such that there are fewer
   unique values than neurons, we can get in a loop of flipping
   case values around neurons.  Thus, rather than verifying
   winners<tptr->ntrain below, we should ideally count how many
   unique values are in the training set, and use that number.
   However, that would be time consuming and protect against an
   extremely unlikely event anyway.
*/

        if ((winners < nout)  &&  (winners < tptr->ntrain)) {
          force win ( tptr , won ) ;
          continue ;
          }

        epoch2 ( rate , kp->learn method , won , &bigcorr , correc ) ;

        sprintf( msg , " correction=%.2lf", 100.0 * bigcorr ) ;
        progress message ( msg ) ;

        if (bigcorr < 1.e-5) { // Trivial improvement?
          if (++n retry > lptr->retries) // If so, start over
            break ;               // unless at user's limit
          initialize () ;         // Use totally random weights
          iter = -1 ;             // End of loop incs this to 0
          rate = kp->rate ;       // Rate starts high again
          continue ;
          }

        if (rate > 0.01)  // Reduce learning rate each time
          rate *= kp->reduction ;

        } // Endless learning loop

/*
   We are done.  Retrieve the best weights.  Learning should have left
   them very close to normalized, but it doesn't hurt to touch them up.
   Unfortunately, this can slightly change the network error.
*/

   copy weights ( this , bestnet ) ;

   for (i=0 ; i<nout ; i++)
     wt norm ( out coefs + i * (nin+1) ) ;

   MEMTEXT ( "KOHNET: Learn scratch" ) ;
   delete bestnet ;
   FREE ( won ) ;
   FREE ( correc ) ;
   if (! kp->learn method)  // Needed only for additive method
     FREE ( work ) ;
   return ;
}

/*
--------------------------------------------------------------------------------

   initialize - Initialize weights

--------------------------------------------------------------------------------
*/

void KohNet::initialize ()
{
   int i ;
   double *optr ;

   zero weights () ;
   shake ( nout * (nin+1) , out coefs , out coefs , 1.0 ) ;
   for (i=0 ; i<nout ; i++) {
     optr = out coefs + i * (nin+1) ;  // This weight vector
     wt norm ( optr ) ;
     }
}
```

```
/*
--------------------------------------------------------------------------------

    epoch1 - Compute the error and correction vector

--------------------------------------------------------------------------------
*/
void KohNet::epoch1 (
    TrainingSet *tptr ,    // Training set
    double rate ,          // Learning rate
    int learn method ,     // 0=additive, 1=subtractive
    int *won ,             // Work vector holds times each neuron won
    double *bigerr ,       // Returns max error length across training set
    double *correc ,       // Work vector nout*(nin+1) long for corrections
    double *work           // Work vector nin+1 long for additive learning
    )
{
    int i, best, size, nwts, tset ;
    double *dptr, normfac, synth, *cptr, *wptr, length, diff ;

    nwts = nout * (nin+1) ;
    size = nin + 1 ;   // Size of each case in training set
/*
    Zero cumulative corrections and winner counts
*/
    i = nwts ;
    while (i--)
        correc[i] = 0.0 ;

    memset ( won , 0 , nout * sizeof(int) ) ;
    *bigerr = 0.0 ;   // Length of biggest error vector
/*
    Cumulate the correction vector 'correc' across the epoch
*/
    for (tset=0 ; tset<tptr->ntrain ; tset++) {
        dptr = tptr->data + size * tset ; // Point to this case
        best = winner ( dptr , &normfac , &synth ) ; // Winning neuron
        ++won[best] ;                   // Record this win
        wptr = out coefs+best*(nin+1) ; // Winner's weights here
        cptr = correc+best*(nin+1) ;    // Corrections summed here
        length = 0.0 ;                  // Length of error vector

        for (i=0 ; i<nin ; i++) {  // Do all inputs
            diff = dptr[i] * normfac - wptr[i] ; // Input minus weight
            length += diff * diff ; // Cumulate length of error
            if (learn method)       // Subtractive method
                cptr[i] += diff ;   // just uses differences
            else                    // Additive more complex
                work[i] = rate * dptr[i] * normfac + wptr[i] ;
            }                       // Loop does actual inputs
        diff = synth - wptr[nin] ; // Don't forget synthetic input
        length += diff * diff ;    // It is part of input too!
        if (learn method)          // Subtractive method
            cptr[nin] += diff ;    // Cumulate across epoch
        else                       // Additive more complex
            work[nin] = rate * synth + wptr[nin] ;

        if (length > *bigerr)      // Keep track of largest error
            *bigerr = length ;

        if (! learn method) {      // Additive method
            wt norm ( work ) ;
            for (i=0 ; i<=nin ; i++)
                cptr[i] += work[i] - wptr[i] ;
            }

        } // Pass through all training sets, cumulating correction vector

    *bigerr = sqrt ( *bigerr ) ;
}


/*
--------------------------------------------------------------------------------

    epoch2 - Adjust weights per corrections from epoch1
```

```
   -------------------------------------------------------------------------
*/

void KohNet::epoch2 (
   double rate ,          // Learning rate
   int learn method ,     // 0-additive, 1-subtractive
   int *won ,             // Work vector holds times each neuron won
   double *bigcorr ,      // Returns length of largest correction vector
   double *correc         // Work vector nout*(nin+1) long for corrections
   )

{
   int i, j ;
   double corr, *cptr, *wptr, length, f, diff ;

   *bigcorr - 0.0 ;                     // Length of largest correction

   for (i-0 ; i<nout ; i++) {           // Apply mean correction to each

      if (! won[i])                     // If this neuron never won
         continue ;                     // might as well skip update

      wptr - out coefs+i*(nin+1) ;      // i's weights here
      cptr - correc+i*(nin+1) ;         // Corrections were summed here

      f - 1.0 / (double) won[i] ;       // Finds mean across epoch
      if (learn method)                 // Subtractive method
         f *- rate ;                    // needs learning rate included

      length - 0.0 ;                    // Will sum length of correction

      for (j-0 ; j<-nin ; j++) {        // Weight vector for this neuron
         corr - f * cptr[j] ;           // Mean correction
         wptr[j] +- corr ;              // Update weight vector
         length +- corr * corr ;        // Sum length of this correction
         }

      if (length > *bigcorr)            // Keep track of biggest correction
         *bigcorr - length ;
      }

/*
   Scale the correction length per learning rate so that we
   are not fooled into thinking we converged when really all
   that happened is that the learning rate got small.
   Note that it can exceed 1.0 if the weights and data
   pointed in opposing directions.
*/

   *bigcorr - sqrt ( *bigcorr ) / rate ;
}


/*
   -------------------------------------------------------------------------

   force win - Force a neuron to win.

   -------------------------------------------------------------------------
*/

void KohNet::force win (
   TrainingSet *tptr ,    // Training set
   int *won               // Work vector holds times each neuron won
   )

{
   int i, tset, best, size, which ;
   double *dptr, normfac, synth, dist, *optr ;

   size - nin + 1 ;  // Size of each training case

/*
   Find the training case which is farthest from its winning neuron.
   It is reasonable to believe that this case is not adequately
   represented by that neuron, and deserves a neuron of its very own.
*/

   dist - 1.e30 ;
   for (tset-0 ; tset<tptr->ntrain ; tset++) {
      dptr - tptr->data + size * tset ; // Point to this case
      best - winner ( dptr , &normfac , &synth ) ; // Winning neuron
```

```
          if (out[best] < dist) {    // Far indicated by low activation
             dist = out[best] ;       // Maintain record
             which = tset ;           // and which case did it
             }
          }

/*
   Now find the non-winning neuron which is most similar to
   the under-represented case found above.
*/

       dptr = tptr->data + size * which ;
       best = winner ( dptr , &normfac , &synth ) ;

       dist = -1.e30 ;
       i = nout ;
       while (i--) {                // Try all neurons
          if (won[i])               // If this one won then skip it
             continue ;             // We want a non-winner
          if (out[i] > dist) {      // High activation means similar
             dist = out[i] ;        // Keep track of best
             which = i ;            // and its subscript
             }
          }

/*
   Use that training case to define the new weights.
   Strictly speaking, we should multiply the inputs by normfac,
   then append synth.  But since we normalize, it is equivalent
   (and faster) to copy the inputs, then append synth / normfac.
*/

       optr = out coefs + which * (nin+1) ;        // Non-winner's weights
       memcpy( optr , dptr , nin*sizeof(double)) ; // become case
       optr[nin] = synth / normfac ;               // Append synth
       wt norm ( optr ) ;                          // Keep normal
   }


/*
--------------------------------------------------------------------------

   wt save - Save weights to disk (called from WT SAVE.CPP)
   wt restore - Restore weights from disk (called from WT SAVE.CPP)

--------------------------------------------------------------------------
*/

int KohNet::wt save ( FILE *fp )
{
   int n ;

   n = nout * (nin+1) ;
   fwrite ( out coefs , n * sizeof(double) , 1 , fp ) ;
   if (ferror ( fp ))
      return 1 ;
   return 0 ;
}

void KohNet::wt restore ( FILE *fp )
{
   int n ;

   n = nout * (nin+1) ;
   fread ( out coefs , n * sizeof(double) , 1 , fp ) ;
   if (ferror ( fp ))
      ok = 0 ;
}

/****************************************************************************/
/*                                                                          */
/*   LAYERNET - All principal routines for LayerNet processing              */
/*                                                                          */
/****************************************************************************/

#include <stdio.h>
#include <string.h>
#include <math.h>
#include <conio.h>
#include <ctype.h>
#include <stdlib.h>
#include "const.h"              // System and limitation constants, typedefs, structs
```

```
#include "classes.h"     // Includes all class headers
#include "funcdefs.h"    // Function prototypes

static void free non null ( void **p ) ;

/*
--------------------------------------------------------------------------------

    Constructor

    The parameter 'executable' determines whether work areas for hidden and
    output neuron activations are also allocated.  These are needed if we
    will ever apply inputs and want to compute outputs.

    In case of malloc failure, we set 'ok' to zero so the user knows about it.
    Also, we always leave unallocated weight pointers set to NULL.  There is no
    hard reason for doing this; calling programs should always know enough not
    to reference them.  However, it is simply good style.  Most compilers are
    much better at producing code that intercepts NULL pointer references than
    just wild pointers.  An ounce of prevention...

--------------------------------------------------------------------------------
*/
LayerNet::LayerNet (
    int out model ,
    int n inputs ,
    int n hidden1 ,
    int n hidden2 ,
    int n outputs ,
    int executable ,   // Also allocate hidden and output neurons?
    int zero           // Zero all weights?
    )
{
    int i, n1, n2, n3 ;

    outmod = out model ;
    nin = n inputs ;
    nhid1 = n hidden1 ;
    nhid2 = n hidden2 ;
    nout = n outputs ;
    exe = executable ;
    neterr = 1.0 ;

    confusion = NULL ;
    hid1 coefs = hid2 coefs = out coefs = hid1 = hid2 = out = NULL ;

    ok = 0 ;    // Indicates failure of malloc (What a pessimist!)

    if (exe  &&  (confusion = (int *) MALLOC ( (nout+1) * sizeof(int))) == NULL)
        return ;

    if (nhid1 == 0) {                  // No hidden layer
        n1 = nout * (nin+1) ;
        if (((out coefs = (double *) MALLOC ( n1 * sizeof(double) )) == NULL)
         || (exe && (out = (double *) MALLOC ( nout * sizeof(double) )) == NULL)){
            free non null ( (void **) &out coefs ) ;
            free non null ( (void **) &confusion ) ;
            return ;
            }
        if (zero) {
            while (n1--)
                out coefs[n1] = 0.0 ;
            }
        }
    else if (nhid2 == 0) {             // One hidden layer
        n1 = nhid1 * (nin+1) ;
        n2 = nout * (nhid1+1) ;
        if (((hid1 coefs = (double *) MALLOC ( n1 * sizeof(double) )) == NULL)
         || ((out coefs = (double *) MALLOC ( n2 * sizeof(double) ))==NULL)
         || (exe && (hid1 = (double *) MALLOC ( nhid1 * sizeof(double) ))==NULL)
         || (exe && (out = (double *) MALLOC ( nout * sizeof(double) )) == NULL)){
            free non null ( (void **) &hid1 coefs ) ;
            free non null ( (void **) &out coefs ) ;
            free non null ( (void **) &hid1 ) ;
            free non null ( (void **) &confusion ) ;
            return ;
            }
        if (zero) {
            while (n1--)
                hid1 coefs[n1] = 0.0 ;
```

```
                      while (n2--)
                         out coefs[n2] - 0.0 ;
                      }
                   }

          else {                              // Two hidden layers
             n1 - nhid1 * (nin+1) ;
             n2 - nhid2 * (nhid1+1) ;
             n3 - nout * (nhid2+1) ;
             if (((hid1 coefs - (double *) MALLOC ( n1 * sizeof(double) )) -- NULL)
               || ((hid2 coefs - (double *) MALLOC ( n2 * sizeof(double) )) -- NULL)
                  ((out coefs - (double *) MALLOC ( n3 * sizeof(double) ))--NULL)
                  (exe && (hid1 - (double *) MALLOC ( nhid1 * sizeof(double) ))--NULL)
                  (exe && (hid2 - (double *) MALLOC ( nhid2 * sizeof(double) ))--NULL)
               || (exe && (out - (double *) MALLOC ( nout * sizeof(double) )) -- NULL)){
                free non null ( (void **) &hid1 coefs ) ;
                free non null ( (void **) &hid2 coefs ) ;
                free non null ( (void **) &out coefs ) ;
                free non null ( (void **) &hid1 ) ;
                free non null ( (void **) &hid2 ) ;
                free non null ( (void **) &confusion ) ;
                return ;
                }
             if (zero) {
                while (n1--)
                   hid1 coefs[n1] - 0.0 ;
                while (n2--)
                   hid2 coefs[n2] - 0.0 ;
                while (n3--)
                   out coefs[n3] - 0.0 ;
                }
             }

       if (exe)
          memset ( confusion , 0 , (nout+1) * sizeof(int) ) ;

       ok - 1 ;               // Indicate to caller that all mallocs succeeded
   }

/*
   Local routine to free non-null pointers
*/

static void free non null ( void **p )
{
   if (*p !- NULL) {
      FREE ( *p ) ;
      *p - NULL ;
      }
   }


/*
   --------------------------------------------------------------------------------

   Destructor

   --------------------------------------------------------------------------------
*/

LayerNet::~LayerNet()
{
   if (! ok)      // If constructor's mallocs failed
      return ;   // there is nothing to free

   FREE ( out coefs ) ;
   if (exe) {
      FREE ( out ) ;
      FREE ( confusion ) ;
      }

   if (nhid1) {
      FREE ( hid1 coefs ) ;
      if (exe)
         FREE ( hid1 ) ;
      if (nhid2) {
         FREE ( hid2 coefs ) ;
         if (exe)
            FREE ( hid2 ) ;
         }
      }
   }
```

```
/*
--------------------------------------------------------------------------------

   copy weights - Copy the weights from one network to another
                  Note that this is NOT like a copy or assignment,
                  as it does not copy other parameters.  In fact,
                  it gets sizes from the calling instance!

--------------------------------------------------------------------------------
*/

void LayerNet::copy weights ( LayerNet *dest , LayerNet *source )
{
   int n ;

   dest->neterr = source->neterr ;
   if (source->exe  &&  dest->exe) // These may be important too!
      memcpy ( dest->confusion , source->confusion , (nout+1) * sizeof(int) ) ;

   if (nhid1 == 0) {                    // No hidden layer
      n = nout * (nin+1) ;
      memcpy ( dest->out coefs , source->out coefs , n * sizeof(double) ) ;
      }

   else if (nhid2 == 0) {               // One hidden layer
      n = nhid1 * (nin+1) ;
      memcpy ( dest->hid1 coefs , source->hid1 coefs , n * sizeof(double) ) ;
      n = nout * (nhid1+1) ;
      memcpy ( dest->out coefs , source->out coefs , n * sizeof(double) ) ;
      }

   else {                               // Two hidden layers
      n = nhid1 * (nin+1) ;
      memcpy ( dest->hid1 coefs , source->hid1 coefs , n * sizeof(double) ) ;
      n = nhid2 * (nhid1+1) ;
      memcpy ( dest->hid2 coefs , source->hid2 coefs , n * sizeof(double) ) ;
      n = nout * (nhid2+1) ;
      memcpy ( dest->out coefs , source->out coefs , n * sizeof(double) ) ;
      }
}


/*
--------------------------------------------------------------------------------

   zero weights - Zero all weights in a network

--------------------------------------------------------------------------------
*/

void LayerNet::zero weights ()
{
   int n ;

   neterr = 1.0 ;

   if (nhid1 == 0) {                    // No hidden layer
      n = nout * (nin+1) ;
      while (n--)
         out coefs[n] = 0.0 ;
      }

   else if (nhid2 == 0) {               // One hidden layer
      n = nhid1 * (nin+1) ;
      while (n--)
         hid1 coefs[n] = 0.0 ;
      n = nout * (nhid1+1) ;
      while (n--)
         out coefs[n] = 0.0 ;
      }

   else {                               // Two hidden layers
      n = nhid1 * (nin+1) ;
      while (n--)
         hid1 coefs[n] = 0.0 ;
      n = nhid2 * (nhid1+1) ;
      while (n--)
         hid2 coefs[n] = 0.0 ;
      n = nout * (nhid2+1) ;
      while (n--)
         out coefs[n] = 0.0 ;
      }
```

```
    }

/*
-----------------------------------------------------------------------------

    trial - Compute the output for a given input by evaluating network

-----------------------------------------------------------------------------
*/

void LayerNet::trial ( double *input )
{
    int i ;

    if (! exe) {     // Should NEVER happen, but good style to aid debugging
        error message ( "Internal error in LayerNet::trial" ) ;
        return ;
        }

    if (nhid1 -- 0) {                    // No hidden layer
        for (i-0 ; i<nout ; i++)
            out[i] - activity ( input , out coefs+i*(nin+1) , nin ) ;
        }

    else if (nhid2 -- 0) {               // One hidden layer
        for (i-0 ; i<nhid1 ; i++)
            hid1[i] - activity ( input , hid1 coefs+i*(nin+1) , nin ) ;
        for (i-0 ; i<nout ; i++)
            out[i] - activity ( hid1 , out coefs+i*(nhid1+1) , nhid1 ) ;
        }

    else {                               // Two hidden layers
        for (i-0 ; i<nhid1 ; i++)
            hid1[i] - activity ( input , hid1 coefs+i*(nin+1) , nin ) ;
        for (i-0 ; i<nhid2 ; i++)
            hid2[i] - activity ( hid1 , hid2 coefs+i*(nhid1+1) , nhid1 ) ;
        for (i-0 ; i<nout ; i++)
            out[i] - activity ( hid2 , out coefs+i*(nhid2+1) , nhid2 ) ;
        }
    }

/*
-----------------------------------------------------------------------------

    learn

-----------------------------------------------------------------------------
*/

void LayerNet::learn ( TrainingSet *tptr , struct LearnParams *lptr )
{
    int i, try, n escape, n retry, bad count ;
    double err, prev err, best err, start of loop error ;
    char msg[80] ;
    SingularValueDecomp *sptr ;
    LayerNet *worknet, *bestnet ;

    if (! exe) {     // Should NEVER happen, but good style to aid debugging
        error message ( "Internal error in LayerNet::learn" ) ;
        return ;
        }

    n escape - n retry - 0 ;

/*
    Allocate scratch memory
*/

    MEMTEXT ( "LAYERNET::learn new worknet, bestnet" ) ;
    worknet - new LayerNet ( outmod , nin , nhid1 , nhid2 , nout , 0 , 0 ) ;
    bestnet - new LayerNet ( outmod , nin , nhid1 , nhid2 , nout , 0 , 1 ) ;

    if ((worknet -- NULL)  ||  (! worknet->ok)
     || (bestnet -- NULL)  ||  (! bestnet->ok)) {
        memory message ( "to learn" ) ;
        if (worknet !- NULL)
            delete worknet ;
        if (bestnet !- NULL)
            delete bestnet ;
        neterr - 1.0 ;
```

```
                    return ;
                    }

/*
    Find initial weight estimates via simulated annealing or genetics
    or simply regression if no hidden layers
*/

    if (lptr->init -- 0)                            // NO INIT
        neterr - trial error ( tptr ) ;

    if ((lptr->init -- 1)  ||  (lptr->init -- 2))   // ANNEAL
        anneal ( tptr , lptr , worknet , 1 ) ;

    else if (lptr->init -- 3) {                     // GENETIC
        if (nhid1)
            gen init ( tptr , lptr ) ;
        else {
            error message ( "Genetic init pointless with no hidden layer" ) ;
            neterr - 1.0 ;
            goto FINISH ;
            }
        }

    else if (lptr->init -- 4) {                     // REGRESSION
        if (nhid1) {
            warning message ( "REGRESS illegal if hidden layer.");
            neterr - 1.0 ;
            goto FINISH ;
            }

        MEMTEXT ( "LAYERNET: new SingularValueDecomp" ) ;
        sptr - new SingularValueDecomp ( tptr->ntrain , nin+1 , 1 ) ;
        if (! sptr->ok) {      // Indicates insufficient memory
            memory message("for regression. Try ANNEAL NOREGRESS." ) ;
            neterr - 1.0 ;   // Flag failure to LayerNet::learn which called us
            delete sptr ;
            }
        neterr - regress ( tptr , sptr ) ;
        MEMTEXT ( "LAYERNET: delete SingularValueDecomp" ) ;
        delete sptr ;
        }

    if (lptr->init  &&  neterr > 0.999999) // Memory allocation failure
        goto FINISH ;
/*
    Initialization is done.  Learning loop is here.
    First, do conjugate gradient optimization, finding local minimum.
    Then anneal to break out of it.  If successful, loop back up to
    do conjugate gradient again.  Otherwise restart totally random.
*/

    copy weights ( bestnet , this ) ;
    best err - neterr ;
    bad count - 0 ;              // Handles flat local mins

    for (try-1 ; ; try++) {

        sprintf ( msg , "Try %d  (best-%lf):", try, 100.0 * best err ) ;
        normal message ( msg ) ;

        start of loop error - neterr ;
        err - conjgrad ( tptr , 1000 , 1.e-8 , lptr->quit err ) ;
        neterr - fabs ( err ) ; // err<0 if user pressed ESCape

        sprintf ( msg , "  Gradient err-%lf", 100.0 * neterr ) ;
        progress message ( msg ) ;

        if (neterr < best err) {    // Keep track of best
            copy weights ( bestnet , this ) ;
            best err - neterr ;
            }

        if (err < lptr->quit err) // err<0 if user pressed ESCape
            break ;

        i - try * 97 + 101 ;    // Insure new seed for anneal
        if (i<0)
            i - -i ;
        slongrand ( (long) i ) ;
```

```
               prev err - neterr ;   // So we can see if anneal helped
               anneal ( tptr , lptr , worknet , 0 ) ;

               sprintf ( msg , "  Anneal err=%lf", 100.0 * neterr ) ;
               progress message ( msg ) ;

               if (neterr < best err) {   // Keep track of best
                  copy weights ( bestnet , this ) ;
                  best err - neterr ;
                  }

               if (best err < lptr->quit err)
                  break ;

               if (neterr < prev err) { // Did we break out of local min?
                  if ((start of loop error - neterr) < 1.e-3)
                     ++bad count ;   // Avoid many unprofitable iters
                  else
                     bad count - 0 ;
                  if (bad count < 4) {
                     ++n escape ;            // For user interest only
                     continue ;              // Escaped, so gradient learn again
                     }
                  }

               if (++n retry > lptr->retries)
                  break ;

               progress message ( "  RESTART" ) ;
               zero weights () ;   // Failed to break out, so retry random
               anneal ( tptr , lptr , worknet , 1 ) ;
               }
FINISH:
      copy weights ( this , bestnet ) ;
      MEMTEXT ( "LAYERNET::learn delete worknet, bestnet" ) ;
      delete worknet ;
      delete bestnet ;
      sprintf ( msg , "%d successful escapes, %d retries", n escape, n retry ) ;
      normal message ( msg ) ;

      return ;
}


/*
--------------------------------------------------------------------------------

   wt save - Save weights to disk (called from WT SAVE.CPP)
   wt restore - Restore weights from disk (called from WT SAVE.CPP)

--------------------------------------------------------------------------------
*/

int LayerNet::wt save ( FILE *fp )
{
   int n ;

   if (nhid1 -- 0) {                    // No hidden layer
      n - nout * (nin+1) ;
      fwrite ( out coefs , n * sizeof(double) , 1 , fp ) ;
      }

   else if (nhid2 -- 0) {               // One hidden layer
      n - nhid1 * (nin+1) ;
      fwrite ( hid1 coefs , n * sizeof(double) , 1 , fp ) ;
      n - nout * (nhid1+1) ;
      fwrite ( out coefs , n * sizeof(double) , 1 , fp ) ;
      }

   else {                               // Two hidden layers
      n - nhid1 * (nin+1) ;
      fwrite ( hid1 coefs , n * sizeof(double) , 1 , fp ) ;
      n - nhid2 * (nhid1+1) ;
      fwrite ( hid2 coefs , n * sizeof(double) , 1 , fp ) ;
      n - nout * (nhid2+1) ;
      fwrite ( out coefs , n * sizeof(double) , 1 , fp ) ;
      }

   if (ferror ( fp ))
      return 1 ;
   return 0 ;
```

```
   }

void LayerNet::wt restore ( FILE *fp )
{
   int n ;

   if (nhid1 == 0) {                    // No hidden layer
      n = nout * (nin+1) ;
      fread ( out coefs , n * sizeof(double) , 1 , fp ) ;
      }

   else if (nhid2 == 0) {               // One hidden layer
      n = nhid1 * (nin+1) ;
      fread ( hid1 coefs , n * sizeof(double) , 1 , fp ) ;
      n = nout * (nhid1+1) ;
      fread ( out coefs , n * sizeof(double) , 1 , fp ) ;
      }

   else {                               // Two hidden layers
      n = nhid1 * (nin+1) ;
      fread ( hid1 coefs , n * sizeof(double) , 1 , fp ) ;
      n = nhid2 * (nhid1+1) ;
      fread ( hid2 coefs , n * sizeof(double) , 1 , fp ) ;
      n = nout * (nhid2+1) ;
      fread ( out coefs , n * sizeof(double) , 1 , fp ) ;
      }

   if (ferror ( fp ))
      ok = 0 ;
}
/******************************************************************************/
/*                                                                          */
/*   NETWORK Routines specific to the Network parent class                  */
/*                                                                          */
/******************************************************************************/

#include <stdio.h>
#include <string.h>
#include <math.h>
#include <conio.h>
#include <ctype.h>
#include <stdlib.h>
#include "const.h"      // System and limitation constants, typedefs, structs
#include "classes.h"    // Includes all class headers
#include "funcdefs.h"   // Function prototypes

/*
--------------------------------------------------------------------------------

   We include a useless destructor to appease errant compilers.
   See the comment in CONST.H regarding BAD COMPILER.

--------------------------------------------------------------------------------
*/

#if BAD COMPILER
Network::~Network()
{
   return ;
}
#endif

/*
--------------------------------------------------------------------------------

   trial error - Compute the mean square error for the entire training set

--------------------------------------------------------------------------------
*/

double Network::trial error ( TrainingSet *tptr )
{
   int i, size, tset, tclass ;
   double tot err, temp, *dptr, diff ;

   if (outmod == OUTMOD CLASSIFY)    // Compute size of each training sample
      size = nin + 1 ;
   else if (outmod == OUTMOD AUTO)
      size = nin ;
   else if (outmod == OUTMOD GENERAL)
      size = nin + nout ;
```

```
        tot err - 0.0 ;   // Total error will be cumulated here

        for (tset-0 ; tset<tptr->ntrain ; tset++) {   // Do all samples

            dptr - tptr->data + size * tset ;        // Point to this sample
            trial ( dptr ) ;                         // Evaluate network for it

            if (outmod -- OUTMOD AUTO) {             // If this is AUTOASSOCIATIVE
                for (i-0 ; i<nout ; i++) {           // then the expected outputs
                    diff - *dptr++ - out[i] ;        // are just the inputs
                    tot err +- diff * diff ;
                    }
                }

            else if (outmod -- OUTMOD CLASSIFY) {    // If this is Classification
                tclass - (int) dptr[nin] - 1 ;       // class is stored after inputs
                for (i-0 ; i<nout ; i++) {           // Recall that train added a
                    if (tclass -- i)                 // fraction so that the above
                        diff - NEURON ON - out[i] ;  // truncation to get tclass is
                    else                             // always safe in any radix
                        diff - NEURON OFF - out[i] ;
                    tot err +- diff * diff ;
                    }
                }

            else if (outmod -- OUTMOD GENERAL) {     // If this is GENERAL output
                dptr +- nin ;                        // outputs stored after inputs
                for (i-0 ; i<nout ; i++) {
                    diff - *dptr++ - out[i] ;
                    tot err +- diff * diff ;
                    }
                }

            } // for all tsets

        tot err /- (double) tptr->ntrain * (double) nout ;
        neterr - tot err ;
        return tot err ;
}
/********************************************************************************/
/*                                                                            */
/*   REGRESS - Use regression to compute LayerNet output weights              */
/*                                                                            */
/********************************************************************************/

#include <stdio.h>
#include <string.h>
#include <math.h>
#include <conio.h>
#include <ctype.h>
#include <stdlib.h>
#include "const.h"        // System and limitation constants, typedefs, structs
#include "classes.h"      // Includes all class headers
#include "funcdefs.h"     // Function prototypes

double LayerNet::regress (
    TrainingSet *tptr ,       // Training set used for regression input
    SingularValueDecomp *sptr // Work areas and needed functions
    )

{
    int i, in, out, tset, nhp1, size, nvars ;
    double *aptr, *bptr, *dptr, err, temp, diff ;


/*
    Compute the size of each training sample in tptr->data and the number
    of independent variables (columns of matrix)
*/

    if (outmod -- OUTMOD CLASSIFY)
        size - nin + 1 ;
    else if (outmod -- OUTMOD AUTO)
        size - nin ;
    else if (outmod -- OUTMOD GENERAL)
        size - nin + nout ;

    if (nhid1 -- 0)          // No hidden layer
        nvars - nin + 1 ;
    else if (nhid2 -- 0)     // One hidden layer
        nvars - nhid1 + 1 ;
```

```
      else                      // Two hidden layers
         nvars - nhid2 + 1 ;

/*
   Pass through training set, building matrix, then find its singular value
   decomposition.  We keep a copy of it so we can compute the error later.
*/

   aptr - sptr->a ;                    // Will build matrix here

   for (tset=0 ; tset<tptr->ntrain ; tset++) { // Do all training samples

      dptr - tptr->data + size * tset ; // Point to this sample

      if (nhid1 -- 0) {              // No hidden layer
         for (i=0 ; i<nin ; i++)     // so matrix is just inputs
            *aptr++ - *dptr++ ;
         }

      else if (nhid2 -- 0) {         // One hidden layer
         for (i=0 ; i<nhid1 ; i++)      // so matrix is hidden1 activations
            *aptr++ - activity ( dptr , hid1 coefs+i*(nin+1) , nin ) ;
         }

      else {                        // Two hidden layers
         for (i=0 ; i<nhid1 ; i++)
            hid1[i] - activity ( dptr , hid1 coefs+i*(nin+1) , nin ) ;
         for (i=0 ; i<nhid2 ; i++)
            *aptr++ - activity ( hid1 , hid2 coefs+i*(nhid1+1) , nhid1 ) ;
         }
      *aptr++ - 1.0 ;   // Bias term is last column of matrix
      } // For each training sample


/*
   Do the singular value decomposition.
   Then solve for weights for each output neuron.
   After each output weight vector is computed (using backsub),
   compute the activation of that output neuron, compare it to
   its desired value in the training set, and cumulate the error.
*/

   sptr->svdcmp () ;

   err - 0.0 ;

   for (out=0 ; out<nout ; out++) {  // For each output neuron

      bptr - sptr->b ;              // Backsub routine wants RHS here

      for (tset=0 ; tset<tptr->ntrain ; tset++) {

         dptr - tptr->data + size * tset ;    // Training sample starts here

         if (outmod -- OUTMOD AUTO) {         // If this is AUTOASSOCIATIVE
            temp - dptr[out] ;                // output is just input
            if (temp > 0.999999)              // Avoid problems in
               temp - 0.999999 ;              // inverse act function
            if (temp < 0.000001)
               temp - 0.000001 ;
            *bptr++ - inverse act ( temp ) ;  // Inverse activation function
            }

         else if (outmod -- OUTMOD CLASSIFY) { // If this is Classification
            if ((int) dptr[nin] -- out+1)     // class identifier past inputs
               *bptr++ - inverse act ( NEURON ON ) ; // Inverse of NEURON ON
            else
               *bptr++ - inverse act ( NEURON OFF ) ;
            }

         else if (outmod -- OUTMOD GENERAL) { // If this is GENERAL output
            temp - dptr[nin+out] ;            // output is just past input
            if (temp > 0.999999)
               temp - 0.999999 ;
            if (temp < 0.000001)
               temp - 0.000001 ;
            *bptr++ - inverse act ( temp ) ;    // Inverse activation function
            }
         } // For all training samples

      bptr - out coefs + out * nvars ;    // Weight vector for this output will
      sptr->backsub ( 1.e-8 , bptr ) ;    // go here.  Find those weights.
```

```
               for (i=0 ; i<nvars ; i++) {    // Limit to reasonable values
                  if (bptr[i] > 5.)
                     bptr[i] = 5. ;
                  if (bptr[i] < -5.)
                     bptr[i] = -5. ;
                  }

/*
   The weights for output neuron 'out' are now in place in out coefs and are
   pointed to by bptr.  Pass through the training set, using the activations
   of the layer just before the output layer, still in sptr->a, to compute
   the activation of the output neuron.  Compare this attained activation to
   the desired in the training sample, and cumulate the mean square error.
   Note that we use nvars-1 in the call to 'activity' because the bias term
   is taken care of in that subroutine.
*/

               for (tset=0 ; tset<tptr->ntrain ; tset++) {// Cumulate err of this output

                  dptr = tptr->data + size * tset ;         // Training sample starts here
                  aptr = sptr->a + tset * nvars ;           // Inputs to output layer
                  diff = activity ( aptr , bptr , nvars-1 ) ; // Find this output

                  if (outmod == OUTMOD_AUTO)                 // If this is AUTOASSOCIATIVE
                     diff -= dptr[out] ;                     // the desired output is input

                  else if (outmod == OUTMOD_CLASSIFY) {      // If this is Classification
                     if ((int) dptr[nin] == out+1)           // class identifier past inputs
                        diff -= NEURON_ON ;
                     else
                        diff -= NEURON_OFF ;
                     }

                  else if (outmod == OUTMOD_GENERAL)         // If this is GENERAL output
                     diff -= dptr[nin+out] ;                 // output is just past input

                  err += diff * diff ;
                  }
               } // For each output

            err /= (double) tptr->ntrain * (double) nout ;
            neterr = err ;
            return err ;
            }
```

```
/*****************************************************************************/
/*                                                                         */
/*   SVDCMP     - SingularValueDecomp object routines for performing singular  */
/*               value decomposition on a matrix, and using backsubstitution   */
/*               to find least squares solutions to simultaneous equations.    */
/*                                                                         */
/*               The decomposition algorithm is yet another implementation of  */
/*               the classic method of Golub and Reinsch (Wilkinson, J.H. and  */
/*               Reinsch, C., 1971, 'Handbook for Automatic Computation' vol. 2)*/
/*               Some tricks have been taken from later sources.  See (Press  */
/*               et al 'Numerical Recipes in C') for a complete list of        */
/*               references.                                                */
/*                                                                         */
/*****************************************************************************/

#include <stdio.h>
#include <string.h>
#include <math.h>
#include <conio.h>
#include <ctype.h>
#include <stdlib.h>
#include "const.h"        // System and limitation constants, typedefs, structs
#include "classes.h"      // Includes all class headers
#include "funcdefs.h"     // Function prototypes

/*
   Prototypes for local subroutines
*/

static double bidiag ( double *a , int rows , int cols , double *w ,
                       double *work ) ;

static void cancel ( int rows , int cols , int lower , int index ,
                     double matnorm , double *a , double *w , double *work ) ;

static void qr ( int rows , int cols , int lower , int index ,
                 double *a , double *v , double *w , double *work ) ;
```

```
static void transforms ( double *a , int rows , int cols , double *w ,
                         double *v , double *work ) ;

static void verify nonneg ( int cols , int index , double *w , double *v ) ;

/*
    Local macros.  RSS computes the root of the sum of squares of
    its arguments.  This clever implementation avoids over/underflow.
    SIGN is the old FORTRAN routine which returns the value of its
    first argument with the sign of its second.
    The variables va, vb and vc are local work areas for these macros.
*/

static double va, vb, vc ;

#define RSS(a,b) ((va=fabs(a)) > (vb=fabs(b)) ? \
                  (vc=vb/va , va*sqrt(vc*vc+1.0)) : \
                  ((vb != 0.0) ? (vc=va/vb , vb*sqrt(vc*vc+1.0)) : 0.0))

#define SIGN(a,b) (va=fabs(a) , (b) >= 0.0 ? va : -va)

/*
-------------------------------------------------------------------------------

    Constructor - This allocates memory for the input/output matrix 'a' and
                  any work areas which it will need (including the public
                  outputs of w and v).  It also allocates 'b' which will be
                  input to the backsub routine.  It does not allocate 'x' which
                  is the output of backsub.

                  If there is a problem (rows < cols, or insufficient memory),
                  it leaves public ok=0.  The user should check for this after
                  allocating with new.

-------------------------------------------------------------------------------
*/

SingularValueDecomp::SingularValueDecomp ( int nrows , int ncols , int preserve)
{
    if (nrows < ncols) {
        rows = cols = ok = 0 ;
        return ;
        }

    a = u = w = v = work = b = NULL ;
    if (((a = (double *) MALLOC ( nrows * ncols * sizeof(double) )) == NULL)
     || (preserve &&
         (u = (double *) MALLOC ( nrows * ncols * sizeof(double)))== NULL)
     || ((w = (double *) MALLOC ( ncols * sizeof(double) )) == NULL)
     || ((v = (double *) MALLOC ( ncols * ncols * sizeof(double) )) == NULL)
     || ((work = (double *) MALLOC ( ncols * sizeof(double) )) == NULL)
     || ((b = (double *) MALLOC ( nrows * sizeof(double) )) == NULL)) {
        if (a != NULL)
            FREE ( a ) ;
        if (u != NULL)
            FREE ( u ) ;
        if (w != NULL)
            FREE ( w ) ;
        if (v != NULL)
            FREE ( v ) ;
        if (work != NULL)
            FREE ( work ) ;
        if (b != NULL)
            FREE ( b ) ;
        rows = cols = ok = 0 ;
        return ;
        }

    rows = nrows ;
    cols = ncols ;
    ok = 1 ;
}

/*
-------------------------------------------------------------------------------

    Destructor - This frees all memory allocated by the constructor.

-------------------------------------------------------------------------------
*/

SingularValueDecomp::~SingularValueDecomp ()
```

```
   {
      if (! ok)     // If constructor's mallocs failed
         return ;   // there is nothing to free

      FREE ( a ) ;
      if (u != NULL)     // This was allocated only if preserve was nonzero
         FREE ( u ) ;
      FREE ( w ) ;
      FREE ( v ) ;
      FREE ( work ) ;
      FREE ( b ) ;
   }

/*
--------------------------------------------------------------------------------

   svdcmp - Perform singular value decomposition on the matrix already stored.

--------------------------------------------------------------------------------
*/

void SingularValueDecomp::svdcmp ()
{
   int cflag, iter, index, lower ;
   double matnorm, *mat ;

   if (u == NULL)     // Do we replace a with u
      mat = a ;
   else {             // or preserve it?
      memcpy ( u , a , rows * cols * sizeof(double) ) ;
      mat = u ;
      }

   matnorm = bidiag ( mat , rows , cols , w , work ) ; // Reduce to bidiagonal
   transforms ( mat , rows , cols , w , v , work ) ;   // Accumulate R&L trans

   for (index=cols-1 ; index>=0 ; index--) { // All singular values
      for (iter=0 ; iter<100 ; iter++) {        // Conservative limit on QR tries
         cflag = 1 ;
         for (lower=index ; lower ; lower--) { // Split?
            if (fabs (work[lower]) + matnorm == matnorm) {
               cflag = 0 ;
               break ;
               }
            if (fabs (w[lower-1]) + matnorm == matnorm)
               break ;
            }
         if (lower && cflag)
            cancel ( rows , cols , lower , index , matnorm , mat , w , work ) ;
         if (lower == index) { // Converged?
            verify nonneg ( cols , index , w , v ) ; // Want nonegative singvals
            break ;
            }
         qr ( rows , cols , lower , index , mat , v , w , work ) ; // Another QR
         }
      }
}

/*
--------------------------------------------------------------------------------

   bidiag - Local routine for Householder reduction to bidiagonal form

--------------------------------------------------------------------------------
*/

static double bidiag (
   double *a ,
   int rows ,
   int cols ,
   double *w ,
   double *work
   )

{
   int col, j, k, nextcol ;
   double pp, qq, denom, sum ;
   double matnorm, scale ;

   matnorm = qq = sum = scale = 0.0 ;
```

```
        for (col-0 ; col<cols ; col++) {

          nextcol - col + 1 ;
          work[col] - scale * qq ;
          qq - sum - scale - 0.0 ;

          for (k-col ; k<rows ; k++)
            scale += fabs ( a[k*cols+col] ) ;
          if (scale > 0.0) {
            for (k-col ; k<rows ; k++) {
              a[k*cols+col] /- scale ;
              sum += a[k*cols+col] * a[k*cols+col] ;
            }
            pp - a[col*cols+col] ;
            qq - -SIGN ( sqrt(sum) , pp ) ;
            denom - pp * qq - sum ;
            a[col*cols+col] - pp - qq ;

            for (j-nextcol ; j<cols ; j++) {
              sum - 0.0 ;
              for (k-col ; k<rows ; k++)
                sum += a[k*cols+col] * a[k*cols+j] ;
              pp - sum / denom ;
              for (k-col ; k<rows ; k++)
                a[k*cols+j] += pp * a[k*cols+col] ;
            }

            for (k-col ; k<rows ; k++)
              a[k*cols+col] *- scale ;
            } // if scale > 0

          w[col] - scale * qq ;


          qq - sum - scale - 0.0 ;

          for (k-nextcol ; k<cols ; k++)
            scale += fabs ( a[col*cols+k] ) ;

          if (scale > 0.0) {
            for (k-nextcol ; k<cols ; k++) {
              a[col*cols+k] /- scale ;
              sum += a[col*cols+k] * a[col*cols+k] ;
            }
            pp - a[col*cols+nextcol] ;
            qq - -SIGN ( sqrt ( sum ) , pp ) ;
            denom - pp * qq - sum ;
            a[col*cols+nextcol] - pp - qq ;
            for (k-nextcol ; k<cols ; k++)
              work[k] - a[col*cols+k] / denom ;
            if (col !- rows-1) {
              for (j-nextcol ; j<rows ; j++) {
                sum - 0.0 ;
                for (k-nextcol ; k<cols ; k++)
                  sum += a[j*cols+k] * a[col*cols+k] ;
                for (k-nextcol ; k<cols ; k++)
                  a[j*cols+k] += sum * work[k] ;
              }
            }
            for (k-nextcol ; k<cols ; k++)
              a[col*cols+k] *- scale ;
          }

        sum - fabs (w[col]) + fabs (work[col]) ;
        if (sum > matnorm)
          matnorm - sum ;
        }
      return matnorm ;
}


/*
-------------------------------------------------------------------------------

   cancel

-------------------------------------------------------------------------------
*/

static void cancel (
   int rows ,
   int cols ,
```

```
      int lower ,
      int index ,
      double matnorm ,
      double *a ,
      double *w ,
      double *work
      )
{
   int col, row ;
   double c, rr, ww, hypot, s, pp, qq ;

   s = 1.0 ;
   for (col=lower ; col<=index ; col++) {
      rr = s * work[col] ;
      if (fabs (rr) + matnorm != matnorm) {
         ww = w[col] ;
         hypot = RSS ( rr , ww ) ;
         w[col] = hypot ;
         c = ww / hypot ;
         s = -rr / hypot ;
         for (row=0 ; row<rows ; row++) {
            pp = a[row*cols+lower-1] ;
            qq = a[row*cols+col] ;
            a[row*cols+lower-1] = qq * s  +  pp * c ;
            a[row*cols+col] = qq * c  -  pp * s ;
            }
         }
      }
}

/*
--------------------------------------------------------------------------------

   Cumulate right and left transforms

--------------------------------------------------------------------------------
*/

static void transforms (
      double *a ,
      int rows ,
      int cols ,
      double *w ,
      double *v ,
      double *work
      )
{
   int col, j, k ;
   double temp, ww, sum ;

/*
   Right
*/

   ww = 0.0 ;  // Insures failure of upcoming if first time
   for (col=cols-1 ; col>=0 ; col--) {
      if (ww != 0.0) {
         for (j=col+1 ; j<cols ; j++)  // Double division avoids underflow
            v[j*cols+col] = (a[col*cols+j] / a[col*cols+col+1]) / ww ;
         for (j=col+1 ; j<cols ; j++) {
            sum = 0.0 ;
            for (k=col+1 ; k<cols ; k++)
               sum += a[col*cols+k] * v[k*cols+j] ;
            for (k=col+1 ; k<cols ; k++)
               v[k*cols+j] += v[k*cols+col] * sum ;
            }
         }
      for (j=col+1 ; j<cols ; j++)
         v[col*cols+j] = v[j*cols+col] = 0.0 ;
      v[col*cols+col] = 1.0 ;
      ww = work[col] ;
      }

/*
   Left
*/

   for (col=cols-1 ; col>=0 ; col--) {

      for (j=col+1 ; j<cols ; j++)
         a[col*cols+j] = 0.0 ;
```

```
            if (w[col] == 0.0) {
                for (j=col ; j<rows ; j++)
                    a[j*cols+col] = 0.0 ;
                }

            else {
                ww = 1.0 / w[col] ;
                for (j=col+1 ; j<cols ; j++) {
                    sum = 0.0 ;
                    for (k=col+1 ; k<rows ; k++)
                        sum += a[k*cols+col] * a[k*cols+j] ;
                    temp = sum / a[col*cols+col] * ww ;
                    for (k=col ; k<rows ; k++)
                        a[k*cols+j] += a[k*cols+col] * temp ;
                    }
                for (j=col ; j<rows ; j++)
                    a[j*cols+col] *= ww ;
                }

            a[col*cols+col] += 1.0 ;
            }
}

/*
--------------------------------------------------------------------------------

    qr

--------------------------------------------------------------------------------
*/

static void qr (
    int rows ,
    int cols ,
    int lower ,
    int index ,
    double *a ,
    double *v ,
    double *w ,
    double *work )
{
    int col, colp1, row ;
    double c, cn, s, sn, thisw, rot1, rot2, hypot, temp, ww ;

    ww = w[index] ;
    sn = work[index] ;
    rot1 = work[index-1] ;
    rot2 = w[index-1] ;
    temp = ((rot2-ww) * (rot2+ww) + (rot1-sn) * (rot1+sn)) / (2.0 * sn * rot2) ;
    hypot = RSS ( temp , 1.0 ) ;
    thisw = w[lower] ;
    cn = ((thisw-ww) * (thisw+ww) + sn *
        ((rot2 / (temp + SIGN(hypot,temp))) - sn )) / thisw ;

    c = s = 1.0 ;

    for (col=lower ; col<index ; col++) {
        colp1 = col+1 ;
        rot1 = work[colp1] ;
        sn = s * rot1 ;
        rot1 = c * rot1 ;
        hypot = RSS ( cn , sn ) ;
        work[col] = hypot ;
        c = cn / hypot ;
        s = sn / hypot ;
        cn = thisw * c  +  rot1 * s ;
        rot1 = rot1 * c  -   thisw * s ;
        rot2 = w[colp1] ;
        sn = rot2 * s ;
        rot2 *= c ;
        for (row=0 ; row<cols ; row++) {
            thisw = v[row*cols+col] ;
            temp = v[row*cols+colp1] ;
            v[row*cols+col] = thisw * c  +  temp * s ;
            v[row*cols+colp1] = temp * c  -   thisw * s ;
            }
        hypot = RSS ( cn , sn ) ;
        w[col] = hypot ;
        if (hypot != 0.0) {
            c = cn / hypot ;
            s = sn / hypot ;
            }
```

```
         cn = c * rot1  +  s * rot2 ;
         thisw = c * rot2  -  s * rot1 ;
         for (row=0 ; row<rows ; row++) {
            rot1 = a[row*cols+col] ;
            rot2 = a[row*cols+colp1] ;
            a[row*cols+col] = rot1 * c  +  rot2 * s ;
            a[row*cols+colp1] = rot2 * c  -  rot1 * s ;
            }
         }
      w[index] = thisw ;
      work[lower] = 0.0 ;
      work[index] = cn ;
}

/*
--------------------------------------------------------------------------------

   verify nonneg - Flip sign of this singular value and its vector if negative

--------------------------------------------------------------------------------
*/

static void verify nonneg (
   int cols ,
   int index ,
   double *w ,
   double *v
   )
{
   int i ;

   if (w[index] < 0.0) {
      w[index] = -w[index] ;
      for (i=0 ; i<cols ; i++)
         v[i*cols+index] = -v[i*cols+index] ;
      }
}


/*
--------------------------------------------------------------------------------

   Backsubstitution algorithm for solving Ax=b where A generated u, w, v
   Inputs are not destroyed, so it may be called with several b's.
   The user must have filled in the public RHS 'b' before calling this.

--------------------------------------------------------------------------------
*/

void SingularValueDecomp::backsub (
   double thresh ,  // Threshold for zeroing singular values.  Typically 1.e-8.
   double *x        // Output of solution
   )
{
   int row, col, cc ;
   double sum, *mat ;

   if (u == NULL)      // Did we replace a with u
      mat = a ;
   else                // or preserve it?
      mat = u ;

/*
   Set the threshold according to the maximum singular value
*/

   sum = 0.0 ;                      // Will hold max w
   for (col=0 ; col<cols ; col++) {
      if (w[col] > sum)
         sum = w[col] ;
      }
   thresh *= sum ;
   if (thresh <= 0.0)     // Avoid dividing by zero in next step
      thresh = 1.e-30 ;

/*
   Find U'b
*/

   for (col=0 ; col<cols ; col++) {
      sum = 0.0 ;
      if (w[col] > thresh) {
```

```
                for (row=0 ; row<rows ; row++)
                    sum += mat[row*cols+col] * b[row] ;
                sum /= w[col] ;
                }
            work[col] = sum ;
            }

/*
    Multiply by V
*/
        for (col=0 ; col<cols ; col++) {
            sum = 0.0 ;
            for (cc=0 ; cc<cols ; cc++)
                sum += v[col*cols+cc] * work[cc] ;
            x[col] = sum ;
            }
    }
```

Bibliography

Aarts, E., and van Laarhoven, P. (1987). *Simulated Annealing: Theory and Practice*. John Wiley and Sons, New York.

Abe, S., Kayama, M., Takenaga, H., and Kitamura, T. (1992). "Neural Networks as a Tool to Generate Pattern Classification Algorithms." *International Joint Conference on Neural Networks*, Baltimore, MD.

Acton, Forman S. (1959). *Analysis of Straight-Line Data*. Dover Publications, New York.

Acton, Forman S. (1970). *Numerical Methods That Work*. Harper & Row, New York.

Anderson, James and Rosenfeld, Edward, eds. (1988). *Neurocomputing: Foundations of Research*. MIT Press, Cambridge, MA.

Austin, Scott (1990). "Genetic Solutions to XOR Problems." *AI Expert*, (December), 52–57.

Avitzur, Ron (1992). "Your Own Handprinting Recognition Engine." *Dr. Dobb's Journal*, (April), 32–37.

Azencott, R., ed. (1992). *Simulated Annealing: Parallelization Techniques*. John Wiley and Sons, New York.

Baba, Norio (1989). "A New Approach for Finding the Global Minimum of Error Function of Neural Networks." *Neural Networks*, **2**:5, 367–373.

Baba, N., and Kozaki, M. (1992). "An Intelligent Forecasting System of Stock Price Using Neural Networks." *International Joint Conference on Neural Networks*, Baltimore, MD.

Barmann, Frank and Biegler-Konig, Friedrich (1992). "On a Class of Efficient Learning Algorithms for Neural Networks." *Neural Networks* **5**: 139–144.

Barnard, Etienne and Casasent, David (1990). "Shift Invariance and the Neocognitron." *Neural Networks*, **3**: 403–410.

Barr, Avron, Cohen, Paul R., and Feigenbaum, Edward A., eds. (vol. I, 1981; vol. II, 1982; vol. III, 1982; vol. IV, 1989). *The Handbook of Artificial Intelligence*. Addison-Wesley Publishing Co., Reading, MA.

Bartlett, E. B. (1991). "Chaotic Time-series Prediction Using Artificial Neural Networks." *Abstracts from 2nd Government Neural Network Applications Workshop,* (September), Session III.

Blum, A. L., and Rivest, R. L. (1992). "Training a 3-Node Neural Network Is NP-Complete." *Neural Networks,* **5**:1, 117–127.

Blum, Edward, and Li, Leong (1991). "Approximation Theory and Feedforward Networks." *Neural Networks* 4: 511–515.

Booker, L. B., Goldberg, D. E., and Holland, J. H. (1989). "Classifier Systems and Genetic Algorithms." *Artificial Intelligence,* **40**: 235–282.

Box, George, and Jenkins, Gwilym (1976). *Time-series Analysis, Forecasting and Control.* Prentice Hall, Englewood Cliffs, NJ.

Brent, Richard (1973). *Algorithms for Minimization without Derivatives.* Prentice-Hall, Englewood Cliffs, NJ.

Brillinger, David R. (1975). *Time Series, Data Analysis and Theory.* Holt, Rinehart and Winston, New York.

Burgin, George (1992). "Using Cerebellar Arithmetic Computers." *AI Expert,* (June), 32–41.

Cacoullos, T. (1966). "Estimation of a Multivariate Density." *Annals of the Institute of Statistical Mathematics,* (Tokyo), **18**:2, 179–189.

Cardaliaguet, Pierre and Euvrard, Guillaume (1992). "Approximation of a Function and Its Derivative with a Neural Network." *Neural Networks,* 5:2, 207–220.

Carpenter, Gail A., and Grossberg, Stephen (1987). "A Massively Parallel Architecture for a Self-Organizing Neural Pattern Recognition Machine." *Academic Press,* (Computer Vision, Graphics, and Image Processing) **37**: 54–115.

Carpenter, Gail A., Grossberg, Stephen, and Reynolds, John H. (1991). "ARTMAP: Supervised Real-Time Learning and Classification of Nonstationary Data by a Self-Organizing Neural Network." *Neural Networks,* 4: 565–588.

Caruana, R. A., and Schaffer, J. D. (1988). "Representation and Hidden Bias: Gray vs. Binary Coding for Genetic Algorithms" in Laird, J. (ed.) *Proceedings of the Fifth International Congress on Machine Learning.* Morgan Kaufmann, San Mateo, CA.

Caudill, Maureen (1988). "Neural Networks Primer, Part IV-The Kohonen Model." *AI Expert*, (August).

Caudill, Maureen (1990). "Using Neural Nets: Fuzzy Decisions." *AI Expert*, (April), 59–64.

Cotter, Neil E., and Guillerm, Thierry J. (1992). "The CMAC and a Theorem of Kolmogorov." *Neural Networks*, **5**: 221–228.

Cottrell, G., Munro, P., and Zipser, D. 1987. "Image Compression by Backpropagation: An Example of Extensional Programming." *ICS Report 8702*, University of California at San Diego.

Cox, Earl (1992). "Solving Problems with Fuzzy Logic." *AI Expert*, (March), 28–37.

Cox, Earl (1992). "Integrating Fuzzy Logic into Neural Nets." *AI Expert*, (June), 43–47.

Crooks, Ted (1992). "Care and Feeding of Neural Networks." *AI Expert*, (July), 36–41.

Davis, D. T., and Hwang, J. N. (1992). "Attentional Focus Training by Boundary Region Data Selection." *International Joint Conference on Neural Networks*, Baltimore, MD.

Davis, Lawrence (1991). *Handbook of Genetic Algorithms.* Van Nostrand Reinhold, New York.

Draper, N. R., and Smith, H. (1966). *Applied Regression Analysis.* John Wiley and Sons, New York.

Eberhart, Russell C., and Dobbins, Roy W., eds. (1990). *Neural Network PC Tools, A Practical Guide.* Academic Press, San Diego, CA.

Fahlmann, Scott E. (1988). "An Empirical Study of Learning Speed in Backpropagation Networks." *CMU Technical Report CMU-CS-88-162*, (June, 1988).

Fakhr, W., Kamel, M., and Elmasry, M. I. (1992). "Probability of Error, Maximum Mutual Information, and Size Minimization of Neural Networks." *International Joint Conference on Neural Networks*, Baltimore, MD.

Finkbeiner, Daniel T., II (1972). *Elements of Linear Algebra*. W. H. Freeman and Co., San Francisco, CA.

Foley, James D., van Dam, Andries, Feiner, Steven K., and Hughes, John F. (1990). *Computer Graphics: Principles and Practice* (Second Edition). Addison-Wesley Publishing Co., Reading, MA.

Forsythe, George E., Malcolm, Michael A., and Moler, Cleve B. (1977). *Computer Methods for Mathematical Computations*. Prentice-Hall, Englewood Cliffs, NJ.

Freeman, James A., and Skapura, David M. (1992). *Neural Networks: Algorithms, Applications, and Programming Techniques*. Addison-Wesley Publishing Co., Reading, MA.

Fu, K. S. , ed. (1971). *Pattern Recognition and Machine Learning*. Plenum Press, New York.

Fukunaga, Keinosuke (1972). *Introduction to Statistical Pattern Recognition*. Academic Press, Orlando, FL.

Fukushima, Kunihiko (1987). "Neural Network Model for Selective Attention in Visual Pattern Recognition and Associative Recall." *Applied Optics*, (December), **26**:23.

Fukushima, Kunihiko (1989). "Analysis of the Process of Visual Pattern Recognition by the Neocognitron." *Neural Networks*, **2**: 413–420.

Gallant, Ronald, and White, Halbert (1992). "On Learning the Derivatives of an Unknown Mapping with Multilayer Feedforward Networks." *Neural Networks*, **2**: 129–138.

Gallinari, P., Thiria, S., Badran, F., and Fogelman-Soulie, F. (1991). "On the Relations between Discriminant Analysis and Multilayer Perceptrons." *Neural Networks*, **4**: 349–360.

Garson, David G. (1991). "Interpreting Neural-Network Connection Weights." *AI Expert*, (April), 47–51.

Gill, Philip E., Murray, Walter, and Wright, Margaret H. (1981). *Practical Optimization*. Academic Press, San Diego, CA.

Glassner, Andrew S., ed. (1990). *Graphics Gems*. Academic Press, San Diego, CA.

Goldberg, David E. (1989). *Genetic Algorithms in Search, Optimization and Machine Learning*. Addison-Wesley, Reading, MA.

Gori, M., and Tesi, A. (1990). "Some Examples of Local Minima during Learning with Back-Propagation." *Third Italian Workshop on Parallel Architectures and Neural Networks (E. R. Caianiello, ed.)*. World Scientific Publishing Co.

Gorlen, Keith E., Orlow, Sanford M., and Plexico, Perry S. (1990). *Data Abstraction and Object-Oriented Programming in C++*. John Wiley & Sons, Chichester, England.

Grossberg, Stephen (1988). *Neural Networks and Natural Intelligence*. The MIT Press, Cambridge, MA.

Guiver, John P., and Klimasauskas, Casimir, C. (1991). "Applying Neural Networks, Part IV: Improving Performance." *PC AI*, (July/August).

Hald, A. (1952). *Statistical Theory with Engineering Applications*. John Wiley and Sons, New York.

Harrington, Steven (1987). *Computer Graphics, A Programming Approach* (Second Edition). McGraw-Hill Book Co., New York.

Hashem, M. (1992). "Sensitivity Analysis for Feedforward Neural Networks with Differentiable Activation Functions." *International Joint Conference on Neural Networks*, Baltimore, MD.

Hastings, Cecil, Jr. (1955). *Approximations for Digital Computers*. Princeton University Press, Princeton, NJ.

Hecht-Nielsen, Robert (1987). "Nearest Matched Filter Classification of Spatiotemporal Patterns." *Applied Optics*, (May 15), **26**:10.

Hecht-Nielsen, Robert (1991). *Neurocomputing*. Addison-Wesley Publishing Co., Reading, MA.

Hecht-Nielsen, Robert (1992). "Theory of the Backpropagation Network." *Neural Networks for Perception, vol. 2*, Harry Wechsler, ed. Academic Press, New York.

Hirose, Yoshio, Yamashita, Koichi, and Hijiya, Shimpei (1991). "Back-Propagation Algorithm Which Varies the Number of Hidden Units." *Neural Networks*, 4:1, 61-66.

Hornik, Kurt, Stinchcombe, Maxwell, and White, Halbert (1989). "Multilayer Feedforward Networks are Universal Approximators." *Neural Networks*, **2**:5, 359–366.

Hornik, Kurt (1991). "Approximation Capabilities of Multilayer Feedforward Networks." *Neural Networks* 4:2, 251–257.

Howell, Jim (1990). "Inside a Neural Network." *AI Expert*, (November), 29–33.

Ito, Y. (1991a). "Representation of Functions by Superpositions of a Step or Sigmoid Function and Their Applications to Neural Network Theory." *Neural Networks*, 4:3, 385–394.

Ito, Y. (1991b). "Approximation of Functions on a Compact Set by Finite Sums of a Sigmoid Function without Scaling." *Neural Networks*, 4:6, 817–826.

Ito, Y. (1992). "Approximation of Continuous Functions on $\mathbf{R}^d$ by Linear Combinations of Shifted Rotations of a Sigmoid Function with and without Scaling." *Neural Networks*, **5**:1, 105–115.

Kalman, B. L., and Kwasny, S. C. (1992). "Why Tanh? Choosing a Sigmoidal Function." *International Joint Conference on Neural Networks*, Baltimore, MD.

Karr, Chuck (1991). "Genetic Algorithms for Fuzzy Controllers." *AI Expert*, (February), 26–33.

Karr, Chuck (1991). "Applying Genetics to Fuzzy Logic." *AI Expert*, (March), 39–43.

Kendall, M., and Stuart, A. (vol. I, 1969; vol. II, 1973; vol. III, 1976). *The Advanced Theory of Statistics*. Hafner Publishing Co., New York.

Kenue, S. K. (1991). "Efficient Activation Functions for the Back-Propagation Neural Network." *SPIE, Proceedings from Intelligent Robots and Computer Vision X: Neural, Biological, and 3-D Methods*, (November).

Kim, M. W., and Arozullah, M. (1992). "Generalized Probabilistic Neural Network-Based Classifiers." *International Joint Conference on Neural Networks*, Baltimore, MD.

Klimasauskas, Casimir C. (1987). *The 1987 Annotated Neuro-Computing Bibliography*. NeuroConnection, Sewickley, PA.

Klimasauskas, Casimir C. (1992). "Making Fuzzy Logic 'Clear'." *Advanced Technology for Developers*, 1 (May), 8–12.

Klimasauskas, Casimir C. (1992). "Hybrid Technologies: more power for the future." *Advanced Technology for Developers*, 1 (August), 17–20.

Klir, George J., and Folger, Tina A. (1988). *Fuzzy Sets, Uncertainty, and Information.* Prentice Hall, Englewood Cliffs, NJ.

Knuth, Donald (1981). *Seminumerical Algorithms.* Addison-Wesley, Reading, MA.

Kohonen, Teuvo (1982). "Self-Organized Formation of Topologically Correct Feature Maps." *Biological Cybernetics*, **43**: 59–69.

Kosko, Bart (1987). "Fuzziness vs. Probability." *Air Force Office of Scientific Research (AFOSR F49620-86-C-0070) and Advanced Research Projects Agency (ARPA Order No. 5794)*, (July).

Kosko, Bart (1988). "Bidirectional Associative Memories." *IEEE Transactions on Systems, Man, and Cybernetics*, (January/February), **18**:1.

Kosko, Bart (1988). "Hidden Patterns in Combined and Adaptive Knowledge Networks." *International Journal of Approximate Reasoning*, vol. 1.

Kosko, Bart (1992). *Neural Networks and Fuzzy Systems.* Prentice Hall, Englewood Cliffs, NJ.

Kreinovich, Vladik Ya. (1991). "Arbitrary Nonlinearity Is Sufficient to Represent All Functions by Neural Networks: A Theorem." *Neural Networks*, 4:3, 381–383.

Kurkova, Vera (1992). "Kolmogorov's Theorem and Multilayer Neural Networks." *Neural Networks*, **5**:3, 501–506.

Lawton, George (1992). "Genetic Algorithms for Schedule Optimization." *AI Expert*, (May), 23–27.

Lu, C. N., Wu, H. T., and Vemuri, S. (1992). "Neural Network Based Short-Term Load Forecasting." *IEEE/PES 1992 Winter Meeting, New York*, (92 WM 125-5 PWRS).

Maren, Alianna, Harston, Craig, and Pap, Robert (1990). *Handbook of Neural Computing Applications.* Academic Press, New York.

Matsuba, I., Masui, H., and Hebishima, S. (1992). "Optimizing Multilayer Neural Networks Using Fractal Dimensions of Time-Series Data." *International Joint Conference on Neural Networks*, Baltimore, MD.

McClelland, James and Rumelhart, David (1988). *Explorations in Parallel Distributed Processing.* MIT Press, Cambridge, MA.

Meisel, W. (1972). *Computer-Oriented Approaches to Pattern Recognition.* Academic Press, New York.

Minsky, Marvin and Papert, Seymour (1969). *Perceptrons.* MIT Press, Cambridge, MA.

Mougeot, M., Azencott, R., and Angeniol, B. (1991). "Image Compression with Back Propagation: Improvement of the Visual Restoration Using Different Cost Functions." *Neural Networks*, 4:4 467–476.

Mucciardi, A., and Gose, E. (1970). "An Algorithm for Automatic Clustering in N-Dimensional Spaces Using Hyperellipsoidal Cells." *IEEE Sys. Sci. Cybernetics Conference* (Pittsburgh, PA).

Musavi, M., Kalantri, K., and Ahmed, W. (1992). "Improving the Performance of Probabilistic Neural Networks." *International Joint Conference on Neural Networks*, Baltimore, MD.

Negoita, Constantin V., and Ralescu, Dan (1987). *Simulation, Knowledge-Based Computing, and Fuzzy Statistics.* Van Nostrand Reinhold Co., New York.

Pao, Yoh-Han (1989). *Adaptive Pattern Recognition and Neural Networks.* Addison-Wesley Publishing Co., Reading, MA.

Parzen, E. (1962). "On Estimation of a Probability Density Function and Mode." *Annals of Mathematical Statistics*, **33:**, 1065–1076.

Pethel, S. D., Bowden, C. M., and Sung, C. C. (1991). "Applications of Neural Net Algorithms to Nonlinear Time Series." *Abstracts from 2nd Government Neural Network Applications Workshop,* (September), Session III.

Polak, E. (1971). *Computational Methods in Optimization.* Academic Press, New York.

Polzleitner, Wolfgang and Wechsler, Harry (1990). "Selective and Focused Invariant Recognition Using Distributed Associative Memories (DAM)." *IEEE Transactions on Pattern Analysis and Machine Intelligence*, (August), **12**:8.

Press, William H., Flannery, B., Teukolsky, S., and Vetterling, W. (1988). *Numerical Recipes in C*. Cambridge University Press, New York.

Raudys, Sarunas J., and Jain, Anil K. (1991). "Small Sample Size Effects in Statistical Pattern Recognition: Recommendations for Practitioners." *IEEE Transactions on Pattern Analysis and Machine Intelligence*, (March), **13**:3.

Reed, R., Oh, S., and Marks, R. J. (1992). "Regularization Using Jittered Training Data." *International Joint Conference on Neural Networks*, Baltimore, MD.

Rich, Elaine (1983). *Artificial Intelligence*. McGraw-Hill Book Co., New York.

Rosenblatt, Frank (1958). "The Perceptron: A Probabilistic Model for Information Storage and Organization in the Brain." *Psychological Review* **65**: 386–408.

Rumelhart, David, McClelland, James and the PDP Research Group (1986). *Parallel Distributed Processing*. MIT Press, Cambridge, MA.

Sabourin, M., and Mitiche, A. (1992). "Optical Character Recognition by a Neural Network." *Neural Networks* **5**: 843–852.

Samad, Tariq (1988). "Backpropagation Is Significantly Faster if the Expected Value of the Source Unit Is Used for Update." *1988 Conference of the International Neural Network Society*.

Samad, Tariq (1991). "Back Propagation with Expected Source Values." *Neural Networks*, 4:5, 615–618.

Schwartz, Tom J. (1991). "Fuzzy Tools for Expert Systems." *AI Expert*, (February), 34–41.

Sedgewick, Robert (1988). *Algorithms*. Addison-Wesley Publishing Co., Reading, MA.

Shapiro, Stuart C., ed. (1990). *Encyclopedia of Artificial Intelligence*. John Wiley & Sons, New York.

Siegel, Sidney (1956). *Nonparametric Statistics for the Behavioral Sciences.* McGraw-Hill Book Co., New York.

Soulie, Francoise Fogelman, Robert, Yves, and Tchuente, Maurice, eds. (1987). *Automata Networks in Computer Science.* Princeton University Press, Princeton, NJ.

Specht, Donald (1990). "Probabilistic Neural Networks." *Neural Networks* **3**: 109–118.

Specht, Donald (1992). "Enhancements to Probabilistic Neural Networks." *International Joint Conference on Neural Networks,* Baltimore, MD.

Specht, Donald F., and Shapiro, Philip D. (1991). "Generalization Accuracy of Probabilistic Neural Networks Compared with Back-Propagation Networks." *Lockheed Missiles & Space Co., Inc. Independent Research Project RDD 360,* I-887-I-892.

Spillman, Richard (1990). "Managing Uncertainty with Belief Functions." *AI Expert,* (May), 44–49.

Stork, David G. (1989). "Self-Organization, Pattern Recognition, and Adaptive Resonance Networks." *Journal of Neural Network Computing,* (Summer).

Strand, E. M., and Jones, W. T. (1992). "An Adaptive Pattern Set Strategy for Enhancing Generalization While Improving Backpropagation Training Efficiency." *International Joint Conference on Neural Networks,* Baltimore, MD.

Styblinski, M. A., and Tang, T.-S. (1990). "Experiments in Nonconvex Optimization: Stochastic Approximation with Function Smoothing and Simulated Annealing." *Neural Networks,* **3:** 467–483.

Sudharsanan, Subramania I., and Sundareshan, Malur K. (1991). "Exponential Stability and a Systematic Synthesis of a Neural Network for Quadratic Minimization." *Neural Networks,* **4:** 599–613.

Sultan, A. F., Swift, G. W., and Fedirchuk, D. J. (1992). "Detection of High Impedance Arcing Faults Using a Multi-Layer Perceptron." *IEEE/PES 1992 Winter Meeting, New York,* (92 WM 207-1 PWRD).

Sussmann, Hector J. (1992). "Uniqueness of the Weights for Minimal Feedforward Nets with a Given Input-Output Map." *Neural Networks,* **5**:4, 589–593.

Tanimoto, Steven L. (1987). *The Elements of Artificial Intelligence.* Computer Science Press, Rockville, MD.

Ulmer, Richard, Jr., and Gorman, John (1989). "Partial Shape Recognition Using Simulated Annealing." *IEEE Proceedings, 1989 Southeastcon.*

Unnikrishnan, K. P., and Venugopal, K. P. (1992). "Learning in Connectionist Networks Using the Alopex Algorithm." *International Joint Conference on Neural Networks,* Baltimore, MD.

van Ooyen, A., and Nienhuis, B. (1992). "Improving the Convergence of the Back-Propagation Algorithm." *Neural Networks,* **5**:3, 465–471.

Wayner, Peter (1991). "Genetic Algorithms." *BYTE,* (January), 361–368.

Webb, Andrew R., and Lowe, David (1990). "The Optimized Internal Representation of Multilayer Classifier Networks Performs Nonlinear Discriminant Analysis." *Neural Networks,* **3**:4, 367–375.

Wenskay, Donald (1990). "Intellectual Property Protection for Neural Networks." *Neural Networks,* **3**:2, 229–236.

Weymaere, Nico and Martens, Jean-Pierre (1991). "A Fast and Robust Learning Algorithm for Feedforward Neural Networks." *Neural Networks,* 4:3, 361–369.

White, Halbert (1989). "Neural-Network Learning and Statistics." *AI Expert,* (December), 48–52.

Wiggins, Ralphe (1992). "Docking a Truck: A Genetic Fuzzy Approach." *AI Expert,* (May), 29–35.

Wirth, Niklaus (1976). *Algorithms + Data Structures = Programs.* Prentice-Hall, Englewood Cliffs, NJ.

Wolpert, David H. (1992). "Stacked Generalization." *Neural Networks,* **5**: 241–259.

Yau, Hung-Chun and Manry, Michael T. (1991). "Iterative Improvement of a Nearest Neighbor Classifier." *Neural Networks*, 4: 517–524.

Zadeh, Lotfi A. (1992). "The Calculus of Fuzzy If/Then Rules." *AI Expert*, (March), 23–27.

Zeidenberg, Matthew (1990). *Neural Network Models in Artificial Intelligence*. Ellis Horwood, New York.

Zhang, Y., Chen, G. P., Malik, O. P., and Hope, G. S. (1992). "An Artificial Neural Network-Based Adaptive Power System Stabilizer." *IEEE/PES 1992 Winter Meeting, New York*. (92 WM 018-2 EC).

Zhou, Yi-Tong and Chellappa (1992). *Artificial Neural Networks for Computer Vision*. Springer-Verlag, New York.

Zornetzer, Steven, Davis, Joel, and Lau, Clifford, eds. (1990). *An Introduction to Neural and Electronic Networks*. Academic Press, New York.

Index